Kitchen Keepsakes

recipes for home cookin'

Bonnie Welch & Deanna White

Cover Design by Pam Hake

Illustrated by Sheila Olson

Kitchen Keepsakes & more Kitchen Keepsakes
Two cookbooks in one!

Specially priced combination
books are available for $19.95, plus $3.50 shipping
(Texas residents add $1.44 sales tax per book).
Quantity discounts are available.

Cover Design by Pam Hake
Text illustrations by Sheila Olson

ISBN: 0-9677932-5-4
Library of Congress Card Number: 00-111718

First Printing	June	2000	5,000 copies
Second Printing	September	2000	15,000 copies
Third Printing	October	2000	15,000 copies
Fourth Printing	November	2000	20,000 copies
Fifth Printing	January	2001	50,000 copies

cookbook resources, llc
541 Doubletree Drive
Highland Village, TX 75077

972/317-0245

www.cookbookresources.com

Manufactured in the USA

cookbook resources ®

Toll Free Orders: 866/229-2665

INTRODUCTION

This book is a collection of recipes that can truly be called keepsakes. They are the ones that have remained favorites in our families for years, and they stir memories of Sunday dinners, backyard picnics at Grandma's, and holiday gatherings. Our mothers and grandmothers prepared them for family, friends, branding and harvest crews.

Having been raised in different parts of the country, our favorite recipes reflect a variety of regional tastes, but whether it's Midwestern, Southern, or Texas-style, it's all down-home.

These foods are ones that we regularly cook (and have frequent requests for!), that do not require expensive or unusual ingredients, and are, for the most part, easy to prepare. Many are our adaptations of old stand-bys, some are family favorites contributed by friends, and all are delicious.

To insure that you find as much pleasure in preparation as we do, we have kitchen-tested all the recipes and edited them for clarity. We have included some menu suggestions—accompaniments we have found to be successful, and those that are capitalized are included within the book. Freezing and quick preparation ideas and tips for using modern kitchen equipment have also been included. In addition, we have included recipes you'll be proud to serve guests at parties, brunches, luncheons or dinners. But mostly, these are recipes you'll be proud to serve your family!

We hope you will find pleasure in preparing, serving, and eating the food from this cookbook, and that our keepsakes will become yours!

DEDICATION

This cookbook is dedicated to those ladies who inspired in us a love for good home cooking—our mothers and our husband's mothers:

Frances Matthews   Jean Sewald

Eileen Welch   Leona White

IN APPRECIATION

The following people were helpful in the creation of this cookbook. They willingly gave us recipes, advice, suggestions, and encouragement. We are most grateful to them.

Bonnie Adam
Chris Bennett
Kathleen Budd
Judy Craig
Zelda Cranmer
Kevin Deets
Edith Eaton
Joanie Graham
Emily Grimes
Sarah Lew Grimes
Noanie Hepp
Mary Hier
Susie Howard
Ruth Jackson
Sid Kelsey
Judy Markoff
Peggy Marvin
Frances Matthews

Kathleen Ness
Sheila Olson
Candy Rayl
Krynn Robinson
Cathy Sewald
Jean Sewald
Sherri Sewald
Dee Smith
Doris Smith
Charlotte Walker
Dixie Welch
Eileen Welch
Kathy Welch
Virginia Welch
Laura Wesley
Leona White
Gladys White
Kathy Williams

A special thank you to our husbands, Jim White and John Welch, and our children, Tanya, Linda, and Will White, and Bob, Andy, and Wesley Welch for their support.

TABLE OF CONTENTS

APPETIZERS AND BEVERAGES 2

EGGS AND CHEESE 24

SOUPS AND SANDWICHES 32

BREADS 48

SALADS 76

MEATS 100

CHICKEN AND FISH 124

VEGETABLES, RICE, AND PASTA 144

DESSERTS 168

PRESERVES, RELISHES, AND SAUCES 218

KIDS' FOOD 230

EQUIVALENT MEASURES 244

INDEX 245

Appetizers
&
Beverages

♥ ♥ ♥ ♥ ♥ ♥ ♥ ♥ ♥ ♥ ♥ ♥ ♥ ♥ ♥ ♥ ♥

SHELLFISH DIP

1—7½ oz. can minced
   clams or flaked crab
8 oz. cream cheese
½ cup sour cream
1 Tbsp. lemon juice
½ tsp. garlic salt
¼ tsp. pepper
¼ tsp. Lawry's seasoned
   salt
¼ cup green olives,
   chopped
¼ cup green onions,
   chopped
1 tsp. Worcestershire sauce

MAKES 2 CUPS
Combine all ingredients and mix well.
Chill. Serve with potato chips or tortilla
chips.

CHILI CON QUESO

½ lb. Velveeta cheese
½ lb. Old English cheese
1 medium onion, chopped
1—10 oz. can Ro-Tel
   tomatoes

MAKES 3 CUPS
Mix all ingredients and cook in top of
double boiler for about 1½ hours.
Serve in a chafing dish or fondue pot
to keep warm. Serve with tortilla or
corn chips.

TOM'S FAMOUS DIP

1 cup sour cream
1 cup mayonnaise
1 tsp. dill weed
1 tsp. parsley flakes
1 tsp. onion flakes
1 tsp. Beaumond seasoning

MAKES 2 CUPS
Mix all ingredients and serve with
crudites, chips, or crackers.

CREAMY ARTICHOKE-CHEESE DIP

2—4 oz. cans artichoke
hearts, partially drained
2—7 oz. cans green chilies,
diced
1 cup mayonnaise
1 cup Parmesan cheese

MAKES 3 CUPS
Combine ingredients and pour into baking dish. Bake uncovered at 350° for 45 minutes to 1 hour. Serve warm with party ryes or club crackers. Cooking blends the flavors just right!

ENCHILADA DIP

½ onion, chopped
2 Tbsp. butter
2 lbs. ground beef
Garlic powder
1 can Mild Old El Paso
Enchilada sauce
1 can Hot Old El Paso
Enchilada sauce
2 pkg. dry enchilada sauce
1—8 oz. can tomato sauce
2 lb. brick Velveeta
cheese, cubed

MAKES 6 CUPS
In a large Dutch oven, saute onion in butter. Add ground beef and season with garlic powder. Cook until onion is tender and beef is browned. Drain grease. Add enchilada sauces and tomato sauce. Stir in cubed cheese and cook over low heat 2-3 hours, stirring occasionally. Serve hot, with stone ground tortilla chips. (You can also use this to make your own enchiladas by placing a mixture of grated cheddar cheese and minced onion in a softened tortilla, rolling it up, placing it seam side down in a baking dish, and covering the whole batch of them with this meat sauce. Sprinkle grated cheese on top and bake at 350° for 30 minutes. You can get 8 enchiladas in a 6 x 9 inch pyrex pan.)

 An experienced hostess will tell you that serving more than six varieties of appetizers is not necessary. Usually four cold ones and two hot ones are ample for a party.

FRESH FRUIT DIP

12 macaroons, crushed
¼ cup packed brown sugar
1 pint dairy sour cream
1 large pineapple

MAKES 3 CUPS

Crush macaroons and combine with brown sugar and sour cream. Chill several hours to soften macaroon crumbs. Do not stir again. Hollow out center of pineapple for serving dish. Fill shell with macaroon dip. Place in center of large platter. Arrange fresh fruits (strawberries, melons, bananas, grapes, etc.) around pineapple. This is good at a brunch.

GOOD 'N EASY GUACAMOLE

2 ripe avocados, peeled
⅓ cup sour cream
1½ Tbsp. packaged taco
    seasoning

MAKES 1 CUP

Mash avocados with fork. Add sour cream and taco seasoning and mix well. Serve with tortilla chips.

BUBBLY BROCCOLI DIP

2 Tbsp. butter
½ lb. fresh mushrooms,
    sliced
½ large onion, chopped
1½ stalks celery, diced
½ can cream of mushroom
    soup
1—10 oz. pkg. frozen
    broccoli, chopped
1—6 oz. tube garlic cheese
½ tsp. lemon juice
Salt and pepper

MAKES 3 CUPS

Saute mushrooms, onion and celery in butter. Cook broccoli according to package directions and drain. Combine all ingredients and warm to almost boiling. Remove from heat. Serve warm in chafing dish or fondue pot with tortilla chips or raw vegetables.

 After peeling an avocado, place the pit in the container with the fruit to keep it from turning brown.

SOMBRERO SPREAD

1—16 oz. can refried beans
1 pkg. taco seasoning
4 Tbsp. Pace's Picante
  sauce
1—7 oz. can green chilies,
  chopped
Guacamole
8 oz. sour cream
Black olives, chopped
Chopped green onions,
  tomatoes and lettuce
Grated cheddar cheese

MAKES 2 CUPS
Mix refried beans with taco seasoning. Layer ingredients on a dinner plate beginning with the beans. Top with chopped green onions, lettuce, tomato and grated cheese. Serve with tortilla chips.

CURRY DIP FOR RAW VEGETABLES

1 pint mayonnaise
2 tsp. curry powder
2 tsp. onion juice
2 tsp. vinegar
2 tsp. horseradish
Assorted raw vegetables

MAKES 2 CUPS
Mix ingredients well and serve with assorted raw vegetables.

DILLED CRAB DIP

1—8 oz. pkg. cream
  cheese, softened
1 cup mayonnaise
¼ cup sour cream
1-1½ tsp. dill weed
2 green onions, minced
1 beef bouillon cube,
  crushed
1 tsp. hot sauce
1—7 oz. can crabmeat,
  rinsed, drained
Assorted fresh vegetables

MAKES 2 CUPS
Beat cream cheese in medium size bowl until light. Beat in mayonnaise and sour cream. Stir in remaining ingredients except fresh vegetables. Refrigerate, covered, several hours to blend flavors. Serve with assorted fresh vegetables.

SMOKED OYSTER DIP

1—8 oz. pkg. cream cheese
1½ cups mayonnaise
4 dashes Tabasco
1 Tbsp. lemon juice
1—4½ oz. can chopped
   black olives
1—3½ oz. can smoked
   oysters, drained and
   chopped

MAKES 2 CUPS
Combine softened cream cheese, mayonnaise, Tabasco and lemon juice. Mix well. Add olives and smoked oysters. Delicious on raw vegetables and crackers.

SPINACH DIP

1—10 oz. pkg. frozen,
   chopped spinach thawed
1—16 oz. carton sour
   cream with chives
1 pkg. Ranch Style
   dressing mix
1 large round loaf of
   rye bread

MAKES 3 CUPS
Combine uncooked spinach, sour cream and Ranch Style dressing mix. Hollow out rye loaf saving pieces of bread for dipping. Spoon dip into loaf.

CARAMEL APPLE DIP

5-6 apples, cut into wedges
14 oz. caramel candy
8 oz. pkg. miniature
   marshmallows
⅔ cup cream or milk

Melt caramel and combine with marshmallows and cream. Stir until smooth. Pour into fondue pot. Dip apple sections in hot caramel mixture.

 When a recipe says "chop very fine" try grating it instead.

SWISS RYES

½ cup bacon, fried and
  crumbled
1 cup Swiss cheese, grated
1—4½ oz. can ripe olives,
  chopped
½ cup green onions,
  minced
1 tsp. Worcestershire sauce
¼ cup mayonnaise
Party rye bread

MAKES 25-30
Combine first six ingredients and mix well. Spread on party ryes. Bake at 375° for 10-12 minutes or until lightly browned.

STUFFED MUSHROOMS WITH BACON

1½ lbs. fresh mushrooms
6 slices bacon, diced
2 Tbsp. green pepper,
  chopped
¼ cup green onion,
  chopped
½ tsp. salt
1—3 oz. pkg. cream cheese
½ tsp. Worcestershire
  sauce
1 Tbsp. butter
½ cup dry bread crumbs

MAKES 25-30
Wash and drain mushrooms. Gently remove and dice stems. Saute bacon and drain on paper towel. Saute the diced mushroom stems, green pepper, and green onion in bacon drippings. Combine this with crumbled bacon, softened cream cheese, salt and Worcestershire sauce. Melt butter in pan and add bread crumbs. Brown crumbs and add to other ingredients. Stuff mushroom caps with mixture. Bake at 375° for 15 minutes. Serve hot.

QUICK STUFFED MUSHROOMS

1 pkg. Jimmy Dean sausage
2 lbs. fresh mushrooms

MAKES 35-40
Wash and drain mushrooms. Gently remove stems. Stuff each cap with raw sausage. Bake on cookie sheet in 350° oven for 20-30 minutes or until sausage is done. Serve hot.

APPETIZERS & BEVERAGES

CHEESE AND BACON HOT RYES

7 slices bacon, fried and
  crumbled
6 oz. cheddar cheese,
  grated
½-1 cup mayonnaise
1 Tbsp. Worcestershire
  sauce
1 small pkg. slivered
  almonds, toasted
1 small onion, chopped
Parmesan cheese
Party ryes

MAKES 3 DOZEN
Combine all ingredients except
Parmesan cheese. Spread on slices
of party rye bread. Sprinkle with
Parmesan cheese and bake at 400°
for 10-15 minutes.

DEVILED HAM PUFFS

1—8 oz. pkg. cream
  cheese, softened
1 egg yolk, beaten
1 tsp. onion juice
½ tsp. baking powder
Salt to taste
¼ tsp. horseradish
¼ tsp. hot sauce
24 party ryes
2—2¼ oz. cans deviled
  ham

MAKES 24
Blend together the cheese, egg yolk,
onion juice, baking powder, salt,
horseradish and hot sauce. Spread
bread with deviled ham and cover
each with a mound of cheese mixture.
Place on cookie sheet and bake in
375° oven for 10-12 minutes or until
puffed and brown. Serve hot. These
can be made ahead and frozen. Remove and allow to thaw before
baking.

WATER CHESTNUTS & BACON ROLL UPS

1 can whole water
  chestnuts
10 strips of bacon, cut in
  half
¼ cup soy sauce
2 Tbsp. brown sugar

MAKES 15-20
Combine soy sauce and brown sugar
in small bowl. Mix well. Add drained
water chestnuts and let marinate 2-6
hours. Wrap each in a bacon strip and
secure with toothpick. Broil until
bacon is done. Serve hot.

HOWDY POTATOES

2 medium baked potatoes
Oil
1 cup sour cream
2 green onions, chopped
1 cup cheddar cheese,
  grated
4 slices bacon, fried and
  crumbled
½ cup fresh mushrooms,
  sliced and sauteed
Salt

MAKES 16
Cut each potato into eight wedges leaving skins on. Deep fry potato wedges at 400° for 1-2 minutes or until golden brown. Arrange in sunburst pattern on platter. Mix sour cream, onions, cheese, bacon, salt and mushrooms and place in center of platter for dipping.

SPINACH APPETIZERS

2—10 oz. pkg. frozen,
  chopped spinach, thawed
  and well drained
2 cups Pepperidge Farm
  Herb Stuffing
4 eggs, well beaten
1 cup onion, finely chopped
½ cup butter, melted
½ cup Parmesan cheese,
  grated
½ tsp. garlic powder
½ tsp. MSG or Accent
½ tsp. pepper
½ tsp. salt
¼ tsp. thyme

MAKES ABOUT 70
Mix all ingredients and chill. Shape into balls and bake at 350° for 20 minutes. Serve hot. This would also be good as a vegetable casserole with a meal. Put all ingredients in a baking dish and bake at 350° about 30-35 minutes.

Use pretzels to skewer your favorite cheese cubes rather than toothpicks.

APPETIZERS & BEVERAGES

♥ ♥ ♥ ♥ ♥ ♥ ♥ ♥ ♥ ♥ ♥ ♥ ♥ ♥ ♥ ♥ ♥

VEGETABLE CRISPS

2 eggs
1 cup cold water
¾ cup flour
Dash salt
Assorted fresh zucchini,
    cauliflower, broccoli,
    onion, or mushrooms

Wash and drain vegetables. Slice zucchini and onions. Break cauliflower and broccoli into flowerets. Stem mushrooms, using both caps and stems. Combine eggs and water. Beat until frothy. Add flour and salt, and beat until well blended. Keep batter cold by setting it in a bowl of ice or refrigerator until ready to use. Dip fresh vegetable pieces or slices into batter. Deep fry at 375° until golden brown. Sprinkle with salt.

SHRIMP BALL

2—4½ oz. cans tiny
    shrimp, rinsed, drained,
    and mashed
½ cup mayonnaise or salad
    dressing
2 Tbsp. minced onion
Worcestershire sauce
    to taste

MAKES 1 CUP
Combine shrimp, mayonnaise, onion, and Worcestershire sauce. Form into a ball, or spoon into a crock. Refrigerate, covered, overnight for the best flavor. Serve with rice crackers.

MAMA WHITE'S CHICKEN LIVER PATE

3 Tbsp. butter
1 lb. chicken livers
¼ tsp. salt
¼ tsp. onion salt
1/8 tsp. pepper
1 medium onion, chopped
3 eggs, hard cooked
⅓ cup mayonnaise
Party ryes

MAKES 40
Melt butter in skillet. Add chicken livers, salt, pepper, and chopped onion. Fry over medium heat for about 15-20 minutes or until livers are done. Grind liver mixture and eggs through food grinder or in food processor. Add more salt and pepper to taste. Add ⅓ cup mayonnaise and mix well. Spread on party ryes.

BEST OF THE WEST SPREAD

¼ cup roasted unblanched
   almonds, chopped fine
2 strips bacon, fried and
   drained
1 cup Velveeta, grated
   and packed
½ cup mayonnaise
¼ tsp. salt
1 Tbsp. green onions
   or chives, chopped

MAKES 1½ CUPS
Finely chop onions, crumble bacon, and mix all ingredients together. Serve with crackers. If you have a food processor, chop almonds, bacon, and green onions first. Add other ingredients and blend well. Spread on crackers or bread rounds. This is delicious!

PARTY RYE SPREADS

HOT CHEDDAR SPREAD:
Grated cheddar cheese
Mayonnaise, enough to
   hold mixture together
Bacon bits

Mix ingredients together. Spread on party rye bread. Broil several minutes until mixture melts.

HAM SPREAD:
8 oz. softened cream
   cheese
1 Tbsp. mayonnaise
1 tsp. prepared mustard
2 Tbsp. drained pickle
   relish
Green onion, chopped
1 cup ham, ground

Mix ingredients together. Spread on party rye bread. These are easy and tasty!

APPETIZERS & BEVERAGES

HOT CRAB MINIATURES

1—7½ oz. can crabmeat,
   drained and flaked
1 Tbsp. minced green
   onion
1 cup Swiss cheese, grated
½ cup mayonnaise
1 tsp. lemon juice
¼ tsp. curry powder
1—5 oz. can water
   chestnuts, chopped and
   drained
1 tube flaky refrigerator
   biscuits

MAKES 30
Combine all ingredients except rolls. Mix well. Separate each roll into three layers. Place on cookie sheet and spoon crabmeat mixture on each. Bake at 400° for 10-12 minutes. Chicken can be substituted for the crabmeat.

SAUSAGE BISCUITS

1 lb. hot sausage
1 lb. sharp cheddar cheese,
   grated
3 cups Bisquick
Cayenne pepper or
   Tabasco sauce (optional)

MAKES 3 DOZEN
Have sausage and cheese at room temperature. Mix uncooked sausage with cheese and Bisquick. Roll into one-inch balls and place on a cookie sheet. (You may freeze these at this point, while on the cookie sheet. When frozen, take off the cookie sheet and put in a freezer bag.) Bake at 400° about 15-20 minutes or until brown. These may be frozen after baking, also.

JUDY'S GREEN CHILI PIE

1—7 oz. can green chilies,
   chopped
2 cups Monterey Jack
   cheese, grated
5 eggs, beaten

MAKES 2-3 DOZEN
Layer in order given in a greased 8 x 11 inch pan. Bake one hour at 325°. Cut into squares and serve hot.

PEOPLE PLEASIN' CHEESEBALLS

8 oz. cream cheese
1 cup sharp cheddar
cheese, grated
1 cup Monterey Jack or
Swiss cheese, grated
1 oz. bleu cheese
2 Tbsp. grated onion
4 drops Tabasco sauce
Parsley, nuts or paprika

Let cream cheese stand at room temperature until softened. Mix all ingredients together. Form into 1 big ball or three small ones. Roll in parsley, nuts or paprika. Serve with assorted crackers.

EASY CHEESE BALL

1—8 oz. pkg. Velveeta
cheese
1—5 oz. jar Old English
cheese
1—3 oz. pkg. cream
cheese
1/8 tsp. garlic powder
½ cup pecans, chopped
Paprika

1 LARGE CHEESEBALL
Have ingredients at room temperature. Mix the three cheeses and garlic powder together with your hands. When they are blended, shape mixture into a ball. Roll in paprika, then in the pecans. Refrigerate until ready to use.

CHEESY PINEAPPLE SPREAD

1—8 oz. pkg. cream cheese
1—8½ oz. can crushed
pineapple, drained
½ cup pecans, chopped
1½ Tbsp. green onions,
chopped
½ tsp. Lawry's seasoned
salt

MAKES 2½ CUPS
Soften cream cheese and mix with other ingredients. Place in small dish or crock; refrigerate. Serve with crackers.

 If cheese becomes dry, try soaking it in buttermilk and it will return to normal.

♥ ♥ ♥ ♥ ♥ ♥ ♥ ♥ ♥ ♥ ♥ ♥ ♥ ♥ ♥ ♥

KATHLEEN'S CHUTNEY DELIGHT

1 cup chutney (see recipe
   in preserves section)
1—8 oz. pkg. cream cheese
½ cup chopped almonds,
   toasted (optional)

This can be served two ways. The cream cheese can be left in its original shape on a dish with the chutney poured over it and the almonds sprinkled on top, or you can soften the cream cheese and mix the ingredients. Best served on club crackers or celery.

CHERRY TOMATO HORS D'OEUVRES

24 cherry tomatoes
1—8 oz. pkg. cream
   cheese, softened
2 Tbsp. ketchup
1 Tbsp. lemon juice
1 Tbsp. horseradish
1 Tbsp. light cream
¼ tsp. paprika
Parsley
Watercress

MAKES 24
Wash tomatoes; dry on paper towels. Cut slice from each stem end. Combine cheese, ketchup, lemon juice, horseradish, cream and paprika. Mix well. Press cheese mixture through pastry bag with No. 6 star tip, making rosettes on each tomato. Decorate each with parsley. Arrange on watercress bed, sprinkle with lemon juice and refrigerate 30 minutes before serving.

CREAM CHEESE BURRITOS

16 oz. cream cheese,
   softened
¼ cup green chilies,
   chopped
½ cup pimento, chopped
½ cup black olives,
   chopped
4 large flour tortillas

MAKES 40 SLICES
Mix the first four ingredients. Spread an equal amount of mixture on each tortilla. Roll, cover and chill, seam side down. (This much can be done up to 7 days in advance.) To serve, slice into ¼ inch slices. Do not freeze.

CHOCOLATE DIPPED STRAWBERRIES

**2 pints strawberries,
  stemmed and dried well**
**1—4 oz. Hershey's
  chocolate bar**
1 large Tbsp. paraffin

Melt chocolate and paraffin in small saucepan. Dip end of strawberries in chocolate. Tip pan if chocolate is too shallow. These are so pretty to look at, so delicious, and so easy to prepare!

 When recipes call for softened cream cheese, warm it in the microwave for 5-10 seconds to soften.

APPETIZERS & BEVERAGES

♥ ♥ ♥ ♥ ♥ ♥ ♥ ♥ ♥ ♥ ♥ ♥ ♥ ♥ ♥ ♥

CREAMY KOOLAID PUNCH

2 pkg. Koolaid (any flavor)
1½ cups sugar
1 cup powdered milk
½ gallon water
½ gallon vanilla ice cream
2 quarts 7-up

SERVES 25
Mix all ingredients. Keep cold.

ORANGE SLUSH

1 cup orange juice
1 Tbsp. honey
½ banana
4 ice cubes

SERVES 1
Blend all ingredients in a blender until slushy and frothy. This is a delicious summertime drink that is filling and nutritious.

APRIL SHOWER ICE CREAM PUNCH

2—6 oz. cans frozen
   lemonade concentrate
1—6 oz. can frozen orange
   juice concentrate
9 cups water
1 qt. lemon sherbet
1 qt. vanilla ice cream

SERVES 25
Mix fruit juices and water in punch bowl. Scoop sherbet and ice cream into punch. Stir gently.

BANANA FRUIT PUNCH

4 cups sugar
6 cups water
48 oz. pineapple juice
2—12 oz. cans frozen
   orange juice concentrate
1—12 oz. can frozen
   lemonade concentrate
5 bananas
3 qts. ginger ale

Mix sugar and water in saucepan. Heat to boiling. Cool. Add pineapple juice, orange juice and lemonade. Mash bananas by hand or in a blender. Add to above mixture. Stir well. Can be frozen at this point in milk cartons. Take out of freezer two hours before serving. When ready to serve, add three quarts ginger ale, and mix well.

♥ ♥ ♥ ♥ ♥ ♥ ♥ ♥ ♥ ♥ ♥ ♥ ♥ ♥ ♥ ♥ ♥

SURE BET PUNCH

1 large can Hawaiian punch
1 pint pineapple sherbet
1 quart 7-Up

SERVES 15
Mix Hawaiian punch and 7-up. Let sherbet float on top.

FRUIT SMOOTHY

1 cup milk
1 cup fresh or frozen
   strawberries
½ cup pineapple chunks
½ cup plain yogurt
¼ cup instant nonfat
   dry milk
1 tsp. sugar
¼ tsp. vanilla
4 ice cubes

SERVES 2
Put all ingredients in blender and puree until thick and smooth.

BONNIE'S ORANGE JULIANA

⅓ cup frozen orange juice
   concentrate
½ cup milk
¼ cup sugar
½ cup water
½ tsp. vanilla
2 scoops vanilla ice cream

MAKES 3 CUPS
Combine ingredients in blender and blend until smooth. Can be made day before and kept in refrigerator.

HOT APPLE CIDER

2 quarts apple cider
½ cup brown sugar
¼ tsp. salt
1 tsp. whole allspice
1 tsp. whole cloves
3 cinnamon sticks
Orange and lemon slices

SERVES 8-10
Heat and mix all ingredients well. Cover and let simmer 15-20 minutes. Strain spices.

APPETIZERS & BEVERAGES

HOT BUTTERED CIDER MIX

1 cup soft butter or
   margarine
1 ⅓ cups light brown sugar
6 Tbsp. honey
2 tsp. nutmeg
2 tsp. cinnamon
2 tsp. vanilla
6 oz. rum, optional
Hot cider

Cream butter and sugar. Add other ingredients. Leave out rum if mixture is to be refrigerated. When ready to serve, add 1 tablespoon of mixture and 1 jigger of rum to each cup of hot cider.

HOT CHOCOLATE

1 cup milk
1 heaping tsp. cocoa
2 heaping tsp. sugar

SERVES 1
Combine cocoa and sugar in pan. Pour in ¼ cup milk and stir over medium heat. As it warms the cocoa will dissolve. Add remainder of milk. Top with marshmallows or whipped cream.

MEXICAN HOT CHOCOLATE

½ cup sugar
⅓ cup unsweetened cocoa
   powder
2 Tbsp. flour
1 tsp. ground cinnamon
½ tsp. salt
1½ cups cold water
6 cups milk
1 Tbsp. vanilla

MAKES 10 SERVINGS
Combine sugar, cocoa powder, flour, cinnamon, and salt in a large saucepan. Stir in cold water and bring to a boil stirring constantly. Reduce heat and simmer, stirring often. Slowly stir in milk and heat almost to boiling. Remove from heat, add vanilla. With a rotary beater or mixer, beat the mixture until it is frothy. Serve in mugs or cups garnishing each with a cinnamon stick or a dollop of whipped cream. This is an unusual and delicious holiday drink.

APPETIZERS & BEVERAGES

DADDY'S EGGNOG

4 eggs, separated
½ cup sugar
¼ tsp. salt
¾ cup bourbon
¾ cup milk
½ pint whipping cream
2 Tbsp. sugar
Nutmeg

MAKES 1 QUART
Cream egg yolks with ½ cup sugar, add ¼ teaspoon salt and beat until fluffy. Add bourbon and milk. Whip ½ pint cream, and fold into the egg yolk mixture. Beat egg whites to soft peaks, adding 2 tablespoons sugar. Fold into the mixture. Refrigerate. Sprinkle nutmeg on top.

GOLDEN WASSAIL

4 cups unsweetened
  pineapple juice
4 cups apple cider
1—12 oz. can apricot
  nectar
1 cup orange juice
6 inches stick cinnamon
1 tsp. whole cloves
1½ cups rum (optional)
Cinnamon sticks

MAKES 9 CUPS
In a large saucepan, combine juices and spices. Heat to boiling; reduce heat and simmer 15 to 20 minutes. Strain. Stir in rum and heat through. Serve with cinnamon stick stirrers. Great at holiday parties.

HOLIDAY PUNCH

3 pieces ginger
1—3 inch stick cinnamon
8 whole cloves
3-4 cardamom seeds
6 lemons
6 small oranges
1 gal. apple cider
1 qt. pineapple juice
½ tsp. salt
Rum, optional

40-50 SERVINGS
Tie spices in a bag of fine cheesecloth. Peel and cut lemons and oranges into thin slices and add to combined cider and pineapple juice. Add spice bag to this mixture and bring to a very low simmering boil. Stir as it simmers for 15 minutes, then add the salt and stir vigorously. Serve hot. May add rum, just before serving, if desired.

APPETIZERS & BEVERAGES

SPICED TEA

1 cup instant tea
2 cups Tang
2 cups sugar
1 envelope lemonade mix
1½ tsp. cinnamon
¾ tsp. ground cloves

MAKES 5½ CUPS
Mix ingredients well. Store in jar or tin. Place a heaping teaspoon in a mug of boiling water for a cup of delicious tea.

SANGRIA

1—12 oz. can Five Alive
   Fruit Punch frozen
   concentrate
2 cups water
1 cup wine, white or rose
Orange, lime or lemon,
   sliced thin

SERVES 8
Mix fruit juice, water and wine in large pitcher. Add ice and float sliced oranges, lemons, or limes in pitcher. This tasty, refreshing, summertime drink is especially good with Mexican food.

BLOODY MARYS

1—32 oz. can tomato juice
8 oz. vodka
¼ tsp. pepper
1-2 Tbsp. Worcestershire
   sauce
1 tsp. sugar
1 Tbsp. salt
Juice of 4 limes
6-8 dashes of Tabasco

SERVES 8
Mix together and serve over ice.

FROZEN DAIQUIRI

1—12 oz. can frozen limeade concentrate
12 oz. light rum
1-2 cups crushed ice
Strawberries, optional

SERVES 4
Place ingredients in a blender and blend until ice is slushy. To make strawberry daiquiries, add ½ pint strawberries before blending.

SKIER'S DELIGHT

1 qt. Burgundy wino
4 oranges, studded with 6 cloves, and sliced
4 lemons, sliced
3 cinnamon sticks, in pieces
1 cup sugar

SERVES 4-6
Heat wine to a simmer, add fruit, spices and sugar. Stir to dissolve sugar. Cook 10 minutes over low heat. Remove fruit pieces and cloves. Serve in heavy mugs on a cold winter evening.

Freeze fresh fruits and use them as you would a block of ice; nectarines, peaches, cherries, and grapes all freeze well.

Eggs

&

Cheese

EGGS & CHEESE

MORNING GLORY BRUNCH CASSEROLE

18 hard-boiled eggs
  sliced thin
1 lb. bacon, cooked
  and drained
¼ cup flour
¼ cup butter
1 cup cream
1 cup milk
1 lb. jar Cheese Whiz
¼ tsp. thyme (crushed leaf)
¼ tsp. marjoram
1/8 tsp. garlic powder
¼ cup chopped parsley,
  fresh if possible

SERVES 8-10

Hard boil eggs, cool and slice. (If you have an egg slicer, it saves a lot of time.) Make a cream sauce, adding flour to melted butter. Gradually add milk and cream, stirring constantly until thick. Add Cheese Whiz and stir until melted. Add seasonings, including half the parsley. In a buttered 9 x 12 inch baking dish, layer egg slices, sauce, crumbled bacon, etc., ending with sauce. Bake about 40 minutes, covered, in a 350° oven. Garnish with fresh parsley. Serve hot and bubbly. This is an exceptional brunch dish, especially when made a day ahead . . . gives the flavors a chance to blend, and the cook an extra hour of sleep! Serve it with Blueberry Muffins (also made ahead), grits, and a fresh Fruit Salad with Poppy Seed Dressing. You will never do better!

FRENCH HAM AND CHEESE SOUFFLE

3 cups cubed French
  bread
3 cups cubed cooked ham
½ lb. cubed cheddar
  cheese
3 Tbsp. flour
1 Tbsp. dry mustard
3 Tbsp. melted butter
4 eggs
3 cups milk
Few drops of Tabasco

SERVES 8

Make a day ahead. Layer ⅓ of the bread, ham and cheese in a buttered 9 x 13 inch dish. Mix flour and mustard. Sprinkle 1 tablespoon flour/mustard mixture over first layer of bread, ham, and cheese mixture. Drizzle 1 tablespoon melted butter over layer. Repeat twice. Beat eggs with milk and Tabasco until frothy. Pour over mixture and cover; chill overnight. Bake uncovered at 350° about 1 hour.

EGGS BENEDICT

4 English muffin halves
2 Tbsp. butter
4 slices of ham or
    Canadian bacon (or 8
    slices bacon, cooked)
4 eggs

HOLLANDAISE SAUCE:
2 egg yolks
2½-3 Tbsp. lemon juice
½ cup cold butter (1 cube)

1 avocado
2 Tbsp. sour cream

SERVES 4
Butter muffin halves and toast under broiler. Fry ham or bacon. Poach eggs. Put ham on muffin and top with egg.

Prepare hollandaise sauce. Combine egg yolks and lemon juice in small saucepan. Mix briskly. Add cube of butter whole, do not cut up. Cook over low heat, stirring constantly until thickened. Spoon hollandaise sauce over each serving. For an extra treat, top each egg with a spoonful of mashed avocado mixed with sour cream. Serve with hot buttered green peas for an added touch.

SUNDAY BRUNCH

1 dozen eggs
1 onion, chopped
3 Tbsp. butter
4-6 medium potatoes,
    diced small
1 lb. sausage, browned
    and crumbled (cooked
    ham or crumbled bacon
    can also be used)
1 cup sharp cheddar
    cheese, grated

SERVES 8
Brown onion in butter. Add diced potatoes, and cook with onion until tender. Layer a greased 9 x 11 inch casserole with potatoes and onions, then a layer of cooked, crumbled sausage. Mix the dozen eggs as though you were going to scramble them, and pour over mixture. Bake uncovered in 300° oven for 30 minutes. Stir every 5-10 minutes so it cooks evenly. Top with grated cheese the last 5 minutes. Do not overcook or eggs will get tough. Serve with Baking Powder Biscuits or Apple Muffins.

 When replacing dried herbs with fresh herbs, use twice the amount.

OMLETTE FOR ONE

1 tsp. butter
2 large eggs, slightly
   beaten
1 tsp. water
Salt
Pepper

FILLINGS:
2-3 Tbsp. grated cheddar
   cheese
2-3 Tbsp. diced ham
1 tsp. chopped green onion
   •
3 Tbsp. Pace's picante
   sauce
   •
2-3 Tbsp. grated Swiss
   cheese
2 slices bacon, fried and
   crumbled
   •
2-3 Tbsp. sauteed
   mushrooms
2-3 Tbsp. Monterey Jack
   cheese, grated

Heat butter in small skillet or omlette pan until it sizzles. Mix beaten eggs with water; pour into skillet, making sure it covers the entire bottom of the pan. Cook over medium high heat until edges begin to set. Sprinkle the filling of your choice on one side of the omlette, then fold the other side over it. Lower heat; cook about 1-2 minutes more. Remove from pan and season with salt and pepper. Omlettes make wonderful Sunday night suppers, especially good with buttered toast and Strawberry Jam.

SAUSAGE SOUFFLE

4 eggs
2 cups milk
1 lb. sausage, browned
   and crumbled (cubed
   ham or crumbled
   bacon can also be used)
¼ cup cheddar cheese,
   grated
1 tsp. dry mustard
½ tsp. salt

SERVES 6
Beat 4 eggs with 2 cups milk, add other ingredients. Pour into greased 10 x 8½ x 2 inch casserole dish. Bake for 45 minutes at 350°, covered with foil, and 15 minutes at 325° uncovered. Serve with Cinnamon Rolls and orange slices dusted with powdered sugar and fresh mint leaves.

❤ ❤ ❤ ❤ ❤ ❤ ❤ ❤ ❤_❤ ❤ ❤ ❤ ❤ ❤ ❤

HAM AND EGG PIE

4 large eggs, beaten
¼ tsp. pepper
¼ tsp. baking powder
½ cup milk
2 cups cooked ham, cubed
1 cup grated cheddar
  cheese
1—9 inch pastry pie shell,
  unbaked

SERVES 6
Preheat oven to 425°. Beat eggs slightly. Add remaining ingredients and mix well. Pour into unbaked pie shell. Bake for 35 minutes or until inserted knife comes out clean. Serve hot or cold.

CHIPPED BEEF AND EGGS

3 Tbsp. butter
¼ cup onion, chopped
¼ cup celery, sliced
2½ oz. sliced processed
  beef, torn into pieces
3 Tbsp. flour
2¼ cups milk
¼ tsp. dried leaf basil
Dash of Tabasco
Salt and pepper to taste
6 eggs, hard-cooked, sliced
Toast triangles or patty
  shells for 6
  (in the frozen food section
  of the supermarket)

SERVES 6
Melt butter in large skillet. Add onion and celery and cook over low heat until tender. Add chipped beef and heat. Blend in flour. Remove from heat and stir in milk, Tabasco, and basil. Return to heat and stir over low heat until mixture thickens and boils. Add eggs and heat through. Serve over toast triangles or in patty shells.

HAM STRATA

2—10 oz. pkg. frozen,
  chopped broccoli
12 slices bread, edges
  trimmed
1½ cups cheddar cheese,
  grated
4 cups ham, diced
6 eggs
3 cups milk
½ tsp. salt
¼ tsp. dry mustard
1 Tbsp. onion flakes

SERVES 6
Cook broccoli according to package directions. Drain well. Butter a 9 x 13 inch casserole dish. Layer bottom with bread slices, grated cheese, ham, and chopped broccoli. Beat eggs and add milk, salt and mustard. Mix well and pour over layered mixture. Sprinkle with onion flakes. Refrigerate 6-8 hours or overnight. Bake, uncovered, one hour and 20 minutes at 325°.

EGGS & CHEESE

♥ ♥ ♥ ♥ ♥ ♥ ♥ ♥ ♥ ♥ ♥ ♥ ♥ ♥ ♥ ♥ ♥

DEVILED EGGS

5 hard-boiled eggs
¼ tsp. salt
¼ tsp. prepared mustard
4 tsp. mayonnaise
1 tsp. vinegar
Paprika or chopped
   parsley

MAKES 10
Halve shelled, cooled hard-boiled eggs lengthwise. Remove yolks and mash; add remaining ingredients and whip until smooth and fluffy. Heap into whites and sprinkle with paprika or chopped parsley.

EGG FU YONG

7 eggs
1—8 oz. can
   water chestnuts, sliced
1 cup small shrimp
1 cup bean shoots
½ green pepper, diced
⅓ onion, diced
1 Tbsp. salad oil
2-3 Tbsp. soy sauce

SAUCE:
¼ cup water
2 Tbsp. cornstarch
2 cups beef bouillon
2 Tbsp. soy sauce

SERVES 4
Beat eggs in bowl. Add water chestnuts, shrimp, bean shoots, pepper, and onion. Mix well. Pour 1 tablespoon oil in skillet and warm. Fill bottom of skillet with 1½-2 cups mixture. With spoon, spread vegetables out evenly around skillet. Cook slowly until egg mixture starts to firm and bottom is slightly golden. When egg mixture starts to set, cut it into four sections with spatula and turn each. Brown other side and serve hot with sauce spooned over top. Sprinkle with soy sauce.

To make sauce, combine cornstarch and water in small saucepan. Add beef bouillon, then soy sauce. Heat and stir until sauce is thick and smooth.

 When hardboiling eggs, put a heaping teaspoon of salt in the water to prevent the shells from cracking.

28

SEAFOOD QUICHE

1—9 inch pastry shell,
  unbaked
2 Tbsp. green onion,
  minced
2-3 Tbsp. butter
1 cup cooked crab, lobster
  or shrimp
3 eggs
1 cup cream
¼ tsp. salt
Pepper
¼ cup Swiss cheese,
  grated

SERVES 4-6
Saute onions in butter. Add fish and cook 2 minutes more. Beat eggs, cream and seasoning. Add cheese, fish and onion. Mix well. Pour into pastry shell and bake at 375° for 25-30 minutes.

PARMESAN QUICHE

1—10 in. cooked pie shell
4 Tbsp. Parmesan cheese,
  grated
½ lb. bacon, fried and
  crumbled
2 whole eggs plus 2 yolks
1 tsp. Dijon mustard
1 tsp. dry mustard
½ tsp. salt
1/8 tsp. cayenne pepper
⅓ cup strained bacon fat
½ cup grated Parmesan
  cheese
2½ cups scalded heavy
  cream
½ lb. bacon, fried
  and crumbled (for
  topping)
Chopped parsley

SERVES 6
Fill pie crust with 4 tablespoons Parmesan cheese and ½ pound bacon pieces. In a bowl, mix eggs and egg yolks; stir in mustards, salt, pepper, bacon fat and the ½ cup Parmesan cheese. Add cream and stir well. Pour mixture into pie crust and bake at 350° for 25 minutes. During last five minutes of baking, scatter the other ½ pound bacon pieces on top. Garnish with chopped parsley.

To prevent a quiche or pumpkin pie crust from becoming soggy, partially bake the pastry shell in a 425° oven for 15 minutes. Brush lightly with beaten egg white or yolk and return to oven for 2 minutes. Pour the filling into the pastry shell just before baking.

Soups

&

Sandwiches

SOUPS & SANDWICHES

♥ ♥ ♥ ♥ ♥ ♥ ♥ ♥ ♥ ♥ ♥ ♥ ♥ ♥ ♥ ♥ ♥

ASPARAGUS WITH CREAM CHEESE

1—10 oz. pkg. frozen
  asparagus, cut into
  1-inch pieces
4 cups regular strength
  chicken broth
Salt
2—3 oz. pkg. cream cheese

SERVES 6

Combine asparagus and broth in saucepan, bring to a boil, and simmer gently for 10 minutes. Add salt to taste. Cut cream cheese into ½ inch cubes and place in each soup bowl. Pour hot asparagus and broth over cream cheese and serve. This is an unusual and tasty first course soup!

BEER CHEESE SOUP

1 stalk celery, chopped
1 carrot, chopped
1 onion, minced
2 Tbsp. butter
½ cup flour
3 cans chicken broth
5 cans cheddar cheese
  soup, undiluted
1 tsp. dry mustard
6 medium potatoes, pared,
  boiled, and diced (or less
  according to your taste)
1 can beer, flat
Fresh cut broccoli, optional
Fresh cut cauliflower,
  optional

SERVES 10

In large soup pot, saute celery, carrot, and onion in butter. Blend together flour and 1 can chicken broth. Add to sauteed vegetables and stir constantly until thickened. Mix in the remaining chicken broth, cheddar cheese soup, dry mustard and potatoes. Stir well. Add flat beer. Cook over low heat, covered, for ½ hour. Add broccoli or cauliflower and cook an additional 20 minutes. This is tasty with big fat submarine sandwiches for a large crowd, or as a first course with steamed shrimp.

BROCCOLI SOUP

2—10 oz. pkg. frozen
   broccoli
¼ cup onion, chopped
2 cups chicken broth
2 Tbsp. butter
1 Tbsp. flour
1½ tsp. salt
Dash pepper
2 cups half and half

SERVES 6

In medium pan, combine onion, chicken broth and broccoli. Bring to boil, simmer for 10 minutes or until broccoli is tender. Puree in blender until very smooth. Melt butter in pan, add flour, salt and pepper. Slowly stir in half and half. Add broccoli puree and cook, stirring constantly until it bubbles.

CREAM OF CARROT SOUP

½ cup cooked rice
4 large carrots (about
   1 lb.), sliced
1 medium onion, chopped
1 small stalk celery,
   chopped (with leaves)
2 tsp. chicken bouillon
   granules
1-1½ cups water
1 tsp. salt
White pepper
¾ cup cream

SERVES 6

Place carrots, onion, and celery in saucepan with water and bouillon. Bring to boil, cover, reduce heat; simmer 15 minutes or until carrots are tender.

When vegetables are tender, drain most of the liquid into a cup and save. Puree vegetables and rice in food processor or blender until smooth. Add salt and pepper, and with machine running, add reserved broth. Return soup to pot. If serving immediately, whisk cream into soup, adjust the seasoning, and heat but don't boil. If serving later, refrigerate without cream and add just before reheating. (If you like cold soups, this one will work beautifully. Add cream to hot soup and chill.)

SOUPS & SANDWICHES

♥ ♥ ♥ ♥ ♥ ♥ ♥ ♥ ♥ ♥ ♥ ♥ ♥ ♥ ♥ ♥ ♥

CHICKEN AND DOUGHIES

1 small chicken, stewed,
  deboned, and cut up
½ tsp. salt
½ tsp. pepper
¼ tsp. onion salt
¼ tsp. poultry seasoning
2 tsp. chicken bouillon
  granules
2 eggs
1½ cups flour

SERVES 6
Cook chicken in 1 quart water which has been seasoned with salt, pepper, onion salt and poultry seasoning. Remove chicken from broth, saving broth. Debone and cut up chicken. Return chicken to broth. Add bouillon and enough water to have 1½ quarts liquid. In bowl, beat eggs with fork. Add flour and work dough with fingers only until all the flour is moistened. (Do not overwork dough.) Bring chicken broth to a boil and drop dough into chicken soup. Break up with fingers as you drop it to make marble size pieces. Let simmer 15 minutes. Season to your liking.

CLAM CHOWDER

1 cup onion, chopped
½ cup salt pork or bacon,
  diced
½ cup butter
1 cup raw potatoes, diced
  fine
½ cup water
2 Tbsp. flour
2 cups milk
1 cup cream
2 cups clams, canned,
  frozen, or fresh

SERVES 6
Saute onion and salt pork or bacon in the butter until tender but not brown. Add potatoes and water and cook until potatoes are soft. Add flour, cook 2 minutes. Add milk and simmer 5 minutes, stirring constantly. Stir in cream and clams and heat through.

 If you over-salt your soup, de-salt it by slicing a raw potato into it. Boil for a short time, then remove the potato.

CORN CHOWDER

2 Tbsp. bacon fat
¼ cup butter
3 large onions, chopped
¼ green pepper, diced
8 medium potatoes, peeled
  and diced
4 cups milk
2 cups whipping cream
5 cups fresh corn kernels,
  or frozen kernels, cooked
¼ cup minced parsley
½-1 tsp. nutmeg
1 tsp. salt
½ tsp. pepper
¼ cup butter
6-8 slices bacon, fried
  crisp and crumbled

SERVES 12
Melt ¼ cup butter and bacon fat in skillet. Add onion and saute over medium heat until tender. Add green pepper and saute 2-3 minutes. Remove from heat. Cook potatoes in boiling water until tender. Drain well. Combine milk and cream in large saucepan and heat slowly. When warm, add all ingredients except ¼ cup butter and bacon. Bring to simmer; remove from heat and let stand at least 3 hours to thicken. Before serving, warm soup. Stir in remaining butter. Thin with milk if desired. Garnish each bowlful with crumbled bacon.

LENTIL SOUP

2 cups ham, cubed
2 cups lentils, washed
  thoroughly
5 cups hot water
1 stalk celery, chopped
1 medium onion, chopped
1 bay leaf
1/8 tsp. garlic powder
2 tsp. salt
1/8 tsp. pepper

SERVES 6
Combine all ingredients and simmer for 2 hours. Remove bay leaf. Puree in a food processor or blender. This makes a thick, hearty soup. Served with fruit and cheese, it makes a delicious winter meal.

CREAM OF MUSHROOM SOUP

1 lb. fresh mushrooms,
   sliced
8 green onions, including
   tops, sliced
5 cups chicken broth
¼ lb. butter
7 Tbsp. flour
½ cup dry sherry
¼ tsp. nutmeg
1 pt. heavy cream

SERVES 8
Place mushrooms in saucepan. Cook covered, over medium heat until nearly dry. Add green onions and cook until dry. Add 2 cups chicken broth. Remove from heat. In heavy 3 quart saucepan, melt butter. Add flour to make a paste, and cook, stirring over medium heat 2-3 minutes. Add vegetables in broth to butter and flour. Add remaining broth. Bring to boil, then reduce heat and simmer 20 minutes. Add sherry and simmer 10 minutes. Remove from heat. Cool 5 minutes. Whisk in cream and nutmeg and heat through. Do not boil.

QUICK MUSHROOM SOUP

1½ lbs. fresh mushrooms,
   sliced
½ cup butter
1 tsp. chicken bouillon
¼ cup water
1 pt. milk
1 pt. cream
1 tsp. salt
1 Tbsp. butter
1 Tbsp. flour

SERVES 4
Saute mushrooms in melted butter. Mix chicken bouillon with water. Pour over mushrooms; let simmer 1 minute. Combine this mixture with milk, cream and salt in a saucepan. Melt 1 tablespoon butter in a cup and add 1 tablespoon flour to make a paste. Stir into soup. Simmer 15-20 minutes.

♥ ♥ ♥ ♥ ♥ ♥ ♥ ♥ ♥ ♥ ♥ ♥ ♥ ♥ ♥ ♥

FRENCH ONION SOUP

4 yellow onions, thinly
   sliced
4 Tbsp. butter
1 qt. beef stock
1½ cups croutons
   (buttered, toasted, and
   cubed French bread)
2 cups grated Swiss
   cheese
½ cup grated Parmesan
   cheese

SERVES 4
Melt butter in skillet. Saute onions until slightly brown. Add onions to beef broth in saucepan. Simmer slowly for 10 minutes. Pour into bowls. Place croutons on top of each bowlful, and either sprinkle Parmesan cheese on top and serve immediately, or cover croutons with Swiss cheese, then Parmesan and bake, covered, at 325° for 15 minutes. Uncover and bake another 10 minutes. Either way is delicious!

CHRISTMAS EVE OYSTER STEW

½ cup butter
2 pts. fresh or canned
   oysters
1 pt. cream
1 qt. milk
1½ tsp. salt
Pepper to taste

SERVES 10
Melt butter in skillet; add oysters. Cook over low heat for 10 minutes. Combine oysters and butter with other ingredients in large saucepan. Simmer, stirring occasionally, for 20 minutes. Reheat before serving. Make this specialty soup a Christmas Eve tradition —it deserves it!

HEARTY POTATO SOUP

6 potatoes, medium to large
2 slices onion, chopped
1 qt. boiling water
1 tsp. salt
¼ cup butter
1 Tbsp. flour
1 qt. milk
1 Tbsp. parsley

SERVES 6
Dice potatoes, or chop in food processor or food chopper. Cook in boiling salted water until mixture becomes thick and potatoes are soft. In large pan, melt butter, add flour, stir until smooth. Add milk, and stir constantly over medium heat, until thickened and smooth. Add potato mixture and chopped parsley. Serve hot.

ROCKY MOUNTAIN SOUP

6 slices bacon, diced
½ cup onion, chopped
2 cloves garlic, crushed
2 cans Ranch-style beans
½ cup rice, cooked
1—8 oz. can stewed
   tomatoes
2 tsp. salt
Dash of pepper and
   paprika
4 cups water

MAKES 6 CUPS
Fry diced bacon in saucepan. Drain. Saute onions and garlic in bacon fat until onions are golden. Add remaining ingredients and simmer 1-1½ hours to allow flavors to blend. Add water as necessary while cooking.

SAUSAGE SOUP

1 lb. bulk sausage
1 cup water
1 medium potato, diced
1 onion, chopped
1 bay leaf
1 tsp. liquid smoke
½ tsp. pepper
½ tsp. summer savory
1—10 oz. pkg. frozen
   mixed vegetables
⅓ cup water
1 tsp. sugar
2 cans cream of chicken
   soup
1 can cream of mushroom
   soup
1 can cream of celery soup
1 soup can milk
½ cup butter
⅔ cup Velveeta cheese,
   grated

SERVES 6-8
Crumble sausage in frying pan and cook until done. Drain fat. In large saucepan mix sausage, water, potato, onion, bay leaf, liquid smoke, pepper and summer savory. In small saucepan, cook the frozen vegetables, water and sugar until they are tender. Pour mixed vegetables into large saucepan, then add remaining ingredients. Stir until well blended and simmer until the potatoes are tender and flavors blended, about 30 minutes. Kids like this soup.

❤ ❤ ❤ ❤ ❤ ❤ ❤ ❤ ❤ ❤ ❤ ❤ ❤ ❤ ❤ ❤ ❤

HOMEMADE VEGETABLE SOUP

1 beef soup bone
2 qts. water
2 bay leaves
1 Tbsp. salt
Pepper to taste
3 stalks celery, sliced
3 large carrots, peeled
　and sliced
4 medium potatoes, pared
　and chopped
2—1 lb. cans whole peeled
　tomatoes
⅓ cup barley
1 large onion, chopped

SERVES 10-12
Place soupbone in large Dutch oven and cover with water. Add bay leaves. Simmer 2 hours. Remove the soup bone and give it to the dog! Let stock cool and skim fat. Add remaining ingredients and simmer 2 more hours. Adjust seasoning. This soup is really better the day after it is made, as the flavors have blended by then. Peas, green beans, corn, or other vegetables can be added to suit your taste.

MOM'S HOT CRABMEAT SANDWICHES

12 slices bread, crust
　removed
1—7 oz. can crabmeat,
　rinsed and drained
1 cup sharp cheese, grated
Onion powder
3 eggs, beaten until frothy
3 cups milk
½ tsp. salt
1 cup sharp cheese, grated
1 can cream of mushroom
　soup

SERVES 6
Butter 6 slices of bread, and lay in bottom of 9 x 11 buttered Pyrex pan. Spread crabmeat on each piece of bread, then cheese. Sprinkle with onion powder, and top with other 6 slices of bread. Mix eggs, milk and salt. Pour over bread mixture and top with 1 cup cheese. Cover. Let stand in refrigerator overnight. Bake 1 hour, uncovered, at 350° and serve with cream of mushroom soup, heated and undiluted on top. This is really delicious and makes a nifty luncheon dish.

SOUPS & SANDWICHES

CARAWAY CRABMEAT SANDWICH

½ lb. mushrooms, sliced
1 Tbsp. butter
6½ oz. can crabmeat,
    drained and flaked
4 green onions, sliced
1 tsp. caraway seeds
Mayonnaise
8 slices bacon, cooked
    and crumbled
8 slices cheddar cheese
8 Kaiser rolls, split

SERVES 8
Saute mushrooms in butter. Combine mushrooms with crabmeat, onions, bacon and caraway seeds and enough mayonnaise to moisten. Spread crabmeat mixture on half of a roll, top with cheese slice, then other half of roll. Cover and bake at 350° for 7 minutes or until cheese melts.

CHEESE BLINTZES

1½ lb. loaf sliced white
    bread, crusts removed
8 oz. cream cheese
1 egg yolk
¼ cup sugar
2 Tbsp. minced onion
½ cup butter, melted
Paprika

MAKES 28
Beat together cream cheese, egg yolk, sugar and onion. Roll bread paper thin between wax paper with rolling pin. Place 1 tablespoon cream cheese mixture on each slice, spread and roll up. Cut in half. Roll in melted butter. Place on waxed paper, seam side down, for half hour to absorb butter. Can be refrigerated or frozen at this point. To freeze, place in freezer uncovered and separated for 1 hour, then store in plastic bag. Bake at 400° for 10 minutes or until lightly browned. Sprinkle with paprika and serve warm. These are delicious luncheon sandwiches. You can also slice them and serve as appetizers.

HOT HAM SANDWICHES

12 Kaiser rolls, split
1—8 oz. tub butter
  or margarine
2 Tbsp. poppy seeds
4 Tbsp. chives
4 Tbsp. prepared mustard
2-3 lbs. ham, sliced very
  thin
24 slices Swiss cheese

MAKES 12 SANDWICHES
Mix butter, seeds, chives and mustard. Spread on buns. Place a slice of cheese on each side of bun and ham in the middle. Wrap in heavy foil. At this point you may either freeze the sandwiches, or bake them. Bake at 375° about 20 minutes if thawed, 45 minutes if frozen. These are great to make ahead and pull out 2-3 at a time. Double the recipe if you have the freezer space.

HAM AND PIMENTO SANDWICH

2 slices bread, spread with
  Durkee's Sandwich
  Spread (can use your
  choice of mustards or
  mayonnaise)
1 slice ham (¼ inch)
1 slice pimento
1 egg, beaten
½ cup milk
Dash salt
Corn flakes, crushed
Butter, melted

MAKES 1
Make a sandwich of ham, pimento, and bread. Dip it in a mixture of egg, milk and a little salt. Roll in corn flakes and fry in butter. Rich but good!

HAM SALAD SANDWICH

1 cup ham, cooked and
   ground
1-2 sweet pickles, chopped,
   or 2 Tbsp. pickle relish
1 Tbsp. onion, chopped
¼-⅓ cup mayonnaise
¼ cup celery, chopped
   (optional)
2-3 eggs, hard cooked,
   chopped fine (optional)

MAKES 6
Combine all ingredients and spread on slices of bread. Try substituting tuna, ground roast beef, additional chopped hard-boiled eggs, or ground chicken for the ham.

MARCO POLOS

6 English muffin halves
1 lb. thinly sliced ham
1 lb. thinly sliced turkey
½ onion, sliced thin
1 tomato, sliced
1 or 2—10 oz. pkgs.
   broccoli, cooked and
   drained

CHEESE SAUCE:
3 Tbsp. butter
3 Tbsp. flour
2 cups milk or
   half and half
1-1½ cups cheddar
   cheese, grated
½ tsp. salt
Paprika

MAKES 6 SANDWICHES
Butter each muffin half and arrange on a cookie sheet. Broil to toast. On each muffin, arrange ham slice, turkey, onion, tomato and 1-2 stalks broccoli.

To make sauce, melt butter in saucepan, stir in flour, then milk, stirring until thickened. Add cheddar cheese and salt; stir until melted. Pour hot cheese sauce over warmed sandwiches (warm 10 minutes in a covered pan at 325°), then sprinkle with paprika. (Sandwiches can also be heated in the microwave after the cheese sauce has been poured over them.) These are a real quick wholemeal sandwich that are great for drop-in guests.

A pastry blender will chop hard-boiled eggs and tuna quickly and finely for salads and sandwiches.

FRENCH BREAD AND MEAT SANDWICH

1 loaf French bread
4 Tbsp. butter, melted
Garlic salt
1 lb. ground beef
3 Tbsp. soy sauce
1 Tbsp. chili powder
4 Tbsp. tomato paste
1 tsp. basil
2 slices chopped onion
1 lb. can dark red
  kidney beans
5 Tbsp. sour cream
1 Tbsp. chili powder
1 slice onion, chopped
1 cup cheddar cheese,
  grated

SERVES 6-8
Cut off top ⅓ of loaf of French bread. Hollow out inside of both sides, saving the bread for crumbs. Brush inside with melted butter and garlic salt. Brown hamburger; drain fat. Add soy sauce, chili powder, tomato paste, basil, and onion. Heat through. In separate bowl, mix beans, sour cream, chili powder, and onion. Place meat in bread shell, pile the bean mixture on top. Sprinkle with cheese. Replace top of bread loaf, place in foil wrapping, and bake at 350° 30-45 minutes. Slice to serve.

GLORIFIED HAMBURGERS

1 cup cabbage, chopped
½ cup carrots, shredded
¾ tsp. salt
¼ tsp. oregano
1/8 tsp. pepper
½ cup onion, chopped
1 Tbsp. water
1½ tsp. Worcestershire
  sauce
1 lb. hamburger, cooked
  and drained
4 Pita breads

SERVES 4
Combine all ingredients except beef and pitas in saucepan. Cook until vegetables are tender. Add meat and heat through. Fill pita bread with mixture; wrap each in foil and bake 15 minutes at 350°.

SOUPS & SANDWICHES

SLOPPY JOES

1 lb. ground beef
1 medium onion, chopped
3 Tbsp. ketchup
3 Tbsp. mustard
1 Tbsp. Heinz 57
   steak sauce
6 hamburger buns

SERVES 6
Brown meat and onion until onion is tender; drain fat. Add other ingredients and heat through. Serve on hamburger buns.

FRENCH DIP

Prime Rib roast, sliced thin
1 pkg. Au Jus mixture
Small French rolls

Layer thin slices of left-over prime rib on split roll. (Also good to spread sour cream and horseradish on roll.) Prepare Au Jus according to package directions. Heat Au Jus to boiling then pour into bowl for dipping sandwiches.

REUBENS

8 slices rye bread
⅓ cup mayonnaise
½ lb. sliced Swiss cheese
½ lb. sliced cooked
   corned beef
1—1 lb. can sauerkraut,
   drained
Butter

SERVES 4
Spread mayonnaise on slices of bread. Arrange cheese, corned beef and warm sauerkraut on slices. Butter outside side of bread, toast in skillet over low heat on both sides. Cover skillet with lid while toasting.

FRENCH BREAD PIZZA

1 loaf French bread
1 can pizza sauce
¾ lb. mozzarella cheese, grated
1 lb. Italian sausage (or topping of your choice), cooked and crumbled

SERVES 4
Cut bread lengthwise, top with sauce, then cheese, then sausage. Bake in 350° oven until thoroughly warmed, and cheese begins to bubble and brown, about 15 minutes.

ITALIAN SAUSAGE SANDWICH

4 small French rolls
2 lb. Italian sausage
2 cups spaghetti sauce

SERVES 4
Cut sausage into 4-inch lengths and fry slowly until done. Split the rolls lengthwise, put sausage on them, and top with warmed spaghetti sauce. Good and fast sandwich.

 To freshen stale pototo chips, crackers, etc., microwave 16 ounces for 30-45 seconds on high.

Breads

BREAD

APPLE BREAD

½ cup shortening
1 cup sugar
2 eggs, beaten
1 cup coarse ground
  apples
1 Tbsp. orange rind
2 cups flour
1 tsp. soda
½ tsp. salt
2 Tbsp. buttermilk
1 tsp. vanilla
½ cup nuts, chopped

MAKES 1 LOAF
Cream shortening, sugar, and eggs until fluffy. Stir in apples and orange rind. Sift dry ingredients and add alternately with buttermilk. Stir in vanilla and nuts. Bake in greased loaf pan at 350° for about 1 hour. Delicious!

APRICOT BREAD

2 cups sugar
1 cup vegetable oil
3 eggs
2 small jars apricot/tapioca
  baby food
1½ tsp. baking powder
½ tsp. salt
2 cups flour
1 tsp. cinnamon
1 cup chopped nuts

MAKES 2 LOAVES
Beat the sugar, oil and eggs well. Add the apricots and mix well. Sift dry ingredients and add to apricot mixture. Stir in chopped nuts. Bake in greased and floured loaf pans. Place in cold oven and turn to 350°. Bake for about 1½ hours.

BANANA BREAD

½ cup butter, softened
1 cup sugar
2 eggs
3 ripe bananas, mashed
2 cups flour
1 tsp. salt
1 tsp. baking soda, dissolved
   in 3 Tbsp. cold water
1 tsp. vanilla
½ cup pecans, chopped

MAKES 1 LOAF
In a mixing bowl, cream butter and sugar. Add eggs and bananas. Beat in remaining ingredients. Pour into a greased 9-inch loaf pan. Bake at 350° for 40-45 minutes.

CHERRY BREAD

¾ cup sugar
½ cup butter or margarine
2 eggs
1 tsp. vanilla
¼ tsp. almond extract
2 cups flour
1 tsp. baking soda
½ tsp. salt
1 cup buttermilk
1 cup nuts, chopped
   (pecans or walnuts)
1—10 oz. jar maraschino
   cherries, chopped (save
   juice)

FROSTING:
1 cup powdered sugar
3 tsp. melted butter
Maraschino juice

MAKES 2 SMALL LOAVES
Cream sugar, butter, eggs, vanilla and almond extract. Mix until fluffy. Mix dry ingredients and add alternately with the buttermilk, ending with flour. Stir in chopped nuts and cherries. Pour into greased loaf pans and bake at 350° for 55-60 minutes. When cool, frost with cherry frosting. This bread is particularly festive at holiday time.

To make frosting, combine sugar and butter. Add maraschino juice, until it's the right spreading consistency for icing. A little red food coloring added to icing makes it prettier.

Always chill fruit breads for easier slicing.

BREAD

DATE AND NUT BREAD

1 Tbsp. butter
1 scant cup sugar
2 eggs, well beaten
2 cups flour
1 tsp. salt
1 tsp. baking powder
1 tsp. baking soda
1 cup boiling water
1 cup dates, chopped
1 cup nuts, chopped

MAKES 1 LOAF
Cream butter and sugar. Add well-beaten eggs, flour, salt and baking powder. Mix well. Dissolve 1 teaspoon baking soda in 1 cup boiling water. Pour this over chopped dates and nuts. Stir well and add to flour mixture. Pour into greased loaf pan and bake 30 minutes at 400°; then lower temperature to 300° and bake another 20-30 minutes. This recipe was sent to a Colorado cook in the 1920's from her American friend living in Peking, China. It is delicious and it NEVER fails. Serve it with a meal, or slice it, spread with thinned cream cheese, and serve as an appetizer.

NONIE'S PINEAPPLE CARROT BREAD

3 eggs
1½ cups salad oil
2 cups sugar
2 cups grated raw carrots
1 small can crushed
   pineapple with juice
2 tsp. vanilla
1 cup chopped nuts
3 cups sifted flour
1 tsp. salt
1 tsp. soda
1 tsp. baking powder
1 Tbsp. cinnamon

MAKES 2 LOAVES
In large mixing bowl, beat eggs, oil, and sugar. Stir in carrots, pineapple with juice, vanilla and nuts. Sift together flour, salt, soda, baking powder and cinnamon. Mix with carrot mixture thoroughly. Pour into two greased loaf pans and bake at 350° about 45 minutes or until done. Can also be baked in a 10 inch tube pan at 350° for 1 hour or until done.

RHUBARB TEA BREAD

3 eggs
1 cup oil
2 cups brown sugar
2 tsp. vanilla
2½ cups rhubarb, chopped
½ cup walnuts, chopped
3 cups flour
2 tsp. soda
2 tsp. cinnamon
1 tsp. salt
½ tsp. baking powder
½ tsp. nutmeg
½ tsp. allspice

MAKES 2 LOAVES
Beat eggs until thick and foamy. Add oil, brown sugar, and vanilla. Beat well. Stir in rhubarb and walnuts. Add remaining ingredients and mix well. Turn into two greased and floured loaf pans. Bake 1 hour at 350°.

ZUCCHINI BREAD

3 eggs, well beaten
2 cups sugar
3 tsp. vanilla
1 cup oil
2 cups shredded zucchini
  (unpeeled)
3 cups flour
½ tsp. baking powder
1 tsp. salt
1 tsp. soda
1 tsp. cinnamon
½ cup nuts, chopped
1 cup coconut, optional
1 cup chocolate chips,
  optional

MAKES 2 LOAVES
Beat eggs until light and fluffy. Add sugar, vanilla, and oil. Blend well. Stir in zucchini. Sift together flour, baking powder, salt, soda and cinnamon. Blend with egg mixture. Fold in nuts and coconut and chocolate chips if desired. Turn into two greased and floured 9 x 5 inch loaf pans. Bake at 350° for 1 hour.

BREAD

EASY BUBBLE BREAD

4 tubes buttermilk
   biscuits
¾ cup sugar
1 Tbsp. cinnamon
½ cup pecans, chopped
1 cup sugar
1 cup pancake syrup
1½ sticks butter

SERVES 8
Cut each biscuit into fourths and roll in mixture of cinnamon and ¾ cup sugar. Grease tube pan. Arrange biscuit pieces in layers, topping each layer with pecans. Sprinkle cinnamon-sugar mixture over top layer, using no more than ½ cup. Let sit 45 minutes before baking (or overnight). Melt together sugar, syrup and butter. Bring to boil and boil 1 minute. Pour over bread and bake at 350° for 1 hour. Turn onto serving dish which should have a lip to catch extra syrup which may run off as it cools.

GRANDMA WHITE'S PURPLE PLUM BUCKLE

½ cup margarine
¾ cup sugar
1 egg
1¾ cup flour
1¾ tsp. baking powder
¼ tsp. salt
½ cup + 1 Tbsp. milk
1 Tbsp. cinnamon
   topping
10-12 purple plums, sliced

CINNAMON TOPPING:
½ cup flour
½ cup sugar
½ tsp. cinnamon
½ stick butter

Combine topping ingredients in bowl and mix until crumbly. Cream ½ cup margarine and sugar, add egg and beat until fluffy. Add dry ingredients and 1 tablespoon of the topping alternately with milk. Pour batter in a 9 x 9 inch greased dish. Arrange the sliced plums on top. Sprinkle topping over plums. Bake 40-45 minutes at 375° or until golden brown. Serve as a coffee cake, or top with ice cream or whipped·cream for dessert.

ORANGE COFFEE CAKE

1 pkg. yeast
½ cup warm water
1 pkg. white cake mix
¼ cup orange juice
2 eggs

STREUSEL TOPPING:
½ cup flour
1 cup brown sugar (packed)
1 Tbsp. cinnamon
¼ cup butter, softened

GLAZE:
1 cup powdered sugar
2 Tbsp. butter, softened
2-3 Tbsp. orange juice

Dissolve yeast in warm water. Blend with cake mix, orange juice, and eggs. Beat well. Spread half the batter (about 2 cups) into a 9 x 13 inch pan. Sprinkle half the streusel topping over batter. Repeat with remaining batter and topping. Bake at 375° for 25-30 minutes. Drizzle glaze over warm cake.

CHOCOLATE CHIP COFFEE RING

1 cup sugar
½ cup butter or margarine
2 cups flour
1 cup sour cream
2 eggs
1 tsp. double-action
    baking powder
1¼ tsp. soda
1 tsp. vanilla
½ cup chocolate chips

TOPPING:
½ cup flour
½ cup packed light brown
    sugar
1½ tsp. cocoa
¼ cup butter
½ cup walnuts or pecans,
    chopped
1½ cup chocolate chips

Preheat oven to 350°. Grease 9 inch tube or Bundt pan. Beat sugar with ½ cup butter until light and fluffy. Add 2 cups flour and next five ingredients; beat at low speed until blended, constantly scraping bowl with rubber spatula. Increase speed to medium; beat 3 minutes. Stir in ½ cup chocolate chips. Spread batter evenly in pan.

In another bowl, measure ½ cup flour, brown sugar and cocoa. With pastry blender, cut in ¼ cup butter until the mixture resembles coarse crumbs. Stir in nuts and chocolate chips. Crumble mixture evenly over batter. Bake 60-65 minutes until cake pulls away from sides of pan. Cool completely. With small spatula, loosen cake from pan and remove.

BREAD

GRANDMA EATON'S COFFEE CAKE

2 cups flour
2 tsp. baking powder
1 tsp. salt
¾ cup sugar
2 rounded Tbsp. Crisco
1 cup milk

TOPPING:
2 Tbsp. melted butter
½ tsp. cinnamon
3 Tbsp. brown sugar

In mixing bowl, combine flour, baking powder, salt, sugar and Crisco. Set aside ¾ cup mixture for topping. Add milk to remainder of flour mixture, and mix until smooth. Pour batter into 8 x 8 inch buttered pan, and crumble topping over it. Bake at 350° for 30 minutes.

Topping: Combine melted butter, cinnamon, brown sugar, and ¾ cup of flour mixture; mix well.

SWEDISH PANCAKES

PANCAKE BATTER:
3 eggs
1¼ cup milk
¾ cup flour
1 Tbsp. sugar
½ tsp. salt

BERRY FILLING:
1 cup berries (strawberries
   or blueberries)
1/8 cup cold water
1 Tbsp. cornstarch
Sugar to taste (1/8-¼ cup)

MAKES 15
Combine batter ingredients in bowl and beat with mixer until smooth. Butter a round teflon skillet. Over medium heat, pour a thin (1/8 inch) layer of batter in bottom of pan. Cook as if making crepes. Cook on both sides for about a minute, or until firm and golden brown. Fill with thickened berry mixture, roll up, and top with powdered sugar and whipped cream.

To make berry mixture, put berries and water in a small saucepan. Add sugar and cornstarch which has been dissolved in 1/8 cup water. Stir over medium heat until thickened. These are a special treat on Sunday morning or for breakfast guests.

BREAD

NEW ORLEANS DOUGHNUTS (BEIGNETS)

1 pkg. active dry yeast
1½ cups warm water
 (105°)
½ cup sugar
1 tsp. salt
2 eggs
1 cup undiluted evaporated
 milk
7 cups flour
¼ cup soft shortening
Oil for frying
Powdered sugar or honey

MAKES 4 DOZEN
In large bowl, sprinkle yeast over water; stir to dissolve. Add sugar, salt, eggs, and milk. Blend with beater. Add 4 cups of flour; beat until smooth. Add shortening; beat in remaining flour. Cover and chill several hours. Dough will keep in refrigerator 4-5 days. Roll on floured board to 1/8 inch thickness. Cut into 2½ inch squares. Deep fry at 360° 2-3 minutes or until lightly browned on both sides. Drain on paper towel. Sprinkle heavily with powdered sugar. Also good with butter or honey. Serve hot at breakfast or brunch.

SOPAPILLAS

1 pkg. yeast
¼ cup water
1½ cups milk
3 Tbsp. shortening, melted
1½ tsp. salt
2 Tbsp. sugar
5 cups flour

MAKES 3 DOZEN
Mix all ingredients and knead briefly. Let rest one hour. Roll very thin, cut into triangles and fry in deep fat until brown on both sides. Dough can be kept for 2 days in refrigerator. Drizzle with honey and serve warm. They will add the perfect finishing touch to your Mexican food dinner.

BREAD

APPLE MUFFINS

1 cup sugar
½ cup margarine, softened
1 cup milk
1 egg
1½ cup flour
1/8 tsp. salt
2 tsp. baking powder
½ tsp. cinnamon
1 tsp. lemon juice
1 cup apples, grated

MAKES ABOUT 20 MUFFINS
Cream sugar and margarine. Add rest of ingredients in order given, being careful not to stir too much. Fill greased or lined muffin tins ⅔ full and bake at 425° for 20-25 minutes.

BLUEBERRY MUFFINS

⅔ cup shortening
1 cup sugar
3 eggs
3 cups flour
2 heaping tsp. baking powder
1 tsp. salt
1 cup milk
1 can blueberries, drained well

MAKES 2 DOZEN MUFFINS
Cream shortening and sugar. Add three eggs, one at a time, beating after each. Sift dry ingredients and add alternately with the 1 cup milk. Fold in 1 can drained blueberries. Fill greased muffin cups ⅔ full and bake at 375° until browned, about 20 minutes. This mixture will keep in the refrigerator 2-3 weeks.

CINNAMON-SUGAR MUFFINS

1½ cups flour
¾ cup sugar
2 tsp. baking powder
¼ tsp. salt
¼ tsp. nutmeg
½ cup milk
1 egg, beaten
⅓ cup butter, melted
1 tsp. cinnamon
½ cup sugar
½ tsp. vanilla
⅓ cup butter, melted

MAKES 2 DOZEN MUFFINS
Mix flour, sugar, baking powder, salt, and nutmeg. Add milk, beaten egg, and ⅓ cup melted butter. Mix well. Fill greased or lined muffin tins ⅔ full and bake at 400° for 20 minutes. Remove while still hot, dip in melted butter, then mixture of sugar, cinnamon and vanilla.

OATMEAL MUFFINS

1 cup quick oats
1 cup buttermilk
1 egg
½ cup brown sugar,
  packed
½ cup vegetable oil
1 cup flour
1 tsp. baking powder
½ tsp. salt
½ tsp. baking soda

MAKES 1 DOZEN MUFFINS
Mix all ingredients and spoon batter into greased muffin tins ⅔ full. Bake at 400° for 15-20 minutes.

ORANGE MUFFINS

1 cup butter or margarine
1 cup sugar
2 eggs
1 tsp. soda
1 cup buttermilk
2 cups sifted flour
2 Tbsp. grated orange rind
Juice of 2 oranges
1 cup brown sugar

MAKES 18-24 MUFFINS
Cream butter and sugar. Add eggs and beat well. Stir soda into buttermilk, and add alternately with flour to batter mixture. Stir in rind. Fill lined or greased muffin tins ⅔ full and bake at 400° for 20-25 minutes. Mix orange juice with brown sugar. Pour over hot muffins that have been poked with fork. Remove from pan immediately.

BREAD

ORANGE HONEY SURPRISE MUFFINS

1 orange, cut into thin
   pieces (peeling, too)
12 Tbsp. honey
1 egg
½ cup milk
¼ cup salad oil
1½ cups flour
½ cup sugar
2 tsp. baking powder
½ tsp. salt

MAKES 1 DOZEN
Heat oven to 400°. Grease 12 muffin cups. Put several pieces of orange and one tablespoon of honey in bottom of each cup. Beat egg; stir in milk and oil. Combine dry ingredients in bowl, mix well and add to milk mixture. Stir ingredients just until flour is moistened. Batter will be lumpy. Fill muffin cups ⅔ full. Bake 20-25 minutes or until golden brown. Serve orange slices up. Serve at brunch or luncheon.

PINEAPPLE MUFFINS

1—9 oz. can undrained
   crushed pineapple
1 cup oatmeal
½ cup sour cream
⅓ cup shortening
⅓ cup brown sugar
1 tsp. grated orange rind
1 egg, beaten
1¼ cup flour
1 tsp. baking powder
½ tsp. soda
1 tsp. salt

MAKES 1 DOZEN
Combine pineapple, oatmeal and sour cream. Let stand 15 minutes. Cream shortening, brown sugar and orange rind. Add beaten egg. Sift together flour, baking powder, soda and salt. Add flour mixture alternately with the pineapple mixture to batter. Fill greased muffin cups ⅔ full. Bake for 25 minutes at 400°.

RAISIN BRAN MUFFINS

15 oz. Raisin Bran
5 cups flour
3 cups sugar
5 tsp. soda
2 tsp. salt
1 cup oil
1 quart buttermilk
4 eggs, beaten

MAKES 5 DOZEN
Combine dry ingredients in a LARGE mixing bowl. Stir until all ingredients are well mixed. Add oil, buttermilk and eggs. Mix until all ingredients are moist. Spoon into greased or lined muffin tin, filling cups ⅔ full. Bake at 400° for 15-20 minutes. This batter keeps well in the refrigerator for two weeks, and makes outstanding muffins!

ONE MINUTE DOUGHNUTS

Tube of refrigerator
   biscuits
Oil for cooking
Chocolate frosting or sugar

Heat oil to 375°. Poke hole in center of biscuit. Deep fry to a golden brown on both sides. Roll in sugar or frost. Quick and easy treat for kids or breakfast.

BREAD

BAKING POWDER BISCUITS

3 cups flour
2 Tbsp. baking powder
1½ tsp. salt
1 cup vegetable shortening
1 cup milk
3 Tbsp. butter, melted
(optional)

MAKES 16-20 BISCUITS
Sift flour, baking powder, and salt together in large bowl. Add shortening and cut into dry ingredients with pastry blender, until it resembles coarse meal. Make a well in the center of mixture and pour in milk. Mix together only long enough to form a soft dough. Knead it for about 30 seconds and roll dough about ½ inch thick. Cut the dough into 2 inch rounds with cookie cutter or water glass. Gather together any remaining dough, roll again, and cut more. Brush with butter if you desire. Arrange biscuits on a cookie sheet, and bake in the middle of oven at 400° for 20 minutes.

EASY BREAKFAST CINNAMON BREAD

1 stick butter or margarine, melted
½ cup brown sugar, packed
½ cup finely chopped nuts
1 pkg. Rhodes frozen dinner rolls
Cinnamon

Grease tube pan well. Pour half the melted butter into pan and sprinkle with brown sugar, cinnamon, and most of the nuts. Put the frozen rolls on top of this, packing them in. Sprinkle with remaining nuts and more cinnamon. Pour remaining half of melted butter over rolls. Cover and let sit out overnight. In the morning, bake in 375° oven for 20-30 minutes. Turn upside down on plate to let topping run down. Serve warm. This is a very easy and delicious way to have hot cinnamon rolls for breakfast.

BREAD

❤ ❤ ❤ ❤ ❤ ❤ ❤ ❤ ❤ ❤ ❤ ❤ ❤ ❤ ❤ ❤

BUTTERSCOTCH ROLLS

1 pkg. butterscotch
 pudding mix
1½ cups milk
1 pkg. yeast
¼ cup warm water
2 eggs, beaten
1 stick oleo, melted
2 tsp. salt
4-4½ cups flour

FILLING:
¼ cup butter, melted
⅔ cup brown sugar
⅔ cup coconut
⅔ cup pecans, chopped
2 Tbsp. flour

FROSTING:
2 Tbsp. butter
2 Tbsp. milk
¼ cup brown sugar
1 cup powdered sugar

MAKES 2 DOZEN
Combine butterscotch pudding and milk in small saucepan. Cook until pudding boils. Let cool. Dissolve yeast in ¼ cup warm water. Combine yeast mixture, cooled pudding, eggs, oleo, salt and 2 cups of the flour in bowl. Beat well. Add enough remaining flour to make a soft dough. Turn onto floured board, knead well, and roll out ¼ inch thick. Combine melted butter, brown sugar, coconut, pecans, and flour in bowl. Spread this filling over dough. Roll up jelly roll style and cut into 1 inch rolls. Place in greased pan. Let rise until double. Bake 25-30 minutes at 375°. Blend together frosting ingredients and frost slightly warm rolls.

ORANGE ROLLS

2 pkg. dry yeast
1 cup lukewarm water
1 tsp. salt
⅓ cup sugar
⅓ cup salad oil
2 eggs, well beaten
4 cups flour

ORANGE BUTTER:
¼ cup frozen orange juice,
 undiluted
1⅓ sticks butter
1 box powdered sugar

MAKES 2 DOZEN
Dissolve the yeast in 1 cup lukewarm water. Add salt, sugar, oil and eggs; beat well. Add flour, 2 cups at a time, beating after each addition. Knead well, place in bowl and cover with damp tea towel. Let rise until more than doubled in bulk. Make into rolls (try cloverleaf style . . . roll the dough into 1 inch balls and drop three at a time in a greased muffin tin.) Let rise again and bake at 375° for 20-25 minutes. Spread warm rolls with orange butter. These are a memorable dinner roll.

61

BREAD

CREAM CHEESE SWEET ROLLS

1 pkg. dry yeast
¼ cup warm water
¾ cup buttermilk
1 egg
2¾ to 3 cups all purpose
   flour
¼ cup butter
¼ cup sugar
1 tsp. baking powder
1 tsp. salt

FILLING:
1—8 oz. pkg. cream
   cheese, softened
½ cup sugar
3 Tbsp. flour
1 egg yolk

Chopped nuts
Strawberry, cherry or
   blueberry preserves
Powdered sugar glaze

MAKES 2-3 DOZEN
Dissolve yeast in warm water. Add buttermilk, egg, 1 cup flour, butter, sugar, baking powder and salt. Mix well for 2 minutes. Stir in enough remaining flour to make soft dough. Let rise.

Roll dough very thin, 1/8 inch thick, and cut into 3 inch squares. Combine filling ingredients and mix well. Place dough square onto greased baking sheets. Place 1 heaping tablespoon filling in center of each square. Bring two diagonally opposite corners to center of each square and pinch together to seal. Let rise. Bake 12-15 minutes at 375°. If you desire, top each square with a spoonful of preserves or powdered sugar glaze. Sprinkle with nuts. These will absolutely melt in your mouth!

♥ ♥ ♥ ♥ ♥ ♥ ♥ ♥ ♥ ♥ ♥ ♥ ♥ ♥ ♥ ♥ ♥

BEER BREAD

3 cups self-rising flour
¼ cup sugar
1 can beer

MAKES 1 LOAF

Pour sugar in bowl. Add beer and stir well. Gradually stir in flour. When well blended, pour into greased loaf pan. Bake at 350° for 1 hour. Great at dinner time but even better for toast the next morning! This is a quick bread that is easy for anyone to make.

EILEEN'S MONKEY BREAD

2 pkg. dry yeast
1 cup lukewarm water
1 cup shortening
¾ cup sugar
1½ tsp. salt
1 cup boiling water
2 eggs, beaten
6 cups flour
1 stick butter, melted

MAKES 2 PANS

Dissolve yeast in warm water. Mix together shortening, sugar, and salt; add boiling water and mix well. Add eggs and stir. Add flour and dissolved yeast to shortening mixture, alternately, until well blended. Knead well. Let rise until double in bulk. Roll to ¼ to ½ inch thickness. Cut in various shapes and sizes. Dip in melted butter and place in tube pans until half full; let rise until doubled. Bake at 350° for 35-45 minutes or until brown. After mixing and rising once, dough may be punched down and refrigerated to be used later. Be sure to cover with damp cloth. Note: Use a tube pan, or a small pan. If put in regular loaf pans, the dough does not get cooked in the middle. This makes a delicious easy bread for your family.

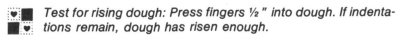 *Test for rising dough: Press fingers ½" into dough. If indentations remain, dough has risen enough.*

BREAD

❤ ❤ ❤ ❤ ❤ ❤ ❤ ❤ ❤ ❤ ❤ ❤ ❤ ❤ ❤ ❤ ❤

MAMA LANG'S CINNAMON ROLLS OR WHITE BREAD

½ cup shortening
½ cup sugar
2 cups boiling water
2 tsp. salt
3 cups flour
2 eggs
2 pkg. yeast
½ cup lukewarm water
4 cups flour

CINNAMON ROLL FILLING:
½ cup softened butter or
  margarine
¾-1 cup brown sugar
2½ tsp. cinnamon
¾ cup walnuts or pecans,
  chopped (optional)
¾ cup raisins (optional)

FROSTING:
2 Tbsp. butter, softened
6-7 Tbsp. milk
1 tsp. vanilla
2 cups powdered sugar

MAKES 4 DOZEN ROLLS, OR 2 LOAVES

Put shortening and sugar in large bowl, cover with boiling water. Let cool. Add salt and 3 cups flour, one at a time. Beat well. Add 2 eggs, then yeast dissolved in water. Stir well. Add 4 cups flour, beating after each cup. Knead well on a floured board. Place in bowl and cover with damp tea towel. Let rise until doubled in bulk; punch down. Put dough in refrigerator, cover with wet cloth and plate, and let sit overnight.

To roll dough for cinnamon rolls, divide in half, and roll to ¼ inch thickness. Spread the dough with softened butter, sprinkle with brown sugar, then cinnamon, raisins and nuts if you choose, and roll in a jelly roll fashion. Seal the edges by pinching them together. Cut into 1 inch rolls and place in a greased muffin tin or pan. Let rise until doubled. Bake at 375° for 10-15 minutes. When cooled, ice with mixture of butter, milk, vanilla and powdered sugar.

To make loaves of bread, divide the dough in half, after it has risen once, roll out, shape into loaves, put in greased loaf pans, cover with damp tea towel and let rise again. Bake at 350° for 20-30 minutes, or until golden brown and hollow-sounding when tapped. Brush with melted butter and immediately set on racks to cool.

♥ ♥ ♥ ♥ ♥ ♥ ♥ ♥ ♥ ♥ ♥ ♥ ♥ ♥ ♥ ♥

WHOLE WHEAT BREAD

6 Tbsp. Crisco, melted
¾ cup scalded milk
4 Tbsp. sugar
3½ tsp. salt
3/8 cup molasses
1½ cup warm water
2 pkg. dry yeast
4½ cups whole wheat flour
2 cups sifted white flour

MAKES 2 LOAVES

Melt shortening, add milk, sugar, salt and molasses. Cool to lukewarm. Dissolve yeast in warm water. Stir milk and molasses mixture into yeast mixture. Add 2 cups whole wheat flour. Beat until bubbly. Stir in remaining flour. Knead well. Place in large bowl and cover with damp tea towel. Let rise until doubled. Punch down, let rise again. Divide into 2 equal parts, and roll out for loaves. Place in greased loaf pans, let rise until doubled. Bake at 375° for 10 minutes, lower the temperature to 350° and bake 20 more minutes. Bread is done when it sounds hollow when tapped. Brush melted butter on top, take out of pans, and cool on wire racks. This whole wheat bread is light and a little sweet, unlike most whole wheat breads. It is a real winner! For something different, try baking one half of this bread in a greased 2 lb. coffee can.

 To form loaves for bread; roll dough into rectangle, 18 x 9 inches. Roll up from short side. Pinch ends and bottom seam to seal and fold ends under. Place seam side down in greased pan. Bake loaves with the top of pan in the middle of the oven.

BREAD

❤ ❤ ❤ ❤ ❤ ❤ ❤ ❤ ❤ ❤ ❤ ❤ ❤ ❤ ❤ ❤

SOURDOUGH BREAD AND STARTER

STARTER:
1 pkg. dry yeast
2 cups warm water
2 cups flour

SOURDOUGH BREAD:
1 pkg. dry yeast
¼ cup warm water
1 tsp. sugar
1 egg
¼ cup vegetable oil
½ cup water
1 tsp. salt
⅓ cup sugar
1 cup sourdough starter
3½ cups flour
Cornmeal
Melted butter

3 CUPS STARTER AND 2 LOAVES
Combine starter ingredients in large bowl (not metal). Mix well and let stand, covered loosely with plastic wrap, at room temperature for 48 hours. To store starter, refrigerate in a jar with a loose-fitting lid. When making bread, stir starter well, pour out required amount and replenish starter with 1 cup flour, 1 cup milk, ⅓ cup sugar. Replenish at least once a week.

Dissolve yeast in water, stir in sugar. Let sit 15 minutes. Mix egg, oil, water, salt, and sugar in large mixing bowl (not metal). Add starter and yeast mixture. Stir well. Blend in 2 cups flour and beat well. Add remainder of flour. Knead well, adding more flour if dough seems sticky. Place dough in a bowl, cover with a damp tea towel and let rise until doubled. Punch down, and knead again for 2-3 minutes. Shape dough, place on greased baking sheets that have been sprinkled with cornmeal; brush with butter. Cover and let rise until doubled. Bake at 350° for about 20-25 minutes. Brush with butter after baking if desired. Once you get in the habit of making this bread, no meal will be complete without it.

When bread is baking, a small dish of water in the oven will help to keep the crust from getting hard.

♥ ♥ ♥ ♥ ♥ ♥ ♥ ♥ ♥ ♥ ♥ ♥ ♥ ♥ ♥ ♥ ♥

CRACKED WHEAT BREAD

½ cup cracked wheat
(bulgar)
2 cups warm water
1 pkg. dry yeast
¼ cup brown sugar
¼ cup white sugar
(scant ¼ cup)
2 tsp. salt
1 Tbsp. vegetable oil
About 5 cups flour

MAKES 2 LOAVES
Soak bulgar in 1 cup warm water 15 minutes. Dissolve yeast in the other cup of water. Add to bulgar. Add sugar, salt, and oil. Mix well. Add flour, a cup at a time, stirring well after each addition. Add flour until a soft dough forms. Let dough rest 10 minutes. Turn out on a floured board and knead well. Place in bowl, cover with damp tea towel, and let rise until doubled. Punch down, let rise again. Cut in half, roll out and place in 2 greased loaf pans. Let rise again. Bake at 375° for 20-25 minutes.

BAR L ROLLS

3 heaping Tbsp. Crisco
1 Tbsp. salt
Scant ½ cup sugar
1 cup hot water
6 cups flour
1 cup lukewarm water
2 pkg. yeast

MAKES 3 DOZEN
Combine Crisco, salt, and sugar in large bowl. Pour 1 cup hot water over mixture and stir until Crisco melts. Add enough flour to make a paste (about 1 cup). Add 1 cup lukewarm water, in which yeast has been dissolved. Mix in remaining flour to form a soft dough. Knead dough well. Place in bowl and cover with damp tea towel; let rise. Punch down when doubled and roll to ½-¾ inch thickness. Cut with cookie cutter and place on greased pans about ½ inch apart. Let rise until doubled. Bake at 400° for 20 minutes or until brown. This was Grandmother's recipe, one she did by look and feel. This written out version produces light and tasty rolls, as close to hers as possible!

BREAD

♥ ♥ ♥ ♥ ♥ ♥ ♥ ♥ ♥ ♥ ♥ ♥ ♥ ♥ ♥ ♥

BRAIDED POTATO BREAD

1 pkg. dry yeast
   dissolved in ¼ cup
   warm water
3½ cups flour
¼ cup sugar
1½ tsp. salt
1 cup mashed potatoes
⅔ cup milk
¼ cup butter or margarine,
   melted
2 eggs
1 tsp. water
1 egg white
2 tsp. poppy seeds

MAKES 1 LOAF

Mix 1½ cups flour, the sugar, and salt in a large mixing bowl. In separate bowl, combine potatoes, milk, butter and eggs, and yeast mixture. Add to flour mixture. Beat 2 minutes on medium speed, scraping bowl occasionally. Stir in enough remaining flour to handle. Knead dough on a well-floured board until smooth and elastic. Place in bowl and let rise in warm place until double in bulk. Punch down and divide the dough into thirds. Shape each third into a roll, 14 inches long. Braid rolls on greased baking sheet, being careful not to stretch dough. Fold ends under loaf. Let rise until almost double. Heat oven to 350°. Beat egg white and water slightly, brush on bread. Sprinkle with poppy seed. Bake until golden brown, about 30-35 minutes. Cool on a wire rack.

CROISSANTS

2 pkg. dry yeast
1 cup warm water
5 cups unsifted flour
¾ cup evaporated milk
1½ tsp. salt
1 egg
⅓ cup sugar
¼ cup butter, melted
1 cup chilled butter
1 egg, beaten with 1
  Tbsp. water

MAKES 3 DOZEN

Sprinkle yeast over warm water in large bowl. Add 1 cup flour, evaporated milk, salt, egg, sugar and melted butter. Beat until smooth. In separate bowl, cut chilled butter into remaining flour until butter particles are the size of peas. Pour yeast batter over the top. Fold in until all flour is moist. Cover bowl with plastic wrap. Chill 4 hours. Can be refrigerated several days. Handle dough as little as possible. Divide in half, keeping other half cool until ready to work. Knead 6-7 times and roll ¼ of the dough into a ¼ inch thick circle on floured board. Cut dough circle into pie shaped wedges. Roll each loosely towards point. Place on ungreased cookie sheet. Cover lightly. Let rise until double. (Don't speed rising by placing them in a warm spot.) When doubled, brush with egg and water mixture. Bake in preheated 400° oven for 12-15 minutes.

BREAD

TEXAS BUTTERMILK BISCUITS

5 cups unbleached flour
3 Tbsp. sugar
1 Tbsp. baking powder
1 tsp. salt
1 cup butter or margarine
2 envelopes dry yeast
¼ cup warm water
2 cups buttermilk
¾ cup butter or margarine, melted

MAKES 3-4 DOZEN
Sift together dry ingredients into a large bowl. Using knife or pastry blender, cut butter into dry mixture until it is like coarse meal. Dissolve yeast in warm water and add to mixture. Add buttermilk and blend thoroughly. Roll or pat into ¼ inch thickness. Cut with cookie cutter or water glass. Dip each biscuit in melted butter, then fold in half and press edges together. Place on a baking sheet and freeze until firm. Package in plastic bags and freeze. May be baked without defrosting at 350° about 15-20 minutes or until golden brown. A versatile, richly-flavored biscuit... good at breakfast or dinner.

HOMESTYLE CORN BREAD

1 cup yellow cornmeal
1 cup flour
¼ cup sugar
4 tsp. baking powder
½ tsp. salt.
1 cup milk
1 egg
¼ cup vegetable oil

MAKES 1 DOZEN MUFFINS, 14 CORN STICKS OR 1 8-INCH SQUARE PAN
Mix cornmeal, flour, sugar, baking powder and salt. Add milk, egg and shortening and beat until smooth. Pour into greased or lined muffin tins, or corn stick pans and bake at 425° 15-20 minutes. It can also be baked in a greased 8-inch square pan at 425° for 20-25 minutes.

♥ ♥ ♥ ♥ ♥ ♥ ♥ ♥ ♥ ♥ ♥ ♥ ♥ ♥ ♥ ♥ ♥

MEXICAN CORN BREAD

1 cup yellow cornmeal
1½ tsp. salt
1 Tbsp. baking powder
2 eggs, beaten
1—8 oz. can cream-style
  corn
⅔ cup corn oil
1—8 oz. carton sour cream
1—4 oz. can green chiles,
  chopped and drained
1 tsp. sugar
2 cups Longhorn cheese,
  grated

SERVES 9
Mix together cornmeal, salt and baking powder; add eggs, corn, oil, and sour cream. Mix well and pour half of the batter into an 8-inch square, greased baking pan. Spread green chiles, 1 cup cheese, and sugar over this. Cover with remaining half of batter. Top with one cup of cheese. Bake 1 hour at 350°.

HUSH PUPPIES

1 cup cornmeal
1 tsp. baking powder
1 tsp. salt
1 tsp. sugar
1 cup flour
1 egg, beaten
¾ cup milk
Dash of Tabasco
1 Tbsp. grated onion

MAKES ABOUT 24
Sift dry ingredients into a bowl. Add beaten egg and milk to cornmeal mixture. Mix in onion and Tabasco. Drop by heaping teaspoons into hot fat (375°) and fry until brown. Drain and serve with a fish fry dinner.

BREAD

❦ ❦ ❦ ❦ ❦ ❦ ❦ ❦ ❦ ❦ ❦ ❦ ❦ ❦ ❦■❦■❦

BEST IRISH SODA BREAD

4½ cups all purpose flour
4 tsp. baking powder
½ tsp. baking soda
1 tsp. salt
3 Tbsp. sugar
1 Tbsp. caraway seeds
1 cup seedless raisins
2 cups buttermilk
Butter
Powdered sugar

Heat oven to 350°. Grease and flour a 9 inch cast iron skillet. (A round cake pan works well also.) Mix 4 cups of flour with baking powder, soda, salt, sugar and caraway seeds. Stir in raisins, making sure they are separated. Add buttermilk all at once and mix with a fork to form a dough. Sprinkle about ¼ cup of remaining flour on a work surface, turn out dough and knead for about 5 minutes until smooth. Use only as much of remaining ¼ cup flour as needed to prevent dough from sticking. Form dough into a smooth, round loaf and press into pan. With a sharp knife, cut a cross ½ inch deep, across top of dough. Bake for one hour or until loaf is lightly browned and sounds hollow when tapped. Remove bread to wire rack, rub top with butter and dust with powdered sugar. Good with extra butter and powdered sugar on each slice.

ONION BREAD

Frozen bread dough or your favorite white bread dough
1 pkg. onion soup mix
1 cup melted butter

Form dough into small balls. Combine onion soup mixture with melted butter. Roll each ball in butter mixture, and arrange in buttered tube pan. Let double and bake at 375° for 45 minutes. Turn cooked bread onto serving plate. Pass remaining butter/onion mixture with bread. Dip each piece into butter mixture before eating.

KATHI'S DILLY BREAD

1 pkg. yeast
¼ cup warm water
1 cup cottage cheese
2 Tbsp. sugar
1 Tbsp. minced onion
1 Tbsp. butter
2 tsp. dill seed
1 tsp. salt
¼ tsp. soda
1 unbeaten egg
2¼-2½ cups flour

Dissolve yeast in water. In bowl combine cottage cheese, sugar, onion, butter, dill seed, salt, soda, egg and softened yeast. Add flour to form stiff dough; beat well after each addition. Cover. Let rise in warm place until light and double in size, 50-60 minutes. Stir down dough. Turn into well greased 8 inch round casserole. Let rise in warm place about 30-40 minutes. Bake at 350° for 40-50 minutes or until golden brown. Brush with butter and sprinkle with dill seed. For a hearty winter lunch, serve this with Homemade Vegetable Soup and a green salad.

Salads

SALADS

RED, WHITE AND BLUEBERRY SALAD

1—3 oz. pkg. raspberry
  gelatin
2 cups water
1 envelope unflavored
  gelatin
½ cup cold water
1 cup half and half
½ cup sugar
1—8 oz. pkg. cream
  cheese, softened
½ cup walnuts, chopped
1 tsp. vanilla
1½ cups frozen blueberries
  (may substitute 1 can
  blueberries)
1—3 oz. pkg. black
  raspberry gelatin
2 cups water

SERVES 10-12
Dissolve raspberry gelatin in 1 cup boiling water. Add 1 cup cold water. Pour into 13 x 9 inch pan or large ring mold. Refrigerate to firm, but not set. Add unflavored gelatin to ½ cup cold water, stir to let soften. Combine half and half, and sugar in small saucepan. Cook over low heat but do not boil. Add unflavored gelatin and let mixture get very warm, but do not boil. Pour into bowl with softened cream cheese and beat with mixer. Add chopped nuts and vanilla. Cool to room temperature. Spoon over raspberry layer. Chill until firm. Dissolve package of black raspberry gelatin in one cup boiling water. Add one cup of cold water and blueberries. (If using canned blueberries, omit the last cup of cold water and pour in the blueberries undrained.) Chill until thick, then pour over cream cheese layer. Chill until firm. This large salad is great for family get-togethers.

BANANA-BERRY GELATIN SALAD

1—3 oz. pkg. strawberry
  gelatin
2 cups water
1—10 oz. pkg. frozen
  strawberries
2 bananas, mashed
1 cup whipped cream

SERVES 4-6
Dissolve gelatin in 1 cup hot water; add frozen strawberries. Add mashed bananas and a cup of cold water. Mix well. Pour into 8 x 8 inch pan or mold. Chill until firm. Spread whipped cream over top. Refrigerate. (A can of crushed pineapple is also good in this salad. Use a large box of gelatin and omit the second cup of water.)

DIVINE RASPBERRY SALAD

Juice from crushed pineapple plus water to make 1 cup
1—3 oz. pkg. lemon gelatin
1½ cups miniature or diced marshmallows
1—8 oz. pkg. cream cheese
½ pint whipping cream
2 Tbsp. sugar
¼ tsp. vanilla
i can crushed pineapple, (2½ cups)
2 cups water
2—3 oz. pkg. raspberry gelatin
1 lb. pkg. frozen raspberries, thawed

SERVES 10-12
Dissolve lemon gelatin in boiling pineapple juice and water. Pour over marshmallows and cream cheese. Beat with mixer. Whip cream, add sugar and vanilla. Add to gelatin mixture. Fold in crushed pineapple, and pour into 9 x 13 inch pan. Allow to set. Dissolve raspberry gelatin in two cups boiling water. Add berries; cool. Spoon over first layer. Refrigerate and let set.

LIME-PEAR GELATIN SALAD

1—3 oz. pkg. lime gelatin
1½ cups water
1—16 oz. can pears, sliced
1—3 oz. pkg. lemon gelatin
1 cup water
1—3 oz. pkg. cream cheese
½ cup water
1 cup cream, whipped

SERVES 8
Dissolve lime gelatin in one cup boiling water. Add ½ cup cold water and undrained pears. Pears may be sliced more if desired. Pour into 8 x 8 inch pan. Refrigerate until firm. Dissolve lemon gelatin in one cup boiling water. Pour over cream cheese and beat with mixer. Mix in ½ cup cold water. Fold in whipped cream. Pour over lime gelatin layer and chill to set.

SALADS

PEACHES 'N CREAM SALAD

2—3 oz. pkg. lemon gelatin
2 cups boiling water
1—3 oz. pkg. cream cheese
1 cup whipping cream
2 Tbsp. sugar
1 cup orange juice
½ cup pecans, chopped
1—1 lb. 6 oz. can peach
   pie filling

SERVES 10-12
Dissolve one package lemon gelatin in one cup boiling water. Pour into bowl with cream cheese. Beat with mixer. Whip cream; sweeten with 2 tablespoons sugar. Add orange juice and whipped cream to cream cheese mixture. Beat with mixer. Add pecans. Pour into 9 x 13 inch pan or mold. Chill until firm. Dissolve second box of gelatin in one cup boiling water. Add the peach pie filling. Let cool. Pour over first layer and chill until firm.

BLUEBERRY SALAD

2—3 oz. pkg. blackberry
   gelatin (or black cherry
   gelatin)
2 cups water
1 small can crushed
   pineapple, drained; save
   juice
2 cups blueberries

TOPPING:
1 carton sour cream (small)
2—3 oz. pkg. cream cheese
½ cup sugar
½ tsp. vanilla

SERVES 10-12
Dissolve gelatin in 2 cups boiling water. Add pineapple juice and enough water to make another cup. Add pineapple and blueberries. Pour into 9 x 13 inch pan. Let set.

Blend topping ingredients and spread over blueberry gelatin mixture. Refrigerate.

Spray the mold for a gelatin salad lightly with Pam before pouring it in. The jello salad will unmold with ease.

$1000 ORANGE SALAD

1—3 oz. pkg. orange
   gelatin
1 cup boiling water
1—8 oz. bottle 7-Up
½ pt. whipping cream
1 small can crushed
   pineapple, drained
1 small jar maraschino
   cherries, drained
2 bananas, sliced
½ cup nuts, chopped
½ cup coconut

SERVES 9-12
Dissolve gelatin in boiling water. Add 7-Up and refrigerate about 45 minutes or until slightly jelled. Whip cream until stiff. Fold whipped cream and remaining ingredients into jello mixture. Pour into 9 x 13 inch pan or mold. Refrigerate until firm.

BING CHERRY GELATIN SALAD

1—1 lb. 4 oz. can bing
   cherries, reserve juice
1—3 oz. pkg. cherry gelatin
1 cup boiling water
1 cup juice from cherries,
   plus water
¼ cup walnuts, chopped
1—3 oz. pkg. cream cheese

SERVES 4-6
Dissolve cherry gelatin in boiling water. Drain juice from cherries and add enough water to make one cup. Add to gelatin. Pour into ring mold. Chill until partially set. Mix cream cheese with walnuts. Roll into marble size balls. Drop cherries and cheese balls alternately into cherry jello. Let set. Also good served with whipped cream on top.

JENNY'S FRUITED COTTAGE CHEESE

To creamed cottage cheese, add pineapple tidbits, seeded red and green grapes, diced apple (with the skin), a few broken nutmeats, and lemon juice to taste. This is a quick and easy salad, perfect with most any meal.

SALADS

MIXED FRUIT SALAD AND DRESSINGS

Oranges, peeled and diced
Apples, diced
Bananas, sliced
Blueberries, whole
Grapes, green or purple
  seedless
Marshmallows, miniature
  or diced
Coconut, flaked
Pineapple, chunked
Walnuts, broken
Cherries, white or bing
Maraschino cherries, halved
Mandarin oranges
Pears, fresh, diced
Cantaloupe balls
Honeydew balls
Watermelon balls
Strawberries

These ingredients can be used in any combination and proportion to suit your family's taste. Serve a fruit salad plain, or with one of the following favorite dressings.

SOUR CREAM-POWDERED SUGAR DRESSING:
½ cup sour cream
2 Tbsp. powdered sugar

Blend and mix into fruit salad.

WHIPPED CREAM DRESSING:
1 cup whipping cream
3-4 Tbsp. sugar
½ tsp. vanilla

Beat the ingredients until the cream is stiff. Mix with fruit.

VANILLA ICE CREAM DRESSING:
1-2 cups vanilla ice cream, softened

Mix the softened ice cream with fruit. This is delicious and easy.

YOGURT-HONEY DRESSING:
1 small carton plain yogurt
3-4 Tbsp. honey

Mix and toss with fruit salad. Use flavored yogurts with special salads. Example: strawberry yogurt with strawberry fruit salad.

POPPY SEED DRESSING:
1¼ cups sugar
2 tsp. dry mustard
2 tsp. salt
⅔ cup vinegar
3 Tbsp. onion juice
2 cups salad oil (not olive oil)
3 Tbsp. poppy seeds

Mix sugar, mustard, salt, and vinegar. Add onion juice and stir it in thoroughly. Add oil slowly, beating constantly until thick. Use a blender, food processor, or mixer for this part. Add poppy seeds and beat until well blended. This dressing is exceptional on any fruit salad. Try it on slices of pink grapefruit and avocado on a bed of lettuce for the best taste treat of all.

FRUIT SALAD DRESSING:
3 egg yolks
2 Tbsp. sugar
Dash of salt
2 Tbsp. vinegar
2 Tbsp. pineapple syrup
1 Tbsp. butter
1 cup whipped cream

Cook egg yolks, sugar, salt, vinegar, pineapple syrup and butter in double boiler until thick, stirring constantly. Cool. Stir into fruit salad. Fold in whipped cream. Chill 24 hours.

CRANBERRY SALAD

1 cup ground, raw cranberries
1 cup sugar
1 small can light cherries (Royal Sweet Cherries), drained
1 small can Bing cherries, drained
½ cup walnuts, chopped
1 cup mandarin oranges, drained (can use cut up fresh orange)
1½ cup whipping cream, whipped and sweetened with 2 Tbsp. sugar
1 cup miniature marshmallows

SERVES 8
Combine cranberries and sugar. Refrigerate overnight. Drain off liquid. Mix in cherries, nuts and oranges. Fold in whipped cream and marshmallows. Pour in serving dish and refrigerate. This is a good holiday salad.

 Heating an orange a moment in the oven will make the inner white skin peel off perfectly.

SALADS

CINNAMON APPLES

½ cup sugar
½ cup water
½ cup cinnamon candies
5-6 apples (Jonathans are best), peeled, cored, and sliced

SERVES 4
Combine sugar, water, and cinnamon candies in saucepan. Heat to dissolve candies and sugar. Add apples. Simmer slowly, covered, for 30 minutes. Uncover and simmer for 1 more hour. Can also be cooked in casserole dish in the oven; leave lid on for ½ hour, then remove lid and bake until syrup thickens, about 1 hour. Syrup will thicken more as it cools. Serve as a cold condiment at lunch or supper. This is a good way to use overripe apples.

PISTACHIO SALAD

1 pkg. instant pistachio pudding
1—8 oz. container whipped topping
1—6½ oz. can crushed pineapple, drained
1 cup small marshmallows
Nuts, chopped (walnuts, pistachios or pecans)

SERVES 6
Make pistachio pudding according to package directions. Add other ingredients and mix. Pour into serving dish; garnish with nuts. Refrigerate. For a variation, try putting this in a graham cracker crust and serving it for dessert! It is delicious either way.

 Scrape the sides of a cucumber with a fork before slicing for a fancy look.

CUCUMBER-VINEGAR SALAD

3 medium cucumbers
¼ medium onion, sliced
   thin
½ cup white vinegar
¼ cup water
2-3 Tbsp. sugar
Pepper to taste
½ tsp. salt

SERVES 4-6
Peel cucumbers and slice thin. Add sliced onion. Stir together vinegar, water, sugar, salt, and pepper. Pour over slices. Cover and refrigerate at least three hours, 7-10 hours is better. This is wonderful to serve with hamburgers at a backyard, summertime picnic.

CUCUMBERS AND SOUR CREAM

3-4 cucumbers, sliced thin
1 tsp. salt
1 small onion, sliced thin
   (or 6 green onions,
   sliced)
1—8 oz. carton sour cream
3 Tbsp. vinegar
1 Tbsp. sugar
2 Tbsp. half and half
Pepper to taste

SERVES 4-6
Mix all ingredients together and let stand 20-30 minutes.

GLORIOUS CUCUMBER SALAD

2—3 oz. pkg. lime-flavored
   gelatin
1½ cups hot water
2 Tbsp. lemon juice
1½ medium cucumbers,
   unpeeled
1 large onion
1 pint creamed cottage
   cheese
1 cup pecans, chopped
2 cups mayonnaise

SERVES 10-12
Dissolve gelatin in hot water. Add lemon juice and cool. In a blender or food processor, grind cucumbers and onion. Strain off juice. Add cucumbers and onion to the gelatin mixture. Then stir in cottage cheese, pecans, and mayonnaise. Mix well. Pour into a 2 quart mold and chill until firm. Good served with chicken or seafood.

SALADS

CAULIFLOWER SALAD

1 head cauliflower, broken
   into buds
1 bunch green onions,
   sliced
1 bunch radishes, sliced
¾ lb. Monterey Jack or
   Longhorn cheese, grated
Pepperoni or ham, sliced
   or cubed into small
   pieces
¼-½ cup Italian dressing

SERVES 6
Layer ingredients in order given. Pour dressing over salad. Cover and let marinate 24 hours in refrigerator.

PEA-CAULIFLOWER SALAD

1—10 oz. pkg. frozen peas,
   cooked and drained
1 head cauliflower, broken
   into pieces
¼-½ cup celery, diced
¼-½ cup onion, diced
½-¾ cup mayonnaise (not
   salad dressing)

SERVES 4-6
Toss all ingredients together the day before serving. Refrigerate.

NEVA'S SALAD

1—8 oz. carton sour cream
¼ cup mayonnaise
3 tsp. vinegar
½ medium onion, minced
1 head cauliflower, broken
   into pieces
1 bunch fresh broccoli,
   broken into pieces
2 carrots, peeled and
   chopped
Salt and pepper to taste
Dash of Tabasco (about 3
   shakes)

SERVES 4-6
Mix all ingredients together the day before serving. Refrigerate.

MARINATED GREEN BEANS

2—20 oz. cans of green
  beans (Blue Lake),
  drained
1 thinly sliced onion
1 Tbsp. salad oil
1 Tbsp. vinegar
Salt and pepper to taste

SOUR CREAM SAUCE:
1 cup sour cream
1 tsp. lemon juice
½ to 1 Tbsp. horseradish
2 tsp. chopped chives
½ cup mayonnaise
¼ tsp. dry mustard
Grated onion to taste

SERVES 6
Combine beans, onion, oil, vinegar, salt and pepper. Let marinate several hours or overnight in the refrigerator. Stir occasionally. Drain. Add sour cream sauce.

To make sour cream sauce, combine all ingredients. Mix well and pour over green bean salad.

BEAN SALAD

1—1 lb. can green beans
1—1 lb. can yellow beans
1—1 lb. can red kidney
  beans
1—1 lb. can garbanzo
  beans (optional)
1—4 oz. can green lima
  beans (optional)
1 red onion, sliced or
  chopped
1 green pepper, sliced or
  chopped

DRESSING:
¾ cup sugar
¾ cup vinegar
¾ cup oil
1¼ Tbsp. dry mustard
1 tsp. salt
1 tsp. pepper

SERVES 8-10
Combine sugar, vinegar, oil and spices in a small saucepan. Bring to boil. Drain beans and combine in large bowl. Pour warm dressing over beans. Add onion and pepper. Stir well. Cover and refrigerate at least 3 hours, overnight is better. Stir occasionally.

SALADS

COPPER CARROT SALAD

2 lbs. carrots (canned),
    drained
1 green pepper, chopped
1 onion, chopped
1 cup tomato soup
½ cup salad oil
1 cup sugar
¾ cup vinegar
1 tsp. Worcestershire
Salt
Pepper
1 tsp. prepared mustard

SERVES 8
Alternate layers of carrots, pepper, and onion. Make a sauce with soup, oil, sugar, vinegar, Worcestershire, salt, pepper, and mustard. Heat until well blended. Pour hot mixture over vegetables and refrigerate several days before using. Will keep 3 weeks. You can also serve this salad as a vegetable by serving warm. It's good with chicken. Or try putting a few of the marinated carrots in a tossed green salad.

ZINGY V-8 ASPIC

1—3 oz. pkg. lemon gelatin
½ cup boiling water
1 cup V-8 juice
½ cup sliced pimento-
    stuffed olives
½ cup finely chopped
    celery
½ tsp. salt
1/8 tsp. Worcestershire
    sauce
Dash Tabasco sauce

SERVES 4-6
Dissolve gelatin in boiling water; cool. Mix in V-8, olives, and celery. Add salt, Worcestershire, and Tabasco to taste. Mix well. Pour into mold and refrigerate until set. This versatile salad complements any meal.

SARAH'S TOMATO ASPIC

1—1 lb. can stewed
   tomatoes
1—3 oz. pkg. lemon
   flavored gelatin
½ tsp. salt
1 Tbsp. vinegar

SERVES 5

Puree tomatoes in food processor or blender; pour into saucepan, saving the can. Bring tomatoes to a boil. Reduce heat; simmer for two minutes. Add gelatin, salt and vinegar; stir until gelatin dissolves. Pour into stewed tomato can. Chill until firm. Puncture bottom of can. Dip in warm water. Unmold on a bed of lettuce. This is a real hit at salad luncheons, and is also good with scrambled eggs at brunch, or with seafood.

MRS. WALKER'S COLE SLAW

Mix equal parts of vinegar, sour cream, and sugar (½ cup each for a big salad). Add shredded red and green cabbage.

CABBAGE PATCH COLE SLAW

5 cups shredded cabbage
1 cup sour cream
¼ cup white vinegar
½ cup vegetable oil
½ tsp. celery seed
½ tsp. salt
3 Tbsp. sugar

SERVES 6

Stir together dressing; pour over cabbage. Toss and chill.

SALADS

SAUERKRAUT SALAD

1 can sauerkraut (2½ cups)
⅓ cup sugar
½ cup green pepper,
  chopped
½ cup carrots, grated
½ cup onion, chopped
½ cup celery, chopped

SERVES 4-6
Drain juice from sauerkraut and add ⅓ cup sugar. Mix to dissolve sugar. Add other ingredients and stir well. Dill seed is also good to add. Let chill at least two hours before serving. Will keep for a couple of weeks in the refrigerator.

ZUCCHINI SALAD

1 medium zucchini,
  chopped
1 cup cheddar or Monterey
  Jack cheese, cubed or
  shredded
1 cup ham, salami or
  pepperoni, sliced or
  cubed
1 hard boiled egg, chopped
½ tomato, chopped

DRESSING:
½ cup oil
½ cup vinegar
¼ cup honey
¼ tsp. garlic, minced
¼ tsp. salt
Pepper
2 Tbsp. grated or minced
  onion
1½ Tbsp. fresh parsley

SERVES 4-6
Combine salad ingredients and toss well. Combine dressing ingredients in pint jar, shake well, and pour over salad. Toss before serving.

24-HOUR LAYERED VEGETABLE SALAD

6 cups lettuce, chopped
6 eggs, hard-boiled
1 lb. bacon, cooked and
crumbled
Salt
Pepper
2 Tbsp. sugar
1—10 oz. pkg. frozen peas,
thawed and uncooked
2 cups Swiss cheese,
grated
¼ cup green onion,
chopped
1 cup Miracle Whip salad
dressing
Paprika

SERVES 12-15
Place 3 cups lettuce in bottom of large bowl; sprinkle with salt, pepper and sugar. Layer sliced eggs on top of lettuce and sprinkle with more salt. Layer in order: peas, remaining lettuce, bacon, and Swiss cheese. Spread salad dressing over top. Cover and chill 24 hours. Garnish with green onion and paprika. Toss before serving. This is especially pretty if served in a large crystal bowl. Makes a very large salad. You can also layer this salad in a 9 x 13 glass baking dish. Make sure to cover the entire top of the salad with the dressing as it seals the lettuce mixture and keeps it crisp. It will stay fresh for several days. Serve by cutting into squares.

WILTED LETTUCE SALAD

4 slices bacon, diced
¼ cup vinegar
2 tsp. sugar
¼ tsp. salt
⅛ tsp. pepper
1 large bunch leaf lettuce,
torn into pieces
5 green onions with tops,
chopped

SERVES 4
Fry bacon until crisp. Remove bacon from grease and set aside. Add vinegar, sugar, salt and pepper to bacon drippings. Tear lettuce into large mixing bowl, and add onion. Heat vinegar mixture to boiling. Pour over lettuce, tossing as you pour. Turn skillet upside down over bowl. Let set 5 minutes. Add bacon and serve immediately.

SALADS

SPINACH SALAD

1 pkg. fresh spinach
4 hard-boiled eggs, sliced
8 strips bacon
1 cup bean sprouts,
  drained
1 small can water
  chestnuts, diced

TANGY DRESSING:
1 cup salad oil
¼ cup wine vinegar
¾ cup sugar
½ tsp. salt
⅓ cup ketchup
2 tsp. Worcestershire sauce
½ onion, quartered

SERVES 6
Fry bacon until crisp. Drain thoroughly and crumble. Wash and drain spinach. Break into bite size pieces. Combine ingredients and toss carefully with Tangy Dressing.

Combine dressing ingredients in blender and puree.

RICH GREEN SALAD

1 head leaf lettuce, washed
  and dried
1—6 oz. jar marinated
  artichoke hearts, drained
  (save oil)
½ cup pitted ripe olives,
  sliced
Croutons
Parmesan cheese

DRESSING:
Juice of ½ lemon
1 tsp. dill weed
¼ cup olive oil
½ tsp. salt
Dash of pepper
Marinade from artichoke
  hearts

SERVES 6
Tear lettuce into small pieces. Cut olives and artichoke hearts into pieces and mix with lettuce. Toss with dressing just before serving; add croutons and Parmesan cheese to taste.

This salad is especially good with steak or prime rib but will complement any entree beautifully.

POTATO SALAD

6 potatoes (medium)
¼ cup red onion, finely
   chopped
1 tsp. salt
1/8 tsp. pepper
¼ cup Italian salad
   dressing
½ cup mayonnaise or salad
   dressing
½ cup celery, chopped
4 eggs, hard-boiled,
   chopped
1 tsp. celery seed

SERVES 6-8
Put unpared potatoes in boiling water, cover and cook until tender. Drain, cool and peel. Cut potatoes in cubes, combine with onion, salt and pepper. Add Italian dressing, cover and refrigerate 2-3 hours. Just before serving, add mayonnaise, celery, eggs, and celery seed. Toss well.

HOT GERMAN POTATO SALAD

2 lbs. potatoes (about 6)
6 slices bacon
1 medium onion, chopped
⅓ cup sugar
⅓ cup vinegar
⅓ cup water
1 tsp. celery seed
Salt
Pepper

SERVES 4
Boil potatoes in their skins. Cook bacon until crisp, then saute the onion in the bacon drippings. Peel cooked potatoes and cut into bite-sized pieces. (Also good with peelings left on.) Crumble bacon over potatoes. Heat bacon drippings, onion, vinegar, sugar, water and celery seed until boiling and pour over hot potatoes. Make sure liquid and potatoes are very hot when mixed together. Mix well. Add salt and pepper to taste, put into 2½ quart casserole and bake, uncovered, 30 minutes at 300°. You can prepare this ahead and refrigerate, as it does taste better the second day. Just be sure to serve it hot. Good with barbecued ribs or sausage.

 Eggs that are several days old are best for boiling as they will peel easier.

SALADS

ARTICHOKE RICE SALAD

1—6 oz. pkg. Chicken
  Rice-a-Roni
2—7 oz. jars marinated
  artichoke hearts
⅓ cup mayonnaise
¼ tsp. curry powder
12 pimento stuffed
  olives, sliced
½ green pepper, chopped
  fine
1 green onion, sliced
  (tops also)

SERVES 8-10
Cook Rice-a-Roni according to package directions. Cool. Drain artichoke hearts, reserving liquid. Combine reserved artichoke liquid and curry powder. Blend well. Add remaining ingredients and mix thoroughly. Chill. This is better if made a day in advance. For a variation, add chopped chicken or ham to make this salad a main course. Makes a large salad.

SOUTH OF THE BORDER SALAD

1 head lettuce, washed and
  drained
1 tomato, chopped
3-4 green onions, chopped
1 small can garbanzo beans
1 avocado, sliced
10 black olives, sliced
¾ cup hamburger, fried
¾ cup tortilla chips,
  slightly crushed
¼ cup cheddar cheese,
  grated
Thousand Island dressing

SERVES 4
Tear lettuce into small pieces. Add tomato, green onions, garbanzos, avocado, and olives. Fry hamburger and drain off grease. Just before serving, add hamburger, chips, and cheese. Add dressing and toss. Excellent with Beef Enchiladas.

 Place an avocado in cornmeal overnight to ripen.

ENSALADA MEXICANA

1 sweet red onion
2 tomatoes
2 small heads lettuce
  (Iceberg, Romaine, or
  leaf)
1 ripe avocado
8 black olives, sliced
1 lb. ground beef
1—1 lb. can Ranch style
  beans (you may
  substitute 1 cup of your
  own cooked pinto beans)
¼ tsp. salt
4 oz. cheddar cheese,
  grated
Tabasco sauce
10 oz. bag tortilla chips,
  slightly crushed
8 oz. bottle Western-style
  or red French dressing

SERVES 8-10
Chop onion, tomatoes, lettuce, avocado, and olives. Refrigerate. Brown ground beef and drain fat. Add beans, salt and a few shakes of Tabasco. Simmer about 15 minutes. When ready to serve, add beef and cheese to refrigerated items. Add crushed chips and toss with dressing. Serve immediately. You may want to add a few more shakes of Tabasco before serving. Makes a great main course meal, especially in the summer.

EASY GUACAMOLE

2 ripe avocados
½ tsp. lemon juice
3-4 Tbsp. Pace's Picante
  sauce
Garlic salt

SERVES 4
Mash 2 ripe avocados. Add lemon juice, Pace's Picante sauce, and some garlic salt to taste. Serve with tortilla chips or on top of burritos.

SALADS

♥ ♥ ♥ ♥ ♥ ♥ ♥ ♥ ♥ ♥ ♥ ♥ ♥ ♥ ♥ ♥ ♥

CRAB LOUIS

3 cups canned crabmeat,
  drained, or frozen cooked
  crabmeat, thawed
3 tomatoes, quartered
4 hard-boiled eggs,
  quartered
5 cups lettuce, torn into
  bite-size pieces

DRESSING:
1½ cups mayonnaise or
  salad dressing
⅓ cup French dressing
⅓ cup chili sauce
2 Tbps. minced green
  onion or chives
2 Tbsp. chopped green
  olives
1 tsp. prepared horseradish
1 tsp. onion juice or
  grated onion
1 tsp. lemon juice
1 tsp. Worcestershire sauce
1/8 tsp. salt
1/8 tsp. pepper
Dash Tabasco

SERVES 4-5
Combine dressing ingredients. Mix thoroughly. On individual serving dishes, arrange crabmeat on lettuce with tomatoes and eggs. Pour dressing over salad. Crabmeat can be combined with the dressing, if you prefer.

TOMATOES AND CRABMEAT

2-3 large red tomatoes,
  sliced thick
1 can King Crabmeat,
  drained

RUSSIAN DRESSING:
½ cup oil
¼ cup wine vinegar
6 Tbsp. sugar
3 Tbsp. ketchup
1 tsp. salt

SERVES 4
Slice tomatoes. Mound King Crab on each slice, then dribble Russian dressing over each. Serve on a bed of lettuce. This is a good accompaniment to smoked ham or turkey.

♥ ♥ ♥ ♥ ♥ ♥ ♥ ♥ ♥ ♥ ♥ ♥ ♥ ♥ ♥ ♥ ♥

MOLDED TUNA SALAD

3 hard-boiled eggs
1 pkg. unflavored gelatin,
  dissolved in ¼ cup cold
  water
1 family-size can tuna,
  drained
½ cup sliced green olives
¼ tsp. onion flakes
2-2½ cups mayonnaise

SERVES 6

Cook gelatin mixture in a double boiler until thin. Add mayonnaise and stir until creamy. Add tuna, eggs, olives, and onion flakes. Pour into mold or loaf pan, and chill. This makes a delicious luncheon dish. Serve with a fresh fruit salad.

CURRIED SHRIMP SALAD

1 lb. shrimp, cooked,
  shelled and chilled
1 cup celery, sliced
3 green onions, chopped
½ cup mayonnaise
½ cup sour cream
Juice of 1 lemon
1½ tsp. curry powder
1 tsp. salt
Pepper

SERVES 6

Cut shrimp in half, lengthwise; add celery and green onions. Mix remaining ingredients to make a sauce; add shrimp. Serve on bed of lettuce. For something different, serve this salad on avocado halves or with quartered tomatoes. Try substituting crabmeat for the shrimp. The curry sauce alone is a good dip for crudites.

SALADS

♥ ♥ ♥ ♥ ♥ ♥ ♥ ♥ ♥ ♥ ♥ ♥ ♥ ♥ ♥ ♥ ♥

TOSSED SHRIMP SALAD

1 bunch salad greens (bibb
  or leaf lettuce)
1½ cups frozen, fresh
  cocktail shrimp
2-3 hard-boiled eggs
1 avocado, sliced
12 cherry tomatoes, halved
1 cup broccoli flowerets
2 Tbsp. green onion,
  chopped
¼ cup celery, chopped
1 small can ripe olives,
  chopped
½ cup grated cheddar
  cheese
Russian or Western Style
  dressing

SERVES 4
Wash and drain lettuce. Tear into bite sized pieces. Add other ingredients and serve with Russian or Western style dressing. This makes a delicious summertime meal in itself.

ITALIAN SCROODLE SALAD

1—8 oz. pkg. scroodle
  macaroni, cooked and
  drained
1—3 oz. pkg. pepperoni,
  diced small (may
  substitute ham)
1½ cup Provolone cheese,
  shredded
3 green onions and tops,
  chopped
1 can garbanzo beans,
  (optional)
Italian dressing

SERVES 4-6
Cook scroodles as directed, rinse with cold water and drain. Combine with other ingredients. Pour dressing over salad and mix well. Let chill 1-2 hours before serving.

SUMMERTIME MACARONI SALAD

3 cups cooked shell
  macaroni (1½ cups
  uncooked)
2 green onions, chopped
¼ cup pimento
1 small can black olives
  (may substitute ¼ cup
  sliced green olives for
  the pimento and black
  olives)
1 cup cheddar cheese,
  grated or cubed
¼ cup celery, chopped
¾ cup salad dressing or
  mayonnaise
½ tsp. salt
¼ tsp. pepper
Dash of garlic salt
2 tsp. celery seed

SERVES 6
Cook macaroni as directed. Drain and rinse with cold water. Combine macaroni with onion, pimento, olives, cheese, and celery. Mix mayonnaise with salt, pepper, garlic salt, and celery seed. Add to the macaroni mixture, blend well. Chill 3-4 hours.

Crack hard boiled eggs and let sit in cold water several minutes for easier peeling.

Meats

MEATS

BARBECUED BRISKET OR RIBS

1½ tsp. salt
1½ tsp. onion salt
3 tsp. celery salt
3 Tbsp. Worcestershire
  sauce
1½ tsp. pepper
4 Tbsp. liquid smoke
4-6 lbs. brisket or ribs
Hickory Barbecue Sauce
  (see recipe in sauce
  section)

SERVES 8-10
Combine all ingredients except barbecue sauce in a cup. Arrange brisket
in foil. Pour salt mixture over brisket
and marinate overnight. Bake
wrapped in foil with marinade at 225°
for 6-8 hours, depending on the size
of brisket. Brisket is delicious with this
juice or with barbecue sauce added
during the last two hours of cooking.
To cook ribs, marinate overnight as
you would the brisket. Before baking,
pour barbecue sauce generously
over ribs and bake, covered tightly at
225° for 6 hours. Serve with Potato
Salad, Cowboy Beans, and Texas
Buttermilk Biscuits for a true western-
style barbecue!

JOANIE'S MARINATED GRILLED STEAK

Juice of one lemon
½ cup soy sauce
3 Tbsp. vegetable oil
2 Tbsp. Worcestershire
  sauce
1 clove garlic, minced
Pepper
Chopped green onion
2 lb. flank steak

SERVES 4
Mix all ingredients in the pan in which
meat is to be marinated. Marinate
steak, turning occasionally, for 4-12
hours in refrigerator. Broil meat over
hot coals to desired doneness.

 *Low cooking temperature keeps the juice and flavor in the
meat, cuts down on shrinkage, and keeps the meat more
tender.*

100

STEAK DIANA

¼ cup butter
1 cup fresh mushrooms,
  sliced
2 Tbsp. minced green
  onion
1/8 tsp. garlic powder
1/8 tsp. salt
1 tsp. lemon juice
1 tsp. Worcestershire sauce
1½ Tbsp. parlsey, chopped
2 Tbsp. butter
1¼ lb. beef tenderloin, cut
  in 2 inch slices

SERVES 4
Melt butter in skillet, add mushrooms, onion, garlic, salt, lemon juice, and Worcestershire sauce. Cook until mushrooms are tender. Add parsley. Pour in small bowl. In skillet melt another 2 tablespoons butter. Cook tenderloin over medium-high heat, 3-4 minutes on each side. Pour mushroom-butter mixture over meat in skillet. Heat thoroughly. Remove from heat, cover and let sit 10-15 minutes, to allow flavors to blend. Heat again to serve. Delicious with Cattlemen's Club Twice Baked Potatoes, green salad and Mud Pie for dessert.

UNATTENDED RIB ROAST

1 standing rib roast,
  any size
Salt and pepper

Preheat oven to 375° 6-7 hours before mealtime. Season roast with salt and pepper and place in roasting pan. Cook, uncovered for 1 hour, then turn off oven. DO NOT OPEN OVEN DOOR. Turn heat on again to 375° 40 minutes before serving. The roast will be medium rare in the center and well done around the edges.

MEATS

♥ ♥ ♥ ♥ ♥ ♥ ♥ ♥ ♥ ♥ ♥ ♥ ♥ ♥ ♥ ♥ ♥

BEST EVER POT ROAST

3-4 lb. arm roast
2 cups water
Lawry's seasoned salt
Pepper
1 bay leaf (optional)
6 potatoes, pared and cut
   in pieces
6-8 carrots, peeled and cut
   in pieces
2 onions, quartered

GRAVY:
3-4 Tbsp. cornstarch
½ cup water
½ tsp. salt
¼ tsp. pepper
1 tsp. Kitchen Bouquet

SERVES 6

Set pot roast in roasting pan, sprinkle liberally with salt and pepper. Add 2 cups water and bay leaf; cover and cook in 250° oven 5-6 hours. About an hour before supper, add vegetables and turn up oven to 325°. In an hour's time you will have a tender, moist pot roast and vegetables with a minimum of fuss. (You can even put the roast in frozen, only do it an hour or so earlier.) Remove meat and vegetables from roaster and set pan on stove top to make gravy. While stirring constantly over medium high heat, add enough cornstarch, dissolved in cold water, to drippings to make desired consistency. Season with salt, pepper and Kitchen Bouquet.

SWISS STEAK

1 arm roast (4 lbs.)
¼ cup flour
½ tsp. salt
¼ tsp. garlic powder
Pepper
2-3 Tbsp. oil
1—16 oz. can tomatoes,
   cut up
1 onion, sliced
1 small green pepper,
   sliced

SERVES 6

Heat oil in large skillet. Season roast with salt, pepper, and garlic powder. Dredge in flour, then brown on both sides in hot oil. Place in roasting pan. Arrange onion and pepper slices on top of roast, then pour tomatoes over top. Cover and bake at 250° for at least 4 hours, more if you have time. Check occasionally to see if it needs water. Makes its own gravy when cooked like this and is so tender it cuts like butter!

SHISH-KA-BOB

1 sirloin steak (about
   2 lbs.), cut into cubes
Italian dressing

Vegetable/Fruit Ideas:
   (Use at least three
   different ones)
Cherry tomatoes (about 10)
Green pepper, quartered (3)
Onion, quartered (3)
Pineapple chunks
Whole mushrooms
Corn on the cob, 2 inch
   pieces

SERVES 4-6
Marinate steak cubes in Italian dressing 4-6 hours in refrigerator. On skewer put pieces of steak alternating with the other selections. Ex: steak, mushroom, tomato, pineapple, steak, etc. This will fill about 4 skewers. Grill outside on charcoal cooker until meat is desired doneness. Serve with Easy Rice, Spinach Salad, and Braided Potato Bread.

EASY BEEF STROGANOFF

1 lb. sirloin steak, cut into
   small cubes or ½ inch
   strips
½ cup flour
3 Tbsp. oil
1/8 tsp. garlic powder
1 pint beef bouillon
1 can cream of mushroom
   soup
1 cup sliced mushrooms
¾ cup sour cream
3-4 cups noodles, cooked
   and drained
Parsley

SERVES 4
Cut steak into cubes or strips. Put ½ cup flour and garlic powder in plastic bag, add meat, and shake to coat meat well. Heat oil in large skillet. Saute meat and mushrooms over medium heat, stirring occasionally. When meat coating is crispy, pour in bouillon and mushroom soup. Mix well. Simmer 20-30 minutes, stirring occasionally. Before serving, stir in sour cream and heat through. Serve over hot noodles. Garnish with parsley.

 Pierce an onion with a fork before cooking. It will retain its shape without falling apart.

MEATS

❤ ❤ ❤ ❤ ❤ ❤ ❤ ❤ ❤ ❤ ❤ ❤ ❤ ❤ ❤ ❤ ❤

CHICKEN FRIED STEAK & CREAM GRAVY

4 cubed steaks or round
   steak (pound round steak
   well with mallet or sharp
   knife)
2 eggs
½-¾ cup flour
Oil
Salt and pepper
6 Tbsp. flour
3 cups milk

SERVES 4

Pound steak well. Divide steak into portion size pieces. Dip into beaten egg, then coat with flour. Pour 1/8 inch oil in bottom of skillet. Have grease fairly hot before putting in steaks. Let fry on one side until well browned, about 4 minutes. Season with salt and pepper. Keeping heat fairly hot, turn steak to brown other side. Place steak on dish and set in 250° oven while making gravy.

To make gravy, drain or add enough oil to have 2-3 tablespoons of grease in pan. Add 6 tablespoons flour and stir well to loosen crumbs on bottom and blend in flour. Add milk slowly, stirring constantly until gravy is desired consistency. Serve with fried or mashed potatoes, Okra and Tomatoes, and Fresh Strawberry Pie for dessert. Wow!

STEAK AND POTATOES

Round steak (1½-2 lbs.)
Meat tenderizer
½-¾ cup flour
3 Tbsp. oil
Lawry's seasoned salt
Pepper
1 can cream of onion soup
1 can cream of mushroom
   soup
1 soup can milk
Potatoes, peeled and sliced
   (as many as your family
   eats)

SERVES 4-5

Sprinkle steak with meat tenderizer and let sit ½-1 hour. Cut steak into single portion pieces and dredge each in flour. Brown on both sides in oil. Season meat with seasoned salt and pepper as it cooks. Remove browned meat and drain on paper towel. Put soups and 1 soup can of milk into frying pan and mix with crusties from meat. Stir well. Grease a 3 quart casserole and layer meat, potatoes, and gravy, ending with gravy. Bake, covered, at 300° for 3-4 hours. This makes a delicious one-pot meal, made early in the day and ready to eat at suppertime. Good with hot biscuits.

CORNED BEEF & CABBAGE

4 lbs. corned beef
1 onion
3-4 potatoes, chunked
3 carrots
3-4 rutabagas (optional)
½-¾ head cabbage, cut in thin wedges

SERVES 8

Place corned beef in large kettle or crockpot. Cover with water. Slice onion and place around beef. Cook all day in crockpot or simmer at least 5-6 hours in kettle. An hour before serving, add carrots, potatoes and rutabagas. Cook 45 minutes; then add cabbage. Simmer until cabbage is tender, about 15-20 minutes. Serve with Irish Soda Bread and Blarney Stones for dessert, and you've got a real St. Patrick's Day feast!

BEEF JERKY

1 lb. flank steak
1 tsp. seasoned salt
½ tsp. garlic powder
½ tsp. onion powder
¼ tsp. pepper
⅓ cup soy sauce
⅓ cup Worcestershire sauce
2 Tbsp. liquid smoke

Pat flank steak dry and slice thinly across grain of meat. In a plastic bag, combine rest of ingredients. Place meat in bag, making sure each slice is coated with marinade. Place in refrigerator overnight. Drain meat on paper towels, blotting well. Place meat on oven rack and cook at 140° for 3 hours. It helps to open the oven door a crack to let moisture escape. Put a piece of foil on oven floor to catch any drippings. Keep in a jar in the refrigerator and watch them disappear!

 Add a little baking soda along with the milk and butter to mashed potatoes to make them fluffy.

MEATS

♥ ♥ ♥ ♥ ♥ ♥ ♥ ♥ ♥ ♥ ♥ ♥ ♥ ♥ ♥ ♥ ♥

LAZY LADY STEW

2 lbs. cubed stew meat
1—1 lb. can tiny peas (may
  substitute 1—10 oz. pkg.
  frozen peas)
1 cup sliced carrots
2 onions, chopped
2 potatoes, pared and
  sliced
1 tsp. salt
Dash of pepper
1 can cream of tomato soup
½ soup can water
1 bay leaf

SERVES 4

Mix all ingredients in a large casserole. Cook, covered, in a 275°
oven for 6 hours. The stew meat can
be put in frozen, but increase the
cooking time by 1 hour. Not only is
this stew delicious, but it is un-
believably easy. Serve with Homestyle Cornbread and a green salad.
(You can easily double or triple these
proportions and feed a crowd.)

HEARTY HODGEPODGE

6 slices bacon
1 medium onion, thinly
  sliced
1 lb. beef shank
¾ lb. ham hock
6 cups water
2 tsp. salt
2—15 oz. cans garbanzo
  beans
3 cups potatoes, diced
1/8 tsp. garlic powder
6 oz. polish sausage,
  thinly sliced

SERVES 4-6

In large heavy kettle, cook bacon until
crisp. Reserve 2 tablespoons drippings. Crumble bacon and set aside.
Saute onion in bacon drippings until
tender. Add beef shank, ham hock,
water, and salt. Cover and simmer 1½
hours. Remove meat from shank and
ham hock; dice. Skim fat from broth.
Return diced meat to soup; add undrained beans, potatoes and garlic.
Simmer, covered for 30 minutes. Add
sausage and bacon. Simmer covered,
15 minutes longer. This is a delicious
stew type meal. Serve with Sourdough Bread.

ZELDA'S CABBAGE ROLLS

1½ lbs. ground beef
½ cup rice
½ tsp. salt
½ tsp. pepper
¾-1 tsp. garlic powder
1 onion, diced
1 egg
1 head cabbage

SAUCE:
2—6 oz. cans tomato sauce
Juice of two lemons
3 Tbsp. flour (rounded)
½ cup sugar

SERVES 4-6
Mix ground beef with rice, salt, pepper, garlic powder, onion, and egg. Dunk cabbage leaves in boiling water to make pliable. Place ¼ cup hamburger mixture on each leaf and wrap. Makes about 12 rolls. Combine ingredients to make sauce. There are several ways to cook these, the best being in a pressure cooker.

Pressure Cooker Method: Heat sauce in the pressure pan. Place cabbage rolls in sauce. Cover and seal. Heat slowly until pressure is on 10 lbs. Cook 10 minutes.

Crockpot Method: Pour half the sauce in the bottom of the crock pot, then add cabbage rolls. Pour remaining sauce over rolls. Cover and cook on high 5-6 hours.

Oven Method: Place rolls in a large greased baking dish. Spoon sauce over rolls and cover dish tightly. Bake at 325° for 1-1½ hours. Check every 20-30 minutes to see if extra liquid is needed. Add water accordingly.

MEATS

CORNY SANDWICH SQUARES

CORNBREAD:
1 cup yellow cornmeal
1 cup white flour
¼ cup sugar
½ tsp. salt
4 tsp. baking powder
1 egg
1 cup milk
¼ cup vegetable oil
1—4 oz. can cream-style
corn
¾ cup Velveeta, grated

FILLING:
1 lb. ground beef, browned
¼-½ cup ketchup
2 Tbsp. sweet pickle relish
½ cup Velveeta, grated
¼ cup Parmesan cheese

SAUCE:
¼ cup cold water
1 Tbsp. cornstarch
1—16 oz. can stewed
tomatoes, cut up
1 tsp. Worcestershire sauce

SERVES 6
Mix cornbread ingredients, adding cream-style corn and ¾ cup cheese. Spread half the batter in a greased 8x8x2 baking pan. In a skillet, brown ground beef, drain off fat. Add ketchup and relish to meat and spread on batter. Sprinkle with ½ cup Velveeta, and the Parmesan. Top with remaining batter. Bake at 350° for 45-55 minutes. Let stand 5 minutes before cutting.

Prepare the sauce by combining water and cornstarch in small saucepan. Stir in tomatoes and Worcestershire. Cook and stir until mixture thickens and bubbles. Serve over cornbread squares. This is an unusual and really delicious meal.

When freezing a casserole dish, line your casserole with foil before filling it, then freeze. When it's frozen solid, slip food and foil from the casserole dish, seal tightly and replace in freezer. The dish can be used while the casserole waits. When ready to bake, slip food from foil, place casserole in the same dish and bake.

❤ ❤ ❤ ❤ ❤ ❤ ❤ ❤ ❤ ❤ ❤ ❤ ❤ ❤ ❤ ❤ ❤

HAMBURGER-SOUR CREAM CASSEROLE

1½ lbs. hamburger
1 onion, chopped
¼ green pepper, chopped
1 can cream of chicken
   soup
1 can cream of mushroom
   soup
1—12 oz. can corn niblets,
   drained
3 cups cooked noodles
   (5 oz.)
1 cup sour cream
½ tsp. salt
¼ tsp. pepper
1—3 oz. can chow mein
   noodles

SERVES 6
In a skillet combine meat, onions, and pepper and brown slowly; drain fat. Add all ingredients except chow mein noodles. Place in a 9 x 13 inch baking dish and top with chow mein noodles. Bake, uncovered, for 25-30 minutes at 350°. Freezes well, but do not put chow mein noodles on top until ready to bake.

GOLDEN BEEF CASSEROLE

2 lbs. lean ground beef
1 medium onion, chopped
½ green pepper, chopped
1—1 lb. can tomatoes
3 Tbsp. ketchup
1 Tbsp. chili powder
1 Tbsp. Heinz 57 steak
   sauce
5 oz. macaroni, cooked and
   drained
½ cup sharp cheddar
   cheese, grated
1 can Golden Mushroom
   soup
Salt and pepper to taste

SERVES 6-8
Brown meat, onions, and green pepper. Drain fat. Add tomatoes, ketchup, steak sauce, chili powder, salt and pepper. Cook, covered, about 30 minutes. Pour mixture into casserole. Add cooked macaroni, stir in mushroom soup and top with grated cheese. Bake, uncovered, at 350° about 30 minutes.

MEATS

TEXAS HASH

1 lb. ground beef
1 large onion, chopped
1 large green pepper,
  chopped
1—1 lb. can tomatoes,
  cut up
½ cup uncooked regular
  rice
2 tsp. chili powder
2 tsp. salt
1/8 tsp. pepper

SERVES 4-6
In large skillet, brown beef, onion, and green pepper. Drain fat. Add tomatoes, rice, chili powder, salt and pepper. Heat through. Pour into 2 quart casserole, cover and bake 1 hour at 350°. You can put this in the microwave if in a hurry and cook on high, turning every 10 minutes for 25 minutes. This is easy, fast, and a hit with the whole family.

MEAT LOAF

2 lbs. ground beef
¼ lb. salt pork, chopped
  fine (leave this out if
  you don't happen to
  have it)
2 eggs, slightly beaten
1 cup milk
3 Tbsp. melted butter
1 Tbsp. horseradish
2 Tbsp. onion, minced
¼ tsp. pepper
¾ Tbsp. salt
1 cup soft bread crumbs
2 strips bacon

SERVES 8
Mix all ingredients, except the bacon and pack into greased loaf pan. Cover with strips of bacon and bake at 350° for 1 hour. Drain fat from meat loaf as soon as you remove from oven.

 Meatloaf will not stick to its pan if you place a strip of bacon at the bottom of the pan before placing your meatloaf in it.

♥ ♥ ♥ ♥ ♥ ♥ ♥ ♥ ♥ ♥ ♥ ♥ ♥ ♥ ♥ ♥ ♥

HOMEMADE PIZZA

DOUGH:
1 pkg. dry yeast
1 cup lukewarm water
1 Tbsp. sugar
1 tsp. salt
2 Tbsp. oil
2½-3 cups flour

TOPPINGS:
1 jar Ragu Pizza Quick
   sauce
¾ lb. mozzarella cheese,
   grated
Pepperoni, sliced
Italian sausage, crumbled
   and browned
Sliced mushrooms, sauteed
Green pepper, diced
Sliced onions

MAKES 2 MEDIUM PIZZAS
In bowl dissolve yeast in warm water. Add sugar, salt and oil. Mix well. Gradually add flour to form a stiff dough. Knead on floured surface until smooth. Place in bowl, cover with a damp towel and let rise until doubled.

Divide dough in half and roll to ¼ inch thickness. Put each round in a medium size cast-iron skillet or pizza pan. Cover with Ragu sauce, grated cheese, then the toppings of your choice. Bake at 400° about 15 minutes or until golden.

PORCUPINE MEATBALLS

1 cup minute rice
1 egg, beaten
1 lb. ground beef
2 tsp. salt
2 tsp. grated onion
Pepper to taste
2½ cups tomato juice
½ tsp. sugar

SERVES 4
Mix ingredients except 2 cups tomato juice and sugar. Shape into meatballs and brown in skillet. Blend remaining juice and sugar. Pour in skillet with meatballs and bring to a boil. Cover and simmer slowly 15-20 minutes. Sprinkle with parsley if desired. Kids love these.

MEATS

SALISBURY STEAK

1½ lbs. ground beef
2 Tbsp. grated onion
1 tsp. salt
¼ tsp. dried marjoram
  leaves, crushed
1/8 tsp. pepper
1 envelope brown gravy mix
1—3 oz. can sliced
  mushrooms, drained
3 Tbsp. red wine (optional)

SERVES 4-6
Combine ground beef, grated onion, salt, marjoram, and pepper; mix well. Divide meat into six portions and shape into patties ¾ inch thick. Broil for 4-5 minutes on each side or until done. Prepare gravy mix according to package directions. Stir in mushrooms. Add wine if desired. Set patties in gravy. Remove from heat and let sit 20-30 minutes to allow flavors to blend. Simmer 5-10 minutes before serving. This is delicious with Italian Green Beans, baked potato and Peach Cobbler for dessert.

SHEPHERD'S PIE

1 lb. ground beef
1 onion, chopped
1—10 oz. can Rotel
  tomatoes
Salt and pepper
1—16 oz. can mixed
  vegetables, drained
4 medium potatoes, cooked
  and mashed
¾ cup cheddar cheese,
  grated

SERVES 4-6
Brown ground beef and onion. Drain grease. In casserole, combine Rotel tomatoes, salt, pepper, mixed vegetables and beef mixture. Top with mashed potatoes and grated cheese. Cook, uncovered at 350° until cheese melts, about 15-20 minutes. Freezes well.

 Try boiling potatoes (unpeeled) for about five minutes, then baking them in a hot oven. They will be thoroughly done in about one-half the usual time.

♥ ♥ ♥ ♥ ♥ ♥ ♥ ♥ ♥ ♥ ♥ ♥ ♥ ♥ ♥ ♥ ♥

TEXAS RED CHILI

1 lb. ground beef
1 medium onion, chopped
1½ Tbsp. chili powder
1¼ tsp. salt
¼ tsp. garlic powder
¼ tsp. black pepper
1/8 tsp. ground cumin
1 Tbsp. vinegar
1—1 lb. can tomato sauce
2 cups water
2 cups pinto beans, cooked (or 1 can Ranch Style beans if you don't have any pinto beans cooked up)

SERVES 4
In a Dutch oven, brown ground beef and onion. Drain off fat. Add vinegar and seasonings. Stir well. Add tomato sauce, beans and water. Simmer over low heat 30 minutes. If you prefer thick chili, put 2 tablespoons flour in a jar, add ½ cup water, cover, and shake until mixed. Pour into chili and stir well. Serve with slices of Longhorn cheese, cold crisp apple, and Mexican Cornbread. The next day put it on hot dogs for a real Coney Island dog!

WEST OF THE PECOS

2 lbs. ground meat
1 large onion, chopped
1 green pepper, chopped
1—4 oz. can sliced mushrooms
2 tsp. chili powder
¼ cup Worcestershire sauce
1 tsp. salt
¼ tsp. pepper
1 can tomato soup
1—10 oz. can Rotel tomatoes
1—16 oz. can cream-style corn
1—12 oz. pkg. noodles, cooked and drained
½ cup Longhorn cheese, grated

SERVES 8-10
In large Dutch oven, brown ground beef, onion, and green pepper. Drain fat. Add mushrooms, chili powder, Worcestershire sauce, salt and pepper. Mix thoroughly. Add can of soup, tomatoes, and corn. Simmer ½ hour. Add cooked noodles, stir well. Top with grated cheese and bake, covered, 1 hour at 325°. This is an extra good goulash. Freezes well.

♥ ♥ ♥ ♥ ♥ ♥ ♥ ♥ ♥ ♥ ♥ ♥ ♥ ♥ ♥ ♥ ♥

GREEN CHILI BURRITOS

SAUCE:
1½ lbs. cooked pork roast,
 cubed
1—10½ oz. can chicken
 broth
1—16 oz. can tomatoes,
 cut up
1—8 oz. can tomato sauce
¼-½ tsp. garlic powder
2—7 oz. cans diced green
 chilies
¼ oz. diced hot peppers
1 tsp. sugar
1 tsp. salt
2 Tbsp. flour, dissolved in
 ¼ cup water

FILLING:
1 lb. ground beef
¼-½ onion, diced
1 or 2—16 oz. cans
 refried beans

TOPPING:
Grated cheddar cheese
Shredded lettuce
Tomato, chopped
Sour cream

White flour tortillas

SERVES 4-6

Simmer pork in broth 5-10 minutes. Add canned tomatoes, tomato sauce, garlic, green chilies, hot peppers, sugar and salt. Let simmer 45 minutes. Thicken slightly with flour.

Brown hamburger and onion; drain grease. Add refried beans and blend together over low heat. Wrap flour tortillas in foil and warm in oven.

To serve: spoon bean and hamburger mixture on warm tortilla. Roll up tortilla and top with chili sauce. Sprinkle with cheese, lettuce and tomato. Top with spoonful of sour cream. The chili sauce freezes well.

BEEF ENCHILADAS

SAUCE:
1 medium onion, minced
2 Tbsp. vegetable oil
2 Tbsp. flour
2 cups chicken broth
¼ tsp. garlic powder
1—4 oz. can chopped, mild green chilies
2 cups canned tomatoes, drained and chopped

FILLING:
1 lb. ground beef
½ onion, chopped
1 tsp. chili powder
1 tsp. vinegar
½ tsp. salt
12 corn tortillas
2 cups grated Longhorn cheese

SERVES 6

Saute onion in oil until soft. Stir in flour and cook for 1 minute. Add broth and garlic powder, cook until thickened. Add chilies and tomatoes and simmer for 10 minutes. Puree sauce in blender or food processor.

Brown meat in large skillet with onion. Drain fat. Add vinegar, chili powder, and salt.

Dip each tortilla in sauce to soften it. Place a large spoonful of meat, a little grated cheese, and a spoonful of sauce in each. Roll up. Place in baking dish (seam side down) and repeat with remaining tortillas. Pour remaining sauce over all, top with cup of grated cheese and bake uncovered at 350° for 15-20 minutes. Serve with Easy Guacamole Salad, tortilla chips, Cowboy Beans, and a mug of frosty beer! This sauce freezes nicely, as do the enchiladas.

MEATS

♥ ♥ ♥ ♥ ♥ ♥ ♥ ♥ ♥■♥■♥■♥■♥■♥ ♥ ♥ ♥

TAMALE PIE

1 cup onion, chopped
1 lb. ground beef
2—8 oz. cans tomato sauce
1—12 oz. can whole kernel
   corn, drained
1 cup ripe olives, chopped
1/8 tsp. garlic powder
1 Tbsp. sugar
1 tsp. salt
2-3 tsp. chili powder
Dash of pepper
1½ cups Longhorn cheese,
   grated

TOPPING:
¾ cup yellow cornmeal
½ tsp. salt
2 cups cold water
1 Tbsp. butter

SERVES 6
In large skillet, brown beef and onion. Drain grease. Add tomato sauce, corn, olives, garlic, sugar, salt, chili powder, and pepper. Simmer about 20 minutes or until thick. Add cheese. Stir until cheese is melted. Pour into a greased 6 x 10 inch baking dish.

To make topping, stir cornmeal and salt into cold water. Stir over medium-low heat until thickened, about 3-4 minutes. Add butter and mix well. Spoon over meat mixture. Bake 40 minutes in 375° oven or until topping is browned.

FANCY TOSTADAS

1—16 oz. can refried beans
Dash Tabasco
¼ cup sliced green onion
4 oz. Monterey Jack
   cheese, grated
1 tomato, chopped
3 cups shredded lettuce
3 green onions, chopped
1 avocado, chopped
3 Tbsp. Italian salad
   dressing (Thousand
   Island is good also)
1 lb. ground beef
1 small onion, chopped
1/8 tsp. garlic powder
1—4 oz. can green chilies
1 can mild enchilada sauce
½ cup tomato juice
7-8 fried tortillas

SERVES 4
Combine refried beans, Tabasco, green onion and Monterey Jack cheese in small bowl. Cover and bake for 25 minutes at 325°. In salad bowl, combine tomato, lettuce, onion, and salad dressing. Brown ground beef, onion and garlic in skillet. Drain grease. Add green chilies, enchilada sauce and tomato juice. Mix well and let simmer 20 minutes. To serve: fry tortillas in ½ inch of oil in small skillet. Turn once. Top with hot refried bean mixture, meat sauce, then salad. Can top with cheese or taco sauce.

MEATS

EGGPLANT PARMESAN

1 lb. ground beef
½ cup onion, chopped
1/8 tsp. garlic powder
1—16 oz. can tomatoes,
    cut up
1—6 oz. can tomato paste
½ tsp. salt
Pepper
¾ Tbsp. Italian seasoning
½ tsp. crushed cayenne
    red pepper
1½ Tbsp. brown sugar
2 small eggplants
¾ cup cracker crumbs
1 egg
8 oz. mozzarella cheese
¾ cup Parmesan cheese

SERVES 6
Brown hamburger, onion and garlic in saucepan. Drain grease. Add cut up tomatoes, tomato paste, salt, pepper, seasoning, red pepper, and sugar to meat. Let simmer ½-1 hour. Peel and slice eggplant. Beat egg. Dip eggplant slices in egg and then cracker crumbs. Melt butter in skillet and brown both sides of eggplant slices. Grease 9 x 13 inch casserole. Arrange eggplant slices in the bottom. Top with tomato mixture. Sprinkle mozzarella and Parmesan cheese over top. Bake uncovered 25 minutes at 350°. Serve with tossed green salad and French bread.

BOB AND GAYLE'S SPAGHETTI SAUCE

1 onion, chopped
1½ lbs. Italian sausage
2—1 lb. cans stewed
    tomatoes
1—8 oz. can tomato sauce
1—6 oz. can tomato paste
¼ cup cooking burgundy
Garlic powder to taste
1 tsp. leaf basil
1 tsp. leaf marjoram
1 tsp. leaf oregano

SERVES 4
Crumble sausage in large skillet and brown along with onion. Drain fat. Add other ingredients and simmer for 45 minutes to 1 hour. Serve over cooked and drained spaghetti with tossed green salad and garlic bread.

Add a little cooking oil to boiling water when making spaghetti to keep it from sticking together. It should also keep the pot from boiling over.

MEATS

LASAGNA

2 lbs. ground beef
½ cup onion, chopped
Garlic salt
1—8 oz. can tomato sauce
1—6 oz. can tomato paste
1—20 oz. can tomatoes,
   cut up
1 tsp. oregano
2 tsp. salt
½ tsp. pepper
1 tsp. sweet basil
1 bay leaf

CHEESE FILLING:
3 cups cottage cheese
½ cup Parmesan cheese
2 Tbsp. parsley flakes
2 beaten eggs
½ tsp. pepper

1 lb. mozzarella cheese,
   grated
1—8 oz. pkg. lasagna
   noodles, cooked and
   drained

SERVES 9-12

Brown ground beef, onion, and garlic salt in large heavy skillet. Drain fat. Add tomato sauce, tomato paste, tomatoes, oregano, salt, pepper, sweet basil, and bay leaf and simmer 20 minutes.

Combine cheese filling ingredients and mix well. In a 9 x 13 inch pan, layer the noodles, meat sauce, cheese filling and mozzarella cheese; then repeat. Bake uncovered at 375° for 30 minutes. Let stand 10 minutes before serving. This is better if made the day before, refrigerated, and then baked. Allow some extra baking time if it has been refrigerated. If you are making this for your family, make two small pans and freeze one.

HAM AND POTATO BAKE

2 Tbsp. onion, chopped
½ cup margarine
½ cup flour
1 tsp. salt
½ tsp. dry mustard
Pepper
1½ cups milk
2 cups cheddar cheese
   grated
½ lb. ham, cut into cubes
   or 1/8 inch slices
6 cups cooked potato,
   sliced

SERVES 6

Saute onion in margarine. Blend in flour and seasonings. Gradually add milk, stirring constantly until thickened. Add 1½ cups cheese, stir until melted. Toss potatoes in cheese sauce. Layer the potato mixture and ham in a buttered casserole. Bake, uncovered, at 350° for 30 minutes. Top with remaining ½ cup cheese. Return to oven until melted.

MEATS

♥ ♥ ♥ ♥ ♥ ♥ ♥ ♥ ♥ ♥ ♥ ♥ ♥ ♥ ♥ ♥ ♥

COMPANY CASSEROLE

24 oz. Jimmy Dean sausage
1 medium onion, chopped
1 cup green pepper,
chopped
1 cup celery, chopped
1 cup uncooked rice
1 can chicken gumbo soup
2 cans cream of mushroom
soup
1 cup mushrooms, sliced
2 cups water (including
liquid from mushrooms)
1½ cups sharp cheddar
cheese, grated
½ cup slivered almonds

SERVES 6-8
Brown sausage, onion, celery, and pepper in a large skillet. Drain grease. Add remaining ingredients. Spoon into large casserole. Bake, covered, at 350° for 1½ hours.

PORK CHOP POTATO SUPPER

4-5 pork chops
1—16 oz. can green beans,
partially drained
2 cans cream of mushroom
soup
3 potatoes, peeled, cut into
fourths
Salt and pepper

SERVES 4-5
Mix green beans, soup, salt, pepper, and potatoes in small roasting pan. Nestle pork chops into mixture. Bake covered at 350° for 1½ hours.

HAM N' BEANS

2 cups dried lima beans
or Great Northern beans,
washed well
1 tsp. salt
1/8 tsp. pepper
2 cups ham, cut in pieces

SERVES 4-6
Soak beans overnight in 6 cups of water. Drain and put in pot with 6 cups of water. Season with salt and pepper. Add ham, and simmer over low heat for 2-3 hours, or until beans are tender. Serve with cornbread and a relish tray of green onions and Deviled Eggs.

MEATS

❤ ❤ ❤ ❤ ❤ ❤ ❤ ❤ ❤ ❤ ❤ ❤ ❤ ❤ ❤ ❤

MILE HIGH PORK CHOP CASSEROLE

4 pork chops
2 Tbsp. oil
1 cup whole grain rice
1 tomato, sliced
1 green pepper, sliced
1 onion, sliced
1 can consomme
Salt and pepper, to taste

SERVES 4

Season pork chops with salt and pepper. In 2 tablespoons oil, brown pork chops on both sides in a skillet. Sprinkle rice in the bottom of a casserole. Lay pork chops on top of rice. Place a slice of onion, green pepper, and tomato on each pork chop. Pour consomme over all. Bake at 350°, covered, for 1½ hours, or until pork chops are tender and rice has absorbed all the moisture.

DARN GOOD BEANS

2 lbs. pinto beans
6 bouillon cubes (beef or chicken)
2-3 lbs. German sausage, cut up (you can substitute Polish or country-style)
3 Tbsp. Worcestershire sauce
1 jalapeno pepper, fresh (you may substitute sliced canned jalapenos)
2 onions, chopped
1 green pepper, chopped
1/8 tsp. garlic powder
1—1 lb. can tomato sauce
Salt to taste

SERVES AN ARMY (really 12-15)

Soak beans overnight. First thing in the morning, drain water from beans, put in a large Dutch oven, cover with fresh water and begin cooking over low heat. Slice sausage very thin, dice all vegetables and spices. Add everything to beans and cook over low heat all day, stirring frequently and adding water as necessary to prevent burning. (You can cook these in a crockpot on high.) Add salt to taste. For thicker bean soup, add 3 tablespoons flour mixed with ½ cup water at least 1 hour before beans are done. These are excellent as is, or spooned over cooked rice and served with hot buttered cornbread.

SWEET AND SOUR PORK

2 lbs. pork loins or
  shoulder, cut into 1 inch
  cubes
¾ cup flour
1 Tbsp. ginger
½ cup oil
1—13½ oz. can pineapple
  chunks, drained, reserve
  juice
½ cup vinegar
½ cup soy sauce
1 Tbsp. Worcestershire
  sauce
¾ cup sugar
2 tsp. salt
½ tsp. pepper
1 green pepper, cut into
  strips
1 can bean sprouts,
  drained
1 or 2 cans water
  chestnuts, sliced and
  drained
1 Tbsp. chili sauce
5 cups cooked rice

SERVES 6

Mix flour and ginger in plastic bag. Add pork cubes and shake well to coat. Heat oil in skillet. Add pork and brown on all sides. Remove meat from pan. Add enough water to the pineapple syrup to measure 1¾ cup. Add remaining flour from bag to skillet and stir. Add water/syrup mixture. Mix until smooth. Add vinegar, soy sauce and Worcestershire sauce. Heat to boiling, stirring constantly. Stir in sugar, salt, pepper and meat. Simmer 1 hour, covered. Add pineapple and green pepper. Cook, uncovered, 10 minutes. Stir in bean sprouts, water chestnuts and chili sauce. Cook 5 more minutes. Serve over hot rice.

 Rice grains stay white and separated if you add a teaspoon of lemon juice to each quart of cooking water.

MEATS

SUKIYAKI

2 Tbsp. cooking oil
1 lb. beef tenderloin,
   sliced thinly across the
   grain
2 Tbsp. sugar
½ cup beef broth
⅓ cup soy sauce
2 cups green onions,
   bias-sliced
1 cup celery, bias-sliced
1—16 oz. can bean sprouts,
   drained
1 cup mushrooms, thinly
   sliced
1—5 oz. can water
   chestnuts, drained and
   thinly sliced
1—5 oz. can bamboo
   shoots, drained
Hot cooked rice

SERVES 4

Heat oil in large skillet or wok. Add beef and cook quickly, turning meat over and over just until browned. Sprinkle with sugar. Combine broth and soy sauce and pour over meat. Push meat to one side. Let soy mixture bubble. In the Japanese style, keep the vegetables in separate groups as you cook them. Add onions, then celery, stir-frying each group over high heat about 1 minute, then pushing aside. Add the other vegetables in separate groups, stir-frying each just until heated through. You don't have to use each of these vegetables to make sukiyaki. You may substitute spinach, snow peas or zucchini, for any of the vegetables mentioned. Serve with hot cooked rice and extra soy sauce. If you are daring and want to try sukiyaki the Japanese way, dip each biteful in beaten raw egg before you eat it. It is really a taste treat!

Chicken
&
Fish

FRIED CHICKEN AND GRAVY

1 large fryer, cut up
3 eggs, beaten
1 cup flour
1-1½ tsp. salt
¼ tsp. pepper
½ tsp. paprika
½ tsp. poultry seasoning
Oil for cooking
6 Tbsp. flour
3 cups milk

SERVES 4

Pour ¼ inch oil in bottom of large skillet. Have it quite hot when you put the pieces of chicken in. Mix flour and seasonings in a plastic bag. Roll each piece of chicken in egg, then coat with seasoned flour. Fry on medium high heat—375° in electric skillet. When first side is golden brown, about 3 minutes, turn each piece. When this side is golden brown, 3-4 minutes, turn down heat, put lid on, leaving a small crack. Let chicken cook slowly for 10 more minutes before turning pieces again. Leave lid on, turning occasionally until the total cooking time from beginning is 40-45 minutes. Turn up heat for 2-4 minutes to crisp. Remove chicken from skillet and put onto platter in a 275-300° oven for 15 minutes while you make gravy and get dinner on the table.

To make gravy, pour out all but 3 tablespoons grease from skillet. Add 6 tablespoons of flour to grease and stir well to loosen chicken crumbs, making a paste. Add 3 cups milk gradually, stirring over medium high heat until desired consistency. Salt and pepper to taste. Serve with Baking Powder Biscuits (gravy on these is great), Country-Style Green Beans, mashed potatoes, and Chocolate Sheet Cake for dessert. Your family will ask for this meal again and again!

 Let cut up chicken soak in salt water overnight for a little extra flavor before frying it the next day.

CHICKEN DIVINE

2—10 oz. pkgs. frozen
   broccoli, cooked and
   drained
6 chicken breast halves,
   boiled and deboned
2 cans cream of chicken
   soup
1 cup mayonnaise
1 Tbsp. lemon juice
½ tsp. curry powder
1 cup grated cheddar
   cheese
Bread crumbs or potato
   chips

SERVES 6

Place cooked, drained broccoli in a greased shallow baking dish. Lay chicken on top of that. Combine soup, mayonnaise, lemon juice and curry powder. Pour over chicken and broccoli. Cover with grated cheese, then bread crumbs or crushed potato chips. Bake uncovered at 350° for 25-30 minutes.

JUDY'S WILD RICE CHICKEN

1 pkg. Uncle Ben's Wild
   Rice Mix
1 pkg. dry onion soup mix
1 can cream of mushroom
   soup
1¾ cup boiling water
¼ cup sherry
4 large chicken breast
   halves
Butter, melted
Salt, pepper to taste
Paprika

SERVES 4

Combine rice, soups, water and sherry in a 9 x 13 inch casserole. Place chicken breasts on top and brush with melted butter, salt, pepper and paprika. Cover and bake at 350° for 1½-2 hours.

CHICKEN & FISH

POTLUCK CHICKEN AND WILD RICE

1 large pkg. Uncle Ben's
   Instant Wild Rice
1 can cream of chicken
   soup
1 can cream of mushroom
   (or cream of celery) soup
2 cups milk
3 lbs. chicken, cut up

SERVES 4-6
Combine wild rice, soups, and milk in roasting pan. Mix well with spoon. Nestle the pieces of chicken into mixture. Cover and bake 1 hour 15 minutes at 350°. Check occasionally. Add more milk if rice begins to get dry. This really is a good potluck dish.

BIRDIE IN THE BAG

6 chicken breast halves
1 can cream of mushroom
   soup
½ cup dry white wine
1 Tbsp. green onion,
   chopped
Pinch of cayenne pepper
Salt and pepper to taste

SERVES 6
Tear off 6 squares of foil and place a chicken breast half on each square. In small saucepan, combine soup, wine, salt, pepper, green onion, and cayenne pepper. Heat and blend to a smooth sauce. Spoon sauce over each chicken breast and wrap securely. Set on cookie sheet and bake for 1 hour in 350° oven. Can be done in 9 x 13 inch casserole without wrapping individually. Cover tightly.

POTATO CHIP CHICKEN

2½ cups potato chips,
  crushed
¼ tsp. garlic salt
Dash of pepper
1 fryer, cut up
½ cup butter, melted

SERVES 4-6

Crush potato chips in plastic bag with a rolling pin. Add garlic salt and pepper to chips and shake well. Dip chicken in melted butter, then shake each piece in potato chips. Place in shallow baking dish, skin side up. Pour remaining butter and crumbs over chicken. Bake uncovered at 375° for 1 hour. Do not turn chicken. The flavor of fried chicken without the work!

CHICKEN CACCIATORE

¼ cup flour
½ tsp. salt
1—2½-3 lb. broiler-fryer
  chicken, cut up
¼ cup olive oil or salad oil
½ cup chopped onion
¼ cup chopped celery
¼ cup chopped green
  pepper
¼ tsp. garlic powder
1—16 oz. can tomatoes,
  cut up
1—8 oz. can tomato sauce
1—3 oz. can sliced
  mushrooms, drained
⅓ cup white wine
1 tsp. salt
½ tsp. dried basil leaves,
  crushed
½ tsp. dried rosemary
  leaves, crushed
Dash pepper

SERVES 4

Combine flour and ½ tsp. salt in plastic or paper bag; add a few pieces of chicken at a time and shake. In an ovenproof skillet, brown chicken in hot oil; remove chicken. In same skillet cook onion, celery, green pepper, and garlic until tender, but not brown. Return chicken to skillet. Combine tomatoes, tomato sauce, mushrooms, wine, salt, basil, rosemary, and pepper. Pour over chicken. Cover and bake at 350° until chicken is tender, about 1 hour. Remove the chicken to warm serving dish. Ladle sauce over top.

CHICKEN & FISH

CHICKEN SPAGHETTI

2 fryers, cut up
3 ribs celery, chopped
1 green pepper, chopped
2 onions, chopped
¼ tsp. garlic powder
1—4 oz. can sliced
  mushrooms, drained
1—10 oz. pkg. spaghetti,
  broken into ⅓'s or halves
1—1 lb. can tomatoes,
  chopped
2 Tbsp. ripe olives,
  chopped
1 can cream of mushroom
  soup
Salt and pepper
Paprika
Worcestershire sauce,
  several dashes
1 lb. Velveeta cheese,
  cubed

SERVES 10-12
Simmer chicken in salted water until tender. Remove chicken and all but 1 quart broth. Bone and dice chicken (you can tear the chicken into pieces and it's a lot less work). Set aside. Put celery, green pepper, onions, garlic powder and mushrooms into broth and cook several minutes. Add spaghetti and cook until it is done. Add remaining ingredients, and chicken, mixing well. Cook over low heat until cheese is melted. You can serve this right out of the Dutch oven immediately, or put it in a casserole and freeze for future use. Bake at 350° until it bubbles, about 30-45 minutes, if it has been frozen or refrigerated. Serve this easy one-pot meal with Spinach Salad, Cracked Wheat Bread, and Moist Coconut Cake. Everyone in your family (kids especially!) will love this meal.

CHICKEN ENCHILADAS

1 large fryer, cooked and
  boned
1 cup chopped onion
1 can cream of mushroom
  soup
1 can cream of chicken
  soup
½ cup chicken broth
2-3 Tbsp. green chilies,
  chopped (more if you
  like it hot)
1 dozen corn tortillas,
  torn into pieces
½ lb. cheddar cheese,
  grated

SERVES 8
Cook chicken in boiling, salted water until tender. Save stock. Debone chicken and cut into pieces. Mix onion, soups, broth, and green chilies in a bowl. Grease a 2 quart casserole and place a layer of tortilla pieces on the bottom. Add a layer of soup mixture, then chicken pieces, then grated cheese. Repeat this process one more time, ending with cheese. Bake at 350° uncovered for 45 minutes. Serve with Guacamole Salad and Sopapillas. Ole!

128

CHICKEN NOODLE CASSEROLE

3 cups (6 oz.) noodles
1 can condensed cream of
  chicken soup
⅓ cup sour cream
⅓ cup milk
1 Tbsp. chopped pimento
1 Tbsp. chopped parsley
⅓ cup chopped celery
Salt and pepper to taste
1 cup diced, cooked
  chicken
Buttered bread crumbs

SERVES 4-6
Cook noodles as package directs. Drain. Combine soup, sour cream, milk, pimento, parsley, celery and seasonings in saucepan. Heat thoroughly. Add chicken and noodles, mixing gently. Pour into greased 1½ quart casserole. Top with buttered bread crumbs. Bake uncovered in 375° oven 30 minutes. Good with tossed green salad, and Sourdough Bread.

CHICKEN AND DUMPLINGS

1 stewing chicken (4-5 lbs.)
  or 2 broiler-fryers (3 lbs.
  each)
1 small onion, sliced
2-3 carrots, sliced
3-4 ribs celery with leaves,
  chopped
1 tsp. salt
4 Tbsp. butter
6 Tbsp. flour
1/8 tsp. paprika
½ cup light cream
White pepper to taste

DUMPLINGS:
2 cups flour
1 tsp. salt
4 tsp. baking powder
1 Tbsp. shortening
¾ cup milk

SERVES 6-8
Simmer chicken, onion, carrots, celery and salt in enough water to cover. Cook until chicken is done, 1½-2 hours. Remove chicken from broth, saving 1 quart. When cool enough to handle, remove skin and bones, and dice meat. Melt butter in a cup. Stir in flour mixed with paprika. Add paste to chicken stock gradually, stirring constantly; cook for 2 minutes. Add chicken, cream, pepper, and adjust seasoning to taste. Spoon dumplings on top of gently bubbling chicken mixture and cover. Cook for 15 minutes without lifting lid. Serve at once.

To make dumplings, sift dry ingredients together. Blend in shortening with pastry blender or fork. Add milk and mix well. Dip teaspoon into cold water then into dough, and spoon dough onto chicken mixture as instructed. These are the best chicken and dumplings you will ever taste.

CHICKEN & FISH

EASY CHICKEN CHOW MEIN

1 chicken, cooked, deboned
   and cut up
1 quart chicken broth,
   reserved from stewed
   chicken
1 large can chow mein
   vegetables
1½ Tbsp. cornstarch
¼ cup water
1—10 oz. pkg. frozen
   Chinese snow peas
Chow Mein noodles
4 cups cooked rice
Soy Sauce

SERVES 4

Simmer chicken in salted water until tender. Remove chicken, debone, and cut into pieces. Reserve 1 quart of chicken broth. Add chicken and chow mein vegetables to broth. Mix cornstarch with ¼ cup water and add to chicken mixture. Add 1 tablespoon soy sauce and simmer 15-25 minutes. Add Chinese peas and simmer 5 more minutes. Serve over hot rice. Let each individual top serving with Chow Mein noodles and season with soy sauce.

HOT CHICKEN SALAD

2 cups cooked chicken
   (bite size)
2 cups chopped celery
½ cup slivered almonds
1 cup mayonnaise
1 cup crushed potato chips
½ cup grated cheddar
   cheese

SERVES 4

Mix the first four ingredients in a baking dish. Refrigerate several hours. Before cooking, cover with potato chips and cheese. Bake uncovered 20 minutes at 350°. This may be served as a cold chicken salad by eliminating the cheese and potato chips. Serve with Frosted Grapes, Croissants and Peach Melba for dessert. This is a light and refreshing summertime lunch.

Frosted Grapes: These are beautiful to look at and better to eat. Use them to garnish your poultry or ham dishes. Wash grapes and separate into small clusters. Beat 1 egg white in a small bowl until just broken up. Dip grapes into egg white. Let excess drip off. Dip grapes into superfine sugar to coat well. Place on a wire rack to dry.

CHICKEN AND BROCCOLI CREPES

4 Tbsp. butter
2 cups fresh mushrooms, sliced
6 Tbsp. flour
Dash salt
3 cups milk
½ cup sharp American cheese, shredded
¼ cup dry white wine
1—10 oz. pkg. frozen, chopped broccoli
2 cups finely chopped, cooked chicken
12-15 main dish crepes

12-15 CREPES
Sauce: In medium saucepan melt butter; saute mushrooms. Blend in flour and salt. Add milk all at once. Cook, stirring constantly, until thickened and bubbly. Stir in cheese and wine. Cook over low heat until cheese melts. Remove ½ cup of sauce; set aside.

Filling:
Cook broccoli according to package directions; drain. Combine drained broccoli, chicken, and ½ cup reserved sauce.

Spread rounded tablespoons of filling over unbrowned side of crepe, leaving ¼ inch rim around edge. Roll up crepe. Place, seam side down, in a skillet or chafing dish. Repeat with remaining crepes. Drizzle sauce over crepes. Cook, covered, over low heat until bubbly.

MAIN DISH CREPES:
1 cup flour
1½ cups milk
2 eggs
1 Tbsp. cooking oil
¼ tsp. salt

15 CREPES
In a bowl combine flour, milk, eggs, and salt; beat with mixer until blended. Heat a lightly greased 6-inch skillet. Remove from heat; spoon in about 2 tablespoons batter. Lift and tilt skillet to spread batter evenly. Return to heat; brown on one side only. (Cook on inverted crepe pan if you have one.) Invert pan and gently remove crepe with a fork. Repeat with remaining batter, greasing skillet occasionally.

CHICKEN ROYALE

4 chicken breasts, deboned
¼ cup flour
½ tsp. salt
¼ tsp. paprika
Dash pepper

HERB STUFFING:
2 cups dry bread crumbs
1 Tbsp. chopped onion
½ tsp. salt
¼ tsp. poultry seasoning
Dash pepper
2 Tbsp. melted butter
¼ cup hot water
⅓ cup melted butter
Chopped parsley

MUSHROOM SAUCE:
½ lb. fresh mushrooms,
  sliced
¼ cup minced onion
2 Tbsp. butter
2 Tbsp. flour
½ cup cream
½ cup sour cream
½ tsp. salt
¼ tsp. pepper

SERVES 4
Combine flour and seasonings in bag, add chicken and shake. Combine bread crumbs, onion, ½ teaspoon salt, poultry seasoning, pepper, 2 tablespoons melted butter and hot water; mix well. Fill middle of chicken breast with stuffing. Roll together and secure with toothpick. Dip chicken in ⅓ cup melted butter, place in baking dish. Drizzle remaining butter over chicken. Bake uncovered at 325° for 45 minutes, turn, cover, and bake additional 45 minutes or until tender. Sprinkle with parsley and serve with Mushroom Sauce.

Sauce: Cook mushrooms and onions lightly in butter until tender. Push mushrooms to one side and stir flour into butter. Add cream, sour cream and seasonings. Heat slowly, stirring constantly, almost to boiling point. Spoon over hot chicken.

Try serving this with Stir-Fried Broccoli and Carrots, Orange Rolls and Cheese Cake. Goodness in every bite!

CHRIS'S CRAB-STUFFED CHICKEN

**8 chicken breast halves,
  boned and skinned**
4 Tbsp. margarine
¼ cup flour
¾ cup milk
¾ cup chicken bouillon
⅓ cup white wine
¼ cup onion, chopped
**7½ oz. can crab, drained
  and flaked**
**3 oz. can chopped
  mushrooms, drained**
½ cup bread crumbs
2 Tbsp. parsley, chopped
½ tsp. salt
Dash of pepper
½ tsp. paprika
**½ cup Swiss cheese,
  grated**

SERVES 8

Place a chicken breast half between 2 pieces of waxed paper and, working from the center, pound the chicken lightly to make it approximately 1/8 inch thick and 8 x 3 inches. Repeat with each piece of chicken and set aside. In a small saucepan, melt 3 tablespoons margarine and blend in flour, then add milk gradually. Add chicken bouillon and wine all at once. Cook until it thickens and bubbles. Set aside. Cook onion in 1 tablespoon margarine until tender, but not brown. Stir in crabmeat, mushrooms, bread crumbs, parsley, salt, and pepper. Stir in ½ cup sauce. Top each chicken piece with the crab mixture, fold in sides and roll up; secure with toothpick. Place seam side down in a large baking dish. Pour balance of sauce over all and bake covered in 350° oven for 1 hour. Uncover and sprinkle with cheese and paprika. Return to oven until cheese melts, about 10 minutes. This is a special occasion dish that will impress your guests. Serve with Rich Green Salad, Whole Wheat Bread, and Chocolate Marengo.

Parsley can be frozen—when you buy a fresh bunch, wash it, trim the stems and dry in a towel. Roll it up in foil and put it in the freezer. When you need chopped parsley, remove it from the freezer and grate it. No chopping board is necessary. Grate the amount you need and return the rest to the freezer.

CHICKEN & FISH

CHICKEN AND DRESSING CASSEROLE

1—8 oz. pkg. Pepperidge
  Farm Herb Seasoned
  Stuffing Mix
1 stick margarine, melted
1 cup water
2½ cups cooked diced
  chicken
½ cup chopped onions
¼ cup green onion tops or
  chives
½ cup celery, chopped
½ cup mayonnaise
¾ tsp. salt
2 eggs, slightly beaten
1½ cups milk
1 can cream of mushroom
  soup, undiluted
1 cup cheddar cheese,
  grated

SERVES 8
Combine stuffing mix, butter, and water; toss lightly. Put half of mixture in buttered 9 x 12 inch shallow casserole. Mix together the chicken, onions, chives, celery, mayonnaise, and salt. Spoon over the stuffing mixture. Top with remaining stuffing mixture. Mix beaten eggs and milk, pour evenly over chicken and stuffing. Cover with foil and refrigerate overnight. One hour before baking, take out of refrigerator and spread cream of mushroom soup over top. Bake uncovered 40 minutes at 325°. Sprinkle grated cheese over top and return to oven for 10 minutes. Serve with Hot Curried Fruit, Orange Rolls, and Dessert Delight for a rich meal. Freezes well.

CORNISH GAME HENS

4 Cornish game hens
¼ cup flour
Salt
Pepper
Pinch of nutmeg
1 tsp. paprika
¼ lb. butter
6 slices onion
1/8 tsp. garlic powder
½ bay leaf
Pinch of thyme
1 can sliced mushrooms
2 slices bacon
2 cups burgundy

SERVES 4
Wipe thawed hens dry. Coat hens in ¼ cup flour, seasoned with salt, pepper, nutmeg and paprika. Melt 2 tablespoons of the butter in a large skillet, and brown hens. Remove and put in a roasting pan. In skillet combine remaining butter, 6 slices of onion, garlic, bay leaf, thyme, and can of sliced mushrooms. Simmer 10 minutes. Pour butter-onion mixture over hens, cover each with bacon; then pour burgundy over hens. Cover and cook at 250° about 2½ hours or more. Serve with Spinach Salad and wild rice.

OLD FASHIONED CHICKEN & NOODLES

1 large chicken
Salt and pepper
2 chicken bouillon cubes

NOODLES:
2½ cups flour
2 eggs
½ tsp. salt
1 tsp. cream of tartar
¾ cup whipping cream

SERVES 6

Cook chicken in 2½ quarts of water. Season with salt and pepper. When tender, debone and cut meat into pieces. Save broth.

Combine flour, eggs, salt and cream of tartar in bowl. Work ingredients with fingers to mix well. Gradually add cream. Continue working dough, adding only enough cream to make a very dry dough that will gather together. Flour a large cutting board or counter-top generously. Roll noodle dough very thin, about 1/8 inch or less. Dust flour over top if sticky. Dough needs to be very dry and flour can be worked in with rolling pin. Roll up dough jelly roll style and slice off noodles about 1/8 inch thick. The noodle rolls should easily shake out. If not, the dough is still too sticky. These noodles don't need to dry, but do dry well if you want to make them ahead of time. Add noodles to 1¾-2 quarts of boiling chicken broth. Add 2 chicken bouillon cubes and let noodles simmer 15 minutes, or until done, before adding chicken. Add chicken, salt and pepper to taste. Chicken and noodles are an all time favorite . . . sure to become a regular in your menu planning. For a variation, substitute beef for the chicken to make hearty beef and noodles.

Throw several ice cubes into meat or chicken broth that has grease to be removed. The grease will stick to the cubes.

CHICKEN & FISH

CHICKEN, QUAIL OR PHEASANT IN CREAM SAUCE

Flour, seasoned with salt,
   pepper, and poultry
   seasoning
2½ lb. chicken, quail or
   pheasant, cut into
   serving size pieces
6 Tbsp. butter
½ lb. mushrooms, sliced
¼ cup almonds, sliced
½ onion, chopped
3 stalks celery, chopped
1 pint cream
1 tsp. salt
¼ tsp. pepper
½ cup dry sherry

SERVES 4

Put flour and seasonings in bag. Shake pieces of meat in flour to coat. Brown in 4 tablespoons melted butter. Remove pieces from skillet to casserole dish. In skillet, saute mushrooms, almonds, onion, and celery in 2 tablespoons butter until tender. Pour sauteed mixture over meat. Cover and bake at 350° for 30 minutes. Mix together cream, salt, pepper, and sherry; add to meat. Cover and bake 45 additional minutes or until birds are tender.

ORANGE-BAKED PHEASANT BREASTS

4 pheasant breasts
⅓ cup flour
1 tsp. salt
1/8 tsp. pepper
½ cup cooking oil
½ tsp. celery seed
1 thinly sliced onion
1 cup fresh orange juice
1 cup water
½ unpeeled orange, cut in
   wedges

SERVES 4

Wash and dry pheasant breasts. Combine flour, salt and pepper and coat breasts with flour mixture. Heat oil in heavy skillet; add pheasant; sprinkle with celery seed. Brown both sides over low heat. Remove pheasant from skillet and place in 2 quart baking dish. Cook onion in same skillet until tender. Add orange juice and water, and bring to boil. Pour over pheasant. Arrange orange wedges over pheasant. Cover and bake in 300° oven for 1 hour. Reduce heat to 250° and bake an additional hour. Delicious with Chicken Rice-a-Roni or Uncle Ben's Wild Rice.

SUSIE'S ROMERTOFF WILD DUCK

1 wild duck, cleaned
½ tsp. salt
¼ tsp. pepper
¼ tsp. garlic powder
½ onion, quartered
½ apple, quartered
1 orange, quartered
3 or 4 cinnamon sticks

SERVES 4
Wash and clean wild duck. Sprinkle with salt, pepper and garlic. Place onion, apple and orange in cavity of duck. Soak Romertoff pot for 15 minutes in a sink full of water. Place duck on sticks of cinnamon in pot and bake at 250-300° for 2 hours. Do not preheat oven. Occasionally baste the duck. Serve with Uncle Ben's Wild Rice. If you do not have a Romertoff cooker (a clay pot cooker), you can use a regular roaster, but add 2-3 cups water.

JOHNNY APPLESEED TURKEY STUFFING

1 stick butter or margarine
1 small onion, chopped
1 cup celery, chopped
2 apples, peeled, cored and chopped
1—10 oz. can chicken broth
1—8 oz. pkg. Pepperidge Farm Herb Seasoned Stuffing
4 slices bacon, crisply fried and crumbled

MAKES ENOUGH TO STUFF AN 8-10 LB. TURKEY
Melt butter. Add onion and celery. Saute until onion is transparent. Add apples and broth. Heat to boiling point. Combine apple mixture with stuffing mix and bacon. Mix well. Just before turkey is ready to be roasted, spoon stuffing in body and neck cavities. This can also be served hot from the saucepan or casserole dish.

Hot applesauce complements all game.

CHICKEN & FISH

MARY'S SCALLOPED OYSTERS

1 lb. butter
1 lb. saltine crackers (more
   or less)
4 cans Geisha whole
   oysters
1 can water chestnuts,
   sliced
Milk to cover
Parsley
Nutmeg
Salt
Pepper

SERVES 12-15

Melt butter and add coarsely crumbled crackers. Toss well. Spread a layer in large casserole. Cover with 1 ½ cans oysters, oyster liquid, ⅓ can water chestnuts. Season with salt, pepper, nutmeg, and parsley. Continue layering until all oysters and water chestnuts are used. Top with buttered crumbs and parsley. Just before heating, add milk to within one inch of crumb top. Cook uncovered at 400° for ½ hour. This is an unusually delicious and easy recipe. The oyster dish will add a gala look and zesty flavor to beef, pork or lamb.

CREAMED SCALLOPS AND MUSHROOMS

1 lb. fresh or frozen
   scallops
2 Tbsp. butter
1 cup fresh mushrooms,
   sliced
¼ cup margarine
¼ cup flour
½ tsp. salt
¼ tsp. pepper
½ cup water
1 ½ cups half and half
½ cup cheddar cheese,
   grated
2 Tbsp. fresh parsley
Paprika

SERVES 4

Thaw, rinse and wipe scallops dry. Saute mushrooms in butter. Set aside. Grease shallow casserole and arrange scallops in bottom. In small saucepan, melt margarine and stir in flour, salt, and pepper until blended. Gradually add half and half, stirring constantly. Add mushrooms and water. Cook, stirring constantly, until thick and smooth. Stir in parsley and pour over scallops. Sprinkle with cheese and paprika on top. Bake uncovered at 350° for 30 minutes or until cheese melts and sauce is bubbly. Serve over rice or toasted patty shells.

DODIE'S CURRIED SCALLOPS

2 lbs. scallops
Seasoned flour (with salt
  and pepper)
8 Tbsp. butter
6 green onions, finely diced
1½ Tbsp. curry powder
⅓ cup dry white wine
5 cups cooked rice

SERVES 4-6
Wash and dry scallops. Dust lightly with seasoned flour. Heat butter in skillet and saute green onions for 3 minutes. Add scallops and cook quickly, turning frequently to brown, about 3 minutes. Sprinkle with curry powder. Add wine and mix well. Serve immediately over rice.

SEAFOOD LUNCHEON DISH

1 can cream of mushroom
  soup
⅔ cup milk
¼ cup cheese, grated
  (Longhorn)
½ cup mayonnaise
2 cups fine noodles,
  crushed slightly
2 cups cooked shrimp
1—6½ oz. can crabmeat,
  drained
1—5 oz. can water
  chestnuts, drained
1 can French fried onion
  rings, crushed

SERVES 6
Mix soup, milk, cheese, and mayonnaise. Fold in uncooked noodles, shrimp, crab, and sliced water chestnuts. Pour into greased 2 quart casserole. Bake, covered, at 325° for 20 minutes. Uncover and bake an additional 10 minutes. Sprinkle with onion rings and bake 10 minutes longer or until noodles are tender. Serve with Banana-Berry Gelatin Salad, Raisin Bran Muffins and Peggy's Lemon Bars.

Try boiling 2-3 lbs. large, raw shrimp in the shell for 10-15 minutes in a broth of beer (2 bottles) seasoned with 1 sliced onion, 1 Tbsp. dill seed, 2 bay leaves, 4-6 peppercorns. Serve with melted butter flavored with garlic powder, Worcestershire sauce, lemon juice, and Tabasco. You'll love it!

CHICKEN & FISH

FISH FRY

Trout, catfish, snapper,
  whitefish, oysters,
  scallops, bass
Cornmeal
Vegetable oil for frying
Lemon juice
Paprika
Dry mustard
Salt and pepper

Skin and fillet fish; cut into strips. Soak fish in lemon juice 5 minutes. Season fish lightly with salt and paprika. Drop fish strips into a bag with cornmeal which has been seasoned with salt, pepper, and dry mustard. Fry fish in hot oil until golden. Serve with ketchup, Tabasco, Hush Puppies, and Cole Slaw. This meal will send the fishermen in your family back for more!

BARBECUED FISH

Scallops, whole fresh
  shrimp, halibut or salmon
Butter
Fresh lemon juice
Salt
Parsley

Baste fish with melted butter mixed with lemon juice, salt and parsley as it cooks on barbecuer. Kabobs can be made using whole scallops, shrimp, and/or chunks of other fish fillets, along with onion pieces, mushrooms, and tomato wedges. A delicious and easy way to fix your favorite fish.

SALMON CROQUETS

1—7¾ oz. can salmon
  drained
5 saltine crackers, crushed
2 eggs, slightly beaten
⅓ onion, chopped
1 tsp. salt
Pepper

SERVES 4
Combine all ingredients in bowl. Form into patties. Fry slowly in butter, turning once, about 7 minutes on each side. Delicious served with Pan Fried Potatoes and Corn Cheese Bake.

SHRIMP AND GREEN NOODLE CASSEROLE

¼ lb. mushrooms, sliced
2 Tbsp. butter
1—12 oz. pkg. green
  noodles
2 cans cream of mushroom
  soup
1½ lb. shrimp, cooked
2 tsp. curry powder
¼ tsp. oregano
¼ tsp. paprika
1 cup sour cream
⅓ cup sherry
½ cup sauterne (wine)
Wheat germ

SERVES 12
Saute mushrooms in butter. Cook green noodles according to package directions. Drain. Combine remaining ingredients and put into greased 2 quart casserole. Bake 45 minutes at 350°. Sprinkle top with wheat germ and return to oven for 5 minutes.

BAKED TROUT

4 small trout, cleaned,
  washed and dried
4 sprigs fresh (or ½ tsp.
  dried) thyme
Juice of 1 lemon
4 thin slices bacon
4 sheets of aluminum foil
4 Tbsp. butter

SERVES 4
Preheat oven to 400°. Place a sprig of fresh thyme inside each trout. Sprinkle with lemon juice; then wrap each trout in a slice of bacon. Grease each sheet of foil with a quarter of the butter. Completely enclose the fish in foil. Place packets on a baking dish and bake for 10 minutes. Lower temperature to 350° and bake for an additional 10 minutes. Serve trout in their foil packages.

COLORADO TROUT

½ lb. bacon
1 large onion, sliced
2-3 fresh, pan-sized trout
½ cup cornmeal
½ cup flour
1½ tsp. salt
Pepper

SERVES 2
Fry and drain bacon. Saute onion in bacon fat. Set onions on plate with bacon. Roll trout in seasoned cornmeal and flour mixture. Fry in hot bacon fat. When trout is almost done, about 10 minutes, top with bacon and onion. Put lid on pan and leave on low heat for 5-10 minutes. This can be done easily at campsite!

Vegetables,
Rice
&
Pasta

VEGETABLES, RICE & PASTA

MARY'S BAKED BEANS

**4—16 oz. Campbell's Old
    Fashioned or Homestyle
    Beans
1 green pepper, chopped
1 medium onion, chopped
2 strips uncooked bacon,
    cut in 1 inch pieces
¼ cup brown sugar
1 Tbsp. Poupon mustard**

SERVES 10
Mix all ingredients and bake uncovered at 325° for 2 hours.

COWBOY BEANS

**2 cups pinto beans, washed
    well
1½ tsp. salt
¼ cup bacon drippings
2-3 tsp. chili powder
¼ tsp. pepper
Cold water to cover
    (about 1-1½ qts.)**

SERVES 8
Put all ingredients in large Dutch oven
or crock pot. Simmer 6-8 hours or
until beans are tender. If cooking in
crock pot, cook on high. To thicken
juice, spoon out about ½ cup beans,
mash with a fork, and return to pot.
These are easiest of all to cook in a
pressure cooker. Set weight at 15
lbs., and cook for 2 hours. These
beans are great with fried chicken,
barbecue, steak, ham, or for Mexican
food fixin's. They freeze well.

VEGETABLES, RICE & PASTA

COUNTRY STYLE GREEN BEANS

1—16 oz. bag frozen green
   beans or fresh green
   beans
¾ cup ham or bacon,
   cut-up
1 Tbsp. instant diced
   onions
1 Tbsp. bacon fat
2½ tsp. salt
6-8 small new potatoes,
   washed and unpeeled
   (optional)

SERVES 6

Cover beans with water in large saucepan. Add other ingredients. Cover with lid and boil for 10 minutes. Remove lid and simmer for 2 hours or until water is cooked down to about 1-2 inches. Remove from heat, cover with lid, and let sit a couple hours, to blend flavors. Before serving, cook 15 more minutes. It's best to let beans cook until most of liquid is gone. Don't let them cook dry and burn. This is also good with new potatoes. If using new potatoes, the peelings can be left on, and cooked whole with beans.

EPICUREAN GREEN BEANS

1 lb. fresh green beans,
   cut into 1 inch pieces,
   or 2—1 lb. cans green
   beans
1 cup fresh mushrooms,
   sliced
1 Tbsp. chopped onion
2 Tbsp. butter
3 Tbsp. flour
Dash pepper
½ tsp. salt
¼ tsp. thyme
2 cups milk
4 slices bacon, cooked
   and crumbled
1—10 oz. pkg. frozen patty
   shells, baked (optional)

SERVES 6

Cook beans in boiling, salted water until tender, about 15 minutes. In 2 quart saucepan, cook mushrooms and onion in butter until tender. Blend in flour, salt, thyme, and pepper. Add milk all at once. Cook, stirring constantly until mixture thickens and bubbles. Stir in beans, heat through. Add bacon. Spoon mixture into prepared patty shells. If desired, garnish with additional crumbled bacon.

VEGETABLES, RICE & PASTA

BUTTERY ITALIAN GREEN BEANS

2—9 oz. pkg. frozen
   Italian green beans
1½ cups fresh mushrooms,
   sliced
6 Tbsp. butter
½ tsp. salt

SERVES 4-6
Cook green beans in boiling salted water for 5 minutes. Drain well. Melt butter in large skillet, saute mushrooms. Add beans to mushrooms in skillet. Sprinkle with salt. Stir and let simmer 5 minutes. Cover with lid and remove from heat until serving time. Before serving, heat thoroughly again. (Better if made ½-1 hour ahead of serving, to allow mushroom and bean flavors to blend.)

SWEET AND SOUR BEANS

1—15 oz. can white lima
   beans, drained
1—15 oz. can green lima
   beans, drained
1—15 oz. can kidney
   beans, drained
1 large can Pork and
   Beans
1½ medium onions, sliced
   or chopped
1 scant cup brown sugar
1 Tbsp. dry mustard
½ cup vinegar
1 tsp. garlic salt
1 tsp. salt
4 slices of bacon,
   chopped

SERVES 12
Combine all ingredients except bacon in large casserole. Mix well and top with chopped bacon. Bake uncovered 2-2½ hours at 350°.

Sprinkle a burnt pan generously with baking soda, dampen slightly, set aside for a few days and rinse.

VEGETABLES, RICE & PASTA

GRANDMOTHER'S ISLAND BEAN CASSEROLE

2—1 lb. cans Blue Lake
   whole green beans
   (save juice)
1 Tbsp. bacon drippings
1½ tsp. dill seed

SAUCE:
6 Tbsp. flour
6 Tbsp. butter, melted
1 cup bean juice
1 cup milk
3 Tbsp. grated onion
1 tsp. black pepper
2½ tsp. mei yen (Spice
   Island)
Bread crumbs or slivered
   almonds

SERVES 6-8
Simmer green beans, drippings, and dill seed at a low temperature for 30 minutes. Make sauce by stirring flour into melted butter, then gradually adding liquids, stirring constantly. Add seasonings, stir well. Stir green beans into sauce, mix and put in casserole dish. Sprinkle bread crumbs or slivered almonds on top. Bake uncovered 20 minutes, or until bubbly, at 350°.

GREEN BEAN CASSEROLE

¼ cup butter
⅓ cup onion, chopped
½ lb. mushrooms, sliced
1—5 oz. can water
   chestnuts, sliced
⅓ cup flour
1 tsp. soy sauce
1/8 tsp. Tabasco
1/8 tsp. salt
1½ cups milk
1 cup cheddar cheese,
   grated
2 or 3—1 lb. cans
   green beans
1 small can French fried
   onion rings
Dash pepper

SERVES 6-8
Melt ¼ cup butter in skillet. Saute onion and mushrooms. Blend in flour; add milk, soy sauce, Tabasco, salt and pepper. Stir over medium heat until smooth. Add cheese and continue cooking until melted. Add onions, mushrooms, and water chestnuts to sauce. Mix well. Drain green beans; place in buttered casserole. Pour sauce over beans and mix. Bake uncovered at 350° for 45 minutes. Arrange onion rings on top and bake additional 10 minutes.

VEGETABLES, RICE & PASTA

GREEN BEANS CAESAR

1½ lbs. fresh green beans
(or 2—1 lb. cans green
beans, heated through; or
2—9 oz. pkg. frozen cut
green beans, cooked and
drained)
2 Tbsp. salad oil
1 Tbsp. vinegar
1 Tbsp. instant minced
onion
¼ tsp. salt
1/8 tsp. garlic powder
1/8 tsp. pepper
2 Tbsp. dry bread crumbs
2 Tbsp. grated Parmesan
cheese
1 Tbsp. butter or
margarine, melted
Paprika

SERVES 6
Place fresh beans cut in pieces, in 1 inch salted water. Cook uncovered until tender, about 10 minutes. Drain well. Heat oven to 350°. Toss beans with oil, vinegar, onion, salt, garlic and pepper. Pour into 1 quart casserole. Stir together crumbs, cheese and butter. Sprinkle over beans. Garnish with paprika. Bake uncovered 15-20 minutes.

ALMOND-BROCCOLI CASSEROLE

2—10 oz. pkg. frozen
broccoli stalks
1—8 oz. can small whole
onions, drain and reserve
juice
1 Tbsp. lemon juice
2 Tbsp. butter
2 Tbsp. flour
1 Tbsp. sugar
½ tsp. salt
1 cup milk
½ cup grated Parmesan
cheese
1/8 cup white wine
1/8 cup juice from onions
½ cup toasted slivered
almonds

SERVES 6-8
Cook broccoli in boiling salted water 8 minutes, drain. Arrange broccoli and onions in bottom of buttered casserole and sprinkle with lemon juice. Melt butter in saucepan, stir in flour; add milk, sugar, and salt. Stir until thick and smooth. Blend in Parmesan cheese, wine and onion juice. Pour over broccoli and onions. Sprinkle with toasted almonds. (To toast: arrange almonds in pie plate in 350° oven, shake occasionally, toast to golden brown.) Bake uncovered at 350° for 25 minutes.

VEGETABLES, RICE & PASTA

♥■♥■♥ ♥ ♥ ♥ ♥ ♥ ♥■♥ ♥ ♥ ♥■♥■♥■♥■♥

STIR-FRIED BROCCOLI AND CARROTS

2 Tbsp. oil
1/8 tsp. garlic powder
½ cup broccoli flowerets
1 cup carrots, sliced thin
1 small onion, cut into rings
¾ cup chicken broth
1 tsp. seasoning salt
1 Tbsp. cornstarch
1 Tbsp. cold water
1 can water chestnuts,
  drained
1 cup sliced mushrooms

SERVES 6
Heat oil, add garlic, broccoli, carrots, and onion; stir fry 1 minute. Add broth and seasoned salt, cover and cook about 3 minutes. Mix cornstarch and water, stir into vegetables. Cook and stir until thickened, about 10 seconds. Add water chestnuts and mushrooms. Cook and stir 30 seconds.

BROCCOLI-CAULIFLOWER CASSEROLE

2—10 oz. pkg. frozen
  broccoli stalks
1—10 oz. pkg. frozen
  cauliflower
2 Tbsp. flour
2 Tbsp. butter
1½ cups milk
1 cup Velveeta cheese,
  diced
Dash pepper
½ tsp. salt
1—4 oz. can mushrooms,
  or ¾ cup fresh
  mushrooms
¼ cup butter
2 cups bread crumbs

SERVES 8
Cook broccoli and cauliflower according to package directions, drain well. Melt butter in saucepan, add flour and stir to make a paste. Gradually add milk, stirring constantly. When sauce is thick and smooth, add Velveeta, salt, pepper, and mushrooms. (If using fresh mushrooms, saute in 1 tablespoon butter.) Arrange broccoli and cauliflower in bottom of buttered casserole and cover with cheese sauce. Melt ¼ cup butter in skillet, add bread crumbs, and stir over low heat for 5 minutes. Sprinkle over casserole. Bake uncovered at 350° for 20 minutes or until hot throughout.

BROCCOLI WITH WALNUTS

3—10 oz. pkg. frozen
chopped broccoli, cooked
and drained
1 stick butter or margarine,
melted
¼ cup flour
1½ Tbsp. instant chicken
broth granules
2 cups milk
⅔ cup hot water
6 Tbsp. butter or margarine
2 cups Pepperidge Farm
stuffing mix
⅔ cup chopped walnuts

SERVES 8
Arrange cooked broccoli in buttered 9 x 13 inch casserole dish. Melt one stick of butter in small saucepan. Add flour and broth granules. Cook a few minutes, stirring constantly. Add milk gradually and stir until smooth and thick. Pour this sauce over broccoli. Melt 6 tablespoons butter in hot water; add stuffing mix and toss thoroughly. Add walnuts and mix. Spoon on top of broccoli and bake uncovered in a 400° oven about 30 minutes. This freezes well. This will be the best broccoli casserole you'll ever taste.

CREAMED CABBAGE

½ head cabbage, sliced
½ small onion, sliced
¼ cup water
Salt and pepper
½ cup cream
1 Tbsp. sugar
1 tsp. cornstarch

SERVES 4
Cover cabbage and onion with water in saucepan. Cook until tender. Drain water. Add cream, sugar, salt and pepper to cabbage. Mix cornstarch with ¼ cup water and add to cabbage. Bring to bubbly stage stirring constantly. Reduce heat and serve.

 When cooking cabbage add a stalk of celery to prevent odor.

CORN CHEESE BAKE

1—3 oz. pkg. cream
  cheese, softened
¼ cup milk
1 Tbsp. butter or margarine
½ tsp. onion salt
1—1 lb. can whole kernel
  corn, drained (or 1—10
  oz. pkg. frozen corn,
  cooked and drained)
Paprika

SERVES 4-5
Combine cream cheese, milk, butter and onion salt in saucepan; stir over low heat until cheese melts. Stir corn into cheese. Pour into small casserole. Sprinkle with paprika. Cook uncovered until bubbly, about 10 minutes, in a 350° oven. Good with Prime Rib or steaks.

CORN PUDDING

2—10 oz. pkg. frozen corn
2 Tbsp. chives
1 Tbsp. sugar
1 tsp. salt
1 tsp. pepper
2 large eggs, beaten
1½ cups whipping cream

SERVES 6-8
Mix all ingredients in 2 quart casserole dish. Cover and bake at 250° for 3-4 hours.

CREAMY EGGPLANT

1 eggplant, peeled and cut
  into chunks
3 Tbsp. butter, melted
⅓ cup cracker crumbs
1 cup cream
¼ cup cheddar cheese,
  grated
2 Tbsp. Parmesan cheese

SERVES 4
Boil eggplant in water 10-15 minutes or until tender. Drain. Add cracker crumbs and melted butter. Arrange in bottom of buttered casserole dish. Pour cream over top and sprinkle with cheeses. Bake uncovered at 350° for 25 minutes or until bubbly throughout.

Add sugar and a little lemon juice, not salt, to the cooking water for corn on the cob. Salt will toughen it.

VEGETABLES, RICE & PASTA

MARINAN'S GARLIC-CHEESE GRITS

6 cups boiling water
1½ cups grits
1½ sticks butter
1½ cups (1 lb.) grated
  American cheese
3 eggs, beaten
1½ tsp. salt
4-6 shakes Tabasco
¼ tsp. minced garlic

SERVES 10
Add grits to boiling water. Reduce heat; simmer 5 minutes stirring constantly. Combine with other ingredients and mix well. Bake uncovered in large buttered bowl for 1 hour 15 minutes at 325°. Good at breakfast with scrambled eggs, hot biscuits and gravy, or at other meals as a potato substitute.

BEST-EVER GREENS

Large saucepan full of
  fresh greens (turnip,
  collard, spinach),
  chopped or whole
2 Tbsp. bacon fat
2-3 pieces bacon, sliced
  into small pieces
1½ tsp. salt

SERVES 4
Pour 1 inch of water in bottom of saucepan. Add greens, fat, bacon and salt. Let simmer, covered, until greens cook down, about 10 minutes. Uncover and let simmer 45 minutes-1 hour. Stir occasionally, making sure they don't cook dry. Let sit in covered pan 2-6 hours for extra flavor . . . the longer, the better. Before serving, cook additional 15 minutes. Eat with vinegar sprinkled on top or with salt and butter.

DORIS' HOMINEY CASSEROLE

1 large can hominey
  (1 lb. 13 oz.)
1 cup sour cream
1—7 oz. can green chilies,
  chopped
1 tsp. salt
1 cup grated cheddar
  cheese

SERVES 4
Combine hominey, sour cream, chilies and salt. Mix well. Cover with grated cheddar cheese. Bake uncovered at 350° until hot and cheese is melted, about 25-30 minutes.

VEGETABLES, RICE & PASTA

COUNTRY FRIED MUSHROOMS

1 lb. fresh mushrooms
3 eggs
1-1½ cups flour
⅓ cup butter
Salt and pepper

SERVES 4-6
Wash mushrooms. Gently pull stems from caps. Save and use them, too! Let sit on towel to dry, or dab excess moisture off. Beat eggs in small bowl. Dip mushrooms and stems in egg, roll in flour. Fry slowly in melted butter, stirring gently. Salt and pepper to taste. After browning on both sides, put lid on loosely and turn down heat. Cook until mushrooms are done—about 20 minutes. These can also be served as the main course as they are very filling.

OKRA AND TOMATOES

2 lbs. okra, washed and
**   sliced (tips and stem**
**   ends removed)**
2 cups water
1 medium onion, sliced
1 Tbsp. vinegar
1½ tsp. salt
2 Tbsp. bacon drippings
1—16 oz. can stewed
**   tomatoes**
½ tsp. sugar
1/8 tsp. pepper

SERVES 6-8
Combine okra, water, onion, vinegar, and 1½ tsp. salt. Cover and cook over medium high heat for 15 minutes. Drain; cook, uncovered, over low heat until all moisture evaporates. Add remaining ingredients; cook over medium heat, turning frequently, 5 minutes.

Try using milk in place of water when cooking peas, limas, or spinach. Adds flavor and nutrition.

VEGETABLES, RICE & PASTA

WEST TEXAS FRIED OKRA

1 lb. okra, sliced with
    stems and tips removed
1 cup cornmeal
Bacon drippings
Salt

SERVES 4

Pour cornmeal in a plastic bag, add okra and shake. Cook okra in bacon drippings stirring over medium high heat until golden brown. Salt well. Drain on paper towel. Serve hot. When okra is prepared this way, it is crunchy and light...a real taste treat!

MOM'S ONION RINGS

1 cup flour
¼ tsp. salt
½ cup (small can)
    evaporated milk
2 Tbsp. salad oil
1 egg white
6 Tbsp. water
2-3 large onions (Bermuda
    onions work best)

SERVES 4

Combine all ingredients except onions. Mix well with beater. Slice onions and take rings apart. Dip in batter and deep fry at 375°, turning once, until golden brown. Sprinkle with salt. Place in warm oven until ready to serve. These never fail!

SOUTHERN STYLE BLACK-EYED PEAS

2 lbs. fresh black-eyed
    peas, washed and
    podded (young tender
    ones can just be
    snapped)
Salt pork, sliced (or ¼ cup
    bacon drippings)
Salt and pepper to taste

SERVES 8

Cover peas with water, add salt pork, salt and pepper. Cook over low heat for 2-3 hours. These are better the second day. It has been a tradition for as long as can be remembered to serve black-eyed peas on New Year's Day as a measure of good luck. It's also fun to hide a thoroughly washed dime in the peas and whoever gets the dime in their portion will become rich in the New Year.

VEGETABLES, RICE & PASTA

CREAMED PEAS

1—16 oz. pkg. frozen peas,
  or 3 cups fresh peas
4 Tbsp. butter
2 Tbsp. flour
1 cup half and half
Heaping tsp. sugar
½ tsp. salt

SERVES 6-8

Cook peas in boiling water for 10 minutes. Pour into colander and drain. Using same saucepan, melt butter over medium heat and stir in flour. Gradually add half and half, stirring constantly until thick and creamy. Stir in sugar, salt and peas. If adding carrots, cook 1 cup sliced carrots until tender in separate saucepan. Add to creamed peas.

COUNTRY POTATOES

12 red or new potatoes
  (baking potatoes can be
  substituted)
6 strips cooked bacon,
  crumbled
2 cups sharp cheddar
  cheese, grated
½ stick butter, melted
Salt and pepper to taste

SERVES 8

Boil potatoes, with skins on, until done. Drain and let cool. Thinly slice the unpeeled potatoes. Butter bottom of 9 x 12 inch baking dish. Put one layer of potatoes, salt, pepper, half of cheese and bacon in casserole. Dribble half of the butter over layer. Make another layer the same way. Bake uncovered at 350° until bubbling hot, about 15 minutes. This potato recipe is guaranteed to please! Freezes well.

SOUR CREAM POTATOES

8-10 medium potatoes,
  pared, cooked and
  mashed
8 oz. cream cheese
¼-½ cup sour cream
Butter
Paprika

SERVES 8

Whip cheese and sour cream until light. Gradually add mashed potatoes to cheese mixture. Top with butter and paprika. Cook 20-25 minutes at 325°. This may be frozen and reheated.

SARAH LEW'S LAYERED POTATO CASSEROLE

4 medium raw potatoes,
  pared and sliced
½ head cabbage, sliced
1½ cups apple, diced
1 medium onion, sliced
Salt and pepper
3 Tbsp. butter
½ pint whipping cream
½ cup Parmesan cheese
¾ cup bread crumbs

SERVES 8
Butter a 3 quart, long, flat casserole. Begin with potatoes as the bottom layer, and layer the cabbage, apple and onion. Place butter dabs on top; pour whipping cream evenly over casserole. Bake 45 minutes at 350°, covered. Uncover and top with Parmesan cheese and bread crumbs; brown an additional 10-15 minutes.

SWEET POTATO CASSEROLE

1 large can sweet
  potatoes
¾ stick margarine or
  butter, melted
1¼ cups sugar
½ tsp. cinnamon
½ tsp. nutmeg
2 eggs

TOPPING:
¾ cup corn flake crumbs
½ cup chopped nuts
½ cup brown sugar
¾ stick melted margarine

SERVES 4-6
Warm potatoes and syrup, and mash to a very smooth consistency. Use a blender, food processor or mixer to do this. Add other ingredients; mix well. Place in 2 quart casserole dish. Bake uncovered 20 minutes at 400°. Spread topping, which has been mixed together, on potatoes and brown for another 10 minutes.

PAN FRIED POTATOES

1 Tbsp. butter
1 Tbsp. Crisco
5 medium potatoes, sliced
   ¼ inch thick
1½ tsp. salt
Pepper
¼-½ purple onion, sliced

SERVES 4

Melt butter and shortening in skillet. Let oil get fairly hot (300°). Add potato slices. Sprinkle with half the salt. Let fry 10 minutes at medium high heat, turning to get most of them browned. Season with remaining salt. Slice onion over potatoes, cover with lid. Let simmer over low heat, 275°, for 15 minutes, stirring occasionally until potatoes are tender. Before serving, turn up heat and remove lid to crisp. Good with Chicken Fried Steak and Cream Gravy.

FAVORITE HASHED BROWN CHEESE CASSEROLE

2—12 oz. pkg. frozen,
   hashed brown potatoes
2 cups sour cream
1 can cream of chicken
   soup (cream of celery or
   cream of mushroom,
   depending on what you
   have!)
1 stick butter or margarine,
   melted
1 tsp. salt
1 Tbsp. minced onion
2 cups shredded cheddar
   cheese
2 cups corn flakes, crushed
¼ cup butter, melted

SERVES 8

Thaw potatoes and drain well. Combine sour cream, soup and butter. Mix well and add salt, onion, and cheese. Blend in potatoes and stir well. Pour mixture into shallow, 2 quart casserole. Mix corn flakes and ¼ cup melted butter and sprinkle on top of potatoes. Bake, uncovered, at 350° for about 50 minutes or until brown and bubbly.

VEGETABLES, RICE & PASTA

CATTLEMEN'S CLUB
TWICE-BAKED POTATOES

5 large potatoes, scrubbed
  and baked
⅓ cup half and half
1 cup sour cream
3 Tbsp. green onions or
  chives, minced
4 strips bacon, fried and
  crumbled
½ tsp. parsley
1 cup cheddar cheese,
  grated
1½-2 tsp. salt
½ tsp. pepper
¼ tsp. garlic salt
1 egg, beaten
⅓ cup butter
½ cup mushrooms, sliced
  and sauteed in butter

SERVES 8-10
Bake potatoes for one hour at 350°
or until tender in center. Cut in half
lengthwise. Scoop out potato carefully as to not tear skins. Mash potatoes with mixer, add half and half
and continue to beat until smooth.
Add all other ingredients and mix well.
Mixture should be somewhat softer
than regular mashed potatoes to prevent drying out when baking again. Fill
skin shells with mashed potato mixture and arrange on cookie sheet. Top
each with extra grated cheese. Bake
at 350° for 20 minutes. Great with
steaks!

CATHY'S PARIS POTATOES

6 medium potatoes
2 cups creamed cottage
  cheese
1 cup sour cream
4 green onions and tops,
  finely chopped
½ tsp. garlic salt
Salt and pepper to taste
1 cup cheddar cheese,
  shredded

SERVES 6
Cook potatoes in boiling salted water
until tender, but not soft. Drain, cool,
and peel. Cut into ½ inch cubes.
Combine potatoes with cottage
cheese, sour cream, onions, garlic
salt, and salt and pepper. Bake uncovered in a greased 2 quart casserole at 350°for 20 minutes. Sprinkle
cheese on top and bake an additional
10 minutes.

♥■

SPINACH SOUFFLE WITH MUSHROOM SAUCE

1 pkg. fresh spinach or
   1—10 oz. pkg. frozen
   chopped spinach
2 Tbsp. butter
¼ cup minced green onion
2 eggs
2 egg yolks
1 cup half and half
½ cup bread crumbs
3 Tbsp. Parmesan cheese

SAUCE:
2 Tbsp. butter
½-¾ lb. mushrooms
1 cup whipping cream
Salt and pepper
1 Tbsp. butter
1 Tbsp. flour
2 Tbsp. minced chives

SERVES 4-6

Cook fresh spinach 2-3 minutes. Drain, squeeze out water and mince. If using frozen spinach, cook for 3-5 minutes and drain. Melt 2 tablespoons butter in small skillet. Saute onion. Combine onion and spinach in large bowl. Mix together the eggs, yolks, and half and half. Add to spinach mixture along with bread crumbs and Parmesan cheese. Turn into 8 x 8 inch baking dish and bake in water bath (set baking dish in larger pan with 1 inch of water). Cover with foil. Bake 50 minutes at 350° or until knife comes out clean.

To prepare sauce, melt butter in small saucepan and saute mushrooms. Add cream and bring to boil. Melt 1 tablespoon butter in a cup and add 1 tablespoon flour. Mix to make a paste. Whisk paste into the boiling cream; reduce heat and mix hard until smooth. Salt and pepper to taste. Spoon over souffle and sprinkle with chives or pour sauce into gravy boat and pass separately. This is a rich and elegant vegetable dish.

VEGETABLES, RICE & PASTA

EASY YELLOW SQUASH

Yellow squash or zucchini
Salt
Pepper
Butter
1 jar Kraft's Jalapeno
   Cheeze Whiz
Paprika

This recipe is a "do it by looking" one. The amount of squash you start out with regulates how much cheese you use. Wash and cut squash. Boil in water until done. Drain well. Add butter, salt and pepper to taste. Stir in Jalapeno Cheeze Whiz until it is melted. Put in buttered casserole and sprinkle with paprika. Bake uncovered at 350° until it bubbles. This is a good, easy way to fix squash.

MEXICAN SQUASH CASSEROLE

2 lbs. yellow or zucchini
   squash, or
3—10 oz. pkg. frozen
   squash
½ onion, chopped
¼ cup butter or
   margarine
1 cup grated longhorn
   cheese
3 eggs, beaten
1 small can evaporated milk
3 Tbsp. chopped green
   chilies
2 cups cracker crumbs
1—2 oz. jar pimentos
Salt and pepper to taste
Grated cheese to cover

SERVES 6-8
Wash squash and slice thin. Partially cover with water, add chopped onion and cook 15 minutes. Drain well and add ¼ cup margarine, grated cheese and beaten eggs. While squash is cooking, pour 1 can evaporated milk over cracker crumbs. When soft, add to squash mixture. Add green chilies, pimentos, salt and pepper and bake uncovered 35 minutes at 325°. Remove from oven, cover generously with cheese and bake 10 more minutes.

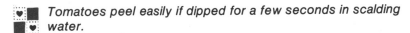 *Tomatoes peel easily if dipped for a few seconds in scalding water.*

SAUTEED SQUASH WITH MUSHROOMS AND ONIONS

3 slices bacon
2-3 zucchini and/or yellow
   summer squash
1 small onion, chopped
½ cup fresh mushrooms,
   whole or sliced
1 tomato
1/8 tsp. salt
Parmesan cheese

SERVES 4

Cook bacon in skillet until crisp. Drain and remove all fat from skillet, except enough to cover bottom of pan. Cut washed squash into 1/8 inch rounds. Saute in bacon fat along with onions and mushrooms until tender. Cut tomato into 6-8 lengthwise slices. Add tomato and crumbled bacon to squash mixture and heat well. Add salt. Turn into serving bowl and sprinkle with Parmesan cheese. Serve with extra Parmesan cheese for individual flavoring. This is a good summertime vegetable dish, especially with barbecued chicken, Onion Bread, and Homemade Vanilla Ice Cream.

BROILED TOMATOES

4 medium size tomatoes,
   cut in half
1 cup bread crumbs
2 Tbsp. butter
Parmesan cheese
Parsley
Salt and pepper to taste

SERVES 4

Place each tomato half on a greased pan. Saute bread crumbs in butter until crisp. Pile bread crumbs on top of tomatoes; sprinkle Parmesan cheese on each. Season with salt and pepper. Place in a 350° oven and bake until tomatoes are soft, about 20-25 minutes. Add a sprig of fresh parsley to each tomato before serving. These are good with ham, Macaroni, Mushroom, Green Bean Casserole and Lemon Pudding Cake for dessert.

VEGETABLES, RICE & PASTA

SPINACH-STUFFED TOMATOES

6 small tomatoes, top ¼
  cut off
½ cup cottage cheese
2 Tbsp. plain yogurt
½ tsp. salt
Dash of pepper
Dash of nutmeg
1—10 oz. pkg. frozen
  chopped spinach, cooked
  and drained well
1 Tbsp. minced fresh onion
2 Tbsp. bread crumbs

SERVES 6
Scoop out tomato seeds and some of the pulp from each tomato. Sprinkle tomato shells with salt and turn upside down to drain. Using blender or food processor, blend cottage cheese, yogurt, ½ tsp. salt, pepper and nutmeg. Mix with spinach, onion, and 1 tablespoon bread crumbs. Spoon mixture into tomato shells and sprinkle with remaining bread crumbs. Place on baking sheet and cook 15-20 minutes at 400°.

CHEESE SAUCE FOR VEGETABLES

3 Tbsp. butter
2 Tbsp. flour
¾ cup half and half
½ cup cheddar cheese,
  grated
¼ tsp. salt
Pepper

Melt butter in small saucepan. Add flour and stir well to make paste. Add half and half. Cook over medium heat, stirring constantly until smooth and thick. Add cheese and cook until melted. Pour over cooked broccoli, cauliflower, or asparagus.

HOT CURRIED FRUIT

¼ cup melted margarine
½ cup brown sugar
2 Tbsp. cornstarch
1 Tbsp. curry powder
1—1 lb. can sliced pears, well drained
1—1 lb. can sliced peaches, well drained
1—1 lb. can pineapple chunks, well drained
1—8 oz. bottle maraschino cherries, well drained
1 cup black pitted cherries
2 bananas, cut in large pieces

SERVES 8
Melt butter in a saucepan; add sugar, cornstarch, and curry powder. Stir until smooth. Mix drained fruit in a 2 quart casserole. Pour sauce over fruit and toss lightly. Bake 40 minutes, uncovered, at 350°. This dish is excellent with a baked ham, or with Chicken and Dressing Casserole.

FRIED APPLE RINGS

4 large, tart, cooking apples, cored
3 Tbsp. butter
⅓ cup brown sugar
½ tsp. ground cinnamon or nutmeg
2 Tbsp. water

SERVES 4-6
Cut apples into ¼ inch thick rounds. Heat butter in large cast iron skillet. Over moderate heat, saute apple rings 3-5 minutes, or until they begin to soften. Sprinkle remaining ingredients, in the order given, and continue to cook 5-7 minutes. Spoon syrup over apples until they are tender and coated with juice. Serve these at brunch or as an accompaniment to ham. These are a real Southern treat!

VEGETABLES, RICE & PASTA

FRIED RICE WITH BACON AND MUSHROOMS

3 Tbsp. bacon drippings
½ cup green onions and
  tops
1 cup celery, diced
1 cup mushrooms, sliced
3 cups cooked rice
  (cooled)
2 Tbsp. soy sauce
1 egg, slightly beaten
½ lb. bacon, fried and
  crumbled

SERVES 6
Saute onions and celery in bacon drippings. Cook until tender. Add mushrooms, rice and soy sauce. Cook 10 minutes on low heat, stirring occasionally. Stir in beaten egg and cook only until egg is done. Add bacon and mix well. Serve this with extra soy sauce. This is a good accompaniment for Sweet and Sour Pork.

EASY RICE

2—10½ oz. cans beef
  consomme
¾ stick butter or margarine
1 small onion, chopped
1—4 oz. can sliced
  mushrooms, drained
1 cup raw rice (not quick)

SERVES 6
Combine ingredients in a casserole and bake uncovered at 325° for 1 hour. You can increase the heat if you want to speed up cooking time or cover if it is cooking too fast.

RICE AND CHILIES

¾ cup Uncle Ben's Rice
  (or any quick cooking
  rice)
Salt to taste
1—6 oz. can chopped
  green chilies
2 cups sour cream
½ lb. Monterey Jack
  cheese, grated
Butter

SERVES 4-5
Cook rice. Combine with sour cream and salt. Arrange half of this mixture in lightly-greased casserole. Place green chilies and half of grated cheese on top. Add the rest of rice mixture. Cover with dots of butter and remaining cheese. Bake uncovered at 350° for 30 minutes.

♥ ♥ ♥ ♥ ♥ ♥ ♥ ♥ ♥ ♥ ♥ ♥ ♥ ♥■♥■♥■♥

MACARONI, MUSHROOMS AND GREEN BEANS

1 pkg. Kraft Macaroni and Cheese Deluxe
1—4 oz. can sliced mushrooms, drained
1—1 lb. can green beans, drained

SERVES 8

Prepare macaroni and cheese according to package directions. While still in saucepan, add mushrooms and green beans (you can add more to suit your taste or use cooked fresh or frozen green beans). Pour mixture into a 2 quart casserole and sprinkle with paprika. Bake uncovered for 10-15 minutes in a 350° oven. This is so easy and delicious . . . it makes an excellent accompaniment for ham or pork chops. Kids love it.

MACARONI AND CHEESE DELUXE

2 cups elbow macaroni
2 quarts boiling water
1 Tbsp. salt
2 Tbsp. butter
2 Tbsp. chopped onion
2 Tbsp. flour
Salt and pepper
2 cups milk
3 cups sharp American cheese, grated
Parsley
1½ tsp. Worcestershire

SERVES 6

Add 1 tablespoon salt to boiling water; add macaroni and cook until tender. Drain. Saute onion in 2 tablespoons melted butter until tender. Stir in flour, salt and pepper. Add milk and stir over low heat until slightly thick and smooth. Add 2 cups of grated cheese, parsley and Worcestershire sauce. Cook slowly until cheese melts. Combine with macaroni. Pour into 2 quart buttered casserole. Top with remaining cup of grated cheese. Bake uncovered until bubbly, about 30 minutes. This old family recipe is a real winner.

♥■
■♥ *Always cook cheese at low temperature. Cheese become tough or stringy if cooked too fast or too long.*

Desserts

DESSERTS

FRESH APPLE CAKE

1 cup oil
2 cups sugar
2 eggs
2¼ cups flour
1 tsp. baking soda
1 tsp. salt
1 tsp. cinnamon
½ tsp. nutmeg
3 cups apples, peeled and
   chopped
1 cup nuts, chopped
1 tsp. vanilla

ICING:
1 stick butter or margarine
1 cup brown sugar
¼ cup evaporated milk

Combine oil and sugar. Add eggs and beat well. Sift dry ingredients into mixture and mix well. Stir in apples, nuts, and vanilla. Blend well. Bake in greased and floured tube pan at 350° for 1½ hours. Makes a large cake that freezes well.

Blend icing ingredients in saucepan. Boil for 2 minutes. Pour over cake while hot. Let icing soak into cake while pouring. Remove from pan when cool.

BLACK BOTTOM CUPCAKES

8 oz. cream cheese
½ cup sugar
1 egg
1/8 tsp. salt
6 oz. semi-sweet
   chocolate bits
1½ cups flour
1 cup sugar
¼ cup cocoa
1 tsp. soda
½ tsp. salt
⅓ cup oil
1 Tbsp. vinegar
1 cup water
1 tsp. vanilla

MAKES 18-20
Soften cream cheese and add sugar, egg and salt. Mix well with beater. Stir in chocolate bits. In separate bowl, combine all other ingredients. Mix well. Fill greased or lined muffin tins ½ full with chocolate mixture. Drop large teaspoonfuls of cream cheese mixture in center of each cupcake. Bake at 350° for 25-30 minutes or until white center is slightly brown. These don't need frosting.

BLARNEY STONES

4 eggs, separated
1 cup sugar
1 cup flour + 2 Tbsp.
1¼ tsp. baking powder
¼ tsp. salt
½ cup boiling water
½ tsp. vanilla

FROSTING:
1 egg yolk (reserved from the cake recipe)
1 cup butter, softened
2½ cups powdered sugar
1 tsp. vanilla
Crushed salted peanuts

Separate eggs, reserving 1 yolk for icing. Beat remaining yolks until thick and lemon colored. Add sugar gradually, beating continuously. Add dry ingredients, sifted together, alternating with boiling water. Add vanilla and beat well. Fold in stiffly beaten egg whites. Bake 30 minutes at 350° in 13 x 9 inch pan. When cool, ice with Blarney Stone Frosting, and cut into squares.

To make frosting, cream together egg yolk, butter and sugar until soft and smooth. Add vanilla. Ice cake and sprinkle crushed salted peanuts on top. Make as a special treat for St. Patrick's Day!!

BROWNIE PUDDING CAKE

1 cup flour
¾ cup sugar
2 Tbsp. cocoa
2 tsp. baking powder
½ tsp. salt
½ cup milk
1 tsp. vanilla
2 Tbsp. oil
¾ cup walnuts
¾ cup brown sugar
¼ cup cocoa
1¾ cup hot water

Mix flour, sugar, cocoa, baking powder, salt, milk, vanilla and oil in bowl. Pour into greased 8 x 8 inch pan. Combine walnuts, brown sugar and cocoa in bowl. Add boiling water to nut mixture and mix well. Pour over batter mixture in pan. Bake at 350° for 45 minutes. Good with vanilla ice cream on top.

DESSERTS

CARROT CAKE

2 cups flour
2 cups sugar
2 tsp. cinnamon
1 tsp. salt
2 tsp. soda
1 cup oil
4 eggs
3 cups grated carrots
1 tsp. vanilla

FROSTING:
1—8 oz. pkg. cream cheese
1 lb. powdered sugar
1 stick butter or margarine
1-2 Tbsp. milk
1 tsp. vanilla
1 cup chopped nuts

Mix dry ingredients. Add oil and vanilla and mix well. Add eggs, one at a time, beating after each egg. Stir in grated carrots. Bake at 350° for 45-60 minutes in a greased and floured 9 x 13 inch pan or in two 9-inch round cake pans.

To make the frosting, cream together cream cheese and butter, blend in powdered sugar and vanilla. Add enough milk to make smooth. Stir in nuts.

CHOCOLATE SHEET CAKE

2 cups flour
2 cups sugar
1 stick margarine
1 cup cold water
4 Tbsp. cocoa
½ cup salad oil
½ cup buttermilk
2 eggs, beaten
1 tsp. soda
1 tsp. vanilla

FROSTING:
1 stick margarine
4 Tbsp. cocoa
6-7 Tbsp. milk
1 lb. powdered sugar
1 tsp. vanilla
1 cup pecans, chopped

In large bowl, combine flour and sugar. In saucepan, combine margarine, water, cocoa, and salad oil. Bring to a boil. Remove from heat, and pour immediately over the flour/sugar mixture. Mix well. Add buttermilk, eggs, soda, and vanilla. Mix well. Pour into well-greased jelly roll pan (17x11x1) and bake 20 minutes at 400°. (You can use a 9 x 13 inch pan, but increase the cooking time.) While cake is in the oven, combine margarine, cocoa, and milk in a saucepan. Bring to a boil. Remove from heat and add powdered sugar, vanilla and nuts. Mix well. Pour over hot cake. From start to finish, this cake takes about 25-30 minutes to make. It is easy, delicious and makes enough to feed a large group of people. It also freezes nicely. After trying this cake, you will never mess with another chocolate layer cake!

QUICK CHOCOLATE-CHERRY CAKE

1 chocolate cake mix
1 can cherry pie filling
2 eggs

FROSTING:
⅓ cup milk
1 cup sugar
5 Tbsp. butter
1 cup chocolate chips

Combine chocolate cake mix, pie filling and two eggs in bowl. Mix well. Pour into greased and floured 9 x 13 inch pan and bake at 350° for 25 minutes or until done to touch.

In saucepan, combine milk, sugar and butter. Heat to boiling and boil 1 minute, stirring constantly. Add chocolate chips and stir well. Let sit for 10-15 minutes, stirring occasionally. Pour warm frosting over cake—will be somewhat runny. This cakes keeps better in the refrigerator. It's an easy and quick cake for spur-of-the-moment guests.

CHOCOLATE CHIP CAKE

1½ cups boiling water
1 cup oatmeal
1 cup brown sugar
1 cup white sugar
½ cup shortening
2 eggs
1½ cup flour
1 tsp. soda
½ tsp. salt
1 Tbsp. cocoa
1 cup chocolate chips
½ cup nuts, chopped

Pour boiling water over oatmeal in small bowl. Stir and let stand 10 minutes. Cream sugars and shortening in separate bowl; add eggs and beat until smooth. Add oatmeal and mix well. Add flour, soda, salt and cocoa. Beat 1 minute. Stir in ½ cup chocolate chips. Pour into greased and floured 8 x 12 inch pan. Sprinke ½ cup chocolate chips and ½ cup nuts over top. Bake at 350° for 35-40 minutes.

Powdered buttermilk is great to have on hand for those recipes that call for buttermilk, especially if you're not a buttermilk drinker.

DESSERTS

CREAMY LAYERED CHOCOLATE MINT CAKE

1 chocolate mint cake mix
1½ large containers
   whipped topping
1/8 cup creme de menthe
   (optional)
2 tsp. mint flavoring
Green food coloring

CHOCOLATE SAUCE:
½ cup sugar
4 tsp. cornstarch
½ cup water
1—1 oz. square
   unsweetened
   chocolate
Dash salt
1 Tbsp. butter
½ tsp. vanilla

Make cake according to directions on box. Pour into 2 layer pans. After baking, remove from pans and freeze. Cut each layer in half while partially frozen, making 4 layers. Add 1/8 cup creme de menthe and the flavoring to whipped topping. Tint with green food coloring. Frost each layer generously with whip cream mixture. Refrigerate. Cake moistens and is better if it can sit at least several hours before serving. Drizzle chocolate sauce over each serving.

To prepare sauce, combine ½ cup sugar and the cornstarch in saucepan. Add water, chocolate and salt. Cook and stir until thickened and bubbly. Remove from heat; stir in butter and vanilla.

CHOCOLATE POUND CAKE

1 cup margarine
½ cup Crisco
3 cups sugar
5 eggs
2 tsp. vanilla
½ cup cocoa
3 cups flour
½ tsp. salt
1 tsp. baking powder
1 cup milk
Powdered sugar, optional

Heat oven to 325°. Grease and flour Bundt pan. Sift flour, salt and baking powder together. Set aside. Cream margarine, Crisco and sugar until fluffy. Add eggs, vanilla and cocoa; beat until smooth. Add sifted dry ingredients alternately with milk, beginning and ending with dry ingredients. Mix well. Take out 2 cups batter and make cupcakes (bake only 30-45 minutes), and pour rest of batter in a greased and floured Bundt pan. Bake at least 1 hour or until done. Cool before removing from pan. Sift powdered sugar onto cake, just before serving. This cake freezes well, and is better 1 or 2 days after it is made as it becomes more moist.

172

SPICED CHOCOLATE ZUCCHINI CAKE

2½ cups unsifted flour
½ cup unsweetened cocoa
1¾ tsp. baking powder
1½ tsp. soda
1 tsp. salt
¾ cup butter or margarine,
  softened
2 cups minus 2 Tbsp.
  sugar
2 tsp. cinnamon
¾ tsp. nutmeg
3 extra large eggs
2 cups shredded,
  unpeeled zucchini
2 tsp. vanilla
½ cup plus 2 Tbsp. milk

FROSTING:
1—3 oz. pkg. cream
  cheese, softened
⅓ cup butter or margarine,
  softened
¾ tsp. cinnamon
4 cups powdered sugar
1 tsp. vanilla
1½-2 Tbsp. milk

Mix flour, cocoa, baking powder, soda and salt. In large bowl, cream butter, sugar, cinnamon and nutmeg until light. Add eggs, mixing well. Stir in zucchini and vanilla. Mix well. Add dry ingredients alternately with milk beginning and ending with flour. Beat well after each addition. Pour batter into two 9-inch layer cake pans, which have been greased and floured (or a 9 x 13 inch oblong pan). Bake at 375° about 30 minutes for round cake pans or 40 minutes for oblong, or until toothpick inserted in middle comes out clean. Cool, then ice with cream cheese frosting.

To make frosting, beat together cream cheese, butter and cinnamon until smooth. Gradually add powdered sugar, mixing until smooth. Stir in vanilla. Gradually add milk until it is the right consistency for spreading. Ice the cake and enjoy! This is a very moist cake that keeps well.

Use cocoa instead of flour when preparing pan for chocolate cake.

DESSERTS

GERMAN CHOCOLATE CAKE

1—4 oz. pkg. German's
   sweet chocolate
½ cup boiling water
1 cup butter
2 cups sugar
4 egg yolks
1 tsp. vanilla
2¼ cups sifted flour
1 tsp. baking soda
½ tsp. salt
1 cup buttermilk
4 egg whites, stiffly
   beaten

**COCONUT PECAN
FROSTING:**
¾ cup evaporated milk
½ cup brown sugar
½ cup sugar
½ cup butter
1 tsp. vanilla
3 egg yolks
1½ cups coconut
1 cup pecans, chopped

Melt the chocolate in the boiling water and let cool. Cream butter and sugar, add yolks, beating well after each. Blend in vanilla and chocolate. Sift flour with salt and soda. Add to chocolate mixture alternating with buttermilk. Beat until smooth. Fold in beaten egg whites. Pour into three 9-inch layer pans, lined with wax paper. Bake at 350° for 30-35 minutes. Cool and frost with Coconut-Pecan Frosting.

Frosting: Combine milk, sugars, butter, and vanilla in saucepan. Bring to full boil, stirring constantly. Remove from heat. Mixture may appear curdled. Quickly stir small amount of hot mixture into beaten egg yolks. Stir this back into saucepan with rest of hot mixture. Return to a boil, stirring constantly. Remove from heat. Add coconut and pecans. Cool, beating occasionally. Ice cake layers when cool.

POPPYSEED CAKE

1 pkg. yellow cake mix
1 pkg. instant vanilla
   pudding
4 eggs
3 Tbsps. poppy seeds
½ tsp. nutmeg
¾ cup cream sherry

Mix ingredients well and pour into a greased and floured Bundt pan. Bake at 350° for 40-45 minutes.

♥ ♥ ♥ ♥ ♥ ♥ ♥ ♥ ♥ ♥ ♥ ♥ ♥ ♥■♥■♥ ♥

DEE'S YELLOW COCONUT CAKE

1 pkg. yellow cake mix
1 small pkg. vanilla instant
  pudding
1¾ cup water
4 eggs
¼ cup oil
2 cups coconut
1 cup walnuts or pecans,
  chopped

FROSTING:
4 Tbsp. butter
2 cups coconut
1—8 oz. pkg. cream
  cheese
2 tsp. milk
3½ cups powdered sugar
½ tsp. vanilla

Combine first five ingredients and beat for 4 minutes. Stir in coconut and nuts. Pour into 3 greased and floured 9-inch pans. Bake for 35 minutes at 350°. Cool in pans and remove.

To make frosting, melt 2 tablespoons butter in skillet. Add 2 cups coconut. Stir over low heat until brown and toasted. In bowl, cream softened cheese and 2 tablespoons butter. Add milk, powdered sugar and vanilla. Mix until smooth. Stir in 1¾ cup of the toasted coconut. Frost cake. Sprinkle remaining ¼ cup toasted coconut on sides and top.

MOIST COCONUT CAKE

1 pkg. yellow cake mix
1½ cups milk
½ cup sugar
1½ cups coconut
3½ cups prepared whipped
  topping, thawed

Prepare cake mix as directed on package, baking in 9 x 13 inch pan. Cool cake 15 minutes. Poke holes down through cake with utility fork. In saucepan combine milk, sugar and ½ cup coconut. Bring to boil, reduce heat and simmer 1 minute. Mixture will be runny. Carefully spoon over warm cake, allowing liquid to soak down through holes. Cool completely. Fold ½ cup of the coconut into whipped topping and spread over cake. Toast remaining ½ cup coconut and sprinkle on top of whipped topping. Chill. Store cake in refrigerator.

DESSERTS

COOKIE CAKE

2 cups flour
2 cups sugar
1 tsp. soda
3½ Tbsp. chocolate syrup
1 stick margarine
1 cup water
⅓ cup buttermilk
2 eggs
1 tsp. vanilla

FROSTING:
1 stick margarine
3½ Tbsp. chocolate syrup
⅓ cup milk
1 lb. powdered sugar
1 tsp. vanilla
1 cup nuts, chopped

Mix flour, sugar, and soda in large bowl. Combine chocolate syrup, margarine and water in saucepan and bring to a boil. Cool boiled mixture slightly and pour over the flour mixture. Add buttermilk, eggs and vanilla, beating well. Pour into a 11 x 16 inch jelly roll pan that has been greased and floured. Bake 20 minutes at 400°

To make frosting, boil margarine, chocolate syrup and milk. Remove from heat, add powdered sugar. Stir in vanilla and nuts. Put on cake as soon as it comes out of the oven. This cake won't last long, as it is really delicious!

EILEEN'S ITALIAN CREAM CAKE

½ cup Crisco
½ cup butter or margarine
1⅔ cup sugar
5 eggs, separated
1 cup buttermilk
¾ tsp. baking soda
½ tsp. salt
2 cups flour, sifted
1 tsp. vanilla
1 cup pecans, chopped
1—3½ oz. can coconut

CREAM CHEESE
FROSTING:
8 oz. cream cheese,
   softened
¼ cup margarine, softened
1 lb. powdered sugar
1 tsp. vanilla
1-2 Tbsp. milk
1 cup chopped pecans

Cream margarine and Crisco; add sugar gradually and beat until fluffy. Add egg yolks, one at a time and beat well after each addition. Add buttermilk alternately with dry ingredients starting and ending with flour. Stir in vanilla, pecans, and coconut. Fold in stiffly-beaten egg whites. Bake in 3 greased and floured 9 inch layer pans at 350° for 30-40 minutes or until done. Cool before removing from pan. Ice with Cream Cheese Frosting.

To make frosting, cream cheese and margarine until smooth. Add remaining ingredients, ending with milk to make the proper spreading consistency. Stir in nuts if desired.

LEMON PUDDING CAKE

3 Tbsp. butter
1 cup sugar
4 eggs, separated
3 Tbsp. flour
¼ tsp. salt
⅓ cup lemon juice
1 cup milk
2 tsp. grated lemon peel
¼ cup sliced almonds
Nutmeg

Cream butter and sugar in bowl. Add egg yolks and beat. Add flour, salt, lemon juice, milk and lemon peel. Mix well. In separate bowl, beat egg whites until stiff. Fold into batter. Pour into 6 x 8 inch buttered dish. Sprinkle almonds over batter. Set in water bath for baking. Bake at 325° for 50-55 minutes. Dust with nutmeg. This will be a favorite!

MISSISSIPPI MUD CAKE

2 sticks margarine
2 cups sugar
4 eggs
1 tsp. vanilla
2 Tbsp. cocoa
1½ cups flour
1 cup nuts, chopped
1 cup coconut

FROSTING:
1 small jar marshmallow
   creme
1—1 lb. box powdered
   sugar
1 stick margarine, softened
½ cup evaporated milk
⅓ cup cocoa
1 tsp. vanilla

Cream margarine and sugar. Add eggs and vanilla and beat well. Combine cocoa, flour, nuts and coconut in bowl and mix with spoon. Add to other ingredients. Mix well. Pour into greased 9 x 13 inch pan. Bake at 350° for 35-45 minutes.

Frosting: Spoon marshmallow creme over warm cake. Let soften, then spread over cake. Blend softened margarine with sugar; add other ingredients, mixing well. Spread over marshmallow layer. This cake is too good to be true!

Cake layers will come out of their pans without sticking if you set the hot pans on a damp cloth when they come out of the oven.

DESSERTS

MOCHA BALLS

4 eggs, separated
1 cup sugar
1 cup flour plus 2 Tbsp.
1¼ tsp. baking powder
¼ tsp. salt
½ cup boiling water
¼ tsp. vanilla

FROSTING:
1 lb. powdered sugar
1 stick butter, softened
5 Tbsp. cocoa
2 tsp. vanilla
4-5 Tbsp. evaporated milk
1 lb. pecans, finely ground

MAKES 36 SQUARES

Separate eggs. Beat yolks until thick and lemon colored. Add sugar gradually, beating continuously. Add dry ingredients, sifted together, alternately with boiling water. Add vanilla and beat well. Fold in stiffly beaten egg whites. Bake 30 minutes at 350° in a 13 x 9 inch pan. When cool, cut into 36 squares.

Make a frosting of sugar, butter, cocoa, vanilla, and canned milk. Heat in double boiler until runny for spreading. Spread all six sides of the sponge cake squares (messy, but worth it) and roll all sides in finely chopped nuts. This is a very old recipe from Germany. It isn't an easy one and it takes time, but it is great for festive occasions. You might think of making mocha balls a part of your Christmas tradition!

ORANGE KISS ME CAKE

1 large orange
½ cup milk
1 cup raisins
⅓ cup walnuts, chopped
2 cups flour
1 cup sugar
1 tsp. soda
1 tsp. salt
½ cup oil
¾ cup milk
2 eggs
⅓ cup orange juice
⅓ cup sugar
1 tsp. cinnamon
¼ cup walnuts, chopped

Squeeze juice from orange. Combine pulp and rind in blender with ½ cup milk to puree. Mix with raisins and walnuts. Sift together flour, sugar, soda, and salt. Add oil and ¾ cup milk. Beat 1½ minutes. Add eggs and beat another minute. Fold in orange-raisin mixture. Pour into 12x8x2 inch greased and floured pan. Bake at 350° for 40-50 minutes. Meanwhile combine ⅓ cup orange juice, ⅓ cup sugar, 1 teaspoon cinnamon, and ¼ cup walnuts. Pour mixture over warm cake.

PINEAPPLE UPSIDE-DOWN CAKE

½ cup butter
1 cup packed brown sugar
1—20 oz. can sliced
  pineapple, drained
Maraschino cherries
1 Supermoist Betty
  Crocker Yellow cake mix,
  or White Cake (below)
12 pecan halves

WHITE CAKE:
3 cups flour
2 cups sugar
3 tsp. baking powder
1 tsp. salt
1½ cups milk
⅔ cup shortening
2 eggs
2 tsp. vanilla

Melt butter in 9 x 13 inch pan. Sprinkle brown sugar over butter. Arrange pineapple slices in butter/brown sugar mixture. Place a maraschino cherry in center of each pineapple slice. Scatter pecan halves between pineapple slices. Prepare cake mix as directed on the package. If making White Cake, combine all ingredients in bowl and mix well. Pour batter over pineapple. Bake 45-55 minutes at 350°. As soon as it is taken out of the oven, invert onto a serving plate. Serve with whipped cream. This recipe can be easily halved and baked in a round layer pan for 35-40 minutes.

MOTHER LINK'S 7-UP POUND CAKE

2 sticks margarine
½ cup Crisco
3 cups sugar
5 eggs
3 cups flour
2 tsp. vanilla
1 tsp. lemon extract
1—7 oz. bottle 7-Up

LEMON GLAZE:
1 cup powdered sugar
Juice of 1 lemon

Do not use cake flour or sift. Stir flour in cannister before measuring. Cream margarine and Crisco. Add sugar slowly and eggs one at a time, beating well after each addition. Add other ingredients except 7-Up and mix well. Slowly add 7-Up, mixing well. Pour into greased and floured Bundt pan and bake 1 hour and 20 minutes at 350°. Let cake sit until cool, then invert onto a cake plate. Drizzle glaze over cake. Freezes well.

Raisins heated a moment in the oven will not sink to the bottom of the cake.

DESESRTS

STRAWBERRY CAKE

1 Duncan Hines white
  cake mix
1—3 oz. pkg. strawberry
  jello
¾ box (10 oz.) frozen
  strawberries, thawed
Scant ½ cup oil
½ cup water
4 eggs

STRAWBERRY ICING:
1 lb. powdered sugar
¼ box frozen strawberries,
  thawed
½ stick butter, softened

Mix cake mix, jello, strawberries, oil and water. Beat well. Add eggs, one at a time, beating well after each egg. Pour into 3 greased and floured 9 inch round cake pans (or a 9 x 13 inch cake pan) and bake at 350° for 30-35 minutes for round pans; 35-40 minutes for 9 x 13 inch. Cake is done when toothpick inserted in the middle comes out clean. When cool, frost with Strawberry Icing.

To make the icing, blend softened butter and powdered sugar. Add frozen strawberries and blend well.

APRICOT SOURS

1½ cups flour
⅔ cup butter
¾ cup dried apricots
  (4 oz.)
2 eggs
1 cup brown sugar, packed
½ tsp. vanilla
½ cup pecans

GLAZE:
¾ cup powdered sugar
2 Tbsp. lemon juice

MAKES 3 DOZEN
Cut butter into flour until mixture is coarse. Press into bottom of a 13x9x2 inch pan. Bake at 350° for 10 minutes. Set aside and cool while preparing apricots. Cover apricots with boiling water and simmer 5-10 minutes. Drain and cool. Chop coarsely (use food processor if you have one) and fold into the following egg mixture. Beat eggs until thick; add brown sugar gradually, beating well after each addition. Blend in vanilla. Add pecans and apricots. Pour over dough crust. Bake at 350° for 20-30 minutes or until wooden pick comes out clean. Glaze immediately with mixture of powdered sugar and lemon juice. Cut into squares.

BUTTER SUGAR COOKIES

1 cup butter
1 cup sugar
½ tsp. vanilla
1 egg
2 cups flour
½ tsp. soda
½ tsp. cream of tartar

MAKES 2 DOZEN
Cream butter and sugar. Add vanilla and egg, then sifted dry ingredients Mix thoroughly. Chill dough. Place on cookie sheet in small balls and flatten with fork dipped in sugar, making sure each cookie is sprinkled with sugar. Bake at 350° until edges just begin to turn golden, about 10 minutes.

This is a good recipe for holiday sugar cookies. After the dough is chilled, roll out a portion to ¼ inch thickness. Using your favorite cookie cutters, cut into shapes; sprinkle with colored sugar, and bake. Can also be baked plain and frosted.

FAVORITE CHOCOLATE CHIP COOKIES

½ cup butter or margarine
½ cup Crisco (try the butter-flavored)
¾ cup white sugar
¾ cup brown sugar, packed
1 tsp. vanilla
2 eggs
2¼ cups unsifted flour
1 tsp. baking soda
1 tsp. salt
2 cups chocolate chips (12 oz.)
1 cup chopped nuts (optional)

MAKES 2-3 DOZEN
Cream butter, shortening, sugar, and vanilla. Add eggs and mix well. Add the dry ingredients and stir until thoroughly mixed. Stir in chocolate chips and nuts. Drop by the heaping teaspoonful onto ungreased cookie sheet and bake at 375° for 8-10 minutes or until golden brown. Remove from cookie sheet and cool.

 When rolling cookie dough, use powdered sugar instead of flour on your board. This will make your cookies a wee bit sweeter but they will not get tough as they sometimes do when they are rolled out on a floured board.

DESSERTS

CHOCOLATE SNOWBALLS

¾ cup butter
½ cup sugar
2 tsp. vanilla
1 egg
2 cups flour
½ tsp. salt
1 cup nuts, chopped
6-oz. chocolate chips
Powdered sugar

MAKES 2 DOZEN
Cream butter and sugar. Add vanilla and egg; mix well. Add flour and salt. Mix well. Stir in chocolate chips and nuts. Roll dough into 1 inch diameter balls and place on greased cookie sheet. Bake for 15-20 minutes in 350° oven. Cool. Roll in powdered sugar.

AUNT VERNA'S DATE COOKIES

2 cups brown sugar
1 cup shortening
2 eggs
3½ cups flour
2 tsp. cream of tartar
1 tsp. soda
1 tsp. salt
1 tsp. vanilla
½ tsp. lemon extract
1 cup chopped dates
1 cup chopped nuts

MAKES 3 DOZEN
Cream sugar and shortening. Add eggs and mix until creamy. Add flour, cream of tartar, soda, salt, vanilla and lemon extract. Mix well. Mix in dates and nuts. Form the dough into a roll, wrap in wax paper, and chill. At this point it can be frozen. Slice off cookies in slices not quite ½ inch thick and bake at 350° for 10-15 minutes.

 When cutting marshmallows or chopping dates, if you dip your scissors into water and cut them wet, the goodies won't stick.

WRANGLER COOKIES

2 large eggs
1 cup sugar
1 cup brown sugar, lightly
  packed
2 sticks butter or margarine
1 tsp. vanilla
1 tsp. soda
½ tsp. baking powder
½ tsp. salt
2 cups flour
2 cups oats
1—6 oz. pkg. chocolate
  chips
¾ cup pecans, chopped
  (optional)

MAKES 2 DOZEN BIG COOKIES
Cream eggs, sugars and butter in a large bowl, until fluffy. Mix in vanilla. Combine dry ingredients and add to creamed mixture. Mix well. Stir in chocolate chips and nuts. The dough will be very stiff. To make an oversize cookie, drop the dough by ¼ cupfuls onto a greased cookie sheet. Put only 6-8 mounds of dough on each sheet as the cookies will spread as they bake. Bake at 350° for 10-15 minutes or until they are golden brown but still spongy on top. Be careful not to overcook, as they are supposed to be chewy. Let cookies cool before removing from the baking sheet. If you prefer a smaller cookie, reduce the baking time accordingly.

HOLLY'S FRUITCAKE COOKIES

2 lb. container of mixed
  candied fruit
1 lb. raisins
1 cup flour
1 cup brown sugar
½ cup margarine
4 eggs
3 Tbsp. buttermilk
½ cup orange juice
1 Tbsp. vanilla
2 cups flour
1 tsp. soda
½ tsp. nutmeg
½ tsp. salt
1½ lb. pecans, whole or
  broken up

MAKES 5 DOZEN
Dust fruit and raisins with 1 cup flour. Cream brown sugar and margarine. Beat in 4 eggs. Add buttermilk, orange juice and vanilla. Mix well. Add 2 cups flour, soda, nutmeg, and salt. Mix well. Add fruit, raisins and nuts. Drop spoonfuls onto greased cookie sheet. Bake at 350° for 14 minutes. Great baked Christmas gift!

DESSERTS

KEEPSAKE COOKIES

COOKIES:
2 cups flour
1 cup butter, softened
½ cup sugar
2 tsp. vanilla

PEANUT BUTTER TOPPING:
¼ cup butter
⅓ cup brown sugar
⅓ cup peanut butter

CHOCOLATE GLAZE:
½ cup semi-sweet
    chocolate pieces
2 Tbsp. milk
⅓ cup sifted powdered
    sugar

MAKES 2 DOZEN
Combine flour, butter, sugar and vanilla in bowl. Mix well. Drop by teaspoon onto greased cookie sheet. Flatten with a glass that has been greased on the bottom then dipped in sugar. Bake at 325° for 15-18 minutes. Spread warm cookie with peanut butter topping. Drizzle with chocolate glaze.

To make topping, cream butter, brown sugar and peanut butter. Mix until light and fluffy. To make glaze, melt chocolate pieces with milk in small saucepan over low heat, stirring constantly. Remove from heat. Add powdered sugar; stir until smooth.

PEANUT BUTTER COOKIES

¼ cup butter
¼ cup Crisco
½ cup peanut butter
½ cup sugar
½ cup brown sugar
1 egg, beaten
1¼ cups flour
½ tsp. baking powder
¾ tsp. soda
¼ tsp. salt
1 cup chocolate chips
    (optional)

MAKES 3 DOZEN
Cream butter, shortening, peanut butter and sugars until fluffy. Add beaten egg and mix well. Blend in dry ingredients. Chill dough. Roll into 1 inch balls and arrange on cookie sheet. Dip a fork in flour or sugar and flatten each with a crisscross pattern. Bake 10-12 minutes at 350°. (Adding the chocolate chips makes this traditional cookie a bit more interesting.)

POTATO CHIP SHORTBREAD COOKIES

½ lb. butter or margarine
½ cup butter-flavored
  Crisco
1 cup sugar
¾ tsp. vanilla
3 cups flour + 2 Tbsp.
1½ cup crushed potato
  chips
½ cup pecans, chopped
  (optional)
Powdered sugar

MAKES 6-7 DOZEN

Cream butter, shortening and sugar well. Add vanilla and flour, stir in potato chips and nuts, if desired. Drop by teaspoonful onto a greased cookie sheet, and bake at 350° for about 15 minutes or until browned around the edges. These cookies do not spread while cooking, and are very rich; therefore, you can make them small and put them closer together on the pan. When done, dust them lightly with powdered sugar. This is a quick, easy cookie, and anyone who eats them will be amazed they have potato chips in them.

ROLLED OAT COOKIES

1 cup margarine
1 cup brown sugar
1 cup white sugar
2 eggs, beaten
1⅓ cup flour
1 tsp. salt
1 tsp. soda
1 tsp. vanilla
3 cups rolled oats
1 cup Rice Krispies
½ cup chopped nuts

MAKES 6 DOZEN

Cream together margarine and sugars. Add beaten eggs and mix well. Sift dry ingredients together and add to butter/sugar mixture. Add vanilla and mix well. Stir in oats, Rice Krispies and nuts. Chill 2-3 hours and roll into 1 inch balls and set on a cookie sheet 2 inches apart. Bake at 350° for about 10 minutes or until golden brown.

Keep cake and cookies moist by placing a piece of bread or apple in the container.

DESSERTS

SNICKERDOODLES

1 cup shortening
1½ cups sugar
2 eggs
2¾ cup flour, sifted
2 tsp. cream of tartar
1 tsp. soda
½ tsp. salt
2 Tbsp. sugar
2 tsp. cinnamon

MAKES 2-3 DOZEN
Cream together shortening, sugar, and eggs. Sift together and stir in flour, cream of tartar, soda and salt. Shape dough into balls the size of walnuts. Roll each in mixture of the sugar and cinnamon. Place 2 inches apart on ungreased cookie sheet. Bake 8-10 minutes at 400°, or until lightly browned.

BEST-EVER THUMB PRINT COOKIES

1 cup butter
½ cup brown sugar
2 egg yolks
1 tsp. vanilla
2 cups flour
½ tsp. salt
2 egg whites, slightly
  beaten
Finely chopped nuts
Butter cream frosting
Crabapple jelly or
  maraschino cherries

MAKES 30-36 COOKIES
Cream butter and brown sugar. Add yolks and vanilla, mix well. Stir in flour and salt. Roll into 1 inch balls. Dip each ball into egg whites then roll in chopped nuts. Place on ungreased cookie sheet. Bake 5 minutes at 375°. Make thumbprint in center of each cookie. Bake 8 minutes longer. At Christmas, these are pretty filled with green Butter Cream Frosting and topped with a spoonful of crabapple jelly or a maraschino cherry.

BUTTER CREAM FROSTING:
⅓ cup soft butter
3 cups powdered sugar
1½ tsp. vanilla
2-3 Tbsp. milk

Frosting: Cream butter and sugar, stir in vanilla and add enough milk to make frosting smooth and spreading consistency.

EVERYBODY'S FAVORITE BROWNIES

¾ cup butter or
   margarine, melted
1 ½ cups sugar
1 ½ tsps. vanilla
3 eggs
¾ cup flour, unsifted
½ cup cocoa
½ tsp. baking powder
½ tsp. salt
1 cup pecans, chopped

MAKES 16
Blend melted butter or margarine with sugar and vanilla. Add eggs and beat well with spoon. Combine flour, cocoa, baking powder and salt. Add to egg mixture gradually, until well blended. Stir in nuts. Spread in greased 8-inch pan. Bake at 350° for 40-45 minutes, or until brownie pulls away from sides of pan. Cool and cut into squares.

CHOCO-MINT BARS

FIRST LAYER:
2 oz. unsweetened
   chocolate
½ cup butter
2 eggs
1 cup sugar
½ cup sifted flour

SECOND LAYER:
1 ½ cups powdered sugar
3 Tbsp. butter
2-3 Tbsp. cream
1 tsp. peppermint extract

THIRD LAYER:
3 oz. semi-sweet or
   unsweetened chocolate
3 Tbsp. butter

MAKES 16 BARS
To make first layer, melt chocolate and butter. Cream eggs with sugar. Add flour and chocolate mixture, mixing well. Pour into 8 x 8 inch pan, bake at 350° for 20 minutes. Turn off oven and let sit an additional 5 minutes.

To prepare second layer, cream sugar and butter. Add other ingredients and mix well. Spread on cooled first layer. Chill. (This layer is prettier tinted green or red.)

For third layer, melt chocolate and butter and pour over peppermint layer.

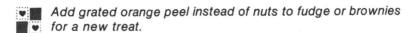 *Add grated orange peel instead of nuts to fudge or brownies for a new treat.*

DESSERTS

PEGGY'S LEMON BARS

CRUST:
2 cups flour
1 cup butter, melted
½ cup powdered sugar

FILLING:
4 eggs
2 cups granulated sugar
1 tsp. baking powder
4 Tbsp. flour
6 Tbsp. lemon juice

MAKES 2-3 DOZEN

Mix crust ingredients. Press into greased 9 x 13 inch glass baking dish, leaving edges some higher than center. Bake at 350° for 20-25 minutes or until crust begins to brown.

To make filling, combine all ingredients and mix well with beater. Pour into baked crust and bake 20-25 minutes at 350°. Bars are done when fairly firm. Chill. Cut into small squares and dust with powdered sugar. Rich and especially good for summer desserts and luncheons.

OATMEAL AND APPLE BUTTER BARS

1 ¼ cups flour
1 cup brown sugar, packed
¾ cup butter or margarine,
   cut up
1 ¼ cups quick-cooking
   oats
¾ cup apple butter

MAKES 16

Mix flour and sugar in large bowl. Cut in butter until mixture resembles coarse crumbs. (If you have a food processor, use it to mix flour, sugar, and butter.) Stir in oats until well mixed. Press half the mixture firmly in greased 8 inch square pan. Spread apple butter to within ½ inch of the edges. Sprinkle remaining oats mixture over apple butter; press carefully but firmly. Bake at 350° for 40 minutes or until lightly browned. Cool, and cut into 2 inch squares. These are simply scrumptious!

PRALINE BARS

1 pkg. graham crackers
2 sticks butter
1 cup light brown sugar
1 cup pecans, chopped

MAKES 24 BARS
Line the bottom of a lightly greased cookie pan (one with sides) with a layer of uncrushed graham crackers. Melt butter in small saucepan, and add 1 cup light brown sugar. Boil for 2 minutes. Remove from heat and add nuts. Pour and spread evenly over crackers. Bake 10 minutes at 350°. Cut while warm. These are extra easy and delicious, too.

PUMPKIN BARS

2 cups flour
1 tsp. soda
½ tsp. salt
1⅔ cup sugar
1 cup oil
4 eggs
2 cups pumpkin
1 cup nuts, chopped
2 tsp. baking powder
1 tsp. pumpkin pie spice or
  ¼ tsp. <u>each</u> cinnamon, allspice, cloves and nutmeg

FROSTING:
1—3 oz. pkg. cream cheese
¼ cup butter
2 Tbsp. cream
1 tsp. vanilla
2 cups powdered sugar

MAKES 4-5 DOZEN BARS
Mix all ingredients well. Pour into two greased and floured 9 x 13 inch pans and bake at 350° for 20-25 minutes.

To make frosting, mix together cream cheese and butter. Combine with other ingredients and mix well. Frost cooled bars. This big recipe makes a good holiday party treat.

 If you break an egg on the floor, sprinkle it heavily with salt and leave it alone for 5-10 minutes. Sweep the dried egg into a dustpan.

DESSERTS

SEVEN LAYER COOKIE

½ cup butter, melted
1 cup graham crackers,
   crushed
1 cup coconut
1 cup butterscotch chips,
   optional
1 cup chocolate chips
1 cup chopped nuts
1—15 oz. can sweetened
   condensed milk

MAKES 2 DOZEN
Combine melted butter with cracker crumbs in 9 x 13 inch pan. Press firmly into pan. Layer in order, the coconut, butterscotch chips, chocolate chips and nuts. Pour sweetened condensed milk evenly over all ingredients. Bake at 350° for 25-30 minutes.

FLAKY PIE CRUST

ONE SINGLE 9 INCH PIE CRUST:
1⅓ cup flour
½ tsp. salt
½ cup Crisco
About 3-4 Tbsp. ice water

MAKES 9 INCH CRUST
Mix salt and flour with one hand. Add Crisco and break up shortening in flour until pieces are pea size. Sprinkle cold water over mixture and toss around with hand. Add enough water until dough holds together when gathered as if making a snowball. Avoid working the dough too much.

To make dough in a food processor, combine flour, salt and Crisco in processor. Blend until mealy. Add ice water, tablespoon at a time with machine running, until dough makes a ball.

Flatten dough on floured surface and roll about an inch larger than pan. Put in pan and trim edges. For a baked pie shell, bake at 450° for 8-10 minutes. (Be sure to prick the bottom and sides.)

 Make at least two pie crusts at a time. Freeze one in a pie pan and it will be ready for the next pie. You'll only have to clean up the mess once.

GRAHAM CRACKER CRUST

1 cellophane wrapped pkg.
   graham crackers (about
   20 crackers)
¼ cup sugar
⅓ cup butter, softened

MAKES ONE 9 INCH CRUST
Crush graham crackers in a food processor, or place in a plastic bag and
crush them with a rolling pin. They
should be finely crushed. Combine
crumbs, sugar and butter and blend
well. Press crumb mixture into 9-inch
pie plate, covering the bottom and
sides evenly. Bake at 375° for 8
minutes and cool.

MERINGUE

3 egg whites, room
   temperature
¼ tsp. cream of tartar
⅓ cup sugar

Beat egg whites and cream of tartar
until foamy. Continue beating, gradually adding sugar. Beat until stiff. You
can't overbeat. Spread onto hot or
warm pie. Seal meringue to edge of
crust. Bake 10 minutes at 375° or
until golden brown.

 A half of teaspoon of baking powder added to the room temperature egg whites before beating seems to "swell" the meringue and make it higher.

DESSERTS

AUNT GINGER'S APRICOT FRIED PIES

FILLING:
16 oz. dried apricots, diced
½ cup cornstarch
3 cups sugar
½ tsp. salt
4 Tbsp. margarine

PASTRY:
4 cups flour
2 tsp. salt
1 cup shortening
¾-1 cup cold water

Crisco for frying

MAKES 12-15 PIES

Stew apricots in small amount of water until tender. Add sugar, salt, margarine and cornstarch and enough water to mix well. Cook several minutes, stirring constantly until thick. Chill fruit before making pies.

To prepare pastry, cut shortening into flour and salt until mealy. Add enough cold water to form pastry dough. Chill dough. Pull off a piece of dough about the size of a peach. Shape into a ball, roll out thin (pie crust thickness) on a floured board to a 6-inch round. Use a saucer as a guide to trim edges. Spoon fruit mixture not quite in the middle of the circle. Dampen edges of the rounds, fold over crust and mash edges together with fork or fingers on both sides. Prick a couple of holes on each side of the pie and fry in deep fat (2 inches of hot oil in a heavy skillet will work fine). These can be frozen before frying.

APPLE PIE

¾ cup sugar
¼ cup flour
½ tsp. nutmeg
½ tsp. cinnamon
Pinch salt
6 cups Granny Smith
    apples, sliced and pared,
    (about 6 medium apples)
2 Tbsps. butter or
    margarine
Pastry for 9-inch two-
    crust pie

Stir together sugar, flour, nutmeg, cinnamon and salt. Mix with apples. Turn into pastry-lined pie pan; dot with butter. Cover with top crust. Slit the top crust, seal and flute. Place in the middle of the oven, and bake at 425° for 40-45 minutes. Although Granny Smith apples are a bit expensive, they make the best apple pie ever!

DIXIE'S BUTTERMILK PIE

9-inch unbaked pie shell
1½ cups sugar
3 Tbsp. flour
2 eggs, well beaten
½ cup butter, melted
1 cup buttermilk
1 tsp. lemon extract
2 tsp. vanilla

SERVES 8
Combine sugar and flour; stir in eggs. Add melted butter and buttermilk, mix well. Stir in vanilla and lemon extract. Pour into chilled pie shell and bake at 425° for 10 minutes. Reduce heat to 350° and bake 35 additional minutes.

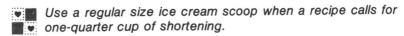 *Use a regular size ice cream scoop when a recipe calls for one-quarter cup of shortening.*

DESSERTS

COCONUT CREAM PIE

9 inch baked pie shell
⅔ cup sugar
¼ cup cornstarch
½ tsp. salt
3 cups milk
4 egg yolks
2 Tbsp. butter
2 tsp. vanilla
¾ cup flaked coconut

SERVES 8

In saucepan combine sugar, cornstarch and salt. Blend milk and egg yolks and add to sugar/cornstarch mixture. Cook over medium heat to boiling, stirring constantly. Boil 1 minute. Remove from heat, add vanilla, butter and coconut. Let cool; stirring occasionally. Pour into cooled pie shell. Top with meringue, sprinkle with coconut. Bake at 400° for 10 minutes or until light golden brown.

CHOCOLATE CREAM PIE

4 egg yolks
3 cups milk
1½ cups sugar
⅓ cup cornstarch
½ tsp. salt
2 oz. unsweetened
   chocolate
1 Tbsp. vanilla
9 inch baked pie shell

SERVES 8

In saucepan combine sugar, cornstarch and salt. Blend milk and egg yolks and add to sugar/cornstarch mixture. Cook over medium heat to boiling, stirring constantly. Boil 1 minute. Remove from heat, add vanilla and melted chocolate. Pour into baked pie shell and top with meringue. Bake at 400° for 10 minutes or until golden brown.

DESSERTS

HERSHEY BAR PIE

9-inch graham cracker
crust
6 small chocolate almond
Hershey bars
16 large marshmallows
½ cup milk
1 cup whipping cream

SERVES 8
Melt candy bars, marshmallows and milk in double boiler. Cool thoroughly. Beat whipping cream until stiff. Fold into chocolate mixture. Pour into prepared graham cracker crust (a regular cooked pastry crust will work, too), and cover with plastic wrap. Refrigerate until serving time. Can be made ahead of time and kept in the freezer.

QUICK LEMON PIE

1 graham cracker crust
½ cup lemon juice (use
fresh lemons for better
results)
1 tsp. grated lemon rind
1⅓ cup sweetened
condensed milk
2 eggs, separated
4 Tbsp. sugar
¼ tsp. cream of tartar

SERVES 6
Combine lemon juice and lemon peel. Gradually stir in sweetened condensed milk. Add egg yolks, and stir until well blended. Pour into cooled graham cracker crust. Beat egg whites, adding cream of tartar and sugar gradually. Beat until almost stiff enough to hold a peak. Pile on pie. Bake at 325° until lightly browned, about 15 minutes. Let cool. If you prefer, you could mound Cool Whip on top (instead of meringue) and sprinkle slivered almonds to garnish.

 Weeping meringue may be caused if any of the filling is exposed to the heat, (not entirely covered). Baking too long or incomplete blending of the sugar are also causes of weeping.

DESSERTS

OLD-FASHIONED LEMON PIE

9-inch baked pie shell
4½ Tbsp. flour
1 cup sugar
1¼ cups water
3 egg yolks
3 tsp. grated lemon rind
¼ cup lemon juice
2 Tbsp. butter

MERINGUE:
3 egg whites, room
   temperature
⅓ tsp. cream of tartar
6 Tbsp. sugar

SERVES 6-8

In top of double boiler, mix flour, sugar, water and egg yolks. Stir over boiling water until it begins to thicken. Put lid on pan and cook without stirring for 10 minutes. Remove from heat and add lemon rind, juice and butter. Mix well and pour into a baked pastry crust.

To make meringue, beat egg whites and cream of tartar, adding sugar gradually, until whites form stiff peaks. Top pie with meringue and bake 10 minutes at 375°.

LUCIOUS LAYERED PIE

1 cup flour
½ cup butter
¼ cup pecans, chopped
1—8 oz. pkg. cream cheese
1—12 oz. carton Cool Whip
1 cup powdered sugar
1 can pie filling (cherry,
   blueberry)
2 large boxes instant
   vanilla pudding
3 cups milk
2 Tbsp. lemon juice

SERVES 12

Combine flour, butter, and pecans in bowl and mix well. Press into 9 x 13 inch pyrex dish. Bake at 350° for 15 minutes. Cool. Combine softened cream cheese, 1 cup of Cool Whip and powdered sugar in bowl and mix well. Spread over cooled crust. Spread pie filling on top of cream cheese layer. To prepare fourth layer, combine instant pudding, milk and lemon juice in bowl and beat until stiff. Spread over pie filling. Top with remaining Cool Whip. Keep refrigerated.

PECAN PIE

9-inch unbaked pie crust
½ cup butter
½ cup brown sugar
1 cup light corn syrup
1 tsp. vanilla
3 eggs
1 cup pecans

SERVES 6-8
Cream butter, add sugar gradually and beat well. Add corn syrup and vanilla. Mix thoroughly. Stir in slightly beaten eggs and pecans. Pour into unbaked 9-inch pie shell, and bake at 450° for 10 minutes. Reduce heat to 350° and finish baking, approximately 45 minutes, or until custard is set.

FOURTH OF JULY STRAWBERRY PIE

9-inch baked pie crust
1—3 oz. pkg. cream cheese
½ cup powdered sugar
½ tsp. vanilla
1 pt. strawberries, whole or halved
½ cup strawberry juice (½ cup strawberries blended with ¼ cup water)
⅔ cup sugar
2 Tbsp. cornstarch
1 cup whipping cream, whipped and sweetened

SERVES 6-8
Soften cream cheese and combine with powdered sugar and vanilla. Beat until smooth. Spread over bottom of cooled baked pie crust. Arrange whole or halved strawberries over bottom. Combine strawberry juice, sugar and cornstarch in saucepan. Mix well. Bring to boil stirring constantly. Simmer for ½ minute. Pour over strawberries in pie shell. Cool. Top each slice with whipped cream.

 Egg whites are easier to beat if first warmed to room temperature.

DESSERTS

FRESH STRAWBERRY PIE

CRUST:
1 stick butter
2 Tbsp. sugar
1 cup flour

FILLING:
1½ pt. strawberries
1 cup water
1 cup sugar
3 Tbsp. cornstarch
2 Tbsp. strawberry jello
Whipped cream

SERVES 6-8
To prepare crust, melt butter and blend with sugar and flour. Press into pie pan. Bake at 350° for 15 minutes.

Slice 1 pint of strawberries and place in cooked pie shell. Puree water and ½ pint strawberries in blender. Combine strawberry juice, sugar and cornstarch in small saucepan. Mix well. Cook over medium heat until clear and thick. Add strawberry jello, mix well. Pour over berries while still warm. Chill several hours. Top with whipped cream.

SOUR CREAM RAISIN PIE

9-inch baked pie shell
1 cup buttermilk
1 cup sour cream
2 large egg yolks or 3
   small yolks, beaten
2 Tbsp. flour
1 Tbsp. cornstarch
¾ cup sugar
¾ cup raisins
¼ cup nuts, chopped big

SERVES 6-8
Combine all ingredients except raisins and nuts in large saucepan. Stir well before heating. Cook over medium heat, stirring constantly. Bring to boil and boil 1 minute. Add raisins and nuts. Put lid on pan and let sit 5-10 minutes. Pour into baked and cooled pie shell. Top with meringue, and bake at 400° about 10 minutes to brown. This pie is guaranteed to be a favorite. It comes highly recommended.

COFFEE CREME MOUSSE

1 lb. small marshmallows
1 cup very strong coffee
1 Tbsp. instant coffee
1 cup heavy cream,
   whipped
¼ tsp. almond extract

SERVES 6

In top of double boiler, melt marshmallows with coffee. Stir and cook until dissolved. Chill mixture until almost set. Fold in one cup heavy cream, whipped. Add almond extract. Pour into a lightly buttered ring mold (or any serving dish), and chill well. Invert and sprinkle top with toasted slivered almonds, or crushed nut brittle.

APPLE CRISP

6-8 medium cooking apples
   (about 6 cups sliced)
½ cup sifted flour
¾ cup firmly packed brown
   sugar
½ cup oats
¾ tsp. cinnamon
¾ tsp. nutmeg
⅓ cup butter or margarine

SERVES 8

Butter a 9x9x2 inch baking dish. Wash, pare, core, and thinly slice apples. Arrange in an even layer in baking dish. Set aside. Mix together flour, sugar, oats, and spices. In a food processor, if you have one, with a pastry blender if not, cut in the butter, until mixture is crumbly. Sprinkle flour, sugar, butter mixture over apples. Bake at 375° for 30 minutes or until crust is crisp and apples are tender. Serve warm, garnished with whipped cream or vanilla ice cream. This is a real treat to serve after a dinner of chili and green salad on the first cold night of the winter.

DESSERTS

❤ ❤ ❤ ❤ ❤ ❤ ❤ ❤ ❤ ❤ ❤ ❤ ❤ ❤ ❤ ❤ ❤

FLAMING BANANA CREPES

12 dessert crepes
2 cups banana, chopped
1 Tbsp. lemon juice
½ cup shredded coconut,
   toasted
1 tsp. ground cinnamon

SERVES 12

Toast coconut in oven until golden. Toss banana with lemon juice to coat. Mix with ¼ cup of coconut and cinnamon. Spoon filling along center of crepe and roll up.

SAUCE:
2 Tbsp. butter
1 Tbsp. light corn syrup
1 pkg. Creamy White
   Frosting Mix (for single
   layer cake)
1 cup evaporated milk
¼ cup rum

To make sauce: Cook butter in saucepan until brown; remove from heat. Stir in corn syrup and frosting mix. Slowly stir in evaporated milk. Heat through, stirring constantly. Add sauce to crepes and sprinkle with remaining coconut. Heat until bubbly. Transfer to warm serving dish. Warm rum just until hot. Ignite; pour over crepes.

DESSERT CREPES:
2 eggs, beaten
⅓ cup milk
⅓ cup water
¾ cup flour
1 Tbsp. melted butter
2 Tbsp. sugar
1 tsp. vanilla

Add milk and water to beaten eggs in mixing bowl. Gradually add flour, stirring constantly with fork until mixture is smooth. Add remaining ingredients and beat until smooth. The batter should have the consistency of fresh cream. Pour thin layer in buttered skillet. Turn once. Brown lightly over medium heat on both sides, or cook on a crepe griddle.

When beating egg whites, make sure the beater and bowl is completely free of fat or grease. (Don't use a plastic bowl.) A trace of grease can prevent the whites from getting stiff.

♥ ♥ ♥ ♥ ♥ ♥ ♥ ♥ ♥ ♥ ♥ ♥ ♥ ♥ ♥ ♥

BANANA PUDDING

½ cup sugar
3 Tbsp. flour
Dash of salt
4 eggs, 3 of them
    separated
2 cups milk
½ tsp. vanilla
Box of vanilla wafers
5-6 medium ripe bananas

MERINGUE TOPPING:
3 egg whites
¼ cup sugar

SERVES 8
Combine ½ cup sugar, flour and salt in the top of double boiler. Mix in 1 whole egg and 3 egg yolks. Stir in milk. Cook, uncovered, stirring constantly until thickened. (Takes about 5 minutes . . . mixture should have the consistency of pudding.) Remove from heat and stir in vanilla. Spread about ¼ cupful on bottom of a 1½ quart casserole. Cover with layer of vanilla wafers, then layer of sliced bananas. Pour about ⅓ of the pudding over this layer, then continue layering wafers, bananas, and pudding until you have 3 layers of each, ending with pudding. Beat remaining 3 egg whites, gradually adding sugar until the mixture forms stiff peaks. Pile on top of pudding and bake at 425° for 5 minutes or until lightly browned.

CHEESE CAKE

Graham cracker crust,
    baked and cooled
12 oz. cream cheese
½ cup sugar
½ tsp. vanilla
2 eggs
1½ cups sour cream
2 Tbsp. sugar
½ tsp. vanilla

SERVES 6-8
Have ingredients at room temperature. Beat cream cheese, sugar, vanilla and eggs at moderate speed until smooth. Pour into graham cracker crust and bake at 325° for 20 minutes. Let cool 15 minutes. Spread with mixture of sour cream, sugar and vanilla. Return to oven for 5 minutes. Chill. Serve this plain, or with strawberries or blueberries poured over each piece. Either way you will get rave reviews.

201

DESSERTS

♥ ♥ ♥ ♥ ♥ ♥ ♥ ♥ ♥ ♥ ♥ ♥ ♥ ♥ ♥ ♥

CHERRY CRUNCH

1—1 lb. 15 oz. can cherry
   pie filling
1 tsp. lemon juice
1 pkg. white cake mix
½ cup nuts, chopped
   (optional)
½ cup butter, melted

SERVES 8-10
Spread pie filling over bottom of a 9-inch square pan. Sprinkle with lemon juice. Combine cake mix, nuts and butter, sprinkle over pie filling. Place in preheated oven at 350° and bake for 45-50 minutes or until golden brown. Serve with ice cream or whipped cream.

PEACH COBBLER

4 cups fresh peaches,
   peeled and sliced
1 Tbsp. cornstarch
¼ cup water
½ cup sugar
¼ tsp. cinnamon

TOPPING:
½ cup flour
½ cup sugar
¼ tsp. salt
½ tsp. baking powder
1 egg
2 Tbsp. butter, melted

SERVES 6-8
Combine water and cornstarch in pan. Stir to dissolve cornstarch. Add fruit, sugar, and cinnamon. Cook until it thickens and boils. Pour into ungreased 2 quart baking dish. Combine flour, sugar, salt and baking powder. Mix together melted butter and egg and add to dry ingredients. Mix well with spoon. Drop spoonfuls of dough over fruit. Bake at 400° for 30-35 minutes or until brown. Other fruits can be substituted in this cobbler, by adjusting the sugar amounts for type of fruit.

SHERRI'S CREAM PUFFS

1 cup water
½ cup butter or margarine
1 cup flour
4 eggs

VANILLA CREAM FILLING:
½ cup sugar
3 Tbsp. cornstarch
¼ tsp. salt
2 cups milk
3 egg yolks
1 Tbsp. butter
1 Tbsp. vanilla

CHOCOLATE SAUCE:
½ cup sugar
4 tsp. cornstarch
½ cup water
1—1 oz. square
   unsweetened chocolate
Dash salt
1 Tbsp. butter
½ tsp. vanilla

MAKES 15
Combine water and butter in saucepan; bring to boil and stir until butter melts. Add flour all at once and stir constantly with wooden spoon until the mixture leaves the sides of the pan and forms a ball. Remove from heat. Immediately add unbeaten eggs one at a time, beating with mixer to a smooth paste after each one. Drop by heaping tablespoonfuls onto a greased baking sheet, about 3 inches apart. Bake in a hot oven (450°) for 15 minutes or until well puffed and delicately browned. Reduce heat to 300° and bake 20 minutes longer; this will bake the center thoroughly but puffs should get no browner. Remove to cake rack to cool. When cool, cut through center with a sharp knife. Fill with vanilla cream filling, whipped cream, ice cream or chocolate pudding. Replace tops and drizzle with chocolate sauce.

To make Cream Filling, combine sugar, cornstarch and salt in saucepan. Mix together milk and egg yolks and gradually stir into sugar mixture. Cook over medium heat, stirring constantly until mixture thickens and boils. Let boil 1 minute. Remove from heat, add butter and vanilla.

To prepare Chocolate Sauce, combine ½ cup sugar and cornstarch. Add water, chocolate and salt. Cook and stir until it thickens and bubbles. Remove from heat; stir in butter and vanilla.

Cream puffs are quick and easy to prepare, and if you're short on time, instant French Vanilla Pudding and warm Hershey's chocolate sauce can provide quick substitutes. This delicious dessert adds a real flair to a brunch.

DESSERTS

CAROL'S DATE PUDDING

1 cup dates, chopped
1 cup boiling water
½ cup white sugar
½ cup brown sugar
1 egg
2 Tbsp. melted oleo
1½ cup flour
½ tsp. salt
1 tsp. baking soda
½ tsp. baking powder
1½ cup brown sugar
1 Tbsp. butter
1½ cup boiling water

SERVES 12
Combine dates and boiling water. Mix and let cool. Mix white sugar, brown sugar, egg and melted oleo. Sift together flour, salt, baking soda, and baking powder; combine with sugar mixture. Mix well. Add dates. Pour into greased 11 x 7 inch pan (9 x 9 inch makes cake thicker). Combine the 1½ cups brown sugar, 1 tablespoon butter and 1½ cups boiling water. Pour over batter. Bake 40 minutes at 375°.

GINGERBREAD

2¼ cups flour
⅓ cup sugar
1 cup dark molasses
¾ cup hot water
½ cup shortening
1 egg
1 tsp. soda
1 tsp. ginger
1 tsp. cinnamon
½ tsp. salt

SERVES 12-16
Combine all ingredients in bowl. Mix well for three minutes. Pour into greased and floured 9 x 9 inch pan. Bake 40-50 minutes at 325°. Serve warm, topped with Lemon Sauce, whipped cream, or butter. What a treat on a cold winter night!

LEMON SAUCE:
½ cup sugar
4 tsp. cornstarch
Dash ground nutmeg
Dash salt
1 cup water
2 beaten egg yolks
2 Tbsp. butter
½ tsp. grated lemon peel
2 Tbsp. lemon juice

MAKES 1 CUP
In saucepan mix sugar, cornstarch, nutmeg, and dash salt. Gradually stir in 1 cup water. Cook and stir over low heat until thickened. Stir half the hot mixture into egg yolks; return to pan. Cook and stir 1 minute. Remove from heat; blend in remaining ingredients. Spoon over hot gingerbread.

♥ ♥ ♥ ♥ ♥ ♥ ♥ ♥ ♥ ♥ ♥ ♥ ♥ ♥ ♥ ♥■♥ ♥

PEACH MELBA

1 cup frozen raspberries
  and juice, thawed
1 tsp. sugar
1 tsp. cornstarch
4 large canned peach
  halves
Vanilla ice cream (or peach)

SERVES 4

Mix raspberries and juice, sugar, and cornstarch over low heat until clear. Strain and cool. Mound ice cream on each peach half, then pour sauce over top. This is an elegant, simple dessert. Serve it with shortbread cookies.

PEANUT BUTTER SAUCE

1 cup sugar
1 Tbsp. white corn syrup
¼ tsp. salt
¾ cup milk
6 Tbsp. peanut butter
¼ tsp. vanilla

MAKES 1 CUP

Mix sugar, corn syrup, salt, and milk and cook over low heat until thickened, stirring constantly. Add peanut butter and blend. Remove from heat and add vanilla when cool. Serve over vanilla or coffee ice cream.

STRAWBERRY SHORTCAKE

1 qt. fresh strawberries,
  sliced
1 cup sugar
2 cups flour
2 Tbsp. sugar
3 tsp. baking powder
1 tsp. salt
⅓ cup shortening
1 cup milk
Butter
Half and half or
  whipped cream

Slice strawberries, add sugar and mash gently. Let sit one-half hour. Combine flour, 2 tablespoons sugar, baking powder and salt in bowl. Cut in shortening until mixture is mealy. Stir in milk. Spread into greased 9" cake pan. Bake 15 minutes at 450° or until golden brown. Slice shortcake while warm. Split each slice and spread with butter. Fill and top with strawberries. Serve warm with cream or sweetened whipped cream.

DESSERTS

RASPBERRY WALNUT TORTE

CRUST:
1 cup flour
⅓ cup powdered sugar
½ cup soft margarine

RASPBERRY LAYER:
2—10 oz. pkgs. frozen
  raspberries
¾ cup walnuts, chopped
2 eggs
½ cup sugar
½ tsp. salt
½ tsp. baking powder
1 tsp. vanilla

SAUCE:
Liquid from raspberries
½ cup water
¼ cup sugar
2 Tbsp. cornstarch
2 drops red food coloring
2 Tbsp. lemon juice
½ cup raspberries
Whipped cream

SERVES 15

Combine 1 cup flour with powdered sugar and softened margarine. Press into 9 x 13 inch pan. Bake 15 minutes at 350°. Cool.

Drain raspberries, reserving juice and ½ cup raspberries for sauce. Spoon raspberries over crust. Sprinkle nuts on top of raspberries. In bowl, beat eggs with the sugar until light and fluffy. Add salt, baking powder and vanilla. Blend well. Pour over nuts and raspberries. Bake at 350° for 30-35 minutes until golden brown.

To prepare sauce, combine raspberry juice, ½ cup water, sugar, cornstarch and food coloring in small saucepan. Cook, stirring constantly until thick and clear. Add lemon juice and ½ cup raspberries.

To serve, cut squares of raspberry torte. Top with whipped cream and spoon sauce over top.

 Use vegetable parer to make chocolate curls to decorate some desserts.

♥ ♥ ♥ ♥ ♥ ♥ ♥ ♥ ♥ ♥ ♥ ♥ ♥ ♥ ♥ ♥ ♥

NANA'S PLUM PUDDING

1 lb. suet, chopped
½ cup flour
1 lb. raisins
1 lb. currants
1 lb. white or seedless
  raisins
1 lb. apples, peeled and
  chopped (about 3 cups)
¼ lb. almonds, chopped
½ lb. citron
1 lb. flour, sifted
1 lb. sugar
½ tsp. cloves
1 tsp. allspice
1 tsp. cinnamon
4 eggs, well-beaten
1 lb. bread crumbs
Milk to moisten (about
  ½ to ¾ cup)
¾ cup brandy
¼ cup brandy for
  igniting

MAKES 2 2-QT. PUDDINGS
SERVES 24
Chop suet and dredge in ½ cup flour. Mix raisins, currants, chopped apples, almonds, and citron in a LARGE bowl. Add suet. Sift flour and add to sugar, cloves, allspice and cinnamon. Combine dry ingredients with raisins. Add eggs, bread crumbs, milk and brandy. Mix well. Pour into 2 greased 2 qt. pudding molds (available at your local kitchen shop). Container should be only ⅔ full and have a tight fitting lid. Place mold on a trivet in a heavy kettle over 2 inches boiling water. Cover kettle. Use high heat, then as steam begins to escape, lower heat to a gentle boil for the rest of cooking. Add water as necessary. Steam for 6 hours. Remove pudding to wire rack; let cool 5 minutes. Invert on serving plate, lift off mold. In a small saucepan, warm the ¼ cup brandy slightly. Ignite with match; pour, blazing, over pudding. Serve with Hard Sauce.

HARD SAUCE
1 cup butter
2 tsp. vanilla
3 Tbsps. sherry, rum
  or brandy
3 cups powdered sugar,
  firmly packed
1/8 tsp. salt

Cream butter until soft and smooth. Stir in flavoring then blend in the sugar, mixed with salt. The mixture should be fairly stiff when finished. Press into a shallow mold or small (5") cake tin. Chill until hard. Serve in slices. Enough for 10 servings.

Your efforts in preparation will be rewarded when you bring in the flaming plum pudding as a final festive touch to Christmas dinner. Nana would garnish her plum pudding with a sprig of holly, and the sight always rivaled the Christmas tree for spectacle. You can freeze leftover pudding or, as Nana did, fry small slices of it in butter for breakfast. If made in smaller molds, they also make wonderful Christmas gifts.

DESSERTS

♥ ♥ ♥ ♥ ♥ ♥ ♥ ♥ ♥ ♥ ♥ ♥ ♥ ♥ ♥ ♥ ♥

PUMPKIN ROLL

4 eggs
1 cup sugar
1 tsp. lemon juice
⅔ cup pumpkin (canned)
1 cup flour
2 tsp. baking powder
1 tsp. ginger
1 tsp. nutmeg
2 tsp. cinnamon

FILLING:
4 Tbsp. butter, softened
6 oz. cream cheese,
   softened
1 cup powdered sugar
½ tsp. vanilla
1 cup nuts, chopped
Powdered sugar

SERVES 15
Beat eggs for about 3 minutes, then add sugar, lemon juice and pumpkin. Combine dry ingredients and fold into batter. Pour into greased jelly roll pan and bake for 15 minutes at 375°. While still warm, transfer cake onto a large tea towel and roll from narrow end. Allow to cool.

To prepare filling, cream butter and cream cheese. Add powdered sugar, vanilla, and nuts; mix well. When cake is cool, roll out and spread with filling. Roll back up (not in the towel), dust with powdered sugar, and slice to serve. Keep wrapped in plastic wrapping in the refrigerator. This is wonderful to have on hand during the holiday season.

DESSERT DELIGHT

1 cup flour
1 cup pecans, chopped
½ cup margarine
1—8 oz. pkg. cream cheese
1 cup powdered sugar
1—12 oz. carton Cool Whip
1 small pkg. instant
   chocolate pudding
1 small pkg. instant
   vanilla pudding
2 cups cold milk

Variation: Substitute 2 small pkgs. instant lemon pudding for a summertime delight.

SERVES 12
Mix together (in a food processor if you have one) flour, pecans and margarine—the mixture should resemble crumbs. Pat into 9 x 13 inch baking dish and bake 15 minutes at 350°. Let cool completely. Cream together cream cheese and powdered sugar. Stir in 1 cup Cool Whip and spread over cooled crust. Whip pudding mixes and milk together until thickened, and spread over cheese layer. Spread remaining Cool Whip on top. Chill before serving. This is a rich dessert, that looks like you worked really hard to put it together. In fact, it is a snap, and is always complimented.

♥ ♥ ♥ ♥ ♥ ♥ ♥ ♥ ♥ ♥ ♥ ♥ ♥ ♥ ♥ ♥ ♥

CHOCOLATE MARENGO

24 chocolate wafers or
  20 Oreos
6 Tbsp. melted butter
4 egg whites
1/8 tsp. cream of tartar
¼ cup sugar
Pinch salt
2 cups heavy cream
1 Tbsp. vanilla
6 oz. semi-sweet
  chocolate
½ cup slivered almonds,
  toasted

CHOCOLATE SAUCE:
½ cup sugar
4 tsp. cornstarch
½ cup water
1—1 oz. square
  unsweetened chocolate
Dash salt
1 Tbsp. butter
½ tsp. vanilla

SERVES 15
Crush wafers or Oreos and combine with melted butter. Press into 8 x 12 inch casserole dish. Bake at 350° for 8 minutes. Beat egg whites and cream of tartar. Gradually add sugar and salt and beat until stiff. In separate bowl, beat cream and vanilla until stiff. Fold cream into whites. Freeze in bowl until crystals form (1-1½ hours). Meanwhile, melt chocolate in double boiler or microwave. Toast almonds lightly in 300° oven and add to chocolate. Keep mixture hot. When frozen mixture is ready, fold chocolate into it. Streaks of chocolate will form. Pour into crust and freeze. Remove from freezer 20-30 minutes before serving. Pass chocolate sauce to be poured over each serving.

To prepare sauce, combine ½ cup sugar and cornstarch in small pan. Add water, chocolate and salt. Cook and stir until thickened and bubbly. Remove from heat; stir in butter and vanilla. This is an elegant dessert.

MUD PIE

1 chocolate cookie crust
  (in the cake mix section
  of your store)
½ gallon coffee ice cream,
  softened
Hershey's chocolate syrup
1—8 oz. carton Cool Whip
Slivered almonds

SERVES 8
Mound coffee ice cream in chocolate cookie crust. Generously drizzle chocolate syrup over ice cream. Pile Cool Whip on top of that, covering it to the edge like a meringue. Sprinkle slivered almonds on top of Cool Whip and freeze. Just before serving, take out of freezer and slice. This is a wonderfully rich dessert that takes about 5 minutes to put together. Your guests will be mightily impressed.

DESSERTS

❤ ❤ ❤ ❤ ❤ ❤ ❤ ❤ ❤ ❤ ❤ ❤ ❤ ❤ ❤ ❤ ❤

OREO ICE CREAM

3 egg yolks
1—14 oz. can sweetened
  condensed milk
2 Tbsp. water
4 tsp. vanilla extract
1 cup coarsely crushed
  Oreo cookies
2 cups whipping cream,
  whipped

SERVES 10
Beat egg yolks in large bowl, stir in sweetened condensed milk, water and vanilla. Fold in cookies and whipped cream. Pour into 2 quart container. Cover and freeze 6 hours or until firm.

STRAWBERRY ICE CREAM

6 pts. fresh strawberries
2 cups sugar
1½ pts. whipping cream
1½ pts. half and half
1/8 tsp. salt

MAKES 4 QUARTS
Cover strawberries with sugar. Let stand an hour, stirring until syrup is formed. Mash. Add remaining ingredients and mix thoroughly. Pour into ice cream freezer container and proceed to freeze.

PEACH ICE CREAM

2½ cups sugar
14 large, ripe peaches,
  peeled and sliced
1/8 tsp. salt
Juice of 1 lemon
1½ pts. whipping cream
1½ pts. half and half
2 tsp. vanilla, optional
2 tsp. almond extract,
  optional

MAKES 4 QUARTS
Sprinkle sugar over peaches; let stand at least 1 hour, stirring occasionally until syrup is formed. Puree in food processor, or mash through a sieve or food mill. Add salt, lemon juice, whipping cream and half and half. Mix well. Pour into container of ice cream freezer and proceed with the freezing process.

HOMEMADE VANILLA ICE CREAM

6 eggs
3 cups sugar
2 Tbsp. vanilla
1½ qts. cream
Milk to fill freezer

Beat eggs until smooth. Add sugar, vanilla and 1 cup milk and beat well. Add remaining ingredients and mix well. Pour into ice cream freezer container and fill to freezer line with milk. Proceed to freeze.

TROPICAL ICE

3 bananas, thoroughly
    mashed
3 oranges, juiced
3 lemons, juiced
3 cups sugar
3 cups milk
1 small can crushed
    pineapple (optional)
Few drops yellow
    food color

Blend ingredients well. Pour into ice cream freezer container, and proceed with the freezing process. (Milk will curdle, but will freeze smooth.) This long-time favorite takes the edge off those hot summer days!

LEMON VELVET ICE CREAM

1 quart plus 1⅓ cups
    whipping cream
4 cups sugar
1 quart plus 1⅓ cups milk
Juice of 8 lemons
2 tsp. lemon extract
1 Tbsp. grated lemon rind
Few drops yellow food
    coloring

Mix ingredients thoroughly. Pour into ice cream freezer container and proceed with freezing process. This rich ice cream tastes just the way it sounds . . . like velvet!

DESSERTS

SINFULLY DELICIOUS DESSERT

24 Oreo sandwich
   cookies, crushed
⅓ cup butter, melted
1 qt. toasted almond ice
   cream
1 small can evaporated
   milk
1—6 oz. pkg. semi-sweet
   chocolate pieces
½ small jar marshmallow
   creme
1 qt. coffee ice cream
1½ cups whipping cream,
   whipped
1½ oz. Kahlua liqueur
Powdered sugar
¼ cup toasted slivered
   almonds

SERVES 15-20
Combine melted butter with cookie crumbs. Press into buttered 9 x 13 inch pan. Bake at 350° for 8 minutes. When cooled, spoon softened almond ice cream over crust. Freeze until firm. In small saucepan, mix evaporated milk and chocolate pieces. Stir constantly over low heat until chocolate melts. Beat in marshmallow creme with a spoon. Cool. Spread over almond ice cream. Let sit in freezer until firm. Spread softened coffee ice cream over chocolate layer. Sprinkle toasted almonds over coffee ice cream. Whip cream, adding powdered sugar to taste and Kahlua. Spread over coffee layer. Garnish with chocolate curls. Freeze. Let sit out 20-30 minutes before serving.

RUTH'S FROSTY STRAWBERRY SQUARES

CRUST:
1 cup flour
¼ cup brown sugar
½ cup softened margarine
½ cup chopped walnuts

TOPPING:
2 egg whites
½ cup sugar
2 Tbsp. lemon juice
1 large container frozen
   strawberries, sliced
½ pt. whipping cream,
   whipped

SERVES 15-20
Stir crust ingredients together. Remove ½ cup mixture to be used for topping. Press remaining crust mixture into 9 x 13 inch pan. Bake 15-20 minutes at 350°. Also bake the ½ cup of crumbs in a pie pan; stir occasionally. Beat egg whites, gradually adding sugar and lemon juice. When whites begin to stiffen, gradually add strawberries, beating mixture until stiff—about 15 minutes. Fold in ½ pint whipped cream. Pour on top of cooled crust. Top with remaining crumbs. Cover and freeze. Delicious luncheon or summertime dessert.

212

ALICE'S NUT GOODIE BARS

1—12 oz. pkg. butterscotch
  chips
1—12 oz. pkg. chocolate
  chips
1 cup chunky peanut butter
1 cup salted peanuts (dry
  roasted can be used)
1—10½ pkg. miniature
  marshmallows

Melt all chips together. Add peanut butter. Stir in nuts and marshmallows. Pour into buttered 9 x 13 inch pan. Cut into candy size pieces.

PECAN MILLIONAIRES

1 pkg. Kraft's caramels
2-3 tsp. water
1½ cups whole pecans
8 Hershey bars, plain
¼ bar paraffin

MAKES 2 DOZEN
Melt caramels with water. Add the pecans. Spoon out on greased wax paper and let cool. Melt Hershey bars and paraffin in double boiler. Dip caramel candies into chocolate mixture and place back on waxed paper to set.

FREDA'S PEANUT BRITTLE

1 cup sugar
½ cup white corn syrup
1 cup raw peanuts
½ tsp. vanilla
3 Tbsp. butter
1 tsp. soda

Combine sugar, syrup and peanuts in a large cast iron skillet. Cook over high heat until sugar turns a rich golden color. Add vanilla and butter to candy. Stir fast, until butter melts. Add soda and and stir very fast. Pour immediately onto a sheet of aluminum foil or buttered cookie sheet. Let harden, then break into pieces with the handle of a knife. The last part of the recipe goes very fast. . . you should have the butter, vanilla, and soda premeasured and ready to add when it's time. Wash the skillet immediately to make clean-up easier.

DESSERTS

MOM'S CARAMEL POPCORN

2 gal. popped popcorn
2 cups brown sugar
2 sticks butter
½ cup white corn syrup
1 tsp. soda
1 tsp. salt

MAKES 2 GALLONS
Combine brown sugar, butter, syrup and salt in saucepan. Heat to boiling, continue to boil 5 minutes, stirring occasionally. Remove from heat, add soda. Mix well. Pour over popped corn, mixing well. Put into 2 large pans. Bake in 200° oven for 1 hour. Stir every 15 minutes.

FUDGE

4 cups sugar
1 stick margarine
1 large can evaporated milk
1—12 oz. pkg. chocolate chips
1 small jar marshmallow creme
1 cup chopped pecans
1 tsp. vanilla

MAKES 2-3 DOZEN
Combine sugar, margarine, and milk in saucepan. Bring to boil. Stir 5 minutes over medium heat to soft ball stage (235° on candy thermometer). Remove from heat, stir in chocolate chips. Add marshmallow creme, nuts, and vanilla. Heat until well blended. Pour into greased pan. Cool. Cut into squares.

PARTY MINTS

1 lb. powdered sugar
¼ cup butter
4 Tbsp. cream
Flavoring of your choice: vanilla, almond, peppermint, orange, lemon to taste
Coloring

MAKES 4-5 DOZEN
Soften butter and combine with sugar and cream. Add flavoring and coloring. Knead well. Press into forms.

PRALINES

1 cup brown sugar
1 cup sugar
½ tsp. soda
1/8 tsp. salt
¾ cup buttermilk
Dash of cream of tartar
2 cups pecans
2 Tbsp. butter
1 ½ tsp. vanilla

MAKES 2 DOZEN
Cook sugars, soda, salt, buttermilk and cream of tartar to softball stage (234° on candy thermometer). Add pecans and butter and cook just a minute more. Remove from heat. Add vanilla. Cool slightly and beat until creamy, but still not too thick. At this point, you must hurry, dropping them by spoonfuls on wax paper, so they do not harden before you spoon them out. These are sure to be a favorite!

ENGLISH TOFFEE

1 cup pecans, chopped
¾ cup brown sugar
½ cup butter
½ cup chocolate chips

Butter a 9 x 9 inch dish. Spread chopped pecans over bottom of dish. Heat sugar and butter to boiling, stirring constantly. Boil over medium heat for 7 minutes. Spread mixture evenly over nuts in pan. Spread with knife to flatten. Sprinkle chocolate pieces over the hot candy. When melted, spread with knife. Cut into squares while hot or break into pieces when cool. A rainy or humid day may affect the success of this recipe.

 Candies cook best in dry cool weather. Always use a wooden spoon to stir the candy, as it will help prevent crystalizing.

Preserves,
Relishes
&
Sauces

PRESERVES, RELISHES & SAUCES

BLUEBERRY-ORANGE MARMALADE

1 medium orange
1 lime or lemon
⅔ cup water
2 pints blueberries
5 cups sugar
½ bottle liquid pectin

MAKES 4 PINTS
Shred or grate orange and lime (or lemon) peel. Combine water and peel in kettle, heat to boiling. Reduce heat, cover and simmer 10 minutes, stirring occasionally. Wash blueberries, drain and mash. Cut white portion off orange and lemon and puree remaining fruit pulp in a blender. Add pulp to cooked peel mixture along with blueberries. Heat fruit mixture to boiling. Reduce heat, cover and simmer 10 minutes. Stir in sugar and heat to full rolling boil, stirring constantly. Stir in pectin, heat again to full rolling boil. Boil hard for 1 minute, stirring constantly. Remove from heat, skim. Ladle into hot jars and adjust lids. Process in boiling water bath 10 minutes.

FRANCES' JALAPENO PEPPER JELLY

¾ lb. bell pepper (2 cups) seeded, and chopped
½ lb. jalapeno peppers, fresh, or 1½ cups seeded, canned hot peppers
6½ cups sugar
1½ cups apple cider vinegar
1—6 oz. bottle liquid pectin

MAKES 4 PINTS
Remove all seeds from peppers before grinding. Grind peppers finely and add to sugar and vinegar. Save juice from ground peppers. Bring peppers, sugar and vinegar to boil and boil for 4-5 minutes. Add bottle of pectin and juice from peppers. Boil for 3 minutes. Pour into sterilized jars and seal with paraffin. This is delicious as a condiment with meat, or great with cheese and crackers. Wear gloves while preparing peppers, or your hands will burn.

PRESERVES, RELISHES & SAUCES

CHOKECHERRY JELLY

3 cups chokecherry juice
6½ cups sugar
1 bottle liquid fruit pectin

MAKES 5 PINTS
To prepare juice, place 3½ pounds chokecherries with 3 cups water in large kettle. Cover and cook 15 minutes. Place in jelly bag and squeeze out juice. Pour juice in large kettle, add sugar and stir. Bring to boil stirring constantly. Stir in pectin, bring to full rolling boil and boil hard 1 minute, stirring constantly. Remove from heat, stir, and skim for 5 minutes. Pour into hot glasses. Cover with paraffin or adjust lids and process in boiling water bath 5 minutes.

This jelly is truly a Colorado native. Chokecherry bushes flourish along the roadsides and grassland areas of the front range, providing those of us lucky enough to discover them before the birds do, a batch of beautiful purple berries just right for making this delicious jelly!

PEACH PRESERVES

1 lb. prepared peaches
¾-1 lb. sugar

MAKES 6 PINTS
To prepare fruit, select peaches at firm, ripe stage. Wash and pare the peaches. Cut into pieces and combine sugar and fruit in alternate layers in a container. Mixture can stand 8-10 hours, overnight, or add the sugar and ¼ cup water for each pound of fruit and cook at once. Stir carefully while heating to a boil. Cook until thick. Fill hot dry jars to ½ inch from top. Seal with paraffin.

PRESERVES, RELISHES & SAUCES

STRAWBERRY JAM

1 qt. strawberries
3 Tbsp. lemon juice
1 qt. sugar

MAKES 2 PINTS
Combine strawberries and lemon juice in kettle. Boil 3 minutes. Add sugar and bring to rolling boil. Boil 9 minutes. Pour into shallow pan. Skim off foam. Lay clean tea towel or cheesecloth over top of pan. Let set, stirring occasionally for 24 hours. Pour into sterilized jars and seal with wax.

CHILI SAUCE

4 qts. ripe tomatoes,
  peeled and chopped
1 cup white onion,
  finely ground
1 cup green pepper,
  finely ground
1 cup sweet red peppers,
  finely ground
2 cups sugar
2 Tbsp. salt
¼ tsp. cayenne pepper
1 Tbsp. whole cloves
3—3 inch sticks whole
  cinnamon
1 Tbsp. mustard seed
3 cups vinegar

MAKES 5 PINTS
Wash vegetables thoroughly. Remove seeds and white portions from peppers before chopping. Combine vegetables, sugar, salt and cayenne in heavy pan. Place over low heat and stir until sugar is dissolved. Cook slowly, stirring occasionally, about 2 hours or until mixture thickens. Add spices, tied in a square of cheesecloth, and vinegar. Cook, stirring occasionally until very thick, about 30 minutes. Remove cheesecloth bag. Pour immediately into hot sterilized jars. Adjust lids and process in boiling water bath 15 minutes. Good on roast beef or hamburgers.

 A simple way to handle the melting of paraffin is to have a permanent paraffin cup or small coffee can in which paraffin is always kept. While jellying, put the cup in a pan of water over low heat. Add new paraffin as needed. When jelly making is completed, let the paraffin harden in the cup. Put in a plastic bag and store with canning equipment.

PRESERVES, RELISHES & SAUCES

CHUTNEY

12 medium apples,
  unpeeled and diced
6 medium green tomatoes,
  diced
1 cup onion, chopped
1 cup green pepper,
  chopped
1 lb. raisins
1 qt. cider vinegar
3 cups brown sugar
3 Tbsp. mustard seed
2 Tbsp. ground ginger
2 tsp. salt
2 tsp. allspice

MAKES 10 PINTS
Combine all ingredients in large kettle. Simmer slowly for 1-1½ hours or until thick. Stir frequently and watch closely at end as it burns easily. Ladle into hot jars; adjust lids. Process in boiling water bath 5 minutes. This is exceptional poured over a brick of cream cheese and served as an appetizer with crackers. Also good on turkey or chicken sandwiches.

POOSE'S CHOW-CHOW

2 large heads cabbage
  (about 8 lbs.)
¼ bushel green tomatoes
  (about 12 lbs.)
6-7 large bell peppers
5-6 large onions
1 cup (or more if you
  prefer) hot green peppers
1 gal. vinegar (white)
5 cups sugar
½ cup salt
1 tsp. allspice
1 tsp. celery seed
1 tsp. alum
1 tsp. turmeric
1 Tbsp. dry mustard
2 Tbsp. pickling spices
½ tsp. ground cloves

MAKES 15-20 PINTS
Grind first five ingredients. Place on a large dish towel and sprinkle with salt. Tie corners of towel together to make a bag. Let stand in the sink for about 2 hours. Tie pickling spices in a cheesecloth bag. Put the bagged spices in bottom of large Dutch oven, and add all other ingredients. If necessary, add enough water to cover the vegetables. Cook about 25 minutes, stirring occasionally. Keep chow-chow at near boiling while filling the hot sterilized jars. Adjust lids and process in boiling water bath 15 minutes. This is a great relish for hot dogs, roast beef, tuna fish, and especially dabbed on top of Cowboy Beans!

 Always wear rubber gloves when working with jalapeno peppers or hot chili peppers. The juice from the peppers will burn your hands.

PRESERVES, RELISHES & SAUCES

GREEN TOMATO RELISH

½ bushel green tomatoes
(48-56 medium)
12 green bell peppers,
seeded
12 red bell peppers,
seeded
6-8 white onions
2 qts. cider vinegar
1 qt. white vinegar
7 cups sugar
½ cup salt
1 cup mustard seed (10 oz.)
3 Tbsp. celery seed
1 Tbsp. cinnamon
1 Tbsp. allspice

MAKES 15-20 PINTS
Grind the vegetables together. A food processor works great. Drain off liquid, using a collander. Put vegetables in large kettle. Add 2 quarts vinegar. Boil 30 minutes, stirring frequently. Drain very well. Add 1 quart vinegar, sugar, salt, and spices. Simmer 3 minutes, pack in hot jars, adjust lids and process in boiling water bath 15 minutes. This is very good on roast beef, but serves the purpose of any good relish. Makes great Christmas presents!

ZUCCHINI RELISH

10 cups finely chopped
zucchini (can also be
grated)
4 cups finely chopped
onion
2 green peppers, chopped
2 red peppers, chopped
(or 1 jar pimentos)
⅓ cup salt
¼ tsp. turmeric
1 tsp. nutmeg
1 tsp. celery seed
1 tsp. pepper
1 Tbsp. cornstarch
2½ cups vinegar
4½ cups sugar

MAKES 6 PINTS
Combine zucchini, onion, green pepper, red pepper and salt in large cooker or canner. Mix well and let stand overnight. Drain and rinse well with cold water. Add remaining ingredients and boil 20-30 minutes. Ladle into hot jars and adjust lids. Process in boiling water bath 15 minutes.

PRESERVES, RELISHES & SAUCES

PICKLED BEETS

2 cups sugar
2 cups water
2 cups vinegar
1 tsp. cloves
1 tsp. allspice
1 Tbsp. cinnamon
15-20 small to medium
   beets

MAKES 5 PINTS

Remove beet tops, leaving roots and about 1 inch of stem. Cover with boiling water and cook until tender. Remove skins and slice beets. The small beets can be pickled whole or can be chunked. Combine liquid, sugar, and spices. Heat to boiling. Add beets and simmer 5 minutes. Pack beets and juice into hot jars. Adjust lids. Process in boiling water bath 30 minutes.

BREAD 'N BUTTER PICKLES

4 qts. cucumbers, sliced
⅓ cup salt
6 medium onions, sliced
   (6 cups)
2 green peppers,
   chopped (1⅔ cup)
3 cloves garlic
3 cups cider vinegar
5 cups sugar
1½ tsp. celery seed
2 Tbsp. mustard seed
1½ tsp. turmeric

MAKES 8 PINTS

Combine cucumbers, onion, green pepper and garlic cloves. Add salt and mix gently. Cover with ice, mix well and let stand 3 hours. Drain well, and remove garlic. Combine remaining ingredients in a large kettle. Boil 10 minutes. Add cucumber mixture to liquid and bring to boiling point. Pack loosely in hot jars; adjust lids. Process in boiling water bath 15 minutes. Note: If you have ½ bushel of cucumbers to pickle, you must quadruple (4x) this recipe.

PRESERVES, RELISHES & SAUCES

CONWAY SPRINGS DILL PICKLES

¼ bushel pickling
  cucumbers
Fresh dill
1 qt. white vinegar
2 qts. water
¾ cup pickling salt
1 Tbsp. alum

MAKES 10 QUARTS

Slice clean cucumbers lengthwise or leave smaller ones whole. Combine vinegar, water, salt, and alum; heat to boiling. Place 3-4 heads of fresh dill in the bottom of clean, hot sterilized jar. Pack pickles standing, tightly as possible, adding 2-3 heads of fresh dill on top. Pour the boiling hot vinegar mixture to cover. Adjust lids and process in boiling water bath 10 minutes. If pickling a few jars at a time, as cucumbers ripen, save the vinegar mixture and reheat it for the next batch. To get a good dill flavor in these pickles, don't open them for at least six weeks after canning.

HOMEMADE V-8 JUICE

7 cups water
½ bushel of tomatoes
1 red beet, peeled and
  quartered
2 carrots, cut in quarters
1 green pepper, quartered
6 onions, quartered
4 Tbsp. salt
¾ cup sugar
¼ cup lemon juice
6 stalks celery
¼ cup vinegar

MAKES 4 QUARTS

Combine all ingredients in large kettle. Let simmer for 2 hours. Run mixture through juicer. Heat juice to boiling and ladle into hot jars; adjust lids. Process in boiling bath 10 minutes.

Subscriber's Privilege Certificate

This certificate entitles bearer to receive Dressage Today at a savings of over $111 off the newsstand price.

☐ 12 issues just $19.95 - Save $51.93! ☐ 24 issues just $31.95 - Save $111.81!

Name _____

Address _____

City/State/Zip _____

E-mail _____ To contact you about your subscription, events and special offers.
                    ☐ Bill me ☐ Payment enclosed

Satisfaction guaranteed or your money back.

For faster service log on to: **save-big.equisearch.com/dressagetoday**

5J5EW

Savings based on annual cover price of $71.88. Canadian orders add $12.00 per year (includes GST). Foreign orders add $24.00 per year. Payment in U.S. currency must accompany all Canadian and foreign orders. Please allow 6-8 weeks for receipt of first issue.

BUSINESS REPLY MAIL
FIRST-CLASS MAIL   PERMIT NO 180   FLAGLER BEACH FL

POSTAGE WILL BE PAID BY ADDRESSEE

Dressage
T O D A Y

PO BOX 420046
PALM COAST   FL   32142-8544

PRESERVES, RELISHES & SAUCES

♥ ♥ ♥ ♥ ♥ ♥ ♥ ♥ ♥ ♥ ♥ ♥ ♥ ♥ ♥ ♥

CREAM CHEESE SAUCE

½ cup milk
8 oz. cream cheese
¼ cup Parmesan cheese
½ Tbsp. onion salt

MAKES 1 ½ CUPS
Warm milk in saucepan. Add cubed cream cheese. Let melt, stirring often. Add Parmesan cheese and onion salt. Delicious on asparagus.

HOLLANDAISE SAUCE

2 egg yolks
2½-3 Tbsp. lemon juice
½ cup cold butter

MAKES 1 CUP
Combine egg yolk and lemon juice in small saucepan. Mix briskly. Add cube of butter whole, do not cut up. Stir over low heat until thickened. Serve immediately. If it looks curdled instead of creamy and smooth, beat vigorously over low heat again.

STEAK BUTTER

1 pint sour cream
1 carton (8 oz.) whipped butter
2-3 Tbsp. minced parsley
¼ tsp. garlic powder
2 Tbsp. chives, chopped
Salt and pepper

MAKES 2 CUPS
Mix all ingredients thoroughly and refrigerate. Remove from refrigerator at least 1 hour before serving. This can be frozen and re-frozen easily. If frozen, let thaw and whip before using. To use, plop one or more tablespoons over steaks while they are hot. Also good on baked potatoes.

PRESERVES, RELISHES & SAUCES

HICKORY BARBECUE SAUCE

1—20 oz. bottle ketchup
½ cup water
¼ cup cider vinegar
1 Tbsp. packed brown
  sugar
1 Tbsp. Worcestershire
  sauce
1 tsp. salt
1 tsp. onion powder
½ tsp. liquid smoke
1/8 tsp. garlic powder

MAKES 3 CUPS
Blend all ingredients in blender or food processor until smooth. Store in refrigerator. Use on ribs, chicken, pork chops, or beef brisket. Also good on sandwiches. Keep this on hand.

TARTAR SAUCE

1 cup mayonnaise
¼ cup dill pickles, chopped
1 Tbsp. chopped pimento
2 Tbsp. grated onion
2 tsp. vinegar
1 tsp. sugar
½ tsp. Tabasco

MAKES 1½ CUPS
Combine all ingredients. Mix well and refrigerate. Serve with fish.

JEZEBEL SAUCE

1—6 oz. jar prepared
  mustard
1—6 oz. jar prepared
  horseradish
1—8 oz. or 10 oz. jar apple
  jelly
1—8 oz. or 10 oz. jar
  pineapple preserves

Mix all ingredients together. No cooking necessary. This sauce is especially good with ham, or poured over cream cheese and served with crackers as an appetizer. Makes a really nice gift, too.

PRESERVES, RELISHES & SAUCES

♥ ♥ ♥ ♥ ♥ ♥ ♥ ♥ ♥ ♥ ♥ ♥ ♥ ♥ ♥ ♥ ♥

THE NEIGHBORS' SAUCY HAM SAUCE

1 cup sour cream
1 Tbsp. horseradish
2 Tbsp. prepared mustard

Add horseradish and mustard to sour cream. So good with ham!

BRANDIED MUSHROOM SAUCE

1 cup whipping cream
3 Tbsp. butter or margarine
2 green onions, chopped
2 cups sliced, fresh
  mushrooms
2 Tbsp. brandy
Salt
Pepper

MAKES 2 CUPS
In a small pan bring unwhipped cream to boil. Stirring constantly, continue to boil about 5 minutes until cream thickens. Remove from heat. Melt butter. Add onions and saute a few minutes until onions are transparent. Add mushrooms. Cook over moderate heat about 4 minutes, stirring constantly. Add brandy and cream. Mix lightly but thoroughly. Add salt and pepper to taste. Heat to serving temperature. Serve as a sauce with sliced, roast turkey or Cornish hens.

Kids' Food

SILLY SALLY SALAD

Body . . . . canned peach half
Arms and legs . . . . small celery sticks
Head . . . . half of a hard cooked egg
Eyes, nose, shoes, buttons . . . . raisins
Mouth . . . . red hot cinnamon candy
Hair . . . . grated yellow cheese
Skirt . . . . piece of lettuce

CELERY BOATS

Celery stalks
Peanut butter
Cream cheese
Pimento cheese
Raisins
Nuts

Clean celery stalks and cut into 2-3 inch lengths. Spread the filling of your choice into each. Top with raisins or nuts.

SUPERMAN STEAK

Make a beef patty, using lean ground beef. Broil, pan fry or grill outside. When done, add cheese and ketchup to make the "Superman" logo. You will be the "Super Hero" with your kids!!!

KIDS' FOOD

COTTONTAIL SALAD

1 chilled pear half
Raisins
1 red hot candy
2 blanched almonds
1 tsp. cottage cheese
2 toothpicks, broken
    in half
Lettuce leaves

Place pear center-down on a bed of lettuce. Add raisins for eyes, red hot for nose, toothpicks for whiskers, almonds for ears, and cottage cheese for tail.

PLUM DELICIOUS CASSEROLE

1 lb. ground beef
1 can cream of chicken
** soup**
½ can water
1—16 oz. pkg. frozen
** Tater Tots**

Brown ground beef. Drain fat. Place in large casserole. Cover with cream of chicken soup, diluted with ½ can water. Place frozen Tater Tots over top and bake uncovered at 350° for 1 hour. Kids like to make and eat this recipe.

SANDWICH IDEAS

Spread 2 slices of bread with butter or cream cheese. Using a cookie cutter, cut each sandwich into shapes. On Valentine's Day, tint the cream cheese with red food coloring, cut each sandwich into the shape of a heart.

Puree peanut butter and banana together, spread on two pieces of bread. Cut sandwich into quarters. Surprise each child with an animal cracker riding atop his sandwich!

PIGS IN THE BLANKET

Pork sausage links or
** hot dogs**
Refrigerated prepared
** biscuits**

Brown sausage or hot dogs. Drain and cool. Roll each biscuit flat, then wrap around sausage. Bake on a cookie sheet at 450° for 10-12 minutes.

 Hairspray removes ballpoint ink. Spray it directly on the surface then wipe away with warm sudsy water.

KIDS' FOOD

ONE MINUTE DONUTS

1 tube of refrigerator
   biscuits
Oil for cooking
Frosting or sugar

MAKES 10
Heat oil to 375°. Poke hole in center of biscuit. Deep fry to a golden brown on both sides. Roll in sugar or frost. Quick and easy. Great breakfast treat for kids.

FRENCH TOAST

1 egg
½ tsp. sugar
1 slice bread

SERVES 1
With fork, beat egg and sugar in pie pan. Dip bread in egg to coat both sides well. Fry in buttered skillet over medium-low heat to lightly brown both sides. Top with butter, powdered sugar, and pancake syrup.

BULL'S EYE EGGS

1 slice bread
1 egg
Butter

SERVES 1
Cut out center of a slice of bread with a biscuit cutter. Butter bread on both sides, then brown one side of bread in moderately hot buttered frying pan. Turn over, then drop egg in center of toast. Cook slowly until egg white is set.

SHERBET FLOAT

Put 1-2 scoops sherbet (your choice of flavors, orange is good) in a tall glass. Pour 7-Up to cover.

STRAWBERRY SODA

Put 2 scoops vanilla ice cream in a tall glass. Pour in strawberry soda to cover.

BOB'S CHOCOLATE SODA

2 Tbsp. chocolate syrup
¼ cup club soda
1-2 large scoops vanilla
  ice cream
¼ cup club soda

SERVES 1
Mix syrup and club soda in a tall glass. Add ice cream. Pour in more soda. Stir to blend and serve at once.

SPARKLING FRUIT PUNCH

2 pkgs. strawberry Koolaid
2 cups sugar
1 can frozen orange juice
  concentrate
1 can frozen lemonade
  concentrate
3-4 qts. water
1 pint ginger ale

Mix ingredients and add 1 pint ginger ale just before serving. Can also use lime Koolaid.

KIDS' FOOD

♥ ♥ ♥ ♥ ♥ ♥ ♥ ♥ ♥ ♥ ♥ ♥ ♥ ♥ ♥ ♥ ♥

YOGURT SUNDAE

Yogurt (your choice of flavor)
Fresh fruit
Honey
Nuts
Maraschino cherry

Freeze the yogurt. Scoop out into an ice cream dish. Add fresh fruit, then honey. Sprinkle with nuts. Top with a maraschino cherry.

ICE CREAM CLOWNS

Place a round scoop ice cream on a piece of cake. Put an ice cream cone upside down on top of the ice cream for a hat. Make a face with cherries, pecan halves for ears, and decorate hat with whipped cream rosettes.

❤ ❤ ❤ ❤ ❤ ❤ ❤❤ ❤ ❤ ❤ ❤ ❤ ❤ ❤ ❤ ❤

PARTY ICE CREAM CONE CAKES

1 Jiffy cake mix, any flavor
12-15 ice cream cones
Frosting

MAKES 12-15
Prepare cake as directed on the box. Spoon batter into cones ½-¾ full. Bake at 350° for 15 minutes or until done. Frost and decorate to fit the occasion.

RAINBOW ICE

Freeze cranberry juice, grape juice, orange juice or left-over juices and syrups from canned fruits in ice cube trays. Sparkle up your lemonade with these ice cube treats!

POPCORN BALLS

40 large marshmallows
¼ cup butter
8-10 cups popped popcorn
Food coloring, optional

MAKES 1 DOZEN
Melt marshmallows and butter over low heat. Add food coloring and mix well. Pour popped corn in large bowl or roasting pan. Pour marshmallow mixture over popcorn while stirring. Mix well to coat all of the corn. Butter your hands and form popcorn mixture into balls.

PUDDING POPS

Combine 1 large package instant pudding with 3 cups of milk. Mix only enough to blend well. Quickly pour into popsicle molds and freeze.

KIDS' FOOD

WHITE CHOCOLATE PRETZELS

**1 pkg. vanilla flavored
  Candiquik
1 pkg. pretzels**

Melt Candiquik in top of double boiler. (Water must be very hot, but not boiling). Remove from heat when melted and dip pretzels in to cover. Set on waxed paper until cool.

S'MORES

**Graham crackers
Marshmallows
Hershey's chocolate bars**

Set 4 squares of candy bar on a graham cracker. Toast a marshmallow, then slip it on chocolate and top with a second graham cracker. Eat like a sandwich. You'll be sure to want s'more!

HAYSTACKS

**1 cup chow mein noodles
1—6 oz. pkg. butterscotch
  chips (may substitute
  chocolate chips)
½ cup chopped nuts or
  salted peanuts**

MAKES 15
Melt chips in microwave or in top of a double boiler. Remove from heat and stir in noodles and nuts. Mix well and drop by teaspoonfuls on greased cookie sheet or waxed paper. Let stand until firm.

TRAIL MIX SNACK

**1—15 oz. box seedless
  raisins
1—12 oz. can Spanish
  peanuts
1—12 oz. pkg. milk
  chocolate chips (may
  substitute carob chips)**

Mix the ingredients together for a high energy, nutritious snack.

♥ ♥ ♥ ♥ ♥ ♥ ♥ ♥ ♥ ♥ ♥ ♥ ♥ ♥ ♥ ♥

E.T. COOKIES

1 cup sugar
1 cup light corn syrup
1 cup peanut butter
5 cups Rice Krispies

ICING:
1—6 oz. pkg. chocolate
   chips
½ cup powdered sugar
2 Tbsp. butter
1 Tbsp. water

MAKES 2 DOZEN
Boil 1 minute the sugar, corn syrup and peanut butter. Stir in Rice Krispies, then press into a buttered 9 x 13 inch pan. Melt chocolate chips in small saucepan with butter and water. Combine with powdered sugar and mix well. Spread on top of Rice Krispies. Cut into squares.

ONE-PAN GRAHAM-BANANA SQUARES

1¼ cups graham cracker
   crumbs
½ cup wheat germ
2 Tbsp. packed brown
   sugar
½ tsp. baking soda
Dash of salt
1 cup mashed bananas
   (2 medium)
⅓ cup peanut butter
2 Tbsp. oil
1 cup semi-sweet chocolate
   chips

MAKES 16
In a 9-inch square baking pan, mix crumbs, wheat germ, sugar, soda and salt. Add bananas, peanut butter, and oil which have been blended together (a food processor will do the trick). Mix until thoroughly blended, using a fork, spatula or your fingers. The dough will be thick. Press evenly into the pan, sprinkle with chocolate chips, and bake at 350° for 30 minutes. Cool and cut in 2-inch squares. This cookie is highly nutritious, easy for kids to make, and an all time favorite.

 Spray your measuring cup with Pam before measuring corn syrup—it will all pour out easily.

KIDS' FOOD

♥ ♥ ♥ ♥ ♥ ♥ ♥ ♥ ♥ ♥ ♥ ♥ ♥ ♥ ♥ ♥ ♥

DOUG'S CHEESEY PRETZELS

1½ cups flour
⅔ cup milk
½ cup cheddar cheese,
   shredded
2 Tbsp. butter or margarine
2 tsp. baking powder
1 tsp. sugar
1 tsp. salt
1 egg, beaten
Coarse salt, onion salt, or
   garlic salt

MAKES 16
Beat first seven ingredients with a fork until well mixed. Divide dough into 16 parts. Make "snakes" with your hands, then form into pretzel shapes or whatever shape you like. Lay carefully on a greased cookie sheet, brush with beaten egg, sprinkle lightly with salt, and bake at 400° for 20 minutes or until golden brown. This is a yummy and nutritious "snake-up" snack. Easy and fun for kids to make and eat!

CHRISTMAS WREATHS

¼ cup butter
1—16 oz. pkg. marsh-
   mallows (40 large
   marshmallows)
5 cups corn flakes
Green food coloring
Cinnamon candies

MAKES 2 DOZEN
Melt butter and marshmallows in large saucepan over low heat, stirring constantly. Remove from heat. Add green food coloring. Mix well. Add corn flakes, mix with melted marshmallows. Shape into small wreaths on wax paper. Place several hot cinnamon candies on wreath for decoration.

240

GINGER COOKIE DOUGH
(for Gingerbread Men)

1 cup shortening
1 cup brown sugar, packed
1 Tbsp. cinnamon
1 Tbsp. ginger
1 cup dark corn syrup
2 eggs
5½ cups flour
1½ tsp. baking soda

ICING:
2 cups powdered sugar
½ tsp. vanilla
2 Tbsp. milk

In a large bowl, cream shortening with brown sugar, cinnamon and ginger until fluffy. Beat in corn syrup and eggs until well-blended. Mix 2 cups flour with baking soda; beat into creamed mixture. Stir in remaining 3½ cups flour, working with hands if necessary to get a smooth dough. Wrap airtight; chill overnight. Roll chilled dough to ¼ inch thickness and cut into desired shapes. Decorate with raisins or red hots, and bake at 375° for 10 minutes. Ice when cooled.

Mix all icing ingredients until smooth and of desired consistency. You can color the icing at this point, or put it in a decorator's tube to outline the gingerbread boys.

JACK-O-LANTERN PIZZAS

4 English muffins, split
1 Tbsp. vegetable oil
1—8 oz. can pizza sauce
8 slices (3½x3½ in.)
    mozzarella cheese

MAKES 8

Place split muffins on a baking sheet. Brush top of each muffin with a little oil. Broil muffins until they are light brown. Remove from oven. Measure one generous tablespoonful of pizza sauce onto each muffin. Spread evenly. Trim corners from cheese slices to make circles. Cut out a jack-o'-lantern face on each circle with a paring knife. Place 1 cheese face on each pizza muffin. Bake pizzas at 400° until the cheese melts, about 8 minutes. This is a fun party treat for Halloween. Can be made ahead and frozen.

PLAY DOUGH

1½ cups salt
3 cups flour
6 Tbsp. cream of tartar
3 cups water
6 Tbsp. oil
Food coloring

Combine all ingredients in large saucepan. Color with food coloring. Mix well and stir over low heat until it feels like "play dough."

EGG YOLK PAINT
(for decorating sugar cookies)

1 egg yolk
¼ tsp. water
Food coloring

Blend well egg yolk and water. Divide mixture among cups in a muffin tin. Add a different food coloring to each cup to make bright colors. Paint designs on cookies with small paintbrushes. If the egg yolk paint thickens, add a few drops of water to thin.

Try removing crayon marks from the wall with toothpaste. It works great.

EQUIVALENT MEASURES

3 teaspoons = 1 tablespoon
16 tablespoons = 1 cup
2 cups = 1 pint
4 cups = 1 quart
2 pints = 1 quart
4 quarts (liquid) = 1 gallon
4 tablespoons = ¼ cup
5⅓ tablespoons = ⅓ cup
1 cup = 8 fluid ounces
pinch or dash is less than 1/8 teaspoon
2 tablespoons = 1 fluid ounce
1 pound = 16 ounces

Substitutions

1 tablespoon cornstarch (for thickening) = 2 tablespoon flour (approximately).

1 cup sifted all-purpose flour = 1 cup plus 2 tablespoons sifted cake flour.

1 square chocolate (oz.) = 3-4 tablespoons cocoa plus ½ tablespoon shortening.

1 teaspoon baking powder = ¼ teaspoon baking soda plus ½ teaspoon cream of tartar.

1 cup bottled milk = ½ cup evaporated milk plus ½ cup water.

1 cup sour milk = 1 cup sweet milk into which 1 tablespoon vinegar or lemon juice has been stirred; or 1 cup buttermilk.

1 cup sweet milk = 1 cup sour milk or buttermilk plus ½ teaspoon baking soda.

1 cup molasses = 1 cup honey.

1 cup sour cream = 1 cup evaporated milk plus 1 tablespoon vinegar or lemon juice.

1 whole egg = 2 egg yolks plus 1 tablespoon water (in cookies) or 2 egg yolks (in custards and similar mixtures).

1 tablespoon fresh herbs = 1 tsp. dry herbs.

1/8 teaspoon garlic powder = 1 small pressed clove of garlic.

1 cup fine crumbs = 24 saltine crackers, 4 slices bread, or 14 squares graham crackers.

INDEX

A

ACCOMPANIMENTS
Blueberry-Orange Marmalade 218
Brandied Mushroom Sauce 227
Bread 'n Butter Pickles 223
Chili Sauce .220
Chokecherry Jelly 219
Chutney 221
Cinnamon Apples 82
Conway Springs Dill Pickles 224
Cream Cheese Sauce 225
Fried Apple Rings 163
Frances' Jalapeno Pepper Jelly 218
Green Tomato Relish 222
Hickory Barbecue Sauce 226
Hollandaise Sauce 225
Homemade V-8 Juice 224
Hot Curried Fruit 163
Jezebel Sauce 226
Johnny Appleseed Turkey Stuffing . . .137
Mary's Scalloped Oysters 138
Neighbor's Ham Sauce, The 227
Peach Preserves 219
Pickled Beets 223
Poose's Chow Chow 221
Strawberry Jam 220
Steak Butter 225
Tartar Sauce 226
Zucchini Relish 222
Alice's Nut Goodie Bars 213
Almond-Broccoli Casserole 148
April Shower Ice Cream Punch 16
APPETIZERS
Cherry Tomato Hors D'oeuvres 14
Chocolate Dipped Strawberries 15
Cream Cheese Burritos 14
Dips
Bubbly Broccoli Dip 4
Caramel Apple Dip 6
Chili Con Queso 2
Creamy Artichoke-Cheese Dip 3
Curry Dip for Raw Vegetables 5
Deviled Ham Puffs 8
Dilled Crab Dip 5
Easy Guacamole 93
Enchilada Dip 3
Fresh Fruit Dip 4
Good 'n Easy Guacamole 4
Shellfish Dip 2
Smoked Oyster Dip 6
Sombrero Spread 5
Spinach Dip 6
Tom's Famous Dip 2
Easy Cheeseball 13
Hot Crab Miniatures 12
Howdy Potatoes 9
Judy's Green Chili Pie 12
People Pleasin' Cheeseballs 13
Quick Stuffed Mushrooms 7
Sausage Biscuits 12
Shrimp Ball 10
Spinach Appetizers 9

Spreads
Best of the West Spread 11
Cheese & Bacon Hot Ryes 8
Cheesy Pineapple Spread 13
Kathleen's Chutney Delight 14
Mama White's Chicken Liver Pate 10
Party Rye Spreads 11
Shrimp Ball 10
Sombrero Spread 5
Swiss Ryes 5
Stuffed Mushrooms with Bacon 7
Vegetable Crisps 10
Water Chestnuts & Bacon Rollups 8
Apple Bread 48
Apple Cake, Fresh 168
Apples, Cinnamon 82
Apple Crisp 199
Apple Muffins 56
Apple Pie .193
Apple Rings, Fried 163
Apricot Bread 48
Apricot Fried Pies, Aunt Ginger's 192
Apricot Sours 180
Artichoke-Cheese Dip, Creamy 3
Artichoke Rice Salad 92
Asparagus with Cream Cheese 32
Aspic, Sarah's Tomato 87
Aspic, Zingy V-8 86
Aunt Ginger's Apricot Fried Pies 192
Aunt Vernon's Date Cookies 182

B

Baking Powder Biscuits 60
Baked Trout 141
Banana-Berry Gelatin Salad 76
Banana Bread 49
Banana Crepes 200
Banana Fruit Punch 16
Banana Pudding 201
Bar L Rolls .67
Barbecue Sauce, Hickory 226
Barbecued Brisket or Ribs 100
Barbecued Fish 140
Bars, Chocomint 187
Bars, Oatmeal and Apple Butter 188
Bars, Peggy's Lemon 188
Bars, Praline 189
Bars, Pumpkin 189
BEANS
Bean Salad 85
Buttery Italian Green Beans 146
Country Style Green Beans 145
Cowboy Beans 144
Darn Good Beans 120
Epicurean Green Beans 145
Grandmother's Island Bean Casserole .147
Green Bean Casserole 147
Green Beans Caesar 148
Ham 'n Beans 119
Lentil Soup 35
Macaroni, Mushrooms and Gr. Beans . .165

245

Marinated Green Beans 85
Mary's Baked Beans 144
Rocky Mountain Soup 38
Sweet and Sour Beans 146

BEEF
Barbecued Brisket or Ribs 100
Beef and Eggs, Chipped 27
Beef Enchiladas 115
Beef Jerky 105
Best Ever Pot Roast 102
Chicken Fried Steak and Cream Gravy . 104
Corned Beef and Cabbage 105
Corny Sandwich Squares 108
Easy Beef Stroganoff 103
Eggplant Parmesan 117
Fancy Tostadas 116
French Bread and Meat Sandwich 43
French Dip 44
Glorified Hamburgers 43
Golden Beef Casserole 109
Green Chili Burritos 114
Hamburger-Sour Cream Casserole . . . 109
Hearty Hodgepodge 106
Joanie's Marinated Grilled Steak 100
Lasagna 118
Lazy Lady Stew 106
Meat Loaf 110
Plum Delicious Casserole 233
Porcupine Meatballs 111
Reubens 44
Salisbury Steak 112
Shepherd's Pie 112
Shish-Ka-Bob 103
Sloppy Joes 44
Steak and Potatoes 104
Steak Diana 101
Sukiyaki 122
Superman Steak 231
Swiss Steak 102
Tamale Pie 116
Texas Hash 110
Texas Red Chili 113
Unattended Rib Roast 101
West of the Pecos 113
Zelda's Cabbage Rolls 107
Beer Bread 63
Beer Cheese Soup 32
Beets, Pickled 223
Beignets, New Orleans Doughnuts 55
Best Ever Greens 152
Best Ever Pot Roast 102
Best Ever Thumb Print Cookies 186
Best Irish Soda Bread 72
Best of the West Spread 11

BEVERAGES
April Shower Ice Cream Punch 16
Banana Fruit Punch 16
Bloody Marys 20
Bob's Chocolate Soda 235
Bonnie's Orange Juliana 17
Creamy Koolaid Punch 16
Daddy's Egg Nog 19
Frozen Daiquiri 21
Fruit Smoothy 17
Golden Wassail 19

Holiday Punch 19
Homemade V-8 Juice 224
Hot Apple Cider 17
Hot Buttered Cider 18
Hot Chocolate 18
Mexican Hot Chocolate 18
Orange Slush 16
Sangria 20
Sherbet Float 235
Skier's Delight 21
Sparkling Fruit Punch 235
Spiced Tea 20
Strawberry Soda 235
Sure Bet Punch 17
Bing Cherry Gelatin Salad 79
Birdie in the Bag 126
Biscuits, Baking Powder 60
Biscuits, Texas Buttermilk 70
Black Bottom Cupcakes 168
Black-Eyed Peas, Southern Style 154
Blarney Stones 169
Bloody Marys 20
Blueberry Muffins 56
Blueberry-Orange Marmalade 218
Blueberry Salad 78
Blueberry Salad, Red, White 76
Bob and Gayle's Spaghetti 117
Bob's Chocolate Soda 235
Bonnie's Orange Juliana 17
Braided Potato Bread 68
Brandied Mushroom Sauce 227
Bread 'n Butter Pickles 223

BREADS
Quick Breads
Apple Bread 48
Apricot Bread 48
Banana Bread 49
Cherry Bread 49
Date and Nut Bread 50
Pineapple Carrot Bread 50
Rhubarb Tea Bread 51
Zucchini Bread 51

Muffins
Apple Muffins 56
Blueberry Muffins 56
Cinnamon-Sugar Muffins 56
Oatmeal Muffins 57
Orange Muffins 57
Orange-Honey Surprise Muffins 58
Pineapple Muffins 58
Raisin Bran Muffins 59

Yeast Breads
Bar L Rolls 67
Braided Potato Bread 68
Butterscotch Rolls 61
Cracked Wheat Bread 67
Cream Cheese Sweet Rolls 62
Croissants 69
Easy Breakfast Cinnamon Bread 60
Eileen's Monkey Bread 63
Kathi's Dilly Bread 73
Mama Lang's Cinnamon Rolls 64
Onion Bread 72
Orange Rolls 61
Sourdough Bread and Starter 66

246

Texas Buttermilk Biscuits 70
Whole Wheat Bread 65

Other

Baking Powder Biscuits 60
Beer Bread 63
Best Irish Soda Bread 72
Chocolate Chip Coffee Ring 53
Easy Bubble Bread 52
Grandma Eaton's Coffee Cake 54
Grandma White's Purple Plum Buckle . . 52
Homestyle Cornbread 70
Hush Puppies 71
Mexican Corn Bread 71
New Orleans Doughnuts 55
One Minute Doughnuts 59
Orange Coffee Cake 53
Sopapillas 55
Swedish Pancakes 54
Brisket, or Ribs, Barbecued 100
Broccoli and Carrots, Stir Fried 149
Broccoli Casserole, Almond 148
Broccoli-Cauliflower Casserole 149
Broccoli Dip, Bubbly 4
Broccoli Soup 33
Broccoli with Walnuts 150
Broiled Tomatoes 161
Brownie Pudding Cake 169
Brownies, Everybody's Favorite 187
Bubble Bread, Easy 52
Bubbly Broccoli Dip 4
Bull's Eye Eggs 234
Burritos, Green Chili 114
Butter, Steak 225
Butter Sugar Cookies 181
Buttermilk Pie, Dixie's 193
Butterscotch Rolls 61
Buttery Italian Green Beans 146

C

Cabbage, Creamed 150
Cabbage Patch Cole Slaw 87
Cabbage Rolls, Zelda's 107
Cacciatore, Chicken 127

CAKES

Black Bottom Cupcakes 168
Blarney Stones 169
Brownie Pudding Cake 169
Carrot Cake 170
Chocolate Chip Cake 171
Chocolate Pound Cake 172
Chocolate Sheet Cake 170
Cookie Cake 176
Creamy Layered Chocolate Mint Cake . 172
Dee's Yellow Coconut Cake 175
Eileen's Italian Cream Cake 176
Fresh Apple Cake 168
German Chocolate Cake 174
Lemon Pudding Cake 177
Mississippi Mud Cake 177
Mocha Balls 178
Moist Coconut Cake 175
Mother Link's 7-Up Pound Cake 179
Orange Kiss Me Cake 178
Party Ice Cream Cone Cakes 237

Pineapple Upside-Down Cake 179
Poppy Seed Cake 174
Quick Chocolate-Cherry Cake 171
Spiced Chocolate-Zucchini Cake 173
Strawberry Cake 180

CANDY

Alice's Nut Goodie Bars 213
English Toffee 215
Freda's Peanut Brittle 213
Fudge 214
Mom's Caramel Popcorn 214
Party Mints 214
Pecan Millionaires 213
Popcorn Balls 237
Pralines 215
White Chocolate Pretzels 238
Caramel Apple Dip 6
Caramel Popcorn, Mom's 214
Caraway Crabmeat Sandwich 40
Carol's Date Pudding 204
Carrot Cake 170
Carrot, Copper Salad 86
Carrot Soup, Cream of 33
Cathy's Paris Potatoes 158
Cattlemen's Club Twice Baked Potatoes . 158
Cauliflower Casserole, Broccoli 149
Cauliflower, Pea Salad 84
Cauliflower, Salad 84
Celery Boats 231

CHEESE & EGGS (See EGGS & CHEESE)

Cheese Blintzes 40
Cheese and Bacon Hot Ryes 8
Cheese Cake 201
Cheese Sauce for Vegetables 162
Cheeseball, Easy 13
Cheeseballs, People Pleasin' 13
Cheesy Pineapple Spread 13
Cherry Gelatin, Bing 79
Cherry Bread 49
Cherry Crunch 202
Cherry Tomato Hors D'oeuvres 14

CHICKEN

Birdie in the Bag 126
Chicken & Broccoli Crepes 131
Chicken Cacciatore 127
Chicken Divine 125
Chicken & Doughies 34
Chicken & Dressing Casserole 134
Chicken & Dumplings 129
Chicken Enchiladas 128
Chicken Noodle Casserole 129
Chicken Royale 132
Chicken Spaghetti 128
Chicken, Quail or Pheasant
   in Cream Sauce 136
Chris' Crab Stuffed Chicken 133
Cornish Game Hens 134
Easy Chicken Chow Mein 130
Fried Chicken & Gravy 124
Hot Chicken Salad 130
Judy's Wild Rice Chicken 125
Old Fashioned Chicken & Noodles . . . 135
Potato Chip Chicken 127
Potluck Chicken & Wild Rice 126
Chicken Fried Steak & Cream Gravy . . 104

247

CHILDREN'S FOOD (See KIDS' FOOD)
Chili Con Queso 2
Chili Sauce 220
Chili, Texas Red 113
Chipped Beef & Eggs 27
Chocolate Cake, German 174
Chocolate-Cherry Cake, Quick 171
Chocolate Chip Cake 171
Chocolate Chip Coffee Ring 53
Chocolate Chip Cookies, Favorite 181
Chocolate Cream Pie 194
Chocolate Dipped Strawberries 15
Chocolate, Hot 18
Chocolate, Mexican Hot 18
Chocolate Marengo 209
Chocolate Mint Cake, Creamy Layered . . 172
Chocolate Pound Cake 172
Chocolate Sauce 203
Chocolate Soda, Bob's 235
Chocolate Sheet Cake 170
Chocolate Snowballs 182
Chokecherry Jelly 219
Chow Mein, Chicken 130
Chow-Chow, Poose's 221
Chris' Crab-Stuffed Chicken 133
Christmas Eve Oyster Stew 37
Christmas Wreaths 240
Chutney 221
Chutney Delight, Kathleen's 14
Cider, Hot Buttered 18
Cider, Hot Apple 17
Cinnamon Apples 82
Cinnamon Bread, Easy Breakfast 60
Cinnamon Rolls, Mama Lang's 64
Cinnamon-Sugar Muffins 56
Clam Chowder 34
Cobbler, Peach 202
Coconut Cake, Dee's Yellow 175
Coconut Cake, Moist 175
Coconut Cream Pie 194
Coffee Cake, Grandma Eaton's 54
Coffee Cake, Orange 53
Coffee Cream Mousse 199
Coffee Ring, Chocolate Chip 53
Cole Slaw, Cabbage Patch 87
Cole Slaw, Mrs. Walker's 87
Colorado Trout 141
Company Casserole 119
Conway Springs Dill Pickles 224
COOKIES AND BARS
Apriot Sours 180
Aunt Vernon's Date Cookies 182
Best Ever Thumb Print Cookies 186
Butter Sugar Cookies 181
Chocolate Snowballs 182
Chocomint Bars 187
Christmas Wreaths 240
E.T. Cookies 239
Everybody's Favorite Brownies 187
Favorite Chocolate Chip Cookies 181
Ginger Cookie Dough 241
Haystacks 238
Holly's Fruitcake Cookies 183
Keepsake Cookies 184
Oatmeal & Apple Butter Bars 188

One Pan Graham-Banana Squares 239
Peanut Butter Cookies 184
Peggy's Lemon Bars 188
Potato Chip Shortbread Cookies 185
Praline Bars 189
Pumpkin Bars 189
Rolled Oat Cookies 185
Seven Layer Cookie 190
Snickerdoodles 186
Wrangler Cookies 183
Cookie Cake 176
Copper Carrot Salad 86
Corn Cheese Bake 151
Corn Chowder 35
Corn Pudding 151
Cornbread, Homestyle 70
Cornbread, Mexican 71
Corned Beef and Cabbage 105
Cornish Game Hens 134
Corny Sandwich Squares 108
Cottage Cheese, Jenny's Fruited 79
Cottontail Salad 232
Country Fried Mushrooms 153
Country Potatoes 155
Cowboy Beans 144
Crab Louis 94
Crabmeat Sandwiches, Mom's Hot 39
Crabmeat Sandwich, Caraway 40
Cracked Wheat Bread 67
Cranberry Salad 81
Cream Cheese Burritos 14
Cream Cheese Sauce 225
Cream Cheese Sweet Rolls 62
Cream of Carrot Soup 33
Cream of Mushroom Soup 36
Cream Puffs, Sherri's 203
Creamed Cabbage 150
Creamed Peas 155
Creamed Scallops & Mushrooms 138
Creamy Artichoke-Cheese Dip 3
Creamy Eggplant 151
Creamy Koolaid 16
Creamy Layered Chocolate Mint Cake . . 172
Crepes, Chicken & Broccoli 131
Crepes, Dessert 200
Crepes, Flaming Banana 200
Crisp, Apple 199
Croissants 69
Croquets, Salmon 140
Crust, Flaky Pie 190
Crust, Graham Cracker 191
Cucumber Salad, Glorious 83
Cucumbers and Sour Cream 83
Cucumber, & Vinegar Salad 83
Cupcakes, Black Bottom 168
Curried Fruit, Hot 163
Curried Shrimp Salad 95
Curry Dip for Raw Vegetables 5

D

Daddy's Egg Nog 19
Daiquiris, Frozen 21
Darn Good Beans 120
Date and Nut Bread 50
Date Cookies, Aunt Vernon's 182

Date Pudding, Carol's 204
Dee's Yellow Coconut Cake 175
DESSERTS
  Cakes 168-180
  Cookies 180-190
  Pies 190-198
  Frozen Desserts 209-210
  Apple Crisp 199
  Banana Pudding 201
  Carol's Date Pudding 204
  Cheese Cake 201
  Cherry Crunch 202
  Coffee Creme Mousse 199
  Dessert Delight 208
  Flaming Banana Crepes 200
  Gingerbread 204
  Nana's Plum Pudding 207
  Peach Cobbler 202
  Peach Melba 205
  Pumpkin Roll 208
  Raspberry Walnut Torte 206
  Sherri's Cream Puffs 203
  Strawberry Shortcake 205
Deviled Eggs 28
Deviled Ham Puffs 8
Dill Pickles, Conway Springs 224
Dilled Crab Dip 5
Dilly Bread, Kathi's 73
DIPS
  Bubbly Broccoli Dip 4
  Caramel Apple Dip 6
  Chili Con Queso 2
  Creamy Artichoke Cheese Dip 3
  Curry Dip for Raw Vegetables 5
  Dilled Crab Dip 5
  Easy Guacamole 93
  Enchilada Dip 3
  Fresh Fruit Dip 4
  Good 'n Easy Guacamole 4
  Shellfish Dip 2
  Smoked Oyster Dip 6
  Sombrero Spread 5
  Spinach Dip 6
  Tom's Famous Dip 2
Divine Raspberry Salad 77
Dixie's Buttermilk Pie 193
Dodie's Curried Scallops 139
Doris' Hominey Casserole 152
Doughnuts, New Orleans 55
Doughnuts, One Minute 59
Doug's Cheesy Pretzels 240
Dressing—Johnny Appleseed Turkey Stfg 137
Dressing—Mary's Scalloped Oysters . . . 138
DRESSINGS, SALAD
  Fruit Salad Dressing 81
  Poppy Seed Dressing 81
  Russian Dressing 94
  Sour Cream-Powdered Sugar Dressing . 80
  Tangy Dressing 90
  Vanilla Ice Cream Dressing 80
  Whipped Cream Dressing 80
  Yogurt-Honey Dressing 80
Duck, Susie's Romertoff 137

E

E.T. Cookies 239

Easy Beef Stroganoff 103
Easy Breakfast Cinnamon Bread 60
Easy Bubble Bread 52
Easy Cheeseball 13
Easy Chicken Chow Mein 130
Easy Guacamole 93
Easy Rice 164
Easy Yellow Squash 160
Egg Nog, Daddy's 19
Egg Yolk Paint 243
Eggplant, Creamy 151
Eggplant, Parmesan 117
EGGS and CHEESE
  Bull's Eye Eggs 234
  Chipped Beef and Eggs 27
  Deviled Eggs 28
  Egg Fu Yong 28
  Eggs Benedict 25
  French Ham and Cheese Souffle 24
  Ham and Egg Pie 27
  Ham Strata 27
  Morning Glory Brunch Casserole 24
  Omlette for One 26
  Parmesan Quiche 29
  Sausage Souffle 26
  Seafood Quiche 29
  Sunday Brunch 25
Eileen's Italian Cream Cake 176
Eileen's Monkey Bread 63
Enchilada Dip 3
Enchiladas, Beef 115
Enchiladas, Chicken 128
English Toffee 215
Ensalada, Mexican 93
Epicurean Green Beans 145
Everybody's Favorite Brownies 187

F

Fancy Tostadas 116
Favorite Chocolate Chip Cookies 181
Favorite Hashed Brwn Cheese Casserole 157

FISH
  Barbecued Fish 140

Clams
    Clam Chowder 34
    Shellfish Dip 2

Crab
    Caraway Crabmeat Sandwiches 40
    Crab Louis 94
    Dilled Crab Dip 5
    Hot Crab Miniatures 12
    Mom's Hot Crabmeat Sandwiches 39
    Tomatoes & Crabmeat 94
    Shellfish Dip 2
    Seafood Quiche 29
  Fish Fry 140
Oyster
    Christmas Eve Oyster Stew 37
    Mary's Scalloped Oysters 138
    Smoked Oyster Dip 6
Salmon
    Barbecued Fish 140
    Salmon Croquets 140
    Seafood Luncheon Dish 139

Shrimp
Beer Boiled Shrimp 139
Barbecued Fish 140
Curried Shrimp Salad 95
Seafood Quiche 29
Shrimp Ball 10
Shrimp & Green Noodle Casserole . . . 141
Tossed Shrimp Salad 96
Trout
Baked Trout 141
Colorado Trout 141
Tuna
Molded Tuna Salad 95
Scallops
Barbecued Fish 140
Creamed Scallops & Mushrooms 138
Dodie's Curried Scallops 139
Flaky Pie Crust 190
Flaming Banana Crepes 200
Float, Sherbet 235
Fourth of July Strawberry Pie 197
Frances' Jalapeno, Pepper Jelly 218
Freda's Peanut Brittle 213
French Bread and Meat Sandwich 43
French Bread Pizza 45
French Dip 44
French Ham & Cheese Souffle 24
French Onion Soup 37
French Toast 234
Fresh Apple Cake 168
Fresh Fruit Dip 4
Fresh Strawberry Pie 198
Fried Apple Rings 163
Fried Chicken & Gravy 124
Fried Rice with Bacon and Mushrooms . . 164
FROSTINGS
Butter Cream Frosting 186
Cream Cheese Frosting 176
Pecan-Coconut Frosting 174
FROZEN DESSERTS
Chocolate Marengo 209
Homemade Vanilla Ice Cream 211
Mud Pie 209
Lemon Velvet Ice Cream 211
Oreo Ice Cream 210
Peach Ice Cream 210
Ruth's Frosty Strawberry Squares 212
Sinfully Delicious Dessert 212
Strawberry Ice Cream 210
Tropical Ice 211
Fruit Dip, Fresh 4
Fruit, Hot Curried 163
Fruit Salad & Dressing, Mixed 80
Fruit Smoothy 17
Fruitcake Cookies, Holly's 183
Frozen Daiquiri 21
Fudge 214

G

GAME
Chicken, Quail/Pheasant in Crm Sauce . 136
Cornish Game Hens 134
Orange Baked Pheasant Breasts 136
Susie's Romertoff Wild Duck 137
German Chocolate Cake 174
German Potato Salad, Hot 91

Ginger Cookie Dough 241
Gingerbread 204
Glorified Hamburgers 43
Glorious Cucumber Salad 83
Golden Beef Casserole 109
Golden Wassail 19
Good 'n Easy Guacamole 4
Goulash—West of the Pecos 113
Graham Cracker Crust 191
Grandma Eaton's Coffee Cake 54
Grandma White's Purple Plum Buckle . . . 52
Grandmother's Island Bean Casserole . . 147
Green Bean Casserole 147
Green Beans, Caesar 148
Green Beans, Country Style 145
Green Beans, Epicurean 145
Green Beans, Macaroni, Mushrooms, and 165
Green Beans, Marinated 85
Green Chili Burritos 114
Green Chili Pie, Judy's 12
Green Tomato Relish 222
Greens, Best Ever 152
Grits, Marinan's Garlic-Cheese 152
Guacamole, Easy 93
Guacamole, Good 'n Easy 4

H

HAM
Deviled Ham, Puffs 8
Ham 'n Beans 119
Ham & Cheese Souffle, French 24
Ham & Egg Pie 27
Ham and Pimento Sandwiches 41
Ham and Potato Bake 118
Ham Salad Sandwich 42
Ham Strata 27
Hot Ham Sandwiches 41
Neighbor's Saucy Ham Sauce, The . . . 227
Hamburger-Sour Cream Casserole 109
Hash, Texas 110
Haystacks 238
Hearty Hodgepodge 106
Hearty Potato Soup 37
Hershey Bar Pie 195
Hickory Barbecue Sauce 226
Holiday Punch 19
Hollandaise Sauce 225
Holly's Fruitcake Cookies 183
Homemade Pizza 111
Homemade V-8 Juice 224
Homemade Vanilla Ice Cream 211
Homemade Vegetable Soup 39
Homestyle Corn Bread 70
Hominey Casserole, Doris' 152
HORS D'OEUVRES (See APPETIZERS)
Hot Apple Cider 17
Hot Buttered Cider 18
Hot Chocolate 18
Hot Chicken Salad 130
Hot Crab Miniatures 12
Hot Curried Fruit 163
Hot German Potato Salad 91
Hot Ham Sandwiches 41
Howdy Potatoes 9
Hush Puppies 71

I

Ice Cream Clowns 236
Ice Cream Cone Cakes 237
Ice Cream, Homemade Vanilla 211
Ice Cream, Lemon Velvet 211
Ice Cream, Oreo 210
Ice Cream, Peach 210
Ice Cream Punch, April Shower 16
Ice Cream, Strawberry 210
Ice, Tropical 211
Ice, Rainbow 237
ICINGS (See FROSTINGS)
Irish Soda Bread, Best 72
Italian Cream Cake, Eileen's 176
Italian Green Beans, Buttery 146
Italian Sausage Sandwich 45
Italian Scroodle Salad 96

J

Jack-o-Lantern Pizzas 242
Jalapeno Pepper Jelly, Frances' 218
Jam, Strawberry 220
Jelly, Chokecherry 219
Jelly, Frances' Jalapeno Pepper 218
Jenny's Fruited Cottage Cheese 79
Jerky, Beef 105
Jezebel Sauce 226
Joanie's Marinated Grilled Steak 100
Johnny Appleseed Turkey Stuffing 137
Judy's Green Chili Pie 12
Judy's Wild Rice Chicken 125

K

Ka-Bobs, Shish 103
Kathi's Dilly Bread 73
Kathleen's Chutney Delight 14
Keepsake Cookies 184
KIDS' FOOD
    Bob's Chocolate Soda 235
    Bull's Eye Eggs 234
    Celery Boats 231
    Christmas Wreaths 240
    Cottontail Salad 232
    Doug's Cheesy Pretzels 240
    E. T. Cookies 239
    Egg Yolk Paint 243
    French Toast 234
    Ginger Cookie Dough 241
    Haystacks 238
    Ice Cream Clowns 236
    Jack-o-Lantern Pizzas 242
    One Minute Doughnuts 234
    One Pan Graham-Banana Squares 239
    Party Ice Cream Cone Cakes 237
    Pigs in the Blanket 233
    Play Dough 243
    Plum Delicious Casserole 233
    Popcorn Balls 237
    Pudding Pops 237
    Rainbow Ice 237
    Sandwich Ideas 233
    Sherbet Float 235
    Silly Sally Salad 230
    S'mores 238
    Sparkling Fruit Punch 235
    Strawberry Soda 235

Superman Steak 231
Trail Mix Snack 238
White Chocolate Pretzels 238
Yogurt Sundae 236

L

Lasagna 118
Layered Potato Casserole 156
Lazy Lady Stew 106
Lemon Bars, Peggy's 188
Lemon Pie, Old Fashion 196
Lemon Pie, Quick 195
Lemon Pudding Cake 177
Lemon Sauce 204
Lemon Velvet Ice Cream 211
Lentil Soup 35
Lettuce, Wilted Salad 89
Lime-Pear Salad 77
Liver Pate, Mama White's Chicken 10
Lucious Layered Pie 196

M

Macaroni and Cheese Deluxe 165
Macaroni, Mushrooms and Green Beans . 165
Macaroni, Summertime Salad 97
Mama Lang's Cinnamon Rolls 64
Mama White's Chicken Liver Pate 10
Marco Polos 42
Marinan's Garlic-Cheese Grits 152
Marinated Green Beans 85
Marinated Grilled Steak, Joanie's 100
Marmalade, Blueberry-Orange 218
Mary's Baked Beans 144
Mary's Scalloped Oysters 138
Meat Loaf 110
MEATS (See Beef, Ham, Pork, Chicken, and
Fish)
Meatballs, Porcupine 111
Meringue 191
MEXICAN FOOD
    Beef Enchiladas 115
    Chicken Enchiladas 128
    Chili Con Queso 2
    Cream Cheese Burritos 14
    Easy Guacamole 93
    Enchilada Dip 3
    Enchilada, Mexican 93
    Fancy Tostada 116
    Good 'n Easy Guacamole 4
    Green Chili Burritos 114
    Judy's Green Chili Pie 12
    Mexican Corn Bread 71
    Mexican Hot Chocolate 18
    Sangria 20
    Sombrero Spread 5
    Sopapillas 55
    South of the Border Salad 92
    Tamale Pie 116
Mexican Corn Bread 71
Mexican Hot Chocolate 18
Mexican Squash Casserole 160
Mile High Pork Chop Casserole 120
Mints, Party 214
Mississippi Mud Cake 177
Mixed Fruit Salad and Dressing 80
Mocha Balls 178

Moist Coconut Cake 175
Molded Tuna Salad 95
Mom's Caramel Popcorn 214
Mom's Hot Crabmeat Sandwiches 39
Mom's Onion Rings 154
Monkey Bread, Eileen's 63
Morning Glory Brunch Casserole 24
Mother Link's 7-Up Pound Cake 179
Mousse, Coffee Creme 199
Mrs. Walkers's Cole Slaw 87
Mud Pie 209

MUFFINS
  Apple Muffins 56
  Blueberry Muffins 56
  Cinnamon-Sugar Muffins 56
  Oatmeal Muffins 57
  Orange Honey Surprise Muffins 58
  Orange Muffins 57
  Pineapple Muffins 58
  Raisin Bran Muffins 59
Mushroom Sauce, Brandied 227
Mushroom Soup, Cream of 36
Mushroom Soup, Quick 36
Mushrooms, Country-Fried 153
Mushrooms, Quick Stuffed 7
Mushrooms with Bacon, Stuffed 7

N

Nana's Plum Pudding 207
Neighbors' Saucy Ham Sauce, The 227
Neva's Salad 84
New Orleans Doughnuts 55
Nut Goodie Bars, Alice's 213

O

Oat Cookies, Rolled 185
Oatmeal & Apple Butter Bars 188
Oatmeal Muffins 57
Okra and Tomatoes 153
Okra, West Texas Fried 154
Old Fashioned Chicken & Noodles 135
Old Fashion Lemon Pie 196
Omlette for One 26
Onion Rings, Mom's 154
Onion Soup, French 37
Orange Baked Pheasant Breasts 136
Orange Coffee Cake 53
Orange Honey Surprise Muffins 58
Orange Juliana, Bonnie's 17
Orange Kiss Me Cake 178
Orange Muffins 57
Orange Rolls 61
Orange Slush .16
Orange, $1000 Salad 79
Oreo Ice Cream 21
Oyster Stew, Christmas Eve 37

P

Paint, Egg Yolk 243
Pan Fried Potatoes 157
Pancakes, Swedish 54
Parmesan Quiche 29
Party Ice Cream Cone Cakes 237
Party Mints 214
Party Rye Spreads 11
Pea Cauliflower Salad 84

Peach Cobbler 202
Peach Ice Cream 210
Peach Melba 205
Peach Preserves 219
Peaches 'n Cream Salad 78
Peanut Brittle, Freda's 213
Peanut Butter Cookies 184
Peanut Butter Sauce 205
Pear Salad, Lime 77
Peas, Creamed 155
Peas, Southern Style Black-Eyed 154
Pecan Millionaires 213
Pecan Pie 197
Peggy's Lemon Bars 188
People Pleasin' Cheeseball 13
Pheasant, Chicken/Quail in Cream Sauce 136
Pheasant, Orange Baked 136
Pickled Beets 223
Pickles, Bread 'n Butter 223
Pickles, Conway Springs Dill 224

PIES
  Apple Pie 193
  Aunt Ginger's Apricot Fried Pies 192
  Chocolate Cream Pie 194
  Coconut Cream Pie 194
  Dixie's Buttermilk Pie 193
  Flaky Pie Crust 190
  Fourth of July Strawberry Pie 197
  Fresh Strawberry Pie 198
  Graham Cracker Crust 191
  Hershey Bar Pie 195
  Lucious Layered Pie 196
  Meringue 191
  Old Fashioned Lemon Pie 196
  Pecan Pie 197
  Quick Lemon Pie 195
  Sour Cream Raisin Pie 198
Pigs in the Blanket 233
Pineapple Carrot Bread 50
Pineapple Muffins 58
Pineapple Spread, Cheesy 13
Pineapple Upside Down Cake 179
Pistachio Salad 82
Pizza, Homemade 111
Pizzas, Jack-o-Lantern 242
Play Dough 243
Plum Buckle, Grandma White's Purple . . .52
Plum Delicious Casserole 233
Plum Pudding 207
Poose's Chow Chow 221
Popcorn Balls 237
Popcorn, Mom's Caramel 214
Poppy Seed Cake 174
Poppy Seed Dressing 81
Porcupine Meatballs 111

PORK
  Mile High Pork Chop Casserole 120
  Pork Chops Potato Supper 119
  Sweet and Sour Pork 121
Potato Chip Chicken 127
Potato Chip Shortbread Cookies 185

POTATOES
  Cattlemen's Twice Baked Potatoes . . . 158
  Country Potatoes 155
  Favorite Hashed Brwn-Chees Casserol 157

Howdy Potatoes 9
Layered Potato Casserole, Sarah Lew's 156
Pan Fried Potatoes 157
Paris Potatoes, Cathy's 158
Potato Bread, Braided 68
Potato Salad 91
Potato Salad, Hot German 91
Potato Soup, Hearty 37
Sour Cream Potatoes 155
Sweet Potato Casserole 156
Potluck Chicken and Wild Rice 126
POULTRY (See CHICKEN)
Powdered Sugar, Sour Cream Dressing . . 80
Praline Bars 189
Pralines 215
Preserves, Peach 219
Pretzels, Doug's Cheesy 240
Pretzels, White Chocolate 238
Pudding, Banana 201
Pudding Pops 237
Pudding, Vanilla Cream 203
Pumpkin Bars 189
Pumpkin Roll 208
PUNCH
April Shower Ice Cream Punch 16
Banana Fruit Punch 10
Creamy Koolaid 16
Golden Wassail 19
Holiday Punch 19
Sparkling Fruit Punch 235
Sure Bet Punch 17

Q

Quail, Chicken or Pheasant
in Cream Sauce 136
Quiche, Parmesan 29
Quiche, Seafood 29
Quick Lemon Pie 195
Quick Mushroom Soup 36
Quick-Stuffed Mushrooms 7

R

Rainbow Ice 237
Raisin Bran Muffins 59
Raspberry Salad, Divine 77
Raspberry Walnut Torte 206
Red, White & Blueberry Salad 76
RELISHES
Chili Sauce 220
Green Tomato Relish 222
Poose's Chow Chow 221
Zucchini Relish 222
Rice, Artichoke Salad 92
Rice & Chilies 164
Rice, Easy 164
Rice with Bacon and Mushrooms, Fried . 164
Rice Green Salad 90
Roast, Best-Ever Pot 102
Roast, Unattended Rib 101
Rocky Mountain Soup 38
ROLLS
Bar L Rolls 67
Butterscotch Rolls 61
Cream Cheese Sweet Rolls 62
Easy Breakfast Cinnamon Bread 60

Mama Lang's Cinnamon Rolls 64
Orange Rolls 61
Texas Buttermilk Biscuits 70
Rolled Oat Cookies 185
Russian Dressing 94
Ruth's Frosty Strawberry Squares 212

S

SALADS
Fruit
Cinnamon Apples 82
Cottontail Salad 232
Cranberry Salad 81
Jenny's Fruited Cottage Cheese 79
Mixed Fruit Salad and Dressing 80
Pistachio Salad 82
Silly Sally Salad 236

Macaroni
Italian Scroodle Salad 96
Summertime Macaroni Salad 97

Meat Salads
Ensalada Mexicana 93
Hot Chicken Salad 130
South of the Border Salad 92

Molded
Banana-Berry Salad 76
Bing Cherry Gelatin Salad 79
Blueberry Salad 78
Divine Raspberry Salad 77
Glorious Cucumber Salad 83
Lime-Pear Salad 77
Peaches 'n Cream Salad 78
Red, White and Blueberry Salad 76
Sarah's Tomato Aspic 87
$1000 Orange Salad 79
Zingy Tomato Aspic 86

Seafood Salads
Crab Louis 94
Curried Shrimp Salad 95
Molded Tuna Salad 95
Tomatoes and Crabmeat 94
Tossed Shrimp Salad 96

Vegetable
Artichoke Rice Salad 92
Bean Salad 85
Cabbage Patch Cole Slaw 87
Cauliflower Salad 84
Copper Carrot Salad 86
Cucumber and Sour Cream Salad 83
Cucumber and Vinegar Salad 83
Easy Guacamole 93
Good 'n Easy Guacamole 4
Hot German Potato Salad 91
Marinated Green Beans 85
Mrs. Walker's Cole Slaw 87
Neva's Salad 84
Pea-Cauliflower Salad 84
Potato Salad 91
Rich Green Salad 90
Sauerkraut Salad 88
Spinach Salad 90
24-Hour Layered Vegetable Salad 89
Wilted Lettuce Salad 89

Zucchini Salad 88
SALAD DRESSINGS (See DRESSINGS)
Salmon Croquet 140
Salisbury Steak 112

SANDWICHES
  Caraway Crabmeat Sandwich 40
  Cheese Blintzes 40
  French Bread and Meat Sandwich 43
  French Bread Pizza 45
  French Dip 44
  Glorified Hamburgers 43
  Ham and Pimento Sandwich 41
  Ham Salad Sandwich 42
  Hot Ham Sandwich 41
  Italian Sausage Sandwich 45
  Marco Polos 42
  Mom's Hot Crabmeat Sandwiches 39
  Reubens 44
  Sandwich Ideas-Kids' 233
  Sloppy Joes 44
Sangria 20
Sarah's Tomato Aspic 87

SAUCES
  Brandied Mushroom Sauce 227
  Cheese Sauce for Vegetables 162
  Chili Sauce 220
  Chocolate Sauce 204
  Cream Cheese Sauce 225
  Hickory Barbecue Sauce 226
  Hollandaise Sauce 225
  Jezebel Sauce 226
  Lemon Sauce 204
  Neighbors' Saucy Ham Sauce, The . . . 227
  Peanut Butter Sauce 205
  Tartar Sauce 226
Sauerkraut Salad 88

SAUSAGE
  Bob and Gayle's Spaghetti 117
  Company Casserole 119
  Darn Good Beans 120
  Italian Sausage Sandwich 45
  Pigs in the Blanket 233
  Sausage Biscuits 12
  Sausage Souffle 26
  Sausage Soup 38
Sauteed Squash with Mushrooms
  and Onions 161
Scallops and Mushrooms, Creamed . . . 138
Scallops, Dodie's Curried 139

SEAFOOD (See FISH)
Seafood Luncheon Dish 139
Seafood Quiche 29
Seven Layer Cookie 190
Shellfish Dip 2
Shepherd's Pie 112
Sherbet Float 235
Sherri's Cream Puffs 203
Shish-Ka-Bob 103
Shortbread Cookies, Potato Chip 185
Shortcake, Strawberry 207
Shrimp and Green Noodle Casserole . . . 141
Shrimp Ball 10
Shrimp Salad, Curried 95
Shrimp Salad, Tossed 96

Silly Sally Salad 230
Sinfully Delicious Dessert 212
Skier's Delight 21
Slaw, Cabbage Patch Cole 87
Slaw, Mrs. Walker's Cole 87
Sloppy Joes 44
Smoked Oyster Dip 6
S'mores 238
Snickerdoodles 186
Soda, Bob's Chocolate 235
Soda, Strawberry 235
Sombrero Spread 5
Sopapillas 55

SOUPS
  Asparagus with Cream Cheese 32
  Beer Cheese Soup 32
  Broccoli Soup 33
  Chicken and Doughies 34
  Christmas Eve Oyster Stew 37
  Clam Chowder 34
  Corn Chowder 35
  Cream of Carrot Soup 33
  Cream of Mushrom Soup 36
  French Onion Soup 37
  Hearty Potato Soup 37
  Homemade Vegetable Soup 39
  Lentil Soup 35
  Quick Mushroom Soup 36
  Rocky Mountain Soup 38
  Sausage Soup 38
Sour Cream Potatoes 155
Sour Cream-Powdered Sugar Dressing . . . 80
Sour Cream Raisin Pie 198
Sourdough Bread and Starter 66
South of the Border Salad 92
Southern Style Black-Eyed Peas 154
Spaghetti, Bob and Gayle's 117
Spaghetti, Chicken 128
Sparkling Fruit Punch 235
Spiced Chocolate Zucchini Cake 173
Spiced Tea 20
Spinach Appetizers 9
Spinach Dip 6
Spinach Salad 90
Spinach Souffle with Mushroom Sauce . . 159
Spinach Stuffed Tomatoes 162

SPREADS
  Best of the West Spread 11
  Cheese and Bacon Hot Ryes 8
  Cheesy Pineapple Spread 13
  Kathleen's Chutney Delight 14
  Mama White's Chicken Liver Pate 10
  Party Rye Spreads 11
  Sombrero Spread 5
  Shrimp Ball 10
  Swiss Ryes 7
Squash Casserole, Mexican 160
Squash, Easy Yellow 160
Squash w/Mushrooms & Onions, Sauteed 161
Steak and Potatoes 104
Steak Butter 225
Steak, Chicken Fried with Cream Gravy . 104
Steak Diana 101
Steak, Joanie's Marinated Grilled 100
Steak, Salisbury 112

Steak, Superman 231
Steak, Swiss 102
Stew—Hearty Hodgepodge 106
Stew, Lazy Lady 106
Stir-Fried Broccoli and Carrots 149
Strawberries, Chocolate Dipped 15
Strawberry Cake 180
Strawberry Jam 220
Strawberry Ice Cream 210
Strawberry Pie, Fourth of July 197
Strawberry Pie, Fresh 198
Strawberry Shortcake 205
Strawberry Soda 235
Strawberry Squares, Ruth's Frosty 212
Stroganoff, Easy Beef 103
Stuffed Mushrooms with Bacon 7
Stuffing, Johnny Appleseed Turkey 137
Sugar Cookies, Butter 181
Sukiyaki 122
Summertime Macaroni Salad 97
Sunday Brunch 25
Superman Steak 231
Susie's Romertoff Wild Duck 137
Sure Bet Punch 17
Swedish Pancakes 54
Sweet and Sour Beans 146
Sweet and Sour Pork 121
Sweet Potato Casserole 156
Swiss Ryes .7
Swiss Steak 102

T

Tamale Pie 116
Tangy Dressing 90
Tartar Sauce 226
Tea, Spiced 20
Texas Buttermilk Biscuits 70
Texas Hash 110
Texas Red Chili 113
Thousand Dollar Orange Salad 79
Thumb Print Cookies, Best Ever 186
Toast, French 234
Toffee, English 215
Tomato, Aspic Sarah's 87
Tomato, Green Relish 222
Tomato Hors D'Oeuvres, Cherry 14
Tomatoes and Crabmeat 94
Tomatoes, Broiled 161
Tom's Famous Dip 2
Torte, Raspberry Walnut 206
Tossed Shrimp Salad 96
Tostadas, Fancy 116
Trail Mix Snack 238
Trout, Baked 141
Trout, Colorado 141
Tuna Salad Molded 95
Twenty-Four Hr Layered Vegetable Salad . 89

U

Unattended Rib Roast 101

V

V-8 Aspic, Zingy 86
V-8 Juice, Homemade 224
Vanilla Creme Pudding 203
Vanilla Ice Cream, Homemade 211

Vanilla Ice Cream 211
Vanilla Ice Cream Dressing 80
Vegetable Crisps 10
Vegetable Soup, Homemade 39
VEGETABLES
Almond-Broccoli Casserole 148
Best Ever Green Beans 152
Broccoli-Cauliflower Casserole 149
Broccoli with Walnuts 150
Broiled Tomatoes 161
Buttery Italian Green Beans 146
Cathy's Paris Potatoes 158
Cattlemen's Club Twice Baked Potatoes 158
Cheese Sauce for Vegetables 162
Corn Cheese Bake 151
Corn Pudding 151
Country Fried Mushrooms 153
Country Potatoes 155
Country Style Green Beans 145
Cowboy Beans 144
Creamed Cabbage 150
Creamed Peas 155
Creamy Eggplant 151
Doris' Hominey Casserole 152
Easy Rice 164
Easy Yellow Squash 160
Epicurean Green Beans 145
Favorite Hashed Brwn-Chees Casserol 157
Fried Apple Rings 163
Fried Rice with Bacon and Mushrooms . 164
Grandmother's Island Bean Casserole . 147
Green Beans Caesar 148
Green Bean Casserole 147
Hot Curried Fruit 163
Macaroni and Cheese Deluxe 165
Macaroni, Mushrooms & Green Beans . 165
Marinan's Garlic-Cheese Grits 152
Mary's Baked Beans 144
Mexican Squash Casserole 160
Mom's Onion Rings 154
Okra and Tomatoes 153
Pan Fried Potatoes 157
Rice and Chilies 164
Sarah Lew's Layered Potato Casserole . 156
Sauteed Sqsh w/Mushrooms & Onions . 161
Sour Cream Potatoes 155
Southern Style Black-Eyed Peas 154
Spinach Souffle with Mushroom Sauce . 159
Spinach Stuffed Tomatoes 162
Stir-Fried Broccoli and Carrots 149
Sweet and Sour Beans 146
Sweet Potato Casserole 156
West Texas Fried Okra 154

W

Wassail, Golden 19
Water Chestnuts and Bacon Roll Ups 8
West of the Pecos 113
Whipped Cream Dressing 80
White Chocolate Pretzels 238
Whole Wheat Bread 65
Wilted Lettuce Salad 89
Wrangler Cookies 183

Y

Yogurt-Honey Dressing 80

Yogurt Sundae 236

Z

Zelda's Cabbage Rolls 107
Zingy V-8 Aspic 86

Zucchini Bread 51
Zucchini Cake, Spiced Chocolate 173
Zucchini Relish 222
Zucchini Salad 88

more Kitchen Keepsakes

recipes for home cookin'

Bonnie Welch & Deanna White

Cover by
Pam Hake

Illustrated by
John Burd

Kitchen Keepsakes & more Kitchen Keepsakes
Two cookbooks in one!

Specially priced combination
books are available for $19.95, plus $3.50 shipping
(Texas residents add $1.44 sales tax per book).
Quantity discounts are available.

Cover Design by Pam Hake
Text illustrations by Sheila Olson

ISBN: 0-9677932-5-4
Library of Congress Card Number: 00-111718

First Printing	June	2000	5,000 copies
Second Printing	September	2000	15,000 copies
Third Printing	October	2000	15,000 copies
Fourth Printing	November	2000	20,000 copies
Fifth Printing	January	2001	50,000 copies

cookbook resources, llc
541 Doubletree Drive
Highland Village, TX 75077

972/317-0245

www.cookbookresources.com

Manufactured in the USA

Toll Free Orders: 866/229-2665

INTRODUCTION

In 1983 when **Kitchen Keepsakes** was first published, we had high hopes for selling our first printing, but little expectation beyond that. The furthest thought from our minds was doing another cookbook. Now, two and a half years and three printings later, we are doing just that. . .another cookbook!

More Kitchen Keepsakes, as the name implies, is an all-new collection of down-home recipes. The 450 recipes we've gathered can best be described as good, old fashioned cooking that is easy to prepare, and a delight to serve family, friends, and guests.

We do not claim these recipes as original. . .most were generously shared by family and friends, while others are our adaptations of recipes from newspapers, magazines, labels, and other cookbooks. As we have done, we encourage you to improvise these recipes to suit your personal taste. After all, cooking is nothing if not self-expression!

As before, we kitchen-tested every recipe* and edited each for clarity. We have selected several **Kitchen Keepsakes** "classic" recipes from our first cookbook to include in this one. They are our favorites and the best of our first book, so we felt it fitting to include them in **More Kitchen Keepsakes**. Their titles are appropriately framed in hearts.

A new feature of this cookbook is a menu section. Drawing from the "keep-sake" recipes in this book, we have compiled a wide variety of menu suggestions from Campfire Breakfast to Do-Ahead Dinner.

We hope you will find this cookbook as useful and complete as **Kitchen Keep-sakes**. We are most grateful for the enthusiastic response to our endeavor, and sincerely appreciate the support and encouragement given us by so many. We are especially appreciative of you, our readers and fellow cooks who, like us, know the pleasure of creating a tasty and satisfying meal. Hats off to home cooking! It is still the best!

*These recipes were tested at an altitude of 6000 feet. Most will not be adversely affected by a change in altitude, but if you desire to make adjustments, consult your state university home extension office for advice.

DEDICATION

We dedicate this cookbook to our fathers:

Jack Matthews   Frank Sewald

They taught us the value of setting goals, showed us how
to work hard to achieve them, and gave us the
confidence to try it on our own.

IN APPRECIATION

The following people were helpful in the creation of this cookbook. They willingly gave us recipes, advice, suggestions, and encouragement. We are most grateful to them.

Kathy Abbas
Jan Allen
Joan Baskin
Chris Bennett
Suzie Bohleen
Cindy Burd
Kathleen Budd
Georgia Culbertson
Cathy Ellis
Lindy Goodman
Joanie Graham
Sarah Lew Grimes
Claudia Previn-Harrison
Ray Harrison
Vera Henderson
Donnie Howard
Lois Jean Howard
Susie Howard
Ruth Jackson
Betsy Joyce
Sid Kelsey
Mary Kuehn
Barbara Kramer

Judy Makens
Peggy Marvin
Adele Matthews
Frances Matthews
Peggy Matthews
Sarah Mills
Judy McLaughlin
The Mountain West crew
Candy Rayl
Kika Retomoles
Cathy Sewald
Jean Sewald
Sherri Sewald
Germaine Tate
Bonnie Van Husen
Barbara Webster
Rita Weingardt
Charlie Welch
Eileen Welch
Gladys White
Leona White
Heather Wilfley
Susan Zimmerman

A special thank you to our artist, Pam Hake. Pam is a 13 year resident of Elizabeth, Colorado. She received her art degree from the University of Colorado and presently works free lance from her home. She paints in several mediums; watercolor and pastels being her favorites. Pam exhibits at various juried shows throughout Colorado.

Our illustrator, John Burd, loves to paint, travel, and teach. A native Coloradan, he has been teaching Drawing and Painting at Douglas County High School in Castle Rock for the past thirteen years. He works in several different mediums but his favorite is watercolors. John also exhibits in 20 to 30 art shows around the county each year.

Bonnie Welch and Deanna White

Bonnie Welch and **Deanna White** have come a long way since the time when, as new brides trying to impress their husbands with their culinary talents, they singed their eyelashes on Flaming Banana Crepes!

Maybe it was then that they realized that cooking doesn't have to be complicated to be appreciated, and began to rely on the good, easy, inexpensive, down-home cooking they had loved as children.

In 1983, Bonnie retired from her teaching job and Deanna from her job as a cattle market analyst to stay home and raise their families. The two Colorado women decided to publish their recipes in the now highly successful **Kitchen Keepsakes**, selling 25,000 copies in 2½ years. **More Kitchen Keepsakes**, a second collection of family style cooking, is being received with equal enthusiasm by America's home cooks!

Deanna, born and raised in a farming community near Longmont, Colorado, and Bonnie, a native of Midland, Texas, credit their mothers with teaching them the art of good home cooking and their fathers with giving them the know-how to start their own business.

But their biggest supporters (and critics) are their husbands and children who were the impetus behind the project and who remain instrumental in keeping it going.

Today Deanna and her husband, Jim, a painting contractor, reside near Castle Rock with their children Tanya, 6, Linda, 5, and Will, 2.

Bonnie, her husband, John, and their three children, Bob, 8, Andy, 5, and Wesley, 4, live on a ranch northwest of Calhan, Colorado, where they have a cow/calf and yearling operation.

TABLE OF CONTENTS

APPETIZERS AND BEVERAGES 1

BRUNCH . . . . ·. . 25

SOUPS AND SANDWICHES 39

BREADS 61

SALADS 93

MEATS 117

CHICKEN AND FISH 143

VEGETABLES, RICE AND PASTA 165

DESSERTS 189

KIDS' FOOD 243

MENU SUGGESTIONS 261

INDEX 271

Appetizers
and
Beverages

APPETIZERS AND BEVERAGES

SUSAN'S SHRIMP AND CRAB DIP

12 oz. cream cheese,
  softened
2 Tbsp. Worcestershire
  sauce
1 Tbsp. lemon juice
1 small onion, minced
2 Tbsp. mayonnaise
12 oz. cocktail sauce
1—6 oz. can crabmeat
1—6 oz. can or ½ lb.
  shrimp, chopped
Parsley, chopped

MAKES 4½ CUPS
Mix cream cheese, Worcestershire sauce, lemon juice, onion and mayonnaise together with mixer, or in a food processor. Spread evenly over a dinner size plate. Pour cocktail sauce over cream cheese layer. Sprinkle crabmeat and shrimp over cocktail sauce. Chill. Sprinkle with parsley. Serve with Ritz or club crackers.

BOUNTIFUL LAYERS

1—8 oz. pkg. cream
  cheese, softened
2 Tbsp. mayonnaise
Worcestershire sauce to
  taste
¼ tsp. garlic powder
2 ripe avocados
Garlic salt
Lemon juice
½ cup Pace Picante sauce
8 oz. baby shrimp (fresh,
  frozen, or canned),
  rinsed and drained
2 green onions, finely
  chopped

SERVES 6–8
Cream together cheese, mayonnaise, Worcestershire sauce and garlic powder. Spread mixture on a rimmed plate. Cover and refrigerate. Just before serving, mash avocados and sprinkle with garlic salt and lemon juice. Frost the chilled cheese mixture with a layer of guacamole; then frost with a layer of Picante sauce; top with shrimp. Sprinkle with green onions and serve with tortilla chips.

 Remember when planning appetizers for your party or dinner "Well begun is half done."

2

APPETIZERS AND BEVERAGES

VEGETABLE DIPPERS

Asparagus spears
Broccoli flowerettes
Carrot sticks or curls
Cauliflower flowerettes
Celery sticks
Cherry tomatoes
Cucumber slices or strips
Pea pods
Green onion curls
Green pepper strips
Radish roses
Zucchini slices
Turnip slices

Keep raw vegetables on ice until ready to serve. Use one of the following dips or, for a last minute dip use Ranch Style dressing.

DILLY DIP

⅔ cup mayonnaise
 (Homemade is good—
 see Index)
⅔ cup sour cream
1 Tbsp. green onion, finely chopped
1 tsp. dried parsley
1 tsp. dill weed
¾ tsp. seasoned salt

MAKES 1½ CUPS
Mix ingredients together and chill. Good with raw vegetables; chips too. Also a good spread for sandwiches.

FRESH VEGETABLE DIP

1—8 oz. carton sour
 cream
1 Tbsp. Miracle Whip
1 pkg. Good Seasons
 Italian dressing mix
1 Tbsp. lemon juice
½–1 avocado, chopped
½–1 tomato, chopped
Dash Tabasco sauce

MAKES 2 CUPS
Combine first four ingredients and mix well. Chill. Before serving, combine mixture with chopped avocado and tomato. Serve with favorite raw vegetables.

APPETIZERS AND BEVERAGES

CREAMY SEAFOOD DILL DIP

1—8 oz. pkg. cream
   cheese, softened
1 cup sour cream
⅓ cup mayonnaise
1—.4 oz. pkg. Hidden
   Valley Ranch Original
   Salad Dressing Mix
2 Tbsp. dill weed
Dash of cayenne
1—6 oz. pkg. frozen crab or
   shrimp, thawed & drained

MAKES 3 CUPS
Mix cream cheese with sour cream and mayonnaise, using electric mixer or food processor, until smooth and creamy. Add dressing mix, dill weed, and cayenne; mix well. Fold in seafood. Serve with toast points, crackers, or potato chips. The seafood may be omitted and the dip served with raw vegetables.

ROQUEFORT DIP

1—8 oz. carton sour cream
1 Tbsp. mayonnaise
¼ tsp. Worcestershire
   sauce
¼ tsp. onion powder
1 tsp. dried parsley
1½ tsp. lemon juice
¼ tsp. salt
3 drops Tabasco
1—4 oz. pkg. Roquefort
   cheese, mashed (bleu
   cheese works)

MAKES 1½ CUPS
Combine all ingredients except Roquefort cheese. When well blended, add crumbled Roquefort. A good dip for raw vegetables, but can also serve as a salad dressing if thinned with a little bit more mayonnaise.

MOZZARELLA VEGETABLE DIP

¾ cup sour cream
¾ cup mayonnaise
¾ tsp. dried parsley flakes
½ tsp. sugar
½ tsp. garlic salt
1 Tbsp. Parmesan cheese
½ cup mozzarella cheese,
   grated
⅛ tsp. onion powder
Raw vegetables for dipping

MAKES 2 CUPS
Combine all dip ingredients. Chill. Serve with raw veggies. If possible, chill overnight before serving to allow flavors time to blend.

APPETIZERS AND BEVERAGES

RIO GRANDE BEAN DIP

1—16 oz. can refried beans
   with green chilies
3 oz. cream cheese
1—4½ oz. can ripe olives,
   chopped
1 Tbsp. chili powder
1/3 cup sour cream
¾ cup grated cheese

MAKES 4 CUPS
In small baking dish, combine beans, cream cheese, olives, chili powder and sour cream. Top with grated cheese. Bake at 350° for 15–20 minutes or until bubbly. Serve with tortilla chips.

SOUTHWESTERN BEAN DIP

1—16 oz. can refried
   beans
½ lb. Jalapeno pepper
   process cheese spread,
   cubed
½ cup chopped onion
¼ cup Picante sauce

MAKES 2 CUPS
In a small saucepan, combine ingredients. Stir over low heat until cheese is melted. Serve hot with tortilla chips.

DIP FOR A CROWD

1 lb. ground beef
1 lb. ground sausage
2 lb. box Velveeta cheese,
   cubed
1 can mushroom soup
   (undiluted)
1—8 oz. jar Picante sauce

MAKES *LOTS*
Brown ground beef and sausage in a large saucepan. Drain grease, add cheese, soup and Picante. Stir until cheese is melted and ingredients are well mixed. Serve with tortilla chips.

APPETIZERS AND BEVERAGES

HOT NACHO DIP

1 lb. ground beef
1 lb. chorizo sausage
1 onion, chopped
1 or 2—8 oz. cans refried
    beans
12 oz. pkg. Monterey Jack
    or Cheddar cheese,
    grated
1—8 oz. jar taco sauce
1 medium avocado,
    chopped
1 medium tomato,
    chopped
1—2½ oz. can ripe olives,
    chopped
½ cup sour cream
Tortilla chips

MAKES 8 CUPS
Brown meat, add onion and cook until onion is transparent. Drain off fat. Spread the refried beans in a 3 quart casserole. Top with meat mixture. Cover with cheese. Pour taco sauce over cheese. (At this point it can be covered and chilled.) Bake at 400° for 25–30 minutes. Garnish with chopped avocado, tomato, olives and sour cream. Serve hot with tortilla chips.

HOMEMADE CHEESE SPREAD

1—8 oz. pkg. cream
    cheese, softened
1/8 tsp. garlic powder
1 tsp. basil
1 tsp. caraway seed
1 tsp. dill weed
1 tsp. chives, chopped
Cracked black or lemon
    pepper

Blend cream cheese with garlic, basil, caraway, dill weed and chives. Pat into round ball. Roll on waxed paper in lemon pepper or cracked black pepper.

Good when made a few days ahead, but you can serve it right away. Serve with assorted crackers.

Salt your food with humor, pepper it with wit, and sprinkle over it the charm of fellowship.

6

FRESH FRUIT DIP

1—8 pkg. cream cheese
½ carton sour cream
4 Tbsp. apricot preserves
¾ cup flaked coconut
½ cup pecans, chopped
  finely

Combine all ingredients and serve with pineapple spears or strawberries.

HEATHER'S HARVEST DIP

8 oz. soft cream cheese
8 oz. sour cream
4 green onions, chopped
¼ tsp. curry powder
5 oz. chutney
6 oz. dry roasted peanuts
5 oz. sunflower seeds
6 oz. raisins

MAKES 4½ CUPS
Mix together and serve with crackers of your choice.

HOT CRAB DIP

1—8 oz. pkg. cream cheese
1—6 oz. can crab meat,
  drained
⅛ tsp. onion powder
1–2 Tbsp. horseradish (or
  to your taste)
1 tsp. lemon juice
Slivered almonds
Paprika

MAKES 2 CUPS
Mix ingredients well. Heat until warm (microwave is best) at 350° for 20 minutes. Top with slivered almonds and sprinkle with paprika. Tasty with crackers!

 A pound package of small-sized snack crackers contains about 200 crackers and a pound of large-sized crackers contains about 100.

APPETIZERS AND BEVERAGES

CHIPPED BEEF DIP

2—8 oz. pkgs. cream cheese
4 Tbsp. milk
5 oz. chipped beef, minced
¼ cup green onion,
    chopped
1 tsp. garlic salt
¼ tsp. pepper
1 cup sour cream
½ cup pecans, chopped
1 Tbsp. horseradish
    (optional)

MAKES 3 CUPS
Mix together cream cheese, milk, chipped beef, onion, garlic salt, pepper; fold in sour cream. Place in 1 quart casserole, arranging pecans on top. Bake at 350° for 20 minutes. Serve warm with crackers.

HOT MUSHROOM DIP

1 pound fresh mushrooms,
    sliced
4 Tbsp. butter
1 Tbsp. grated onion
1 Tbsp. prepared Dijon
    mustard
½ tsp. salt
⅛ tsp. garlic powder
2 Tbsp. parsley, chopped
¼ tsp. Tabasco
1 cup sour cream

MAKES 3 CUPS
Saute sliced mushrooms in butter for two minutes. Add remaining ingredients and cook over medium heat for ten minutes or until mushrooms are tender. Serve hot in a chafing dish with tortilla chips for dipping. This is also excellent as a sauce with charcoaled steaks.

EASY CRAB SPREAD

1—8 oz. pkg. cream cheese
1—6 oz. can crabmeat,
    drained
Cocktail sauce

MAKES 2 CUPS
Set cream cheese on serving dish. Top with crabmeat. Pour cocktail sauce generously over the top. Serve with Ritz or club crackers.

To make this a little fancier, soften cream cheese, mix with crabmeat and form into a ball before topping with cocktail sauce.

JALAPENO SPREAD

½ lb. Velveeta cheese, grated
1 cup mayonnaise
2 fresh jalapeno peppers, seeded and grated
$1/_8$ tsp. onion powder
Garlic salt to taste

MAKES 2 CUPS
Combine all ingredients. (Canned jaiapeno slices can be used if fresh cannot be found.) Serve as a spread with crackers. Will keep in the refrigerator for several weeks, so it's a good appetizer to have on hand.

VERA'S BACON-CHEESE SPREAD

24 oz. cream cheese, softened
1 bell pepper, chopped
1—4 oz. can chopped green chilies
1 medium onion, chopped fine
¼ cup mayonnaise
2 Tbsp. lemon juice
1 tsp. garlic salt
½ tsp. garlic powder
1 tsp. seasoned salt
1 lb. bacon, cooked and crumbled (reserve some for garnish)

MAKES 3 CUPS
Combine all ingredients in a food processor until well blended. Pour into a lightly greased 3-cup mold and refrigerate overnight. Unmold on a serving platter or tray and garnish with crumbled bacon. Serve with toast points or crackers. This is a **wonderful** appetizer. Men love it!

APPETIZERS AND BEVERAGES

LEMON PEPPER CHEESE SPREAD

2—8 oz. pkgs. cream
  cheese, softened
¼ tsp. garlic powder
2 tsp. caraway seeds
2 tsp. basil
2 tsp. dehydrated chopped
  chives
2 tsp. dill weed
Lemon pepper

MAKES 2 CUPS

Blend cream cheese with garlic, caraway seeds, basil, chives and dill weed. Pat into a round, flattened shape. Roll in lemon pepper to cover all sides. Wrap in plastic wrap and refrigerate several days to allow flavors to blend. Serve with assorted crackers.

DELICIOUS FRUIT 'N CHEESE SPREAD

1—8 oz. pkg. cream cheese
4 oz. Cheddar cheese,
  grated
¼ cup chopped dried
  apricots or apricot
  preserves
¼ cup currants or raisins
2 Tbsp. pecans, chopped

MAKES 2 CUPS

In food processor or blender, process cream cheese and Cheddar cheese until smooth. Fold in apricots, currants and pecans. Spread on favorite fruit bread or sandwich bread. Nice to serve with a salad at luncheons.

MARINATED MUSHROOMS

1 cup Wesson oil
4 Tbsp. mustard seed
1 tsp. garlic powder
2 tsp. garlic salt
1 tsp. lemon pepper
2 tsp. seasoning salt
1 tsp. Tabasco
2 bay leaves
4 Tbsp. lemon juice
1½ lbs. small, fresh
  mushrooms

MAKES 30–40

Combine all ingredients except lemon juice and mushrooms in medium-sized bowl. Stir, cover and refrigerate overnight. Next day, bring mixture to a boil in an uncovered skillet. Simmer 15 minutes. When cool, add lemon juice and mushrooms and refrigerate in covered container until ready to use. Best if allowed to marinate several days before using. Will keep a week in refrigerator (gently shake container occasionally). To serve, drain off most of the oil, leaving as much mustard seed as possible on the mushrooms. Serve with toothpicks.

APPETIZERS AND BEVERAGES

❧ ❧ ❧ ❧ ❧ ❧ ❧ ❧ ❧ ❧ ❧ ❧ ❧ ❧ ❧ ❧ ❧ ❧

OYSTERS FLORENTINE

10 flaky biscuits or sheet
   of prepared pastry
10 Tbsp. Swiss cheese,
   grated
10 large or 20 small fresh
   shucked oysters
4 Tbsp. butter, melted
¾ cup Stouffer's Spinach
   Souffle, thawed
Thin lemon slices,
   quartered

MAKES 20 APPETIZERS

Cut pastry into 1½-inch squares or peel biscuits in half and flatten slightly. Bake 4 minutes in 400° oven. Cool slightly. Spoon ½ tablespoon Swiss cheese onto each pastry. Pat oysters dry on paper towels; halve, if large. Dip oysters in melted butter and place on cheese. Drizzle with any remaining butter. Top each oyster with 1 tablespoon Spinach Souffle mixture. Bake 20-25 minutes at 425° or until heated through. Garnish with lemon triangles. Serve hot.

CALF FRIES
a.k.a.
ROCKY MOUNTAIN OYSTERS

Calf fries (Rocky Mountain
   oysters)
Eggs
Flour

Oil for deep frying
Salt & pepper to taste

Leave calf fries frozen when removing outer membrane. Dip in hot water, then peel off membrane. Cut into 1 inch slices if large. Set on paper towel and pat dry. Dip each in beaten egg, then shake in plastic bag containing flour. Fry in about 1½ inches of oil in a heavy skillet until golden brown. Salt and pepper to taste. Good as an hors d'oeuvre with Picante sauce, cocktail sauce, or sour cream mixed with horseradish and garlic salt to taste.

At branding time we make them the main course with Cowboy beans (pinto beans), buttermilk biscuits and fried okra. The old West lives on!

11

APPETIZERS AND BEVERAGES

COCKTAIL FRANKS

1 lb. all-beef frankfurters
1—12 oz. bottle extra hot barbecue sauce (or use homemade, see Index)
2 tsp. celery seed
1 Tbsp. vinegar
⅛ tsp. garlic powder

Diagonally slice each frankfurter into 6 pieces. Combine remaining ingredients and franks. Refrigerate overnight or at least four hours. To serve, heat sauce and franks. Provide toothpicks for spearing.

HOT FRIED CHEESE STICKS

1 cup flour
½ tsp. garlic salt
½ cup cornmeal
1½ tsp. parsley
½ tsp. basil
¾ tsp. oregano
1 lb. mozzarella cheese, cut into 20 rectangular pieces
½ cup buttermilk
Oil for frying

MAKES 20
Combine first six ingredients in bowl. Mix well. Dip each piece of cheese in buttermilk then roll in cornmeal mixture to coat completely. Deep fry in hot oil (370°) until golden brown. Serve hot.

SPEEDY SPINACH MUSHROOM CAPS

1 lb. fresh mushrooms
1—12 oz. pkg. Stouffer's Spinach Souffle, thawed
½ cup butter, melted
⅓ cup Parmesan cheese

MAKES 25–30
Cut stems off mushrooms, and chop, reserving mushroom caps. Mix chopped stems into thawed spinach. Dip whole mushroom caps into melted butter. Stuff each cap with spinach mixture. Sprinkle with Parmesan cheese. Bake at 350° for 15–20 minutes, until puffy and lightly browned. These taste like you spent more time than you did!

APPETIZERS AND BEVERAGES

BACON-FILLED CHERRY TOMATOES

1 lb. bacon, fried &
  crumbled
¼ cup green onion, finely
  chopped
2 Tbsp. parsley, chopped
2 Tbsp. Parmesan cheese
½ cup Miracle Whip
24 cherry tomatoes

MAKES 24
In medium bowl, combine all ingredients except tomatoes. Cut a thin slice off the top of each tomato. With small spoon or melon scoop, hollow out tomato. Fill tomatoes with bacon mixture. Refrigerate several hours to blend flavors. These are colorful as well as tasty.

PARTY TOMATOES

1 basket cherry tomatoes
1—8 oz. pkg. cream cheese
¼–½ tsp. garlic salt
Pepper
Dash Worcestershire
  sauce
2 Tbsp. green onion,
  finely chopped
6½ oz. canned or frozen
  shrimp, rinsed and
  drained
Parsley, chopped

MAKES 15–20
Cut tomatoes in half. Scoop out and discard insides. Mix cream cheese until creamy (warm in the microwave to soften). Mix in garlic salt, pepper, Worcestershire sauce and onion. Blend in shrimp. Stuff tomato halves with mixture. Garnish with fresh parsley. Chill until ready to serve.

CRABBIES

1—6 oz. jar Olde English
  Cheese Spread
½ cup butter, softened
¼ tsp. salt
¼ tsp. garlic powder
1 Tbsp. mayonnaise
1—6 oz. can crabmeat
6 English muffins, split

MAKES 48 QUARTERS
Blend the cheese, butter, seasonings and mayonnaise. Stir in crabmeat. Spread on English muffin halves. Cut into quarters. Bake at 400° for 10 minutes or until lightly browned. These may be frozen before baking. Simply set quarters on a baking sheet and freeze until solid; then store in plastic bags. Bake without thawing.

APPETIZERS AND BEVERAGES

LONE STAR CHEDDAR BITES

6 English muffins, split
½ lb. Olde English
cheese, grated
½ cup ripe olives,
chopped
½ cup green onions,
chopped
½ cup mayonnaise (try
Homemade, see Index)
½ tsp. curry powder

MAKES 24 APPETIZERS
Combine cheese, olives, onion, mayonnaise and curry powder. Spread on muffin halves. Cut into quarters. Bake at 400° for 5 minutes. Quarters may be frozen before cooking . . . just place them on a cookie sheet, freeze, then transfer to a plastic bag and store in the freezer. May be used as needed and cooked without thawing.

MUCHOS NACHOS

Tortilla chips
Cheddar cheese, grated
Black olives, sliced
Refried beans
Green chilies, sliced
Green onions, chopped

Cover a plate with chips. Top with desired amounts of each ingredient. Cover with another layer of chips. Top with more cheese, chilies and olives. Heat in microwave or under broiler until cheese is melted.

BAR-B-QUE BEEF BITES

1 lb. ground beef, lean
½ cup barbecue sauce
1 egg, slightly beaten
1 cup sharp Cheddar
cheese, grated
2—10 oz. pkgs.
refrigerated buttermilk
flaky biscuits

MAKES 48
Brown ground beef and drain well. Add barbecue sauce and egg and mix well. Set aside. Gently separate the biscuits into 48 circles. Press each circle into the bottom and up the sides of tiny muffin tins. Spoon beef mixture into each pastry shell. Top with grated Cheddar cheese. Bake 8–10 minutes at 400°. Remove from tins and serve hot. May be prepared a day in advance, covered and refrigerated. Reheat for 5 minutes at 350° to serve.

APPETIZERS AND BEVERAGES

QUICK AND EASY CHEESE BALL

2—8 oz. pkgs. cream cheese
1—7 oz. pkg. Good Seasons
  Italian dressing mix or
  Cheese Garlic dressing
¾ cup pecans, chopped,
  or paprika and parsley

1 LARGE CHEESEBALL
Combine softened cheese and dry dressing mix thoroughly. Form into ball, roll in nuts. For a colorful change, roll in paprika then parsley flakes. Serve with crackers.

CHILI POWDER CHEESE ROLL

1—8 oz. pkg. cream
  cheese, softened
1 cup Olde English pro-
  cessed cheese, grated
¼ tsp. garlic salt
2 Tbsp. toasted sesame
  seeds
1 Tbsp. chili powder

MAKES 1 ROLL
Combine cream cheese, Olde English cheese and garlic salt. Stir in sesame seeds. (To toast, spread seeds on a cookie sheet and bake at 350° for about 5 minutes until golden. Watch carefully.) Shape mixture into a roll (10×1¼ inches). Spread chili powder on wax paper and coat outside of cheese roll with chili powder by rolling over the wax paper. Chill. Serve with crackers.

ALMOND CRANBERRY PUNCH

3 pints chilled cranberry
  juice
½ cup chilled bottled lime
  juice or small can
  limeade
⅓ cup sugar
½ tsp. almond extract
2½ qts. ginger ale

MAKES 20 (½ CUP) SERVINGS
Pour first five ingredients in punch bowl. Stir until sugar is dissolved. Add ginger ale before serving and stir. Add ice block or mold.

A punch cup holds ½ cup of a beverage. The servings have therefore been measured as ½ cup equalling one serving.

APPETIZERS AND BEVERAGES

CREAMY FRUIT FLOAT

1 cup sliced strawberries
1 cup milk
⅓ cup sugar
1 pint orange sherbet
1—8 oz. can crushed pine-
apple, undrained

MAKES 8 (½ CUP) SERVINGS
Combine all ingredients in food processor or blender and blend until
smooth. Garnish with strawberry leaf
or mint.

FRUIT PARTY PUNCH

1—6 oz. can frozen orange
juice concentrate
1—6 oz. can frozen
lemonade concentrate
3 cups pineapple juice
1½ quarts cranberry juice

MAKES 24 (½ CUP) SERVINGS
Add water to orange juice and lemonade concentrates, according to package directions. Mix with other liquids
and chill.

CRANBERRY ORANGE PUNCH

6 cups cranberry juice
1 cup frozen orange juice
concentrate
3 Tbsp. lemon juice
1¼ cups pineapple juice
3 cups ice water

MAKES 24 (½ CUP) SERVINGS
Mix ingredients and chill. Serve plain
over an ice block, or with fruit sherbet
floating on top.

GOLDEN SUMMER PUNCH

2—12 oz. cans frozen orange
juice concentrate
2—12 oz. cans frozen lemon
juice concentrate
1 large can apricot nectar
2 large cans pineapple
juice
4 quarts water

MAKES 60 (½ CUP) SERVINGS
Combine ingredients and chill. Add
rum to spike.

APPETIZERS AND BEVERAGES

LIME COOLER PUNCH

1 cup lime juice or 2 small
   cans limeade
½ cup granulated sugar
2 quarts water
1 pint lime sherbet
1 pint pineapple sherbet
Lime slices
Mint leaves

MAKES 24 (½ CUP) SERVINGS
Combine lime juice and sugar and stir
until sugar is dissolved. Add all other
ingredients except sherbets. Just before serving fold in the lime and pineapple sherbet. Garnish with lime slices
and mint leaves.

LIME PUNCH

1 large pkg. lime jello
3½ cups boiling water
1 cup sugar
2—6 oz. cans frozen
   lemonade
1 large can pineapple
   juice
6 cups cold water
1 qt. ginger ale

MAKES 30 (½ CUP) SERVINGS
Combine jello, boiling water and sugar.
Stir until dissolved. Add lemonade,
pineapple juice, cold water and ginger
ale.

GRAPE PUNCH

1½ quarts (6 cups) apple
   juice
1 quart (4 cups) grape
   juice
1—6 oz. can frozen
   lemonade concentrate
32 oz. bottle (4 cups)
   lemon-lime flavored carbonated beverage

MAKES 28 (½ CUP) SERVINGS
In punch bowl, combine all ingredients.
Make an ice ring of frozen apple juice
and water with slices of golden and red
apples and grapes. It is pretty with this
punch.

 *Add carbonated beverages just before serving time and mix gently only
enough to blend, so "bubbles" remain.*

17

APPETIZERS AND BEVERAGES

PINEAPPLE SHERBET PUNCH

1—6 oz. can frozen pink
  lemonade concentrate
1—6 oz. can frozen orange
  juice concentrate
4½ cups water
1 pint pineapple sherbet
1 pint vanilla ice cream
1 quart ginger ale

MAKES 24 (½ CUP) SERVINGS
Pour lemonade, orange juice concentrate and water in punch bowl. Stir to blend. Fold in sherbet and ice cream. Add ginger ale. Serve at once.

PARTY PUNCH

1 pkg. cherry Kool-Aid
1 pkg. strawberry Kool-Aid
2 cups sugar
3 quarts water
1—6 oz. can frozen orange
  juice concentrate
1—6 oz. can frozen
  lemonade concentrate
1 quart ginger ale

MAKES 32 (½ CUP) SERVINGS
Dissolve Kool-Aid in water, add sugar, stir to dissolve sugar. Add juice concentrates and chill. Just before serving, add ginger ale.

STRAWBERRY-PINEAPPLE PUNCH

1—6 oz. can frozen
  lemonade concentrate
1—8 oz. can crushed
  pineapple
1—10 oz. pkg. frozen
  strawberries
2 quarts ginger ale, chilled
Crushed ice

MAKES 30 (½ CUP) SERVINGS
Put lemonade concentrate, pineapple, strawberries in blender or food processor. Blend until completely smooth. Combine with ginger ale and pour over crushed ice in punch bowl.

To make a fruit- or flower-filled ice ring, first freeze the ring filled ⅓ full with water. Add desired garnish or decoration, and add water to fill ⅔ full. Freeze again. Then completely fill with water and freeze again.

APPETIZERS AND BEVERAGES

❧ ❧ ❧ ❧ ❧ ❧ ❧ ❧ ❧ ❧ ❧ ❧ ❧ ❧ ❧ ❧ ❧ ❧ ❧ ❧

STRAWBERRY PUNCH

1—3 oz. pkg. strawberry
flavored gelatin
1 cup boiling water
2—6 oz. cans frozen pink
lemonade concentrate
1—6 oz. can frozen orange
juice concentrate
6 cups cold water
28 oz. bottle (3½ cups)
ginger ale or 7-Up
1 pint fresh strawberries
with stems, frozen

MAKES 30 (½ CUP) SERVINGS
Dissolve gelatin in boiling water; cool.
Combine gelatin mixture, lemonade
concentrate, orange juice concentrate
and cold water in large punch bowl.
Before serving, stir in ginger ale and
frozen strawberries.

CHRISTMAS COFFEE PUNCH

½ gallon cold strong
coffee
2 tsp. vanilla
1 tsp. cinnamon
½ gallon chocolate ice
cream
½ gallon vanilla ice cream
1 pint heavy cream,
whipped

MAKES ABOUT 30 (½ CUP) SERVINGS
Combine coffee, vanilla, and cinnamon. Chill well. Immediately before
serving, pour coffee into a large punch
bowl. Spoon in ice cream in chunks.
Fold in whipped cream and serve.

ORANGE JULIUS

½ cup frozen orange juice
concentrate
½ cup milk
½ cup water
½ tsp. vanilla
6 ice cubes

MAKES 4 SMALL SERVINGS
Combine all ingredients in a blender
until smooth. This is a real hit with kids.

 One gallon of punch makes 30 ½-cup servings.

APPETIZERS AND BEVERAGES

HOT CRANBERRY-APPLE CIDER

2 quarts apple cider
1 can cranberry juice
   concentrate
3 cinnamon sticks
1 tsp. whole allspice
1 tsp. whole cloves
Orange slices
1½ cups water

MAKES 20 (½ CUP) SERVINGS
Combine all ingredients in large kettle. Let simmer at least 15–20 minutes. Strain spices before serving.

HOT SPICED NECTAR

3 cups apricot nectar
2 cups orange juice
1 cup water
2 Tbsp. lime juice
½ cup brown sugar
10 cinnamon sticks
6–8 whole cloves

MAKES 12 (½ CUP) SERVINGS
Combine all ingredients in large saucepan and simmer 15–20 minutes. Strain spices and serve hot.

TEXAS TEA

8 cups water
1½ cups sugar
1 lemon
2 cups strong tea, using 3
   tea bags
Juice of 3 lemons
Juice of 2 oranges
1 tsp. vanilla
2 tsp. almond extract
Garnishes:
   Thinly sliced oranges,
   thinly sliced lemons, or
   fresh mint

MAKES 10 CUPS
Boil water, sugar and sliced lemon for 5 minutes. Add tea, juices, vanilla and almond extract. Heat and serve hot with a slice of orange. Can also be served cold with an orange or lemon slice or fresh mint.

 Coffee stored in the refrigerator or freezer will retain its fresh flavor.

APPETIZERS AND BEVERAGES

CINNAMON COCOA MOCHA MIX

4 cups nonfat dry milk powder
1 cup non-dairy coffee creamer
2½ cups instant presweetened cocoa mix
½ cup instant coffee crystals
1½ cups powdered sugar
1 Tbsp. ground cinnamon
1 tsp. ground allspice
¼ cup cocoa

MAKES 10 CUPS
Combine all ingredients in large bowl and mix well. To make 1 serving, measure ⅓ cup of dry mix into a mug. Fill with boiling water, stir and top with whipped cream. Store dry mixture in tightly covered container.

WOLFENSBURGER PASS HOT CHOCOLATE

1—15 oz. can sweetened condensed milk
4 oz. semi-sweet cooking chocolate
1 cup whipping cream, whipped
6 cups milk

MAKES 15 (½ CUP) SERVINGS
In a small saucepan, mix condensed milk and chocolate pieces. (Can also be melted in microwave.) Stir constantly over low heat until chocolate melts. Cool to room temperature and fold in whipped cream. Mix ¼ cup of chocolate mix with ¾ cup warm milk. Can be stored in refrigerator up to one week in covered container.

APPETIZERS AND BEVERAGES

❧❧❧❧❧❧❧❧❧❧❧❧❧❧❧❧❧❧❧❧❧

IRISH COFFEE EGGNOG PUNCH

2 qts. commercial
   refrigerated eggnog
1/3 cup firmly packed brown
   sugar
3 Tbsps. instant coffee
   granules
½ tsp. cinnamon
½ tsp. nutmeg
1 cup Irish whiskey
   (optional) *
1 qt. coffee ice cream,
   scooped into balls

Garnishes: Sweetened
   whipped cream, freshly
   grated nutmeg

*Substitute ½ tsp. rum
   extract if you choose

Makes about 3 quarts
Combine first five ingredients in a large mixing bowl; beat at low speed with an electric mixer until sugar dissolves. Chill 15 minutes; stir again until coffee granules dissolve. Stir in whiskey if desired. Cover and chill at least 1 hour. Pour into a punch bowl. Spoon in ice cream. Garnish, if desired.

CHAMPAGNE PUNCH

2 cups sugar
2 cups water
Juice of 6 lemons
2 cups apricot nectar
1—6 oz. can frozen orange
   juice concentrate
3 cups apple juice
2 cups pineapple juice
2—12 oz. cans ginger ale
2 fifths champagne

SERVES 50 (½ CUP SERVINGS)
Boil sugar and water for 1 minute and cool. Add juices. May freeze at this point. If so, thaw 1 hour before serving. Add ginger ale and champagne. Serve over an ice block in a punch bowl.

APPETIZERS AND BEVERAGES

❦ ❦ ❦ ❦ ❦ ❦ ❦ ❦ ❦ ❦ ❦ ❦ ❦ ❦ ❦ ❦ ❦ ❦ ❦

JOAN'S COFFEE RUM PUNCH

1—2 oz. jar instant coffee
2 cups boiling water
2 cups sugar
1 quart milk
1 quart half and half
1 quart carbonated water,
   chilled
1 cup rum

MAKES 24 (½ CUP) SERVINGS
Mix instant coffee with boiling water
and sugar. Chill 2–3 hours or overnight.
When ready to serve, add milk, half
and half, carbonated water and rum.
Serve cold. This is good over ice, but
it isn't necessary to serve it that way.
It is **so** good you might plan on everyone drinking more than just a half-cup
serving!!

RUM SLUSH

1—6 oz. can frozen
   lemonade concentrate
1—6 oz. can frozen limeade
   concentrate
1—46 oz. can pineapple-
   grapefruit juice
3 cups light rum

SERVES 20
Mix all ingredients and freeze at least
24 hours before serving. Keeps indefi-
nitely in the freezer, slushy, and ready
to take the edge off a hot summer's
day. Garnish with mint leaves if desired.

T LAZY S MARGARITAS

3 shots tequila
1 shot triple sec
1—6 oz. can limeade
1—12 oz. can 7-Up, ginger
   ale, or Fresca
15–20 ice cubes (1½ cups
   crushed ice)
Coarse salt
Lime

4–6 SERVINGS
Pour tequila, triple sec, limeade and
7-Up into a blender. Add ice and continue blending until slushy. Rub the
rims of glasses with a slice of fresh
lime and dip rims in coarse salt. Pour
mixture into prepared glasses.

Brunch

BRUNCH

EGGS FRIED JUST RIGHT

Eggs
Bacon or sausage
drippings
Salt & pepper

After frying bacon or sausage, break eggs into skillet, over medium-low heat. DO NOT fry too fast over hot burner. Salt and pepper to taste. Add a tablespoon of water and place a lid on the skillet. The grease will spatter and cook the top of the egg. When prepared this way, you will have a nice "over-easy" fried egg—cooked on top, still somewhat runny in the middle and no crispy edges. Cook a little longer to set the middle.

Eggs can also be broken into skillet, the grease spooned over top of egg while tilting skillet slightly. Cook to desired doneness.

SCRAMBLED EGGS

1 dozen eggs
⅓—½ cup cold milk
Salt
Pepper
Butter

EXTRAS:
Diced ham
Chopped green chilies
Chopped smoked sausage

SERVES 6
Break eggs into a bowl. Whisk in cold milk. Season with salt and pepper. Add any extras. Melt butter in a large skillet over medium high heat. Cook stirring constantly, until fluffy, and still a little bit loose. Turn immediately on serving platter. Eggs will continue to cook after removing them from the pan, so they are easy to overcook. Then they get tough and rubbery. Soak pan in cold water immediately.

Scrambled eggs are the ultimate comfort food. Served with hot sausage and biscuits, they are a terrific way to start the day, a solace after a hard day at work when you forgot to thaw the pork chops, and a satisfying late-night snack after a night out on the town.

BISCUITS 'N GRAVY

BISCUITS
2 cups flour
3 tsp. baking powder
1 tsp. salt
¼ cup shortening
¾ cup milk

GRAVY
5 Tbsp. bacon drippings
6 Tbsp. flour
2½ cups milk
Salt & pepper

Bacon, fried just right
Eggs, cooked just right
Home grown tomatoes

SERVES 4
To prepare biscuits, combine flour, baking powder and salt in bowl. Cut in shortening until it resembles crumbs. Stir in milk. Can be rolled ½ inch thick and cut into biscuits, or pat dough into 8×8 inch greased pan. Bake 10–12 minutes in 450° oven or until golden brown. Cut into squares.

To prepare gravy, stir flour into bacon drippings. Add milk and stir, over medium high heat, until smooth and thick. Salt and pepper to taste.

Heap plates with bacon, biscuits, gravy, eggs and a couple of slices of tomato and enjoy the sunrise!

SPRING OMELET

4 Tbsp. butter
1—10 oz. pkg. frozen
  asparagus, or com-
  parable fresh amount
1–1½ cups fresh
  mushrooms, sliced
¾ tsp. dillweed
4 eggs
2 Tbsp. milk
½ tsp. celery salt
Dash pepper
2 Tbsp. vegetable oil
2 slices bacon, fried
½ cup Cheddar cheese,
  grated

MAKES TWO
Melt butter in skillet and add asparagus, mushrooms, and dillweed. Cook and stir until mushrooms are tender. In small bowl, combine eggs, milk, celery salt and pepper. Beat with fork or whisk until well mixed. In an eight-inch omelet pan or skillet, heat 1 tablespoon oil over medium high heat. When a drop of water sizzles in the pan, pour in egg mixture. Cook gently, lifting edges so uncooked portion flows underneath, until eggs are set. Spoon asparagus filling onto omelet, add strip of bacon and roll up. Sprinkle with cheese. Repeat for second omelet. This can also be served with a Hollandaise Sauce (see Index) or Cheddar Cheese sauce (see Index) in place of Cheddar cheese.

BRUNCH

BREAKFAST PIZZA

1 lb. pork sausage
1—8 oz. pkg. refrigerated
    crescent rolls
1 cup frozen loose-pack
    hashed browns
    potatoes, thawed
1 cup shredded sharp
    Cheddar cheese
5 eggs, beaten
¼ cup milk
½ tsp. salt
½ tsp. pepper
2 Tbsp. Parmesan cheese,
    grated

SERVES 6–8
Cook sausage in medium skillet until brown; drain and set aside. Separate crescent dough into 8 triangles. Place with elongated points toward center of greased 12-inch pizza pan. Press bottom and sides to form a crust. Seal perforations. Spoon sausage over dough. Sprinkle with hashed browns and Cheddar cheese. Combine eggs, milk, salt and pepper; pour over sausage mixture. Bake at 375° for 25 minutes. Sprinkle with parmesan cheese and bake an additional 5 minutes.

HUEVOS RANCHEROS

1 egg
1 corn tortilla
2 Tbsp. Picante sauce
Grated cheese (Longhorn
    or Monterey Jack)
Oil for frying

SERVES 1
Heat oil in skillet and fry tortilla. Drain. Fry egg, then place on the tortilla. Spoon Picante sauce over egg and top with grated cheese. Place under the broiler a few seconds to melt cheese. Serve with refried beans for a fast, easy lunch or Sunday night supper.

LONGHORN BRUNCH CASSEROLE

1 lb. Jimmy Dean hot
sausage (may use regular)
2—4 oz. cans green chilies
1 lb. Longhorn cheese,
   grated
1 lb. Monterey Jack
   cheese, grated
9 eggs, beaten
1 cup milk
2 Tbsp. flour
Paprika

SERVES 10–12

Brown sausage and drain well. In a lightly greased 9×13 inch Pyrex baking dish, layer sausage with cheeses and chilies. Combine eggs, milk, and flour in a food processor. Pour over sausage, etc. Sprinkle with paprika and bake at 350° for 40–45 minutes.

SWISS BACON & TOMATO STACKS

SWISS SAUCE:
1 cup American cheese,
   grated
1 cup Swiss cheese, grated
1¼ cups half and half
1 tsp. dry mustard
½–1 tsp. Worcestershire
   sauce
2 egg yolks, beaten

BREAD CRUMBS:
2 Tbsp. butter
1 cup soft bread crumbs
¼ cup grated Parmesan
   cheese
1 Tbsp. chopped chives
1 tsp. paprika

12 slices bacon
6 thick tomato slices
6 English muffin halves,
   buttered & toasted

SERVES 6

In heavy saucepan, mix American cheese, Swiss cheese, half and half, dry mustard and Worcestershire sauce. Stir constantly over low heat, until melted. Stir 1 cup of hot sauce into egg yolks; mix well. Add egg yolk mixture to hot mixture in saucepan. Stir constantly over medium heat until thick.

In small saucepan, melt butter; add breadcrumbs, Parmesan cheese, chives and paprika. Toss and set aside.

In large skillet, fry bacon until crisp. Remove bacon and drain all but 3 tablespoons of drippings. Cook tomato slices in reserved drippings for 2 minutes. Butter and toast muffins. Place a tomato slice and 2 slices of bacon on top of each muffin. (Can also add an egg!) Ladle sauce over muffin stacks. Top with bread crumb mixture. Bake 15 minutes at 350°.

BRUNCH

CRUSTLESS QUICHE

1 cup Swiss cheese, grated
8–10 slices bacon, cooked
   and crumbled
¼ cup onion, minced
4 eggs
14 oz. small curd cottage
   cheese
1 pkg. frozen chopped
   spinach, cooked with
   1 tsp. salt, then drained
½ tsp. salt
½ tsp. pepper
1 tsp. Worcestershire sauce
3 dashes Tabasco sauce

SERVES 8–10

Sprinkle cheese, bacon, and onion in that order in a 10-inch greased pie plate. Beat remaining ingredients until well blended. Pour over bacon mixture. Bake at 350° for 35–40 minutes. Let stand 10–15 minutes before cutting.

QUICK AND EASY QUICHE

½ cup butter, melted
1½ cups milk
¼ tsp. salt
Dash of pepper
½ cup biscuit mix
1 cup Swiss cheese, grated
½ cup chopped ham or
   crumbled, crisp bacon
3 eggs, beaten

SERVES 6

Mix melted butter, milk, salt, pepper and biscuit mix in blender or food processor, or mix well with a beater. Pour into a greased, glass 10 inch pie dish. Sprinkle batter with cheese and ham or bacon. Push the meat below the surface with the back of a spoon. Pour eggs over the ham and cheese. Microwave for 18 minutes or bake in oven 40 minutes at 375°.

OLD SOUTH SHORTCAKE

1 cup cornmeal
1 cup flour
¼ cup sugar
4 tsp. baking powder
½ tsp. salt
¼ cup milk
2 eggs
¼ cup vegetable
   shortening
2 tsp. prepared mustard
1—8 oz. can cream style
   corn
½ cup Swiss cheese,
   grated
1—3 oz. can chopped
   mushrooms, drained
1 cup Swiss cheese, grated

CREAM SAUCE:
2 Tbsp. butter
2 Tbsp. flour
¾ cup chicken broth
¾ cup half-and-half
2 egg yolks, slightly
   beaten
1 cup cubed cooked
   chicken or turkey
1 cup cubed cooked ham

SERVES 5

In medium bowl combine cornmeal, flour, sugar, baking powder, salt, milk, eggs, shortening, mustard, corn and cheese. Mix well. Spread about 1 cup of the batter in a greased 8x8 inch baking dish. Sprinkle on mushrooms, and 1 cup of cheese. Top with remaining batter. Bake at 350° for 35 minutes or until cornbread is golden brown. Prepare cream sauce and ladle over cornbread squares.

To prepare sauce melt butter in saucepan, blend in flour. Add chicken broth and half-and-half. Stir constantly over medium-high heat until sauce thickens and bubbles. Blend ¾ cup of the sauce into beaten egg yolks; mix well. Add egg yolk mixture to hot sauce. Stir in chicken and ham. Stir constantly over medium-high heat until heated through. Keep warm. Kids love this on toast.

BRUNCH

CHEESE AND SAUSAGE GRITS

1 lb. sausage
¼ tsp. garlic powder
Dash Tabasco
½ tsp. salt
⅛ tsp. pepper
1 cup instant grits
2 cups boiling water
1 cup extra sharp Cheddar
   cheese, grated
¼ cup butter, melted
2 large eggs, beaten
4 oz. mild green chilies,
   optional

Brown sausage and drain. Add Tabasco sauce, garlic powder, salt and pepper. Set aside. Cook grits in 2 cups boiling water. Add all ingredients to grits and stir until well mixed. Pour into buttered 9x13 inch baking dish. Bake, uncovered, at 350° for 45 minutes to 1 hour or until set in middle. This is also good served at supper without the sausage and green chilies.

SILVER DOLLAR PANCAKES

2 eggs
2 cups buttermilk
4 Tbsp. oil
2 cups flour
2 Tbsp. + 2 tsp. sugar
2 tsp. baking powder
1 tsp. soda
1 tsp. salt

MAKES 10–12 4-INCH PANCAKES
Beat egg. Add remaining ingredients in order listed and beat until just smooth. Drop by the tablespoonful onto a hot griddle, cook, and serve with butter and warmed syrup. We used to think pancakes were pancakes until we tasted these!

BUTTERMILK WAFFLES

1¾ cups flour
1 tsp. baking powder
1 tsp. soda
½ tsp. salt
2 cups buttermilk
⅓ cup oil
2 eggs, slightly beaten

MAKES 6 WAFFLES
Preheat waffle iron. Mix dry ingredients, then add buttermilk, oil, and eggs. Mix well. Pour about ¾ cup batter in the middle of the waffle iron. Spread to about 1 inch of the edge. Waffle is ready when steam quits escaping from the iron. Serve immediately with hot butter and syrup. These freeze well.

BRUNCH

STRAWBERRY FRENCH TOAST

2 slices French bread, cut
   1 inch thick
3 Tbsp. strawberry
   preserves
1 Tbsp. chopped pecans
1 egg, slightly beaten
4 Tbsp. milk
1½ tsp. sugar
2 drops vanilla
2 Tbsp. butter
2 Tbsp. powdered sugar
¼ cup fresh strawberries

SERVES 2

Make pocket in bread: cut each slice of French bread in half through crust on one side, keeping one side uncut. In small bowl, mix together preserves and pecans. Stuff half of the mixture into each pocket. Mix together the egg, milk, sugar and vanilla in pie pan. Melt butter in skillet. Dip both sides of bread slices into egg mixture. Cook on buttered griddle until lightly browned on both sides. Sprinkle with powdered sugar and top with strawberries. This is also good served with peaches and peach or apricot preserves replacing the strawberries. Sprinkle with toasted, slivered almonds.

JOANIE'S BIRTHDAY BRUNCH SANDWICHES

4 slices sourdough bread,
   lightly toasted & buttered
8 eggs, scrambled or
   poached
6 oz. crab, fresh or frozen
1 tomato, sliced
½ red onion, sliced thin
Fresh spinach leaves
4 slices Swiss cheese

HOLLANDAISE SAUCE:
2 egg yolks
2½–3 Tbsp. lemon juice
½ cup cold butter

SERVES 4

Place toasted bread on cookie sheet. Top each with eggs, spinach leaves, tomato, onion, crab and a slice of Swiss cheese. Bake in 325° oven until cheese is melted and sandwiches are heated through. Drizzle hollandaise (or cheese sauce) over sandwich.

To prepare hollandaise sauce, combine egg yolks and lemon juice in small saucepan. Mix briskly. Add cube of butter whole, do not cut up. Cook over low heat, stirring constantly until thickened.

33

BRUNCH

HOLIDAY BRUNCH DISH

15 slices white sandwich
   bread
2 cups chopped ham
1 cup sharp Cheddar
   cheese, grated
1 cup Monterey Jack
   cheese, grated
1—4 oz. can chopped
   green chilies
7 eggs
½ Tbsp. dry mustard
1 tsp. salt
3 cups milk
1 cup cornflakes, crushed
¼ cup butter, melted

SERVES 10
Remove crusts from bread and cut slices in half. Butter a 9×13 inch glass baking dish, and place half the bread in the bottom. Layer with ham, cheese, and green chilies. Cover with remaining bread. Beat eggs with dry mustard, salt and milk. Pour over casserole and cover. Place in the refrigerator overnight (or for 12 hours). Before baking, cover with cornflakes and drizzle with butter. Bake at 350° for 40 minutes. This is a good company brunch dish.

BANANA SPLIT STACK

Waffles or pancakes
Strawberry yogurt
Banana yogurt
Crushed pineapple or
   pineapple ice cream
   topping
Bananas, sliced
Pecans, chopped
Strawberries, sliced

SAUCE:
1—6 oz. pkg. butterscotch
   chips
⅓ cup evaporated milk or
   cream
12 large marshmallows

Stack waffles or pancakes with layers of various toppings between each waffle. Pour butterscotch sauce over stack and sprinkle with chopped nuts. Everyone will enjoy making their favorite "banana split."

To make sauce, combine butterscotch chips, milk and marshmallows in small saucepan. Stir over low heat until mixture is melted and smooth.

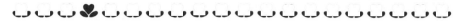

BLUEBERRY LEMON PANCAKES

PANCAKES:
1 cup flour
2 Tbsp. sugar
1 Tbsp. baking powder
½ tsp. salt
¼ tsp. baking soda
1 egg
½ cup milk
½ cup lemon yogurt
2 Tbsp. vegetable oil
Vegetable oil
1 cup fresh or frozen
   blueberries

TOPPING:
1 cup lemon yogurt
1 cup Cool Whip
½ cup fresh or frozen
   blueberries
Butter
Powdered sugar

SERVES 3–4
In medium bowl, mix flour, sugar, baking powder, salt and baking soda. Mix in egg, milk, ½ cup lemon yogurt and 2 tablespoons oil. Beat until fairly smooth. Brush preheated griddle with oil. Pour ¼ cup batter for each pancake and sprinkle each with two tablespoons blueberries. Cook until golden brown; turn and cook other side.

In small bowl, combine other cup of yogurt and Cool Whip. Top each pancake with butter, yogurt-whipped cream mixture, a tablespoon of blueberries and powdered sugar.

BRUNCH

GERMAN APPLE PANCAKE

PANCAKE:
3 large eggs
¾ cup milk
¾ cup flour
½ tsp. salt
1½ Tbsp. butter

APPLE FILLING:
4 Tbsp. butter
1 lb. Granny Smith apples,
    peeled and thinly sliced
¼ cup sugar
1 tsp. cinnamon

Confectioner's sugar
Whipped cream
Vanilla ice cream

SERVES 6–8
Beat eggs, milk, flour and salt until smooth. Melt 1½ tablespoons butter in a heavy 12-inch cast iron skillet. When it is very hot, pour the batter into the skillet and put it in a 450° oven. Bake for 15 minutes, watching to see if the batter puffs up. If so, prick with a fork to deflate. After 15 minutes, lower the temperature to 350° and bake for another 10 minutes. The pancake should be light brown and crisp.

Meanwhile, melt the 4 tablespoons of butter in a skillet, and saute the apples with sugar and cinnamon until tender. When pancake is done, slide it onto a serving platter and pour the apples over the top. Sprinkle with powdered sugar and cut into pie-shaped wedges. This is excellent for breakfast with link sausages and scrambled eggs. Would also be good for dessert with whipped cream or ice cream on top.

 Rub butter or margarine over cut portion of cheese to keep it from drying out.

AEBLESKIVERS

4 eggs, separated
2 cups sour cream
2 Tbsp. oil
2 cups Bisquick or dry
   pancake mix
4 cardamon seeds, peeled
   and crushed (optional)
Thinly sliced cooking
   apples (optional)

MAKES 26–30

Beat egg whites until stiff. Mix other ingredients well and fold in egg whites. Fill cups in hot Aebleskiver pan (available in most kitchen shops) two-thirds full. Turn with a utility fork when golden brown on the bottom, and cook on the other side. Be sure pan is not so hot that the Aebleskivers don't cook in the middle. Serve with hot syrup.

Aebleskivers are Danish apple pancakes, and though they can be cooked on a griddle the same way as a regular pancake, the Aebleskiver pan is fun to use. For an authentic version, top each batter-filled cup with a thin slice of apple. It will sink during cooking, and end up in the middle of the Aebleskiver.

Soups
and
Sandwiches

SOUPS AND SANDWICHES

CREAM OF ASPARAGUS SOUP

¼ cup butter
¼ cup onion, chopped
½ cup celery, chopped
1 lb. fresh or frozen
   asparagus
5 cups chicken stock
3 Tbsp. flour
4 oz. cream cheese
Salt, and white pepper
Hard boiled egg, chopped
   for garnish (optional)

SERVES 6
Saute onion and celery in butter until tender. Cook asparagus for 3–5 minutes; drain. Cut off ½-inch of tips and save. Puree asparagus with some of the chicken stock. Stir flour into onion, celery and butter; pour chicken broth over mixture and stir well with whisk until smooth. Add cheese. Heat soup and add tips. Garnish with egg. A very tasty and elegant soup.

CHILLED AVOCADO SOUP

2 ripe avocados, mashed
   well
1 cup consomme
1 cup sour cream
½ tsp. onion juice (or
   more to taste)
1 tsp. lemon juice
Salt to taste
Dash chili powder

SERVES 4
Combine mashed avocado, consomme and sour cream. Whisk well to blend. Season with salt, juices and chili powder. Chill and serve very cold with tortilla chips. This is a very rich soup. . .would be delicious at a spring or summer luncheon as a first course.

SOUPS AND SANDWICHES

BROCCOLI CHEESE SOUP

1 cup boiling water
2 chicken bouillon cubes
3 Tbsp. butter
2 Tbsp. finely chopped
  onion
1 cup sliced fresh
  mushrooms
3 Tbsp. flour
2 cups half and half
½ tsp. Worcestershire
  sauce
⅛ tsp. oregano
½ lb. sharp Cheddar
  cheese, grated
2 cups fresh broccoli,
  chopped

SERVES 4
Pour water over bouillon cubes in saucepan and stir until dissolved. In small skillet, melt butter and lightly saute onions and mushrooms. Stir flour into mixture. Add to bouillon and water, blend, and add remaining ingredients. Cover over low heat for 3–4 hours. May use a crockpot.

CREAM OF CAULIFLOWER SOUP

1 large cauliflower
¼ cup butter
2 Tbsp. chopped onion
3 small celery ribs,
  minced
¼ cup flour
4 cups chicken stock
2 cups half and half
Salt
Grated cheese for garnish

SERVES 6
Cook cauliflower until tender. Drain, add 1 cup chicken stock and puree in food processor or blender. Can be pureed smooth or left with some pieces. Melt butter in saucepan and saute onion and celery until tender. Stir in flour. Add chicken broth and stir well until bubbly. Over low heat, add cauliflower and half and half; do not bring to boil. Add salt to taste. Garnish each bowl with grated cheese.

SOUPS AND SANDWICHES

FAMILY TIME STEW

2 Tbsps. olive oil
4 boneless, skinless
   chicken breast halves,
   cut into 1-inch pieces
1 cup onion, chopped
½ green pepper, chopped
½ yellow pepper, chopped
¼ tsp. garlic powder
2—14 oz. cans stewed
   tomatoes
1—15 oz. can pinto beans,
   drained
¾ cup medium picante
   sauce
1 Tbsp. chili powder
1 Tbsp. cumin

GARNISH:
½ cup Cheddar cheese,
   grated
6 Tbsp. sour cream

SERVES 6

In a large Dutch oven, heat olive oil over medium heat. Add chicken, onion, bell peppers, and garlic, and cook until chicken is white throughout. Add tomatoes, beans, picante sauce, chili powder, and cumin. Reduce heat to low and simmer 25 minutes or up to 2 hours. Place in individual serving bowls and top with cheese and sour cream.

This filling soup is a real hit with the family!

Ideas for soup garnishes:

For Clear Soups: Chopped parsley, vegetable curls or thin slices, thin slices of avocado, chopped hard-cooked egg, sliced stuffed olives, croutons

For Cream Soups: Salted whipped cream, chopped toasted almonds, minced chives, toasted croutons, cheese popcorn, pimiento, sliced mushrooms

For Chowders and Meat Soups: Thin slices frankfurters in pea or bean soups, sliced lemon in fish chowder, chopped parsley, and chopped crisp bacon

MEXICAN CHEESE SOUP

½ cup onion, finely
  chopped
½ cup carrots, grated
½ cup celery, thinly sliced
6 Tbsp. butter
6 Tbsp. flour
1 tsp. paprika
1 tsp. dry mustard
1 tsp. Worcestershire
  sauce
2 cups chicken broth
1 cup milk
½ tsp. Liquid Smoke
1—8 oz. jar pasteurized
  process cheese spread
  with jalapenos or
  pimiento
Tortilla chips
Grated Cheddar cheese
Chili powder
Chopped green chilies

SERVES 4–6
Saute onion, carrots and celery in butter until tender. Stir in flour, paprika, dry mustard and Worcestershire sauce until blended. Add chicken broth and milk. Stir over medium heat until thick. Stir in Liquid Smoke and cheese spread. Simmer 10–15 minutes. To serve, top each bowl of soup with grated Cheddar cheese, lightly crushed tortilla chips, sliced chilies, if desired, and a sprinkle of chili powder.

RED BEANS AND RICE

1 lb. dry red beans
8 cups water
1 meaty ham bone or ham
  hocks
2 onions, chopped
¼ tsp. garlic powder
2 bay leaves
Tabasco sauce
Salt and pepper to taste

SERVES 6–8
Place ingredients in a heavy Dutch oven or stockpot. Bring to a boil, then lower heat and simmer, stirring occasionally for about 4 hours. When they are soft enough, mash some of the beans against the side of the pot to thicken the sauce. Serve over hot, cooked rice. (Soaking the beans overnight cuts the cooking time in half.)

SOUPS AND SANDWICHES

COLD-DAY CHOWDER

8 slices bacon, cut up
1 cup onion, chopped
5 medium potatoes, peeled and cubed
1 cup water
1—10 oz. can cream of chicken soup
1 cup sour cream
1¾ cup milk
½ tsp. salt
Dash pepper

SERVES 6
Fry bacon until crisp. Remove bacon and saute onion in drippings. Remove onion and drain. Cook cubed potatoes in 1 cup water until tender. Add soup, onion and bacon, sour cream, milk, and seasonings. Save some bacon to use as garnish for each bowl of soup. Simmer to heat through, but do not boil.

CHUCKWAGON SOUP

1 lb. hamburger meat
1 medium onion, chopped
3 stalks celery, chopped
3 carrots, sliced
4 potatoes, peeled and cubed (or rice, barley or noodles)
1—10 oz. pkg. frozen mixed vegetables (or add corn, peas, beans or any other vegetable to taste)
1—16 oz. can tomatoes (or tomato sauce)
Water to cover
4 beef bouillon cubes
¼ tsp. black pepper
1½ tsp. salt
¼ tsp. garlic powder
Cheddar cheese, grated
Flour & water mixture to thicken

SERVES 6–8
In a large saucepan, brown the hamburger with the onion. Drain fat. Add celery, carrots, potatoes, frozen mixed vegetables and tomatoes. Add water, then seasonings. Bring to a boil, reduce heat and simmer until vegetables are tender. Ladle into bowls and top each generously with grated cheese. As with any soup, this is better the second day as flavors have blended. This is also a good soup to make when there are little dabs of leftover vegetables to use, and it's definitely one you can make your own with dashes of your favorite seasonings.

 Make soups at least several hours ahead of serving and let set to allow flavors to blend.

GAZPACHO

1 cup tomatoes, peeled
   and finely chopped
½ cup bell pepper, finely
   chopped and seeded
½ cup celery, finely
   chopped
½ cup cucumber, peeled
   and finely chopped
¼ cup green onion, finely
   chopped
¼ cup parsley, finely
   chopped
⅛ tsp. garlic powder
3 Tbsp. tarragon wine
   vinegar
2 Tbsp. olive oil
1 tsp. salt
¼ tsp. pepper
½ tsp. Worcestershire
   sauce
1—46 oz. can V-8 juice
1 cup sour cream (for
   garnish)
Chopped parsley

SERVES 8–10
Combine all ingredients except sour cream and chill well. Top each bowlful wih a dollop of sour cream and sprinkle with chopped parsley. This cold soup is delicious at brunch as a first course with chicken crepes and fruit salad.

SOUPS AND SANDWICHES

HEARTY WHITE BEAN CHILI

2 Tbsps. oil
1 small onion, chopped
1 yellow or red pepper,
  chopped
Garlic powder to taste
1—4 oz. can chopped
  green chilies
½ tsp. ginger
½ tsp. salt
½ tsp. sage
½ tsp. cumin
2 chicken breasts, cooked
  and diced
3 Tbsps. butter, melted
¼ cup flour
½ cup cream
2 cups chicken broth
1 cup frozen corn
1—15 oz. can Great
  Northern beans

SERVES 4
Sauté onion and pepper and garlic powder in oil until cooked. Mix with green chilies, spices, and chicken and set aside. In a Dutch oven, combine butter and flour and cook over medium heat until blended. Stir in liquids until smooth. Add onion/chicken mixture, corn, and beans. Cook over low heat for about 30 minutes. Can also be cooked in a crockpot on low.

ARIZONA SOUP

4 cups beef broth
1—14 oz. can diced
  tomatoes
1 tsp. dried oregano
½ tsp. ground cumin
½ tsp. pepper
1 lb. lean ground beef
¼ cup Minute rice
1 large egg
½ tsp. salt
½ cup green onions, thinly
  sliced
¼ cup fresh cilantro,
  chopped

SERVES 4
In a 6 qt. saucepan, combine broth, tomatoes, ½ tsp. oregano and ¼ tsp. each cumin, garlic powder, and pepper. Cover pan and bring to a boil.

In a bowl, mix beef, rice, egg, salt, and remaining oregano, cumin, garlic powder, and pepper. When broth is boiling, drop beef mixture in 1-inch balls into broth. Cover pan, reduce heat, and simmer about 10 minutes. Stir in green onions and cilantro. Serve immediately.

 Good character—like good soup—is usually homemade.

SOUPS AND SANDWICHES

MINESTRONE

Water
2–3 lbs. stew meat or beef shank
1 med. onion, diced
2 carrots, diced
2 stalks celery with tops, sliced
1—16 oz. can tomatoes, chopped
1—10 oz. pkg. frozen vegetables
2 tsp. salt
1 zucchini, sliced
1 cup shredded cabbage
1 Tbsp. dried basil
¼ tsp. garlic powder
1 tsp. oregano
½ cup vermicelli or 1—16 oz. can garbanzo beans

SERVES 10–12

Cover meat with water. Salt and pepper to taste. Cook in pressure cooker or crock pot until tender. Remove meat from bones and cut into pieces. Add beef and remaining ingredients to 2 cups of meat stock in crock pot. Cover and cook on low 6–8 hours or high for 4 hours. To serve, sprinkle each bowl with Parmesan cheese. Serve with Herb Buttered Bread (see Index) on a cold snowy day.

POTATO HAM SOUP

1 cup potatoes, diced
¼ cup onions, diced
½ cup celery, sliced
¼ tsp. pepper
½ tsp. salt
2 cups water
3 Tbsp. butter, melted
1½ Tbsp. flour
2 cups milk
1 cup ham, diced

SERVES 4–6

Combine first six ingredients. Simmer until vegetables are tender. Combine flour and melted butter. Add butter, milk and diced ham to vegetables. Heat just to boiling. Let set a couple of hours to allow flavors to blend.

SOUPS AND SANDWICHES

NINE BEAN SOUP

2 cups Bean Soup Mix
2 quarts water
1 lb. ham, diced
1 large onion, minced
¼ tsp. minced garlic
½ tsp. salt
½–1 cup sliced carrots
¼–½ cup celery, sliced
1—16 oz. can tomatoes
1—10 oz. can Ro-tel
  tomatoes (with green
  chilies)

SERVES 12–15
Wash bean mixture and soak overnight. Drain. Add two quarts water and ham, onion, garlic and salt. Bring to a boil and simmer 2–3 hours or until beans are tender. Add remaining ingredients. Simmer 30 minutes.

BEAN SOUP MIX
1—16 oz. pkg. dried black
  beans
1—16 oz. pkg. dried pinto
  beans
1—16 oz. pkg. dried split
  peas
1—16 oz. pkg. dried baby
  Lima beans
1—16 oz. pkg. dried Northern white beans
1—16 oz. pkg. dried barley
1—16 oz. pkg. dried garbanzo beans
1—16 oz. pkg. dried kidney
  beans
1—16 oz. pkg. dried black-
  eyed peas

Mix all together in **large** bowl. Store. This is fun to give as a gift. Pour 2 cups of beans in a jar and give along with the recipe.

SOUPS AND SANDWICHES

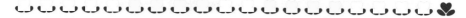

SEAFOOD CHOWDER

1 medium onion, chopped
½ cup celery, diced
3 Tbsp. butter
1—10¾ oz. can New
 England clam chowder
½ lb. cooked shrimp (chop
 if large), rinsed &
 drained
¾ cup chicken broth
¾ cup half and half
½ cup Cheddar cheese,
 grated
Parsley, chopped
Salt & pepper to taste

SERVES 4
Saute onion and celery in butter until
tender. Add remaining ingredients, except parsley. Stir over medium heat until cheese is melted. Season with salt
and pepper. Garnish with parsley.

CREAM OF SPINACH SOUP

¼–½ lb. fresh mushrooms,
 sliced
1 Tbsp. grated onion
3 Tbsp. butter
1—10 oz. pkg. frozen
 spinach
1 cup milk
3 Tbsp. butter
3 Tbsp. flour
1 cup chicken stock
1 tsp. chicken bouillon
2 cups cream
1 Tbsp. Parmesan cheese
Parmesan cheese, for
 garnish
Hard boiled egg, chopped
 for garnish (optional)

SERVES 3
Saute mushrooms and onion in butter
until tender; set aside. Cook spinach for
5 minutes; drain. Puree spinach with
milk in blender or food processor. Melt
3 tablespoons butter in saucepan; add
flour and stir to make a paste. Add
chicken stock and chicken bouillon,
and stir with whisk until smooth. Add
cream, mushrooms, spinach mixture
and Parmesan cheese. Heat soup well.
Better if it can sit a while before serving to allow flavors to blend. Garnish
with Parmesan cheese or chopped
egg.

 Try seasoning canned tomato soup with dried minced onion or a little dill.

SOUPS AND SANDWICHES

TORTILLA SOUP

5 chicken bouillon cubes
5 cups water
1—10 oz. can mild enchilada sauce (Rosarita is good)
1—16 oz. can stewed tomatoes
1 medium onion, diced (or 1 Tbsp. dried minced onion)
⅛ tsp. garlic powder
3 cups Longhorn cheese, grated
Tortilla chips (not Fritos— try Candy's Authentic tortilla chips)

SERVES 6–8
Combine first six ingredients in a large pot. Simmer for about 20 minutes. Coarsely crush tortilla chips in a bowl, and cover with broth ¾ full. Top generously with grated cheese. This quick and easy version of tortilla soup is one the whole family will love. It is very filling, so when offered with a salad, it makes a satisfying meal.

BAR-B-QUE BEEF SANDWICHES

1 3–4 lb. chuck roast
1 medium onion, chopped
Salt
Pepper
Bay leaf
Water to cover
Barbecue Sauce (see Index or use store-bought)

ENOUGH FOR 12–15 SANDWICHES
Place chuck roast in a large pan. Add seasonings and water to cover. Simmer 4 to 5 hours (you can do this in a crock pot) or until meat falls off the bone. Remove from broth, let cool slightly, then pull strands of beef, removing pieces of fat as you go. Pour Barbecue Sauce over all the shredded beef and heat in a saucepan for about 30 minutes, or simmer another hour or so in the crock pot to let the flavors blend. Mound hot beef on buns or club rolls, and serve with potato salad and pinto beans. This meat mixture freezes well, so you can make a large batch at once and have it on hand. You can also use the shredded beef on French Dip-type sandwiches, and the broth for soup base, if you choose.

SOUPS AND SANDWICHES

CANADIAN BACON SANDWICHES

6 slices rye bread, or
   whole wheat muffins
Butter or mayonnaise
12 strips bacon, chopped
6 Tbsp. green onion,
   chopped
3 tsp. fresh parsley,
   chopped
2 cups sliced, fresh
   mushrooms
12 slices Canadian bacon
6 slices Swiss cheese
½ cup black olives
6 thin green pepper rings
   (optional)

MAKES 6 SANDWICHES
Spread each slice of bread with butter or mayonnaise. Saute chopped bacon, onion, mushrooms and parsley for 5–10 minutes or until mushrooms are tender. Drain grease. Arrange 2 slices Canadian bacon on each bread slice and top with mushroom mixture. Add 1 slice of cheese. Sprinkle with chopped olives and green pepper ring. Place sandwiches on baking sheet and broil for 5 minutes or until cheese melts. Serve open-faced.

GRILLED CHEESEBURGERS ON RYE

1 lb. lean ground beef
4 slices Cheddar cheese
1—4 oz. can chopped
   green chilies
8 slices rye bread
¼ cup butter or margarine

SERVES 4
Make four beef patties and cook to desired doneness. Place a slice of cheese on each and top with a spoonful of green chilies (more or less according to taste). Place each patty between two slices of bread. Spread both sides of sandwich with butter, and grill in hot iron skillet.

 To get the last bit of mayonnaise or ketchup out of the jar or bottle, add a little vinegar into the jar, put the top on and lightly shake.

SOUPS AND SANDWICHES

CHICKEN SWISSWICHES

1½ cups cooked chicken,
   diced
⅓ cup mayonnaise
¼ cup celery, diced
¼ cup Swiss cheese,
   grated
8 slices bread
1—10 oz. pkg. frozen
   asparagus spears,
   cooked 3 minutes and
   drained
½ cup butter
1 pkg. seasoned coating
   mix for chicken

SERVES 4
Combine chicken, mayonnaise, celery and cheese. Spread on 4 slices of the bread. Arrange a couple of asparagus spears atop filling. Top with other slice of bread. Melt butter in skillet and brush butter on both outer sides of bread. Coat sandwiches with seasoned coating mix; brown on both sides in remaining butter in skillet.

TERIYAKI CHICKEN SANDWICH

Teriyaki marinade sauce
Boned chicken breasts
Provolone cheese, sliced
Mayonnaise
Tomato slices
Lettuce
Kaiser or crescent rolls

Marinate chicken breasts overnight in teriyaki sauce. Barbecue on grill, basting with marinade. When done, top each piece with cheese; let melt. Place on half of roll spread with mayonnaise. Top with spoonful of marinade, tomato slice, lettuce, and top of roll. Serve hot.

These are also good cold. Grill ahead of time and melt cheese on top. Keep in container with some of the marinade. Great picnic sandwich.

SOUPS AND SANDWICHES

CHICKEN CLUB SANDWICHES

3 slices bacon
1 cup cubed cooked
 chicken
2 Tbsp. celery, chopped
2 Tbsp. pimiento, chopped
Salt & pepper
2 Tbsp. sour cream
2 Tbsp. mayonnaise
4 English muffin halves
4 slices tomato
1 avocado, peeled and
 sliced

MAKES 4 SANDWICHES
Cook bacon in skillet until crisp. Crumble bacon and set aside. Cook and stir chicken, celery and pimiento in drippings until heated through. Season with salt and pepper. Spoon into bowl with bacon and mix well with sour cream and mayonnaise. Toast muffin halves, cut-side down in skillet with remaining drippings. Spoon chicken mixture onto muffins. Top with tomato and avocado slices. So good!

SOUTHWESTERN SUBMARINE SANDWICH

Breast of turkey, thinly
 sliced
Ham, thinly sliced
Summer sausage, thinly
 sliced
Baby Swiss cheese, sliced
Green chile strips (use
 canned)
Miracle Whip salad
 dressing
Club rolls

Split club rolls and spread each side with Miracle Whip. Layer turkey, ham, summer sausage, cheese and chile strips on each sandwich. Top with other half of roll and serve. Get all the meats and cheese for this sandwich at the deli section of your grocery store. Mix and match types of meats according to your preference, but don't leave out the green chile. . .it adds a special zip to an already good combination.

SOUPS AND SANDWICHES

HOT ROAST BEEF SANDWICH

2 Tbsp. butter
2 slices cooked roast beef
2 slices whole wheat
  bread, toasted
1 Tbsp. butter
1 Tbsp. flour
½ cup beef broth
1 tsp. Worcestershire
  sauce
Salt and pepper

MUSTARD SAUCE:
2 Tbsp. sour cream
1 tsp. Dijon-style mustard

SERVES 2
Melt 2 tablespoons butter in medium skillet. Cook and turn roast beef in butter until heated through. Place on toast and keep warm. Melt 1 tablespoon butter in skillet, stir in flour. Add beef broth and Worcestershire sauce and cook over medium heat until thickened and bubbly. Season to taste with salt and pepper. Spoon over roast beef and toast. Combine sour cream and mustard in small bowl. Drizzle over top of sandwich. Dad will love these!

GRILLED ROAST BEEF SANDWICHES

2 cups roast beef, cooked
  and ground
2 heaping Tbsp. pickle
  relish
1 Tbsp. onion, chopped
¼ cup mayonnaise or
  Miracle Whip
Garlic salt to taste
8 slices bread
Butter

MAKES 4 SANDWICHES
Combine all ingredients and spread on slices of bread. Butter outsides of both sides of the sandwich and grill over medium heat until outsides are browned and the roast beef filling is hot. Serve with a bowl of hot soup on a cold day for a hearty lunch.

SOUPS AND SANDWICHES

HAM 'N AVOCADO CRESCENTS

1—8 oz. can crescent din-
  ner rolls
4 tsp. horseradish mustard
4 thin slices ham
8 slices Swiss cheese
1 avocado, peeled and cut
  into 8 wedges

MAKES 8
Spread each rectangle with 1 teaspoon of mustard, top with 1 slice of ham and 1 cheese slice. Cut each rectangle in half, forming two triangles. Place avocado on wide end of each triangle and roll sandwich to the point. Place point side down on ungreased cookie sheet. Bake at 375° for 12–15 minutes or until golden brown.

HIGH COUNTRY HOT DOGS

1 tsp. dried minced onion
1—12 oz. can beer
1 Tbsp. Worcestershire
  sauce
½ cup chili sauce
12 all-beef hot dogs,
  quartered
6 club rolls, split

SERVES 6
Mix all ingredients together in a saucepan. Simmer for 30 minutes. Serve on split rolls.

SOUPS AND SANDWICHES

ITALIAN SAUSAGE ROLL

1 lb. Italian sausage (or
  pepperoni, sliced)
½ onion, chopped
Bell pepper, chopped
  (optional)
1—3 oz. can mushrooms,
  or 1 cup sliced fresh
1—10 oz. pkg. Mozzarella
  cheese, grated
1 loaf frozen bread dough
½ tsp. garlic salt
½ tsp. pepper
2 Tbsp. butter
Garlic salt
Ragu pizza sauce

SERVES 4

Fry sausage in skillet with onion, pepper and mushrooms; drain. Add half of the grated Mozzarella cheese. Roll out dough to ¼-inch thickness. Spread sausage mixture on dough and top with remaining half of grated cheese. Sprinkle with ½ teaspoon of the garlic salt and the pepper. Roll dough and mixture jelly roll-style and pinch ends of dough together. Brush with melted butter and sprinkle with garlic salt. Bake at 350° for 15–20 minutes or until golden brown. Warm pizza sauce. Slice roll and top each serving with sauce, or use sauce for dipping. Mama mia!

PIZZA BURGERS

2 lbs. ground beef
¼ bottle chili sauce
1 Tbsp. oregano
¼ tsp. salt
⅛ tsp. pepper
1—10 oz. can tomato soup
¼ cup Parmesan cheese
½ tsp. garlic salt
8 oz. Mozzarella cheese,
  grated
8 hamburger buns

SERVES 6–8

Brown ground beef and drain well. Add all ingredients except Mozzarella cheese and let simmer 5–10 minutes. Sprinkle grated cheese over hamburger mixture in skillet. Cover and let simmer until cheese melts. Use spatula to place filling into bun.

SOUPS AND SANDWICHES

PIMIENTO CHEESE SPREAD

8 oz. Olde English
  processed cheese,
  grated
¼ tsp. onion powder
1—4 oz. jar pimiento,
  plus liquid
Mayonnaise
Cayenne pepper, optional

MAKES 1 PINT
Stir together the grated cheese and onion powder. Add pimiento and enough mayonnaise to make mixture as moist as desired. Season with cayenne pepper, if desired, and refrigerate overnight to mellow the flavors. Makes excellent sandwiches, or spread for celery.

BEEF AND KRAUT SANDWICH

¹/₃ cup Miracle Whip
¼ cup pickle relish
2 Tbsps. Dijon mustard
1 tsp. Worcestershire sauce
1 cup shaved roast beef
1 cup Swiss cheese,
  shredded
1—16 oz. can sauerkraut,
  drained
12 slices rye bread

SERVES 6
Combine first 4 ingredients; mix well. Stir in roast beef, cheese, and sauerkraut; cover and chill. Spread beef mixture evenly on 6 slices of bread, top with remaining bread.

Great to keep on hand for lunch!

SOUPS AND SANDWICHES

HERO SANDWICH

1—16 oz. loaf Italian bread
2 Tbsps. Miracle Whip
1 tsp. spicy mustard
¼ cup ripe olives, chopped
¼ cup red onion, finely
chopped
1 lb. thinly sliced roast beef
1—8 oz. pkg. sliced Swiss
cheese

SERVES 4–6
Slice bread in half horizontally. Combine salad dressing, mustard, olives, and onion, stirring well. Spread on cut surfaces of bread.

Layer beef and cheese alternately on the bottom half of the cut loaf. Cover with top half. Cut sandwich into 4–6 slices; wrap each in foil. Bake at 400° for 20 minutes.

HOT TURKEY ROYALE

1—10 oz. pkg. frozen
asparagus spears, or
broccoli
2 Tbsp. butter
4 slices cooked or smoked
turkey
2 whole wheat muffin
halves
1 Tbsp. flour
½ cup chicken broth
1 Tbsp. white wine
Salt and pepper
Chopped green onions

MAKES 2 SANDWICHES
Cook asparagus three minutes and drain. Melt butter in skillet. Cook and turn turkey in butter until heated through. Spoon asparagus on top of turkey. Butter and toast muffins under broiler. Place turkey and asparagus on toasted muffins. Stir flour into juices in skillet; add butter if necessary. Add chicken broth and wine. Cook and stir over medium-high heat until mixture thickens and bubbles. Season with salt and pepper. Spoon sauce over turkey and asparagus. Sprinkle with green onions.

 Keep bags of potato chips closed by clipping shut with a clothespin.

SOUPS AND SANDWICHES

SAUSAGE AND CHEESE SANDWICHES

1 lb. regular Jimmy Dean
sausage
1 lb. Velveeta, cubed
12 slices rye bread

**MAKES 12 OPEN-FACED
SANDWICHES**
Brown sausage in skillet. Drain grease.
Add cheese, and stir until melted.
Spread on slices of rye bread. Toast
under broiler immediately, arrange
slices on cookie sheet and freeze.
When frozen, remove from cookie
sheet and store, frozen, in a plastic bag.
Use as needed by baking unthawed
sandwiches at 400° for 8–10 minutes.
These make great after school snacks
for growing boys. Also make good ap-
petizers when spread on party ryes.

BATH TUB PICKLES

½ bushel pickling
cucumbers
Fresh dill
Garlic cloves
Dried hot chilies
Alum

VINEGAR SOLUTION:
2 quarts cider vinegar
3 quarts water
¾ cup pickling salt

MAKES 1 DOZEN QUARTS
This is a recipe to use when you have
a bunch of cucumbers to pickle at
once. The method saves processing
time so it makes sense to use it when
you have a dozen or more quarts to
process.

Place dill, garlic cloves, 1 **small** dry hot
chili, ⅛ teaspoon alum in the bottom
of a quart jar. Pack with cucumbers;
whole, sliced, or spears. Pour boiling
vinegar solution to ½-inch head space.
Seal with hot lids and rings. Place
packed jars in the bathtub. Cover with
hottest tap water, at least 1 inch water
over jars. Leave until cooled. Check
seals and store. Don't do the laundry
while you're making these, because
you need all the hottest water for the
tub!

Breads

P.B.KORTON SONS.
WORCESTER MASS
3

Young L
Bisc

John Burd

BREADS

APPLESAUCE BREAD

1 cup quick oats
1²/₃ cup flour
1 tsp. soda
1 tsp. cinnamon
½ tsp. salt
¼ tsp. baking powder
½ cup margarine,
    softened
¾ cup sugar
2 eggs
1 cup applesauce
1 tsp. sugar
¼ tsp. cinnamon

MAKES 1 LOAF
Combine dry ingredients and set aside. Cream margarine and sugar until light and fluffy. Add eggs and beat well. Add dry ingredients, alternately with applesauce, beating until smooth after each addition. Pour batter into a lightly greased 9x5x3-inch loaf pan. Mix 1 teaspoon sugar and ¼ teaspoon cinnamon and sprinkle on top of loaf. Bake at 350° for 45 minutes. Delicious and nutritious. . . great snack for kids!

BLUEBERRY LEMON BREAD

2 eggs
1 cup sugar
1 cup milk
3 Tbsp. shortening, melted
3 cups flour
4 tsp. baking powder
1½ tsp. Salt
1 tsp. vanilla
1 tsp. grated lemon rind
1—10 oz. pkg. frozen
    blueberries, thawed
½ cup walnuts, chopped

MAKES 1 LOAF
Beat eggs in mixing bowl. Beat in sugar; then milk and shortening. Add dry ingredients, then vanilla and lemon rind; stir to blend. Stir in blueberries and walnuts. Pour into greased loaf pan. Bake in 350° oven for 1 hour or until bread tests done. Cool in pan for 10 minutes, remove from pan.

CACHE LA POUDRE FRUIT BREAD

½ cup margarine
1 cup sugar
3 eggs, beaten
3 bananas, mashed
2 cups flour
1 tsp. soda
¼ cup nuts, chopped
¼ cup chocolate chips
¼ cup maraschino cherries, chopped

MAKES 1 LOAF
Cream margarine and sugar. Add eggs and bananas and mix well. Stir in flour and soda. Fold in nuts, chocolate chips and cherries. Pour into greased and floured loaf pan. Bake 1 hour at 350°.

CARIBBEAN NUT BREAD

4 Tbsp. butter
1 cup sugar
1 egg
4 cups + 2 Tbsp. flour
1 tsp. baking powder
4 tsp. finely grated orange peel
1 tsp. baking soda
1 tsp. salt
1 cup orange juice
8 oz. pitted dates, chopped
½ cup pecans, chopped

MAKES 1 LOAF
Cream butter, sugar, and egg until fluffy. Stir in flour, baking powder, orange peel, baking soda, salt and orange juice; mix well. Add pecans and dates. Bake in greased loaf pan at 350° for about 1 hour, or until it tests done.

BREADS

LEMON BREAD

1 cup butter or margarine
2 cups sugar
4 eggs, separated
3¼ cups flour
2 tsp. baking powder
1 tsp. salt
1¼ cups milk
1 cup pecans, finely
  chopped
2 Tbsp. grated lemon rind
½ cup fresh lemon juice
½ cup powdered sugar

MAKES 3 LOAVES
Cream butter and sugar well. Add egg yolks and beat well. Mix dry ingredients, then add to egg yolk mixture alternately with milk; blend well. Fold in stiffly beaten egg whites, nuts and lemon rind. Turn into three greased and floured 8½"x4½" loaf pans. Bake at 350° for 1 hour or until tested done.

Mix lemon juice and powdered sugar. Prick tops of loaves and spoon lemon juice mixture over hot loaves. Cool, remove from pan, wrap and refrigerate 24 hours for easier slicing. Try making these up and freezing them to have on hand for hostess gifts.

ORANGE NUT BREAD

¾ cup sugar
3 Tbsp. butter
2 eggs
1 cup orange rind, finely
  chopped
½ cup chopped walnuts
2¼ cups sifted flour
3 tsp. baking powder
1 tsp. salt
1 cup milk

MAKES 1 LOAF
Cream sugar and butter. Add eggs and beat until smooth. Mix dry ingredients and add alternately with the milk, beating well. Pour into greased loaf pan and bake at 350° for 55–60 minutes. Serve at a luncheon with a fruit salad.

POPPY SEED BREAD

3 cups flour
½ tsp. salt
1½ tsp. baking powder
2 Tbsp. poppy seeds
2 cups sugar
1½ cups oil
3 eggs
1½ tsp. vanilla
1½ tsp. almond extract
1½ cups milk

TOPPING:
¼ cup orange juice
¾ cup sugar
½ tsp. almond extract

MAKES 2 LARGE LOAVES
Combine flour, salt, baking powder and poppy seeds, in a large bowl and set aside. Cream sugar, oil, eggs, vanilla and almond extract. Add dry ingredients to the sugar mixture alternately with milk, beginning and ending with dry ingredients. Bake at 350° in 2 greased loaf pans for 40–60 minutes or until they test done.

Combine orange juice, sugar, and almond extract and drizzle this mixture over the top of the baked bread. Cool. This bread is also good without the glaze.

STRAWBERRY BREAD

3 cups flour
1 tsp. baking soda
1 tsp. salt
1 Tbsp. cinnamon
2 cups sugar
4 eggs
1¼ cups oil
2—10 oz. pkgs. frozen
  strawberries, thawed
  (reserve ½ cup juice)
1 cup pecans, chopped

SPREAD:
½ cup strawberry juice
1—8 oz. pkg. cream cheese

MAKES 2 LOAVES
In a large bowl, mix together the dry ingredients. Add eggs and oil and blend well. Stir in strawberries and pecans. Mix well. Pour into 2 greased and floured loaf pans and bake 1 hour at 350°. Cool, remove from pans and refrigerate overnight for easier slicing. Freezes well. This bread is also good toasted for breakfast.

To make spread, combine strawberry juice and cream cheese to a spreadable consistency. A blender or food processor works well for this. Slice bread and spread with mixture. Make into finger sandwiches for brunch. Or, cut a loaf lengthways into 3 sections, put filling on each layer, stack together and slice for a layered-cake effect.

BREADS

PUMPKIN DATE BREAD

3⅓ cups flour
3 cups sugar
1 tsp. salt
2 tsp. soda
1 tsp. nutmeg
2 cups pumpkin
1 cup oil
4 eggs, beaten
⅔ cup water
1 cup nuts, chopped
1 cup dates, chopped

MAKES 3 LOAVES

Mix flour, sugar, salt, soda and nutmeg. Add the pumpkin, oil, eggs and water. Mix until smooth and add nuts and dates. Pour into greased and floured loaf pans, and bake at 350° for 1 hour.

BAKED APPLE MUFFINS

1½ cups flour
1¾ tsp. baking powder
½ tsp. salt
½ tsp. nutmeg
½ cup sugar
1 egg
⅓ cup oil
¼ cup milk
½ cup grated apple or
　¾ cup applesauce

TOPPING:
¼ cup butter, melted
⅔ cup sugar
2 tsp. cinnamon

MAKES 12

Mix dry ingredients in a bowl. Add egg, oil and milk. Blend well, add grated apple. Fill muffin cups ⅔ full. Bake at 400° for about 20 minutes. Remove from pan and while still warm, brush with melted butter and roll in sugar and cinnamon mixture.

BREADS

THE BEST BRAN MUFFINS

4 cups All-Bran cereal
2 cups boiling water
1 cup shortening
2½ cups sugar
4 eggs, beaten
4 cups buttermilk
5 cups flour
5 tsp. baking soda
1 tsp. salt
2 cups 100% Bran cereal

MAKES 6 DOZEN MUFFINS
Soak All-Bran in boiling water for a few minutes. In a large bowl, cream shortening and sugar. Add eggs and buttermilk and blend well. Add All-Bran, flour, soda, salt and 100% Bran. Combine thoroughly. Fill greased or paper-lined muffin tins ⅔ full and bake at 400° for 25 minutes. Batter will keep for six weeks in refrigerator if tightly covered. Bake up as many as you need for breakfast or brunch. Watch out... they're addictive!

CRANBERRY-ALMOND MUFFINS

3 cups flour
½ cup sugar
2 tsp. baking powder
1 tsp. baking soda
¼ tsp. salt
1—16 oz. container sour cream
⅓ cup milk
¼ cup salad oil
½ tsp. almond extract
2 eggs
1½ cups cranberries, coarsely chopped
2 Tbsp. sliced blanched almonds

MAKES 18
In large bowl, mix together first five ingredients. In separate bowl, beat together the sour cream, milk, salad oil, almond extract and eggs until blended. Stir sour cream mixture into flour mixture just until flour is moist. Gently fold in cranberries and almonds. Spoon greased muffin cups ⅔ full and bake at 375° for 25–30 minutes.

BREADS

SUSAN'S PUMPKIN MUFFINS

4 oz. cream cheese
¼ cup butter
1¼ cup sugar
2 eggs
2 cups canned pumpkin
½ tsp. vanilla
2 cups flour
1 tsp. baking soda
½ tsp. salt
½ tsp. cinnamon
½ tsp. pumpkin pie spice
²/₃ cup pecans, chopped
Sugar

MAKES 18
Cream together butter, cream cheese and sugar. Mix in eggs, canned pumpkin and vanilla. Sift together flour, baking soda, salt, cinnamon and pumpkin pie spice. Mix with pumpkin mixture. Stir in pecans. Pour batter into greased muffin tins filling ²/₃ full and bake at 375° 20–25 minutes. Sprinkle sugar over warm muffins. This also makes a nice bread. Bake in greased loaf pan 50–60 minutes.

PEACH MUFFINS

²/₃ cup shortening
1 cup sugar
3 eggs
3 cups flour
2 heaping tsp. baking powder
1 tsp. salt
1 cup milk
1—16 oz. can peaches, drained and diced

TOPPING:
¹/₃ cup sugar
½ tsp. cinnamon

MAKES 2 DOZEN MUFFINS
Cream shortening and sugar. Add three eggs, one at a time, beating after each. Sift dry ingredients and all alternately with the cup of milk. Fold in peaches. Fill greased muffin cups ²/₃ full. Combine topping ingredients and sprinkle on each muffin. Bake at 375° until browned, about 20 minutes.

Stir muffin batter only until dry ingredients are moistened, the batter will appear lumpy. The muffins will be tender and have a shiny, brown, rough crust. If batter is beaten until smooth, muffins will be tough, the crust will be dull and the texture uneven and tunneled.

BREADS

RHUBARB MUFFINS

1¼ cup brown sugar
½ cup vegetable oil
1 egg
2 tsp. vanilla
1 cup buttermilk
2½ cups flour
1 tsp. soda
1 tsp. baking powder
½ tsp. salt
1½ cups rhubarb, finely
   chopped
½ cup walnuts, chopped

TOPPING:
1 Tbsp. butter, melted
⅓ cup sugar
1 tsp. cinnamon

MAKES 18 MUFFINS
Cream together the brown sugar and vegetable oil. Mix in egg, vanilla and buttermilk. Add dry ingredients and blend well. Fold in rhubarb and nuts. Fill greased muffin tins ⅔ full and bake at 400° for 20–25 minutes. When done, dip each muffin top into melted butter then the cinnamon and sugar mixture.

DUTCH BABIES

1 cup flour
1 cup milk
5 eggs
1 cube butter, melted

OTHER TOPPINGS:
Orange marmalade
Cooked apples with cinna-
   mon and sugar
Fresh strawberries
Banana slices sauteed in
   butter and powdered
   sugar
Yogurt
Honey butter (whip in
   some cream & vanilla
   for a special treat)

SERVES 4–6
Combine the flour, milk and eggs with half of the butter. Place other half of the melted butter in the bottom of a 9×13-inch Pyrex baking dish. Pour batter over butter. Bake at 425° for 15–20 minutes. Cut into squares and serve with syrup and powdered sugar, or with your choice of toppings.

BREADS

APPLE COFFEE CAKE

¾ cup sugar
¼ cup soft shortening
1 egg
½ cup milk
½ cup raisins
1½ cups flour
2 tsp. baking powder
½ tsp. salt
4 apples, cored, peeled
  and sliced

TOPPING:
½ cup sugar
⅔ cup flour
⅔ cup quick cooking oats
½ cup butter
1 tsp. cinnamon
2 Tbsp. sugar

SERVES 4-6
Mix sugar, shortening and egg until smooth. Stir in milk and raisins. Add dry ingredients to creamed mixture. Pour mixture into 9×9-inch greased and floured pan. Arrange apple slices on top of batter; press into batter slightly with spoon. Combine topping ingredients until crumbly. Sprinkle over apples. Bake at 375° for 30-35 minutes or until toothpick in center comes out clean. Serve warm.

BIJOU SPRINGS COFFEE CAKE

CRUMB MIXTURE:
2½ cups flour
1½ cups brown sugar,
  packed
½ cup sugar
½ tsp. salt
1 tsp. cinnamon
¾ cup butter, softened

1 cup pecans, chopped

BATTER:
1 tsp. baking soda
1 egg
1 cup buttermilk

TOPPING:
¼ cup nut mixture
½ tsp. cinnamon
¼ heaping tsp. nutmeg
2 Tbsp. sugar

SERVES 12
Combine flour, brown sugar, sugar, salt and cinnamon. Blend in butter until mixture is like coarse crumbs. Remove 1½ cups crumb mixture and mix with nuts. Press 1¼ cups nut mixture into bottom of 9×13 inch pan. Reserve ¼ cup nut mixture for topping. You should now have 1 cup nut mixture left. Add it to the remaining crumb mixture, then blend in baking soda, egg and buttermilk. Mix well. Pour batter over nut mixture in pan. Combine topping ingredients and sprinkle over batter. Bake at 350° for 40-45 minutes. Freezes well.

STROH RANCH COFFEE CAKE

2 pkg. crescent rolls
2—8 oz. pkg. cream
  cheese, softened
¾ cup sugar
1 tsp. lemon juice
1 tsp. vanilla
1 egg yolk, save white
Chopped almonds

Lightly grease a 9x13 inch pan. Line bottom of pan with one package of rolls. Mix cream cheese, sugar, lemon juice, vanilla, and egg yolk and pour over roll dough. Layer second package of rolls on top of cream cheese mixture. Pinch edges of rolls together. Brush slightly beaten egg white on roll dough and sprinkle with almonds. Bake at 350° for 30–40 minutes.

CRUNCHY GRANOLA COFFEE CAKE

3 cups granola cereal
  (try C.W. Post)
1½ cups brown sugar,
  packed
3 tsp. cinnamon
2—8 oz. pkgs. refrigerator
  biscuits
½ cup butter, melted

SERVES 8
Combine granola, brown sugar and cinnamon in a small bowl and mix well. Grease a bundt or tube pan, and sprinkle some of the granola mixture in the bottom of the pan. Divide each biscuit in half, then dip each biscuit piece in melted butter, then in granola mixture, making sure they are coated generously. Arrange coated biscuits in overlapping layers, sprinkle again with any leftover granola and drizzle with any remaining butter. Bake at 350° for 30 minutes. Immediately turn out and serve.

BREADS

VICTORIAN COFFEE CAKE

1 white cake mix,
   preferably pudding type
¾ cup oil
½ cup sugar
1 tsp. vanilla
4 eggs
1 cup sour cream
1 cup pecans, chopped
1½ tsp. cinnamon
3 Tbsp. brown sugar

GLAZE:
1 Tbsp. butter
1 cup powdered sugar
¼ tsp. vanilla
Milk

SERVES 10–12
Mix together the cake mix, oil, sugar and vanilla. Add eggs and mix well. Mix in sour cream and pecans. Pour half of the batter in bundt or 9×13 inch pan. Sprinkle with the mixture of cinnamon and brown sugar. Top with remainder of the batter. Bake at 350° for 40–60 minutes depending on the pan used. Test with toothpick for doneness.

Before serving, drizzle with glaze made by combining butter, powdered sugar, vanilla and milk and mixing until smooth. This coffee cake is especially good...try it next Sunday morning.

ORANGE MARMALADE BREAD

¼ cup pecans, chopped
½ cup butter, melted
1—12 oz. jar orange
   marmalade
2—8 oz. pkgs. refrigerator
   biscuits

SERVES 6–8
Lightly grease a bundt or tube pan. Sprinkle nuts in the bottom of the pan, pour some of the butter over the nuts. Separate biscuits and divide each in half. Dip each piece in melted butter, then in orange marmalade. Arrange coated biscuits in overlapping layers. Drizzle with any remaining butter, and bake at 350° for about 30 minutes. Immediately turn out and serve.

TWO QUICK BREAKFAST COFFEE CAKES

VERSION I:
½ cup brown sugar
1 cup sugar
1 tsp. cinnamon
1—12 oz. tube refrigerator
   flaky biscuits
⅓ cup pecans, chopped
¼–½ cup raisins
5 Tbsp. butter, melted
6 maraschino cherries,
   halved

SERVES 4–6
Combine dry ingredients with nuts in bowl. Melt butter in separate bowl. Cut each biscuit into fourths and dip in melted butter, then roll generously in sugar and nut mixture. Place in greased loaf pan. Add cherries and raisins after first layer of biscuit squares. Drizzle with any remaining butter and sprinkle with any remaining sugar and nuts. Bake 35 minutes in 350° oven. This recipe can easily be doubled and cooked in a bundt or angel food pan. Increase cooking time slightly.

VERSION II:
1—3 oz. pkg. regular
   coconut cream pudding
   mix
½ cup packed brown
   sugar
½ cup pecans, chopped
1 tsp. ground cinnamon
1—12 oz. tube refrigerator
   flaky biscuits
5 Tbsp. butter, melted

SERVES 4–6
Combine pudding mix, brown sugar, pecans and cinnamon in bowl. Cut each biscuit into fourths and dip in melted butter, then roll generously in dry mixture. Place in greased loaf pan. Drizzle with remaining butter and sprinkle with remaining pudding mixture. Bake 35 minutes in 350° oven.

BREADS

NO-KNEAD BREAKFAST TWISTS

¾ cup milk, scalded
½ cup sugar
2 tsp. salt
½ cup margarine
½ cup warm water
2 pkgs. yeast
1 egg
4 cups flour
½ cup sugar
½ tsp. cinnamon
½ cup butter, melted

MAKES 4 DOZEN

Stir together milk, sugar, salt and margarine. Cool to lukewarm. In a large bowl, pour in warm water. Sprinkle yeast on it and stir to dissolve. Add milk mixture, egg and 2 cups flour. Beat until smooth. Stir in remaining 2 cups flour to make a stiff batter. Cover tightly and refrigerate at least 2 hours. Dough may be kept in refrigerator 3 days.

When chilled, divide in half. Roll ¼-inch thick to an 8×16 inch rectangle. Brush with melted butter. Sprinkle cinnamon and sugar on dough and fold into thirds. Slice with a sharp knife. Twist each slice and place on a lightly greased cookie sheet. Bake 10–12 minutes at 375° until golden brown. Repeat for second half of dough. Dough may also be used for biscuits ... just roll out and cut with biscuit cutter. Place on cookie sheet and bake as directed.

 To scald milk, bring it almost to the boiling point. When the edges begin to bubble remove immediately from burner.

MRS. VAN HUSEN'S ORANGE BOWKNOTS

1¼ cups milk, scalded
½ cup shortening
⅓ cup sugar
1 tsp. salt
2 pkgs. yeast
2 eggs, well beaten
¼ cup orange juice
2 Tbsp. grated orange rind
5 cups flour

ORANGE FROSTING:
4 Tbsp. orange juice
2 tsp. grated orange rind
2 cups sifted powdered
  sugar

MAKES 4 DOZEN BOWKNOTS
Combine milk, shortening, sugar and salt; cool to lukewarm. Sprinkle yeast on this mixture, stir to dissolve. Add eggs, orange juice and peel, and beat thoroughly. Add flour and mix to a soft dough. Knead lightly on a floured surface. Place in a greased bowl, cover with a damp tea towel, and let rise until doubled. Punch down. Roll dough ½-inch thick; cut in strips about 6 inches long. Tie each in a knot. Arrange on a greased baking sheet. Cover, let rise until doubled, then bake at 400° for about 12 minutes. Frost with Orange Frosting.

LAZY MORNING BLUEBERRY ROLLS

2—7½ oz. pkgs. refrigerated
  flaky biscuits
2 Tbsp. butter, melted
¼ cup sugar
⅔ cup blueberry pie filling

GLAZE:
½ cup powdered sugar
1 Tbsp. milk
⅛ tsp. vanilla extract

SERVES 6
With your hands, roll two biscuits together into a 14 inch rope. Roll in melted butter and the sugar. Coil the rope on greased baking pan. Do the rest of the biscuits the same way. Flatten each coil with a spatula. Bake at 400° for 12 minutes or until golden brown. Top each spiral with a heaping tablespoon of blueberry pie filling. In a small bowl, mix powdered sugar, milk and vanilla. Beat until smooth. Drizzle warm rolls with glaze.

BREADS

QUICK CARAMEL STICKY BUNS

1—1 lb. loaf frozen bread
dough

TOPPING:
1 cup brown sugar
½ cup butter
¼ cup water
½ cup chopped pecans or
walnuts

FILLING:
3 Tbsp. soft butter
1½ tsp. ground cinnamon
3 Tbsp. sugar
½ cup chopped pecans or
walnuts

MAKES 12–15 ROLLS
Thaw dough according to package directions. To make topping, mix sugar, butter and water in a small saucepan over moderate heat. Bring to a boil and boil 5 minutes, stirring frequently; reduce heat slightly if syrup boils up too high. Pour into 9×13 inch pan. Sprinkle nuts evenly over syrup.

Roll dough out to a 9×14 rectangle. Spread butter over dough. Mix cinnamon with the sugar and sprinkle over the buttered dough. Sprinkle with nuts. Starting from one long side, roll dough like a jelly roll. Cut into 12 slices and arrange evenly over topping. Cover with a damp tea towel, and let rise in warm place 40–60 minutes or until double in volume. Bake at 350° for about 30 minutes or until buns are medium brown. Let stand 5 minutes. Invert onto a platter and serve warm.

JUDI'S PAN DE LOTE

1 cup Bisquick
1 egg
½ cup milk
2 Tbsp. sugar
2 Tbsp. margarine, melted
1—8 oz. can creamed corn
1—4 oz. can chopped
green chilies
½ lb. grated Monterey
Jack cheese

Mix together Bisquick, egg, milk, sugar, margarine and corn. Pour half of the mixture into a greased 2-quart casserole. Top with chilies and cheese. Pour remaining batter over top. Bake 35 minutes at 400°. Great with fried catfish.

HEAVENLY BISCUITS

1 pkg. dry yeast
5 Tbsp. warm water
5 cups flour
5 tsp. baking powder
½ tsp. soda
1 tsp. salt
3 Tbsp. sugar
1 cup shortening
2 cups buttermilk

MAKES 5–6 DOZEN

Sprinkle yeast over warm water, then stir to dissolve. Set aside. Sift dry ingredients together. Add shortening and blend, using a pastry blender or a food processor, until mixture resembles crumbs. Add buttermilk to yeast mixture and stir well. Add dry ingredients and mix well. Turn on a floured board and knead lightly. Roll and cut with biscuit cutter. Place on cookie sheets and bake at 450° for 8–10 minutes or until *lightly* browned. Dough will keep in the refrigerator and can be used as needed. These light, flavorful biscuits have become a regular at mealtime.

BOSTON BROWN BREAD

1½ cup raisins
1½ cups water
2 Tbsp. shortening
1 cup sugar
1 egg
2 Tbsp. molasses
1 tsp. salt
2 tsp. soda
2¾ cups flour

MAKES 1 LOAF

Combine raisins and water in small saucepan and simmer for 7 minutes over medium heat in covered pan. In large bowl, cream together shortening and sugar. Add egg, molasses and salt and mix thoroughly; stir in raisins. Sift together soda and flour and mix with creamed mixture. Pour into greased, floured pan or coffee cans so that the batter has room to double in size. Bread will be quite crusty unless baked in a covered pan or dish. Cover with foil or turn a loaf pan upside down on top of loaf and bake at 325° for 1 hour.

BREADS

PARMESAN BREAD STICKS

Day-old sandwich bread (can use hot dog or hamburger buns, too)
Butter, melted
Parmesan cheese

Variation: garlic salt, onion salt, or seasoned salt

Melt butter in a shallow bowl. Lay a slice of bread in butter, coating both sides. (Trim the crusts off the bread if you're doing these for a dinner party and want them to look pretty and uniform.) Then lay the bread slice on a cookie sheet. Sprinkle with Parmesan cheese, turn and sprinkle the other side. Using a sharp paring knife, cut each piece of bread into 5–6 skinny slices. Bake at 250° until toasty and golden brown. For something different try seasoning the bread slices with one of the variations. These are good as snacks, with soup, or as an appetizer. Can be stored in an air-tight container for several weeks.

COWBOY CORN CAKES

2 cups yellow cornmeal
½ cup flour
2 tsp. salt
2 cups boiling water
2 Tbsps. corn oil

SERVES 4–6
In a bowl, combine the cornmeal, flour, and salt. Stir in boiling water and form the mixture into 10–12 patties. Heat the oil in a large skillet over medium-high heat. Fry the patties 3–5 minutes on each side or until browned.

These are great with chili or stew, but wait until you try them for breakfast, served with bacon and eggs or topped with butter and syrup!

GERMAINE'S QUICK ONION ROLLS

1—12 oz. can flaky
  biscuits
1 cup sour cream
1½ Tbsp. minced onion
1 Tbsp. poppy seed

SERVES 4
Arrange biscuits in pie pan. In small bowl combine sour cream, minced onion and egg. Pour over biscuits. Sprinkle with poppy seed. Bake at 350° for 30 minutes.

HOMEMADE HAMBURGER BUNS

1 pkg. yeast
1 cup warm water
6 cups flour
4 tsp. baking powder
2 tsp. salt
¼ tsp. soda
2 cups buttermilk

MAKES 2½ DOZEN
Dissolve yeast in warm water. Set aside. Combine dry ingredients. Add buttermilk to yeast mixture, then stir into dry ingredients. Mix well. Roll out on a floured board, and cut with a biscuit cutter. Bake at 450° until brown. Store unused dough in a covered bowl in the refrigerator. Will last up to 2 weeks. This recipe makes a hard-roll type bun.

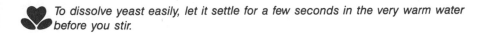

To dissolve yeast easily, let it settle for a few seconds in the very warm water before you stir.

BREADS

GRANDMOTHER'S BUTTERMILK BISCUITS

2 cups flour
½ tsp. salt
4 tsp. baking powder
½ tsp. soda
⅓ cup shortening
1 cup buttermilk

MAKES 16
Combine dry ingredients in a food processor. Add shortening and process just until mixture resembles crumbs. Add buttermilk all at once and process until dough makes a ball and spins around the processor. (You can, of course, do this all by hand like Grandmother did.) Turn onto a floured board and knead lightly 4 or 5 times. Roll to a 1–1½ inch thickness and cut with biscuit cutter. Place on a lightly greased baking sheet and with sides touching. Bake at 450° for 12 to 15 minutes, or **just until** the tops are lightly browned for a light, tender, old-fashioned biscuit.

JALAPENO MUFFINS

2 cups flour
2 Tbsp. sugar
3 tsp. baking powder
½ tsp. salt
½ cup Cheddar cheese, grated
2 Tbsp. chopped jalapeno peppers or green chiles
1 cup milk
¼ cup oil
1 egg, beaten

MAKES 1 DOZEN MUFFINS
Combine dry ingredients with cheese and peppers. Add milk, oil and egg and stir to moisten. Fill lined muffin cups ⅔ full. Bake at 400° for about 20 minutes or until golden brown.

Either the previous or the following recipe provides a nice alternative to cornbread. They go well with chili, stews, or casseroles. Try either as an accompaniment to Texas Red Chile or Lazy Lady Stew (see Index).

QUICK ONION CHEESE BISCUITS

½ cup chopped onion
2 Tbsp. butter
1 egg
½ cup milk
1½ cups biscuit mix
1 cup Cheddar cheese, grated
2 tsp. parsley flakes

SERVES 4–6
Saute onion in melted butter in small skillet until tender (do not brown). Set aside to cool. Combine egg and milk in bowl. Add biscuit mix, stirring just enough to moisten. Stir in cooked onion, ½ cup cheese and parsley flakes. Spread batter in greased 8-inch square baking pan. Sprinkle with ½ cup cheese. Bake in 400° oven for 20 minutes.

HERB BUTTERED BREAD

1 cup butter or margarine, softened
2 Tbsp. green onion, finely chopped
2 Tbsp. ripe olives, finely chopped
1 tsp. dried parsley
1 tsp. dried basil
½ tsp. dried thyme, crushed
½ tsp. dried marjoram, crushed
½ tsp. dried tarragon, crushed
1 loaf French bread, sliced diagonally

Combine ingredients and spread on slices of French bread. Wrap loaf in foil and heat at 350° for 15–20 minutes.

BREADS

CHEESE AND HERB BREAD

1 loaf French bread
1 pkg. Swiss cheese,
    sliced
¾ cup butter, melted
¼ tsp. garlic powder
1 Tbsp. dried parsley
2 slices bacon

SERVES 6-8
Slice the bread in 2-3 inch slices, making sure you do not cut all the way through. (For ease, buy Earth Grains sliced French bread.) Cut each slice of cheese in half to make triangles and put 1 triangle in between each slice of bread. Add garlic powder and parsley to melted butter and spoon between each slice and drizzle over top. Place 2 slices of bacon on top of the loaf, wrap in heavy foil and heat thoroughly at 350° for 15-20 minutes. Fold back foil and **broil** until bacon is cooked. This freezes well, uncooked. Just thaw before cooking according to directions.

NAVAJO FRY BREAD

1 cup flour
1 Tbsp. baking powder
½ tsp. salt
½ cup milk
Vegetable shortening for
    frying

MAKES 6 SERVINGS
Mix dry ingredients, add milk, turn dough onto a floured board and knead lightly 4 or 5 times. Roll to ⅛-¼ inch thickness (very thin). Cut into 2 inch squares. Fry in hot shortening (about 2 inches deep). Bread should puff up immediately. . . if it doesn't, your oil is not hot enough. When brown on both sides, remove and drain on paper towels. Serve hot with honey, OR roll in a mixture of granulated sugar and cinnamon. Can also be made bigger and topped with seasoned ground beef, lettuce, tomato and grated cheese for a tasty Navajo Taco.

GRANDMA WHITE'S ALL BRAN ROLLS

¼ cup shortening
¾ cup sugar
1 cup bran
1½ tsp. salt
1 cup boiling water
2 pkgs. yeast
1 cup lukewarm water
2 eggs
6 cups flour

MAKES 25–30 ROLLS
Combine shortening, sugar, bran and salt in mixing bowl. Pour cup of boiling water over ingredients and mix well. Cool to lukewarm. Dissolve yeast in 1 cup of lukewarm water. When dissolved add to bran mixture. Beat in eggs and 2 cups flour. Mix in remaining 4 cups flour. Knead dough. Place in greased bowl, turn dough and cover with damp tea towel; let rise until double in bulk. Punch down and form dough into rolls. Place on lightly greased baking sheet; let rise until almost double, about 45 minutes. Bake in 350° oven for 20–25 minutes.

BUTTER BUNS

⅔ cup warm water
1 pkg. yeast
2 Tbsp. sugar
½ tsp. salt
¼ cup shortening or butter (try butter-flavored Crisco)
1 egg
1⅔ cups flour

MAKES 1 DOZEN
In a bowl, dissolve yeast in water. Add sugar, salt, shortening, egg and 1 cup flour. Mix well. Add remaining flour and mix until smooth. Fill greased muffin tins half full. Allow batter to rise in a warm place until doubled. Bake at 375° for 20 minutes. This is a quick yeast-bread recipe that produces light, tasty rolls, and is especially handy when you don't have time to make a conventional yeast roll for dinner.

 For tender crust, brush rolls with salad oil or melted butter before baking. For crisp crust, brush with milk or 1 beaten egg diluted with 1 tablespoon milk.

BREADS

POTATO ROLLS

2 med. potatoes, peeled
  and cubed
½ cup shortening
¾ cup sugar
1 cup milk, scalded
2 eggs, beaten
2 pkgs. yeast
½ Tbsp. salt
4 cups flour

MAKES 2 DOZEN
Boil potatoes in enough water to cover. When tender, drain and mash. Add shortening, sugar, scalded milk and eggs. Cool to lukewarm. Add yeast and stir to dissolve. Add salt and flour to make a manageable dough. Knead well, then place in a bowl and cover with a damp cloth. Let rise until doubled. Punch down. May store in refrigerator at this point. Roll dough into 1½ inch thickness. Cut out rolls and place on a lightly greased cookie sheet. Let rise until doubled, then bake at 400° until browned, about 15–20 minutes.

HARVEST BATTER BREAD

¼ cup warm water
2 pkgs. yeast
1 cup milk
2 Tbsp. honey
1 tsp. salt
3½ cups whole wheat flour
3 eggs
1 cup sour cream
½ cup toasted wheat
  germ

MAKES 1 LOAF
Dissolve yeast in warm water. Heat milk to lukewarm. Stir milk, honey, salt and 1 cup of whole wheat flour into yeast mixture and beat for 2 minutes. Add eggs and sour cream and beat for additional 2 minutes. Add remaining flour and wheat germ and beat for 1 minute. The batter will be thick. Cover and let rise until double in bulk, about 1 hour. Punch dough down and place in loaf pan. Cover and let rise about 30 minutes. Bake in 350° oven for 35 minutes or until hollow-sounding when tapped. This is a very simple bread to make and is light textured.

 To reheat rolls place in plain paper bag, sprinkle bag lightly with water, and place in hot oven 3 to 5 minutes before serving.

HONEY-WHEAT BREAD

1 pkg. yeast
1 cup warm water
½ cup honey
1 Tbsp. salt
2 Tbsp. oil
1 cup milk, scalded
3 cups white flour,
   unbleached
1 cup wheat germ
1½ cups whole wheat flour

MAKES 2 LOAVES

Dissolve yeast in water. Combine honey, salt, oil and cooled milk in large bowl. Add yeast mixture. Beat in 2 cups flour, then stir in 1 more cup of flour, wheat germ, and whole wheat flour. It should form a fairly stiff dough. Knead well, until smooth and satiny. Let rise until doubled in bulk. Punch down and divide in half. Shape into 2 loaves. Place in two 5×9 inch pans which have been lightly greased. Cover with a damp tea towel and let rise in a warm place for 2½ hours. Bake at 350° for 50 minutes or until loaf sounds hollow when tapped. Cool on a wire rack. Makes a delicious, full-flavored bread.

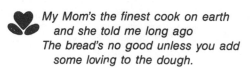

*My Mom's the finest cook on earth
and she told me long ago
The bread's no good unless you add
some loving to the dough.*

BREADS

CRUSTY FRENCH BREAD

2 cups warm water
1 pkg. yeast
1 Tbsp. sugar
2 tsp. salt
5–5½ cups flour
1 egg white, beaten

MAKES 2 LOAVES
Pour water into a large bowl. Sprinkle on yeast and stir until dissolved. Add sugar, salt, and 3 cups flour. Stir to mix; then beat until smooth and shiny. Stir in 2 (or 2½) more cups of flour to make a stiff dough. This part is easy to do in a food processor.

Turn out dough on a floured board and knead until satiny and smooth—5–7 minutes. Shape into a smooth ball. Turn into a lightly greased bowl, cover with a damp tea towel, and let rise until doubled (about 1 hour).

Punch down, divide in halves and shape each portion into a ball. Place balls on a lightly floured board and let stand 5 minutes.

Rub a little shortening on the palms of hands. Start shaping the loaves by rolling ball of dough at center and gently working the hands toward the ends of the loaf. Do this several times to get well-shaped, long, slender loaves.

Place 2 loaves about 4 inches apart on lightly greased baking sheet. With sharp knife, cut diagonal gashes about ¾-inch deep, 1½ inches apart, into the top of each loaf. Cover and let rise until a little more than doubled. Bake in a 425° oven 30–35 minutes. Remove from oven. Brush with egg white and return to oven for 2 minutes. Remove from oven, transfer to wire racks to cool, and brush with butter for a soft loaf.

CRUSTY ROLLS: Bake 1 loaf of French bread and use other half of dough to make rolls. Cut the dough into 12 equal pieces. Shape each piece into a smooth ball by folding the edges under. Place the rolls 3 inches apart on a lightly greased baking sheet. With a sharp knife or kitchen scissors, cut a cross ½-inch deep in top of each roll. Cover and let rise until doubled. Bake at 425° for 15–20 minutes. Remove from oven, brush rolls with egg white and return to oven for 2 minutes. Remove from baking sheet. Brush with melted butter to make softer tops.

Serve hot with a meal, or use for sandwiches. For a variation, sprinkle tops with sesame seeds or poppy seeds after brushing with egg white.

Don't let the length of these instructions scare you . . . this bread is **very** easy to make with consistently good results.

RAISIN BREAD

1 pkg. yeast
1½ cups warm water
4 to 5 cups flour
1 tsp. salt
⅓ cup sugar
3 Tbsp. butter or
  margarine, softened
1 tsp. cinnamon
½ cup dark raisins

MAKES 1 LOAF

Soften yeast in ½ cup warm water and set aside. In a large bowl combine 4 cups flour with the salt. Set aside 2 tablespoons of the sugar and stir remaining sugar into the flour mixture. Cut butter into the flour, then add yeast mixture and remaining 1 cup of water all at once. Stir until well mixed, adding more flour if necessary to make a workable dough. Turn onto a floured board and knead until smooth and shiny. Place in a bowl, cover with a damp tea towel and allow to rise until doubled. Punch down dough, roll into a 12×8 inch rectangle. Lightly brush dough with water. Stir cinnamon into reserved 2 tablespoons of sugar and sprinkle over dough. Top with raisins, then roll jelly-roll style. Pinch seams and fit into a greased loaf pan, seam-side down. Let rise, covered, until double. Bake at 350° about 50–60 minutes. Brush with butter. While hot, remove from pan and cool on wire rack.

*At high altitudes, the rising time of bread is shortened. Since the development of a good flavor in bread partially depends on the length of the rising period, it is a good idea to punch the dough down **twice** to give time for the flavor to develop. It is also known that flours tend to be drier in high, dry climates. Because they are able to absorb more liquid, less flour may be needed to make the dough the proper consistency.*

BREADS

SUNFLOWER WHOLE WHEAT BREAD

3 cups warm water
¾ cup honey
2 pkgs. dry yeast
¼ cup butter, softened
4 cups whole wheat flour
4 cups white flour
2 tsp. salt
1 cup dry roasted
   sunflower seeds

MAKES 2 LOAVES

In large mixing bowl, combine and mix together the water, honey and yeast until yeast is softened. Blend in melted butter, whole wheat flour, 1 cup white flour, salt and sunflower seeds into the yeast mixture with electric mixer for 7 minutes on low speed. Slowly add 3 more cups white flour, beating with a wooden spoon until a stiff dough forms. Add flour if dough is sticky. Turn dough out onto board and knead 8–10 minutes or until dough is smooth and elastic. Place in a greased bowl and turn the dough to grease its top. Cover bowl with damp towel and set in a warm place until it has doubled in bulk, about 1 hour. Punch down and knead dough for 1 minute. Divide dough in half, shape into two loaves and place in greased bread pans. Place loaves in a warm place and allow to rise to top of pans, about 45 minutes. Bake in pre-heated 350° oven for about 1 hour or until loaves are hollow-sounding when tops are tapped. Turn loaves onto a rack to cool. So good toasted for breakfast!

After your bread is baked, lay it on its side on a cooling rack. The wires from the rack leave a slight impression on the bread at just the right places for slicing.

WHOLE WHEAT SESAME BREAD

3 pkgs. dry yeast
¾ cup warm water
½ tsp. sugar
3 cups lukewarm milk
⅓ cup oil
⅓ cup brown sugar
¼ cup molasses
⅓ cup sesame seeds
2 eggs
1 Tbsp. salt
3 cups whole wheat flour
7–8 cups white flour
1 egg, beaten
Sesame seeds

MAKES 3 LOAVES

Dissolve yeast in ¾ cup warm water; stir in sugar. In large bowl combine milk, oil, brown sugar, molasses, and sesame seeds; mix well. Add yeast mixture, 2 eggs, salt and whole wheat flour; mix well. Add white flour, 1 cup at a time, mixing well until well blended. Turn out to knead, using additional flour as necessary to prevent sticking. Knead about 7 minutes or until smooth and elastic. Put dough in a greased bowl, turn once to grease top, and cover. Put in a warm place and let rise about 1 hour or until doubled. Punch down. Shape into 3 loaves and put in greased loaf pans. Cover and let rise about ½ hour or until dough is above top of pans. Brush tops with beaten egg and sprinkle with additional sesame seeds. Bake at 350° for 45 minutes or until bread sounds hollow when tapped. Turn onto racks to cool. More wheat flour can be used in place of white flour, making a denser, heartier-type bread.

BREADS

CRAB APPLE JELLY

4 lbs. crab apples
4–6 cups cold water
Sugar

MAKES 4 PINTS

Wash apples and cut out any bad spots. Quarter the apples and place them, complete with peel and core, in a Dutch oven. Pour in enough cold water to cover apples. Place a pan over high heat and bring to a boil. Reduce heat and simmer for 1 hour or until apples are tender and mushy.

Pour the apples and liquid into a jelly bag and leave overnight for the juice to strain into a pan.

Measure the final amount of juice and pour it back into the pan. Add 1¾ cups sugar for every 2 cups juice.

Place the pan over low heat and stir the juice to dissolve the sugar. Increase heat and bring to a boil. Skim foam from surface and boil briskly for about 10 minutes or until setting point is reached. Juice will sheet off the spoon. Pour into hot, dry jelly jars, seal with paraffin, and store in a cool place.

Crab apple jelly is about the prettiest jelly there is. It is delicious on toast and biscuits, and makes a tasty accompaniment for pork. Crab apples are naturally high in pectin, so their juice jells easily. Remember, though, the riper the apple, the less pectin, so the more you have to cook it to reach the setting point.

Grandmother used the spoon test for determining the jellying point for jellies. Dip a metal spoon into boiling juice mixture and hold it at least 12 inches above the kettle, out of the steam and let the liquid run off the sides. As it is reaching the jellying point, the jelly will run off in drops. When it reaches the jellying point, the drops slide together and drop off the spoon in a sheet. At this stage, remove jelly from heat at once.

APPLE BUTTER

4 lbs. apples
2 cups apple cider
Brown sugar
3 tsp. cinnamon
1½ tsp. cloves
½ tsp. allspice

MAKES 3 PINTS

Use Jonathan, Winesap, Granny Smith, or other cooking apples for best results. Peel and core apples. Slice apples and place in a large pot. Add cider and cook slowly until soft. Mash well. Add ½ cup brown sugar for each cup pulp. (Add a little more if you like it dark.) Stir in spices, and cook over low heat, stirring constantly, until sugar is dissolved. Continue to cook until mixture is very thick and sheets from the spoon. Watch stirring, so that mixture doesn't scorch on the bottom. Another way to test if it is done is to place a small amount on a plate. When no ring of liquid separates around the edge of the butter it is done. Pour into hot sterilized jars, seal and store.

Breathes there a man with taste so nought
Who never in his life thought,
"These store-bought jams don't make the grade.
Where are the ones like Mother made?"

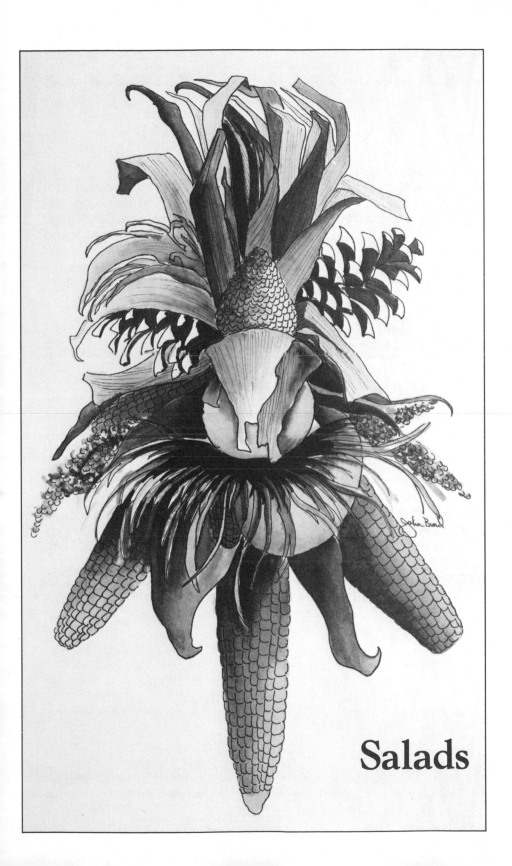

Salads

SALADS

DREAMY APRICOT SALAD

2—3 oz. pkgs. apricot jello
⅔ cup water
2 Tbsp. sugar
2—4½ oz. jars apricot
  baby food
1—20 oz. can crushed
  pineapple, drained
1—14 oz. can Eagle Brand
  milk
1—8 oz. pkg. cream
  cheese, softened
1½ cup nuts, chopped

SERVES 15
Combine jello, water and sugar in a small saucepan. Bring to boiling, stirring to dissolve. Remove from heat. Cool, stir in fruit. Combine milk and cream cheese, beating until smooth. Stir in jello mixture and nuts. Pour into a 9×13 inch Pyrex dish and chill.

CRANBERRY RELISH MOLD

1—9 oz. can crushed
  pineapple
1—3 oz. pkg. raspberry
  gelatin
½ cup boiling water
½ cup sugar
1 Tbsp. lemon juice
1 cup fresh cranberries,
  ground
½ cup pecans, chopped
1 cup celery, chopped
1 unpeeled orange, seeds
  removed, and ground

SERVES 6–8
Drain pineapple, reserving syrup. Add enough water to syrup to make ½ cup. Dissolve gelatin and sugar in ½ cup boiling water. Add reserved syrup and lemon juice. Stir in remaining ingredients. Chill until partially set. Add remaining ingredients. Pour into ring mold and chill overnight.

A teaspoon of vinegar added to any gelatin recipe will keep molded salads from losing their shape so soon after unmolding. . . will not affect the taste of the salad.

CRANBERRY MOUSSE

1—20 oz. can crushed
  pineapple
1—6 oz. pkg. strawberry
  gelatin
1 cup water
1—1 lb. can whole berry
  cranberry sauce
3 Tbsp. fresh lemon juice
1 tsp. fresh grated lemon
  peel
¼ tsp. ground nutmeg
⅓ cup pecans, chopped
2 cups sour cream

SERVES 12–15
Drain pineapple and reserve juice. Add juice to water and bring to a boil. Pour over gelatin and stir to dissolve. Blend in cranberry sauce. Add lemon juice, peel and nutmeg. Chill until mixture thickens slightly. Blend sour cream into gelatin mixture. Fold in pineapple and pecans. Pour into 2 quart mold. Chill.

ORANGE SHERBET SALAD

2—3 oz. pkgs. orange jello
1½ cups boiling water
1 cup sour cream
2 cups orange sherbet
1—11 oz. can mandarin
  oranges, drained

SERVES 8–10
Dissolve jello in boiling water. Whisk in sour cream and sherbet until sherbet is melted and mixture is smooth. Chill until slightly thick, stir in oranges. Pour into 1½ quart mold and chill until firm. This is a very refreshing salad.

MOLDED PEACH MELBA

3 oz. pkg. raspberry
  flavored gelatin
1 cup boiling water
1 cup cold water
1 cup fresh raspberries
3 oz. pkg. peach flavor
  gelatin
¾ cup boiling water
2 med. peaches, peeled
  and sliced
1 Tbsp. lemon juice
1 cup whipped topping or
  whipped cream

SERVES 12
Dissolve raspberry gelatin in 1 cup boiling water. Stir in cold water and raspberries. Pour into mold. Refrigerate until firm. Meanwhile, dissolve peach gelatin in ¾ cup boiling water and cool. In blender or food processor combine peaches and lemon juice and blend until smooth. Add pureed mixture to peach gelatin and refrigerate until thickened. Fold in whipped topping. Pour over raspberry mixture. Refrigerate until firm.

SALADS

RASPBERRY PRETZEL SALAD

2 cups pretzels, crushed
3 Tbsps. sugar
¾ cup butter or margarine, melted
1—8 oz. pkg. cream cheese, softened
½ cup powdered sugar
1½ cups Cool Whip
2 cups miniature marshmallows
2—3 oz. pkg. raspberry gelatin
2 cups boiling water
2—10 oz. pkg. frozen raspberries

Crush pretzels; mix with sugar and butter. Press into a 9×13 inch pan, and bake at 350° for 15 minutes. Set aside to cool. Cream softened cheese, add sugar and beat well. Fold in Cool Whip and marshmallows. Spread over cooked crust.

Dissolve jello in water and stir in raspberries, separating them as you stir. Chill until thick. Spread this over cream layer. Chill and refrigerate until ready to serve.

FRONT RANGE APPLE SALAD

½ cup sugar
1 Tbsp. flour
1 egg
1 Tbsp. vinegar
1—9 oz. can pineapple chunks, drained
Pineapple juice
1 cup cream, whipped
1 cup miniature marshmallows
1/3 cup salted or honey roasted peanuts, chopped big
2 cups diced apples

SERVES 6–8
Mix sugar and flour in saucepan. Add egg, vinegar and pineapple juice. Cook, stirring constantly, until thick. Chill thoroughly. Fold in whipped cream. Mix lightly with remaining ingredients.

STUFFED CINNAMON APPLES

6 apples
⅔ cup red cinnamon
   candies
2 cups water
5 oz. pkg. cream cheese
2 Tbsp. milk
1 tsp. lemon juice
⅓ cup pitted dates, chopped
9 oz. can crushed pineapple,
   drained
3 Tbsp. pecans, chopped

SERVES 6
Pare and core apples. Add candies to water; cook until dissolved. Add apples and simmer, uncovered, spooning syrup over apples occasionally, until apples are tender, about 15 minutes. Chill in syrup for several hours. Blend softened cream cheese, milk, lemon juice, dates, pineapple and nuts. Stuff apple centers with cream cheese mixture.

RUTH'S CHERRY SALAD

1—9 oz. carton Cool Whip
1—21 oz. can cherry pie
   filling
1—16 oz. can crushed
   pineapple
1½ cups coconut
1 cup pecans
2 cups miniature
   marshmallows

SERVES 10
Combine all ingredients in bowl, folding gently but thoroughly. Refrigerate.

CRANBERRY FREEZE

1—16 oz. can whole
   cranberry sauce
1—8¾ oz. can crushed
   pineapple, drained
1 cup sour cream
¼ cup powdered sugar

SERVES 6
Combine cranberry sauce and drained pineapple. Add powdered sugar to sour cream and blend, then stir into fruit mixture, mixing well. Line a loaf pan with foil and pour in fruit. Freeze until firm. Remove frozen salad and foil from the pan. Let set a few minutes, remove foil and cut in slices. Arrange slices on a bed of lettuce to serve. This is an excellent salad for Thanksgiving or Christmas. . .a little tart, a little sweet, and really pretty.

SALADS

FAMILY FRUIT SALAD

1—16 oz. can peach slices, drained
2 bananas, sliced
1—6 oz. can frozen lemonade, thawed & undiluted
½ pt. whipping cream
1 tsp. sugar

SERVES 8
Mash peaches and bananas until mushy. Stir in lemonade. Whip cream with sugar until thick. Fold into fruit mixture and pour into a 1 quart milk carton (or a foil-lined loaf pan). Freeze until firm. When ready to serve, remove from freezer a few minutes ahead of time. Peel carton to expose the amount of salad needed and slice into individual servings. Arrange on a bed of lettuce. This salad will keep for weeks in the freezer.

FIVE CUP SALAD

1 cup mandarin oranges, drained
1 cup pineapple chunks, drained
1 cup flaked coconut
1 cup miniature marshmallows
1 cup sour cream
1 banana, sliced (optional)

SERVES 6
Combine ingredients and stir gently to mix. Refrigerate at least 1 hour before serving, but if you're in a real hurry, you don't even have to do that. This old stand-by is a favorite with men.

FRUIT SALAD COATING

½ box lemon jello
Juice from canned pineapple

Dissolve jello in the reserved pineapple juice, and toss together with a fruit salad. Fruits such as apples and bananas will not darken when tossed in this dressing.

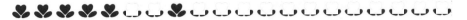

FRUIT PLATTER
WITH HONEY-LEMON DRESSING

**Assorted fruits cut into
  wedges or slices:**
Cantaloupe
Kiwi
Pineapple
Watermelon
Oranges
Grapes
Honeydew
Banana
Apples

DRESSING:
3 oz. cream cheese
2 Tbsp. honey
3 Tbsp. lemon juice
½ tsp. grated lemon peel

Combine dressing ingredients in small bowl. Arrange assorted fruits around bowl for dipping.

Also see Fresh Fruit Dip in Appetizers and Beverages section.

MANDARIN ORANGE SALAD

60 Ritz crackers, crushed
½ cup butter, melted
¼ cup sugar
**1—6 oz. can orange juice
  concentrate**
**1 can sweetened con-
  densed milk**
1—8 oz. carton Cool Whip
**2 small cans mandarin
  oranges, drained**

SERVES 12–15
Mix together cracker crumbs, butter and sugar. (Set aside ⅓ cup of mixture.) Press into 9×13 inch pan. In medium bowl, mix together orange juice, condensed milk and Cool Whip. Fold in mandarin oranges. Pour and spread over crust. Top with remaining crumbs. Refrigerate. This also makes a cool, summer dessert.

SALADS

ORANGE SALAD

1 lb. cottage cheese
1—3 oz. pkg. orange jello
1—8¼ oz. can crushed
  pineapple, drained
1—11 oz. can mandarin
  oranges, drained
1 cup Cool Whip

SERVES 4–6
Mix dry jello with cottage cheese. Add fruit and mix well. Fold in Cool Whip. Chill.

WINED FRUIT MEDLEY

3 fresh ripe pears, cut into
  pieces
2 oranges, peeled, cut into
  pieces
1 cup grapes, halved and
  seeded
2 bananas, sliced
½ cup orange juice
½ cup dry white wine

SERVES 6
Toss pears, oranges, grapes and bananas together. Combine orange juice and wine. Pour over fruits, mixing gently until fruits are well dressed. Chill. Serve in sherbet glasses.

 When you forget to chill a fruit salad or beverage, stick it in the freezer for 20 minutes. Set your timer to help you remember to take it out.

BROCCOLI SALAD

2 bunches broccoli
2 cups fresh mushrooms,
  sliced
4 eggs, hard-cooked and
  chopped
2—8 oz. cans water
  chestnuts, sliced

DRESSING:
⅓ cup ketchup
¾ cup sugar
¼ cup vinegar
2 Tbsp. Worcestershire
  sauce
½ tsp. salt
1 medium onion, quartered
1 cup salad oil

SERVES 12
Combine dressing ingredients in a blender or food processor. Combine vegetables and pour half the dressing to cover. Toss gently. The reserved dressing will keep and is delicious on a salad of fresh spinach.

COMPANY SALAD

2 bunches broccoli
  flowerettes
1 head cauliflower, cut up
4 green onions, chopped
  (tops, too)
2 cups cherry tomatoes
  (whole)

DRESSING:
1 cup mayonnaise
½ cup sour cream
1 Tbsp. vinegar
2 Tbsp. sugar
Salt and pepper to taste

SERVES 6-8
Wash, cut up, and put in a salad bowl all the vegetables. Mix together the dressing ingredients, pour over vegetables, and stir gently to coat. Cover and marinate in the refrigerator 3–4 hours.

SALADS

JAZZY BEAN-AVOCADO SALAD

2—16 oz. cans kidney
  beans
1—15 oz. can garbanzo
  beans
¼ cup sliced green onion
½ cup salad oil
¼ cup vinegar
¼ cup lemon juice
2 Tbsp. sugar
¾ tsp. chili powder
½ tsp. salt
⅛ tsp. garlic salt
⅛ tsp. pepper
Lettuce
3–4 avocados, halved and
  seeded

SERVES 6–8
Drain beans; toss with onion in large bowl. Mix oil, vinegar, lemon juice, sugar, chili powder, salt, garlic salt and pepper. Pour over beans. Chill. Arrange lettuce on platter; place avocados on lettuce. Spoon bean salad over avocados.

MARINATED BLACK EYED PEAS

1—16 oz. can black-eyed
  peas
¼ cup red onion, chopped
½ green pepper, chopped
1½ cups Bernstein's Italian
  dressing

SERVES 4
Drain and rinse black-eyed peas. Add onion and green pepper. Pour dressing over and stir gently. Marinate in the refrigerator, covered, for at least four hours.

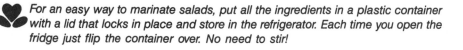

For an easy way to marinate salads, put all the ingredients in a plastic container with a lid that locks in place and store in the refrigerator. Each time you open the fridge just flip the container over. No need to stir!

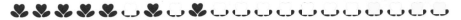

COLORFUL CABBAGE SALAD

1 cup oil
1 tsp. salt
1 cup sugar
1 cup white vinegar
1 tsp. dry mustard
1 tsp. celery seed
2 cups red cabbage, shredded
2 cups white cabbage, shredded
1 red onion, sliced thin
1 cup carrots, grated
1 cup celery, sliced
½ green pepper, sliced thin

SERVES 10
Combine oil, salt, sugar, vinegar, mustard and celery seed in saucepan and heat to dissolve sugar. Pour over the vegetables while hot. Cover and refrigerate. Let set for 24 hours in refrigerator before serving.

CALICO SALAD

1—16 oz. can diced carrots, drained
1—16 oz. can corn, drained
1—16 oz. can green beans, drained (or yellow wax beans)
1 medium bell pepper, chopped
1 red bell pepper, chopped
1 onion, chopped
1 tsp. salt
¾ cup sugar
⅔ cup vinegar
⅓ cup oil

SERVES 10
Combine vegetables. Mix together salt, sugar, vinegar and oil. Add to vegetables and toss gently to coat. Refrigerate overnight. Makes a really pretty salad.

Wooden salad bowls should be rinsed and dried immediately, not washed and soaked. Every now and then, rub vegetable oil on the inside and outside of the bowl to rejuvenate it.

SALADS

CAULIFLOWER SALAD

2 cups cauliflower, thinly
  sliced
½ cup olives, chopped
¼ cup green pepper,
  chopped finely
¼ cup pimento, chopped
  finely
3 Tbsp. onion, chopped
4½ Tbsp. salad oil
1½ Tbsp. lemon juice
½ Tbsp. wine vinegar
1 Tbsp. sugar
1 tsp. salt
Dash of pepper

SERVES 4–6
In medium bowl, combine cauliflower, olives, green pepper, pimiento and onion. In pint jar, mix salad oil, lemon juice, vinegar, sugar, salt and pepper. Shake well to mix. Pour over vegetables, Toss and refrigerate at least one hour.

MOLDED CUCUMBER SALAD

1 pkg. lime-flavored gelatin
1 cup boiling water
1 tsp. salt
2 Tbsps. lemon juice
1 cup sour cream
¼ cup mayonnaise
1½ cup cucumber, finely
  cut
3 Tbsps. green onion,
  minced
1 Tbsp. green pepper,
  chopped

Dissolve gelatin in water. Add salt and lemon juice. Cool to room temperature and add sour cream and mayonnaise. Chill until syrupy and fold in cucumber, onions, and green pepper. Pour into an 8–inch ring mold and chill until firm. This is also good on crackers as an appetizer. Serve on a bed of lettuce as a salad.

Put a little zest into tossed lettuce and tomato salad! Chop the small, upper ends of celery stalks very find and put into a jar. Cover the celery bits with half vinegar and half water, then add a teaspoon of sugar. Shake well and refrigerate. Add a few teaspoonfuls to your tossed salad. Will keep for days.

PEA 'N CHEESE SALAD

1—16 oz. pkg. frozen peas,
  cooked 2 minutes and
  drained
4 oz. Cheddar cheese,
  cubed (small) or grated
2 hard-cooked eggs,
  chopped
¼ cup celery, chopped
  finely
2 Tbsp. green onion,
  chopped
2 Tbsp. pimiento, chopped
⅓ cup mayonnaise
¼ tsp. salt
¼ tsp. hot pepper sauce

SERVES 6
In large bowl, combine all ingredients
and toss well. Cover and refrigerate
several hours or overnight.

SAUCY SALAD

DRESSING:
¼ cup vinegar
Juice of 1 lemon
¼ cup undiluted frozen
  orange juice
½ tsp. salt
2 tsp. grated orange peel
¼ cup sugar
½ tsp. dry mustard
1 cup salad oil

3 grapefruits or oranges,
  peeled and sectioned
2 large, ripe avocados,
  peeled and sliced
1 large Bermuda onion,
  sliced
½ cup chopped walnuts
7 cups crisp salad greens

SERVES 6
Mix dressing ingredients and pour over
grapefruit, avocado and onion rings.
Cover and refrigerate at least 2 hours.
Before serving, stir in nuts, then pour
all over salad greens. Toss gently to
coat.

SALADS

ORANGE-BEET SALAD

2 oranges, sliced and
   peeled
1—8¼ oz. can sliced
   pickled beets
1 small purple onion, thinly
   sliced
Bibb lettuce leaves
½ cup creamy Italian
   dressing

SERVES 4
Arrange orange and beet slices on Bibb lettuce. Top with onion slice (or rings it you prefer). Pour dressing over top and serve.

BARN-RAISING SALAD

½ cup slivered almonds,
   toasted
½ large bunch spinach,
   torn into bite-sized
   pieces
½ head cauliflower, broken
   into flowerets, then cut
   in ¼-inch slices
1 large avocado, cubed
Lemon juice

DRESSING:
6 Tbsp. salad oil
3 Tbsp. white wine vinegar
¼ tsp. minced garlic or
   1 clove, minced
½ tsp. salt
½ tsp. dry mustard
½ tsp. dry basil leaves
¼ tsp. pepper
Dash nutmeg

MAKES 4 SERVINGS
Spread nuts in pan and toast in a 350° oven until lightly browned. Dip avocado cubes or slices in lemon juice to coat. Combine vegetables and nuts. In a jar, combine oil, vinegar, garlic, salt, mustard, basil, pepper and nutmeg; shake well to blend. Pour over vegetables and toss. This salad doesn't wilt readily, so it is good to take for potluck dinner.

FRESH SPINACH SALAD
WITH SOUR CREAM DRESSING

2 lbs. fresh spinach,
 stemmed and torn in
 pieces
8 hard-cooked eggs, finely
 chopped
1 lb. fresh mushrooms,
 sliced
1 can garbanzo beans,
 drained
1 can red kidney beans,
 drained

DRESSING:
½ cup green onion,
 coarsely chopped
½ cup mayonnaise
½ tsp. minced garlic
2½ Tbsp. white wine
 vinegar
1½ tsp. salt
1½ tsp. dry mustard
¼ tsp. white pepper
1½ cups sour cream

SERVES 10–12
Arrange spinach on eight plates. Sprinkle egg over spinach. Arrange mushrooms on egg. Sprinkle on garbanzo and kidney beans. In a blender or food processor, combine onion, mayonnaise, garlic, vinegar, salt, mustard and pepper; whirl until smooth. Pour mixture into a bowl and stir in sour cream. Serve salad with dressing in a side dish to be spooned over top.

APPLEWOOD SPINACH SALAD

1 pkg. fresh spinach
1 cup dried curd cottage
 cheese
1 cup pecans, coarsely
 broken
1 cup sour cream
½ cup sugar
3 Tbsp. vinegar
1½ tsp. dry mustard
3–4 tsp. horseradish
½ tsp. salt

Wash spinach and tear into bite sized pieces. Combine spinach, pecans and cottage cheese. Combine remaining ingredients in pint jar and shake. Pour over spinach mixture and toss well. Serve with Sunflower Whole Wheat Bread and Chocolate Cheesecake for a great luncheon. Very different!

SALADS

SUSIE'S TOMATO AND ONION SALAD

6 large tomatoes, sliced
2 Bermuda onions, sliced

DRESSING:
2 Tbsp. lemon juice
1 tsp. dried dill weed
   (more if you have fresh)
2 tsp. sugar
1¼ tsp. salt
½ tsp. pepper
1 tsp. celery seed

SERVES 8
Arrange tomato and onion slices in overlapping layers on a serving plate. Combine dressing ingredients, stirring well to dissolve sugar. Pour mixture over tomatoes and onions, cover and chill thoroughly.

This is a delicious salad with almost any entree. . .especially good in the summer with vine-ripened tomatoes, fresh dill, and fresh fish! Also good to serve as a condiment for hamburgers and sandwiches.

FIRE AND ICE TOMATOES

6 tomatoes, chunked
1 large green pepper,
   chopped
1 red onion, chopped
1 cucumber sliced

DRESSING:
¾ cup vinegar
1½ tsp. celery salt
1½ tsp. mustard seed
½ tsp. salt
4½ tsp. sugar
⅛ tsp. cayenne pepper
⅛ tsp. black pepper
¼ tsp. water

SERVES 6
Combine tomatoes, green pepper and onion in a bowl. Mix all dressing ingredients in a saucepan and boil for one minute. Pour over tomato mixture. Cool, then add the sliced cucumber. Chill and serve.

MARINATED VEGETABLES

DRESSING:
1½ cups vegetable oil
½ cup red wine vinegar
3 Tbsp. tarragon vinegar
3 Tbsp. minced onion
1 tsp. sugar
1 tsp. dry mustard
1½ tsp. salt
¼ tsp. pepper
1 tsp. dried basil

2 doz. whole cherry
  tomatoes
3 stalks celery, sliced
1 lb. fresh mushrooms,
  sliced
1 green pepper, seeded
  and chopped
1 head cauliflower, cut up
1 bunch broccoli, cut up
1 yellow squash, unpeeled
  and sliced

SERVES 10–12
Combine dressing ingredients and mix well. Combine all the vegetables in a large bowl and pour the dressing over. Marinate, covered, in the refrigerator 4–5 hours or overnight.

SALADS

MARINATED ZUCCHINI SALAD

2 cups unpeeled zucchini
or yellow squash, thinly
sliced
½ cup fresh mushrooms,
halved
2 med. tomatoes, thinly
sliced
1 small red onion, sliced
½ med. lemon, thinly
sliced
½ cup olive or salad oil
2 Tbsp. vinegar
2 Tbsp. fresh lemon juice
¾ tsp. salt
⅛ tsp. pepper
¼ tsp. minced garlic
2 cups salad greens, torn
into bite-sized pieces

SERVES 8
Combine zucchini, tomatoes, mushrooms, onion and lemon slices. Shake
together in a jar the oil, vinegar, lemon
juice, salt, pepper and garlic. Pour vinegar mixture over vegetables. Refrigerate, covered, for several hours. Place
greens in a bowl. Spoon marinated
vegetables on top. Toss lightly.

CASHEW CHICKEN SALAD
WITH DIJON DRESSING

2 cups cooked, chopped
chicken
¾ cup cashew nuts
¾ cup bean sprouts
6 cups lettuce, torn into
pieces (leaf, Bibb, red-
tip lettuce is best)

DRESSING:
1 cup mayonnaise
2 Tbsp. Dijon mustard
2 Tbsp. lemon juice
2 Tbsp. sugar

SERVES 4
Toss salad ingredients together. Mix
dressing ingredients and whisk until
well blended. Top each salad serving
with dressing. This is a delicious salad
for luncheon. The dressing also would
be good on a spinach salad, for something different.

CHICKEN STUFFED MELON

2 med. cantaloupes
2 cups cold cooked
   chicken, diced
½ cup seedless green
   grapes
Seeds from 1 pomegranate
1 small kiwi, sliced

LIME-HONEY DRESSING:
4 Tbsp. lime juice
4 Tbsp. honey
¼ tsp. ground coriander
¼ tsp. nutmeg

**GRAND MARNIER
   DRESSING:**
1 cup sweetened, whipped
   cream
4 oz. cream cheese
¼ cup fresh orange juice
2-3 Tbsp. Grand Marnier

SERVES 4
Cut each cantaloupe in half. Can be made fancier by making zigzag cuts. Scoop out and discard seeds. With spoon or grapefruit knife, remove melon fruit and cut into bite-sized pieces. Drain shell and pieces. Mix cantaloupe pieces with chicken; spoon into melon shell. Top with grapes and pomegranate seeds. Garnish with sliced kiwi. Prepare one of the dressings and serve in separate bowl along with salads.

To prepare Lime-Honey Dressing, combine ingredients in pint jar and shake well.

To prepare Grand Marnier Dressing, soften cream cheese in microwave, beat in whipped cream with mixer or in food processor until smooth. Add remaining ingredients and mix well.

CHICKEN SALAD WITH GREEN CHILIES

2 cups cooked, chopped
   chicken
1 cup carrots, grated
1—4 oz. can chopped
   green chilies
¼ tsp. onion powder
2 tsp. vinegar
2 tsp. salad oil
Salt (sparingly)
6 level Tbsp. mayonnaise
1 med. avocado
Lettuce leaves
Sliced black olives

SERVES 4-6
Combine chicken, carrots, chilies, onion powder, vinegar, oil and salt. Chill. Before serving, add mayonnaise and mix well. Serve on lettuce leaves, garnishing each serving with wedges of avocado. May also serve in an avocado half. Garnish with black olives.

SALADS

CRAB-STUFFED AVOCADO SALAD

1 lb. crabmeat or imitation
  crabmeat
½ cup Miracle Whip
2-3 Tbsp. minced green
  onions
¾ cup Cheddar cheese,
  grated
¼ cup ripe olives, sliced
⅓ cup celery, sliced
1 Tbsp. fresh lemon juice
White pepper
Salt
3 avocados, halved

SERVES 3
Combine all ingredients and mix well.
Spoon into avocado halves. An easy
but fancy luncheon dish!

COASTAL SHRIMP SALAD

2 lbs. med. size shrimp,
  cooked and shelled
1-2 avocados, cubed
1 head iceberg lettuce,
  shredded

DRESSING
¼ cup olive oil
¼ cup white wine vinegar
2 Tbsp. lemon juice
½ tsp. garlic salt
¼ tsp. seasoned pepper
½ cup minced green onion
½ tsp. dill weed

SERVES 4
Combine shrimp, avocado and lettuce
in a salad bowl. Combine dressing ingredients in a jar and shake well. Pour
over salad and toss well.

MAIN DISH PASTA SALAD

1—12 oz. pkg. tri-colored
  rotini noodles
12 oz. summer sausage
1—6 oz. jar marinated
  artichokes, cut in half
1—16 oz. can whole ripe
  olives, sliced
1 green pepper, cut in thin
  strips
1 red pepper, cut in thin
  strips
8 oz. cherry tomatoes, cut
  in half
1 bunch green onions,
  sliced
8 oz. fresh mushrooms,
  sliced
1 head broccoli, cut into
  small flowerettes
12 oz. Mozzarella, cubed
¼ cup Parmesan cheese,
  grated

DRESSING:
2 Tbsp. Dijon mustard
½ cup red wine vinegar
2 tsp. sugar
1 tsp. salt
1 tsp. black pepper
¼ cup fresh parsley,
  minced
1 Tbsp. fresh chives
½-1 tsp. oregano
½-1 tsp. thyme
1 cup olive oil

SERVES 15–20
Cook noodles according to package directions, drain. Cut sausage into thin slices, then strips. Mix noodles and sausage with other ingredients in a large bowl. Toss with dressing. Chill before serving.

To prepare dressing measure mustard in a bowl. Whisk in vinegar, sugar, salt, pepper and herbs. Continue to whisk mixture while slowly dribbling in olive oil until mixture thickens. Adjust seasonings to taste.

You will love this salad for potlucks, salad luncheons, or family reunions.

SALADS

DYNAMITE MACARONI SALAD

3 cups cooked macaroni,
  rinsed
½ cup mayonnaise
1–2 tsp. chili powder
Salt to taste

SERVES 4
Combine ingredients, toss and chill. This is an unusual twist to macaroni salad that is quite good. Fresh chili powder is best but remember, it is hotter, so you might need to use less.

SESAME SEED SALAD

6 oz. pkg. Rotini (pasta
  twists)
¼ cup sesame seeds
½ cup salad oil
⅓ cup soy sauce
⅓ cup white wine vinegar
  (distilled white works)
3 Tbsp. sugar
½ tsp. salt
¼ tsp. pepper
1—10 oz. pkg. fresh spinach
½ cup green onion, thinly
  sliced, including tops

SERVES 8
Combine sesame seeds and ¼ cup oil in a frying pan. Cook over medium heat until seeds are golden. Cool. Stir in remaining oil, soy sauce, salt and pepper, vinegar and sugar. Pour over cooked pasta. Toss gently. Cover and chill at least 2 hours; overnight is better. Add washed, torn spinach leaves and onion to serve. This unusual salad is absolutely delicious. . .perfect for salad luncheons!

HOMEMADE MAYONNAISE

1 whole egg
1 egg yolk
½ tsp. garlic salt
½ tsp. table salt
1 tsp. dry mustard
½ tsp. cayenne pepper
Juice of ½ lemon
1 Tbsp. red wine vinegar
1½ cups vegetable oil,
  CHILLED

MAKES 1 PINT
Beat egg and egg yolk until light and lemon-colored. Add spices, lemon juice, and vinegar. (Do this in a food processor or blender.) With machine running, pour cold oil in a thin stream into mixture. In a flash, you will have delicious, fresh mayonnaise. . .great for having on hand, or for gift-giving!

MUSTARD VINAIGRETTE

¼ cup red wine vinegar
¾ cup olive oil
¹/₈ tsp. onion powder
1–2 Tbsp. Dijon mustard
Freshly ground pepper

MAKES 1 CUP
Mix ingredients together several hours before serving and chill. Whisk again just before serving.

RANCH STYLE DRESSING

2 tsp. onion powder
¼ tsp. garlic powder
½ tsp. salt
2 Tbsp. dried parsley flakes
1 cup mayonnaise
1 cup buttermilk

MAKES 2 CUPS
Combine all ingredients and mix.

SESAME SEED SALAD DRESSING

¼ cup sesame seeds
¼ cup cider vinegar
¹/₃ cup vegetable oil
3 Tbsp. sugar
1½ tsp. salt
½ tsp. freshly ground black
    pepper (less if you use
    ground pepper)

MAKES 1 CUP
Saute sesame seeds in a small saucepan over medium heat until golden, about 3 minutes. Stir frequently. Combine the sesame seeds with the remaining ingredients and whisk for one minute. Refrigerate and reblend before serving. Delicious on a tossed salad!

MACARONI AND GREEN PEA SALAD

3 cups cooked macaroni,
    rinsed
1 cup green peas, blanched
¼–½ cup mayonnaise
3 green onions, finely
    chopped
1 Tbsp. pimientos, chopped
Salt and pepper

SERVES 4–6
Combine ingredients, toss and chill. You can use frozen peas without blanching if you're in a hurry.

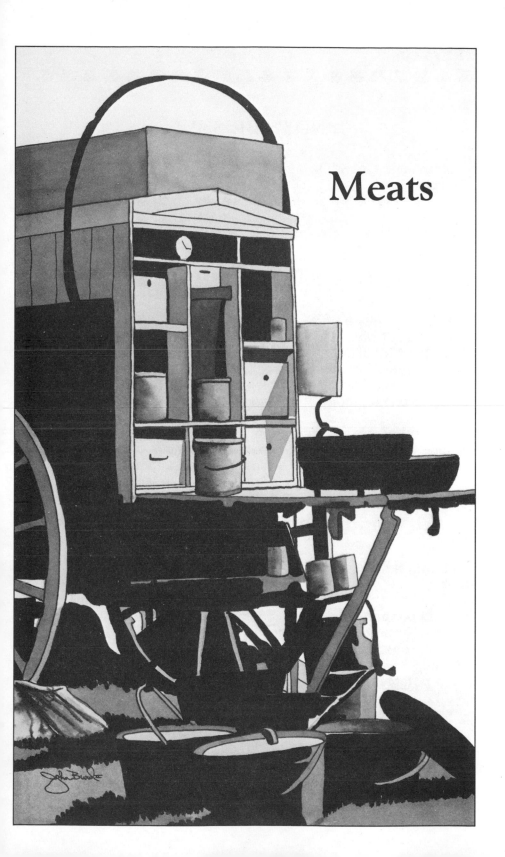

Meats

MEATS

LINDY'S BRISKET

1—12 oz. jar Heinz Chile
  Sauce
1 envelope dry onion soup
  mix
1—3–4 lb. brisket

SERVES 6
Place brisket in a large roasting pan. Sprinkle dry onion soup mix on top, then pour chile sauce over. Cover and bake at 225° for 6–8 hours.

HOT BARBECUED RIBS

6 lbs. country-style pork
  ribs or beef ribs
¼ cup light molasses
¼ cup prepared mustard
¼ cup lemon juice
1 Tbsp. Worcestershire
  sauce
½ tsp. bottled hot pepper
  sauce
¼ tsp. salt
Lemon slices

SERVES 10
Simmer ribs, uncovered, in salted water until tender, about 1 hour. Meanwhile, in small saucepan, gradually blend molasses into mustard; stir in lemon juice, Worcestershire sauce, hot pepper sauce, and salt. Heat to boiling. Grill ribs over slow to medium coals for 15 minutes on each side, brushing often with barbecue sauce. Garnish ribs with lemon slices.

SMOTHERED STEAK 'N MUSHROOMS

2 lbs. round steak
Flour
Oil
Salt and pepper
1 onion, cut into eighths
¼–½ lb. mushrooms,
  sliced
Sliced potatoes, optional
2—10½ oz. cans cream of
  mushroom soup

SERVES 4
Cut steak into individual portion sizes. Dredge in flour and brown in oil. Salt and pepper to taste. In same skillet, or roasting pan, lay meat on bottom, top with onions and mushrooms. Potato slices can be added, too, if you like. Top with soup. Cover and cook at 300° for 2½ hours or simmer on low in covered skillet.

SAUCY MEATBALLS

1½ lbs. lean ground beef
¾ cup evaporated milk
½ cup chopped onion
1 cup quick oats
1 egg
¼ tsp. garlic powder
¼ tsp. pepper
1 tsp. salt
1 Tbsp. chili powder

SAUCE:
1 cup ketchup
¾ cup brown sugar
¼ tsp. garlic powder
¼ cup chopped onion
1 Tbsp. liquid smoke

MAKES 4 DOZEN
Combine meatball ingredients, shape into balls, and place in one layer in a baking pan.

Combine sauce ingredients and mix well. Pour evenly over meatballs. Bake at 350° for 1 hour. Serve hot.

This dish serves well from a crock pot taken to potluck dinners.

PLATTE RIVER STEAK

6 cubed beef steaks
1½ tsp. salt
¼ tsp. lemon pepper
2 Tbsp. oil
2 cans sliced mushrooms
½ cup dry white or red
  wine
½ cup green pepper,
  chopped
1 small onion, chopped

SERVES 6
Sprinkle steaks with salt and lemon pepper. In a greased skillet, cook over medium heat until brown; 5 to 10 minutes on each side. Stir in mushrooms (with liquid), wine, green pepper and onion. Simmer 10–15 minutes.

MEATS

MUSHROOM STUFFED STEAK

1 round steak, ½-inch thick
½ lb. fresh mushrooms
½ cup parsley, chopped
½ cup onion, chopped
1 cup sharp Cheddar
  cheese, grated
¼ cup flour
1 tsp. salt
⅛ tsp. pepper
3 Tbsp. shortening
1—10½ oz. can condensed
  consomme
½ tsp. dry mustard

SERVES 4

Cut steak into four portions and pound to ¼-inch thickness. Remove mushroom caps from stems; chop stems and reserve caps. Combine stems, parsley, onion and cheese in a bowl; set aside 1 cup of mixture. Divide remaining mixture evenly and place in center of each piece of steak. Roll steak pieces around stuffing and fasten with toothpicks. Combine flour, salt and pepper. Dredge meat in seasoned flour. Brown in shortening. Drain drippings. Combine consomme and dry mustard; add to steak rolls in skillet. Add mushroom caps. Cover tightly and cook slowly over low heat for 45 minutes. Add reserved mushroom mixture and continue cooking 45 minutes or until meat is tender. If gravy is desired, thicken pan juices with flour and add water and a little Kitchen Bouquet.

STOCK SHOW STEAK

3 Tbsp. butter
1 med. onion, chopped
1 cup mushrooms, chopped
1 cup bread crumbs (use
  2-3 slices of bread,
  toasted and torn up)
¼ cup fresh parsley, chopped (or 2 tsp. dried)
½ tsp. salt
¼ tsp. pepper
2 lb. tenderloin or sirloin
  steak, about 1½" thick

SERVES 6

In a 10-inch skillet over medium heat, melt butter, add onion and cook until translucent. Add mushrooms and saute about 5 minutes. Stir in bread crumbs, parsley, salt and pepper. Cut a long horizontal slit in side of steak to form a pocket. Stuff bread mixture into pocket and secure with toothpicks. Season steak with salt and pepper and place on broiling pan. Broil 8–10 minutes per side, turning once. To serve, remove toothpicks and slice. Serve with Parsley Potatoes (see Index).

RUNNING W PEPPER STEAK

3 Tbsp. peppercorns
8—½-inch thick slices
  beef tenderloin
3 Tbsp. butter
2 Tbsp. oil (olive oil if you
  have it)
Salt to taste
¼ cup beef broth or 1
  bouillon cube dissolved
  in ¼ cup water
1 Tbsp. butter

SERVES 4
Put the peppercorns in a plastic bag and crush them gently with a rolling pin into irregular pieces. Press the crushed pepper into both sides of the steaks. Heat the butter and oil in a large, heavy skillet over high heat. Brown the steaks on both sides and cook to desired degree of doneness. Season with salt. Remove the steaks to a warm serving platter. Reduce heat and add the beef broth. Stir well to loosen the crumbs from the bottom. Continue cooking until sauce has reduced slightly, stir in the butter, pour over the steaks and serve.

MARINADE FOR BEEF

1 cup oil
½ cup lemon juice
2 tsp. paprika
4 Tbsp. Worcestershire
  sauce
Dash Tabasco sauce
4 Tbsp. vinegar
4 Tbsp. salt
4 Tbsp. sugar
½ tsp. garlic powder

Mix all ingredients together. Marinate scored flank steak or shish-kabob at least 24 hours. Barbecue or broil to taste. The marinade will keep in the refrigerator for several days. This all-purpose marinade also will work well on sirloin or other types of steaks. . . . The more tender the steak, the less amount of time needed to marinate.

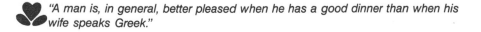

"A man is, in general, better pleased when he has a good dinner than when his wife speaks Greek."

121

MEATS

ZESTY BEEF 'N ZUCCHINI

1¼ lbs. chuck steak,
   ½" thick
2 Tbsp. orange juice
¼ tsp. garlic powder
2 medium tomatoes,
   peeled and chopped
¾ cup tomato sauce
½ tsp. dried basil leaves
½ tsp. dried marjoram leaves
½ tsp. sugar
¼ tsp. finely grated orange
   peel
Salt and pepper
4 med. zucchini, sliced
3 Tbsp. butter
¼ cup Parmesan cheese
½ tsp. herb seasoning

SERVES 4

Cut steak into strips. Combine orange juice and garlic; sprinkle over beef, turning to coat. Cover and let stand 20 minutes. Simmer tomatoes, tomato sauce, basil, marjoram, sugar and orange peel in small saucepan 20 minutes, stirring occasionally. Season with salt and pepper. Saute zucchini in nonstick frying pan in melted butter until tender. Sprinkle with Parmesan cheese and herb seasoning and toss. Remove from pan and keep warm. Cook beef over medium high heat 4–7 minutes, stirring constantly. Season with salt and pepper. Add sauce and bring to boil. Spoon over zucchini on serving plate.

AUNT PEGGY'S BEEF BURGUNDY

⅛ lb. salt pork, diced
12 small white onions
3 lbs. round steak, cut in
   2" cubes
2–3 Tbsp. flour
2 tsp. salt
¼ tsp. ground marjoram
¼ tsp. ground thyme
⅛ tsp. pepper
1 cup Burgundy wine
1 cup beef bouillon
8 oz. mushrooms, halved
1 Tbsp. snipped parsley
Cooked noodles

SERVES 8

In a deep, heavy pan stir the diced salt pork and 12 onions until onions are golden brown. Remove onions and set aside. In the same pan, add the round steak and brown well, over medium high heat. Sprinkle with flour and seasonings. Stir in wine and bouillon, then add sauteed onions. Cover and cook 4–5 hours over lowest heat, or in a covered casserole in a 250° oven. Add mushrooms 45 minutes before the end and check again for seasoning. Garnish with parsley and serve with hot buttered noodles.

SNOW PEAS AND BEEF

2 Tbsp. dry sherry
4 Tbsp. soy sauce
4 tsp. cornstarch
¼ tsp. garlic powder
1 lb. top beef sirloin, cut
  into thin strips
2 Tbsp. vegetable oil
¼ lb. fresh mushrooms,
  sliced
1—8 oz. pkg. frozen snow
  peas, thawed
1 tsp. sugar
½ tsp. MSG, optional
1 cup canned consomme
1½ tsp. cornstarch
1 Tbsp. water

SERVES 2
Combine sherry, 2 tablespoons soy sauce, 4 teaspoons cornstarch and garlic. Add beef; mix well. Let stand 15 minutes. Saute beef in hot oil in skillet until color disappears, stirring constantly. Add mushrooms; cook 3 minutes. Remove meat and mushrooms from skillet; set aside. Add snow peas to skillet and saute 2 minutes. Return beef and mushrooms to skillet. Add 2 tablespoons soy sauce, sugar, MSG and consomme. Dissolve 1½ teaspoons cornstarch in water; stir into sauce in skillet. Simmer until sauce thickens.

LIVER AND ONIONS

1 lb. calves liver
Bacon drippings
Flour
Salt and pepper to taste
1—10½ oz. can French
  Onion soup
½ soup can water

SERVES 4
Heat bacon drippings in a large skillet over medium high heat. Dredge liver in seasoned flour. Brown both sides in skillet. Pour soup and water over liver, stir to loosen crumbs, cover and reduce heat. Cook about 15–20 minutes more or until gravy is thickened.

MEATS

WORKING WOMAN'S ROAST

1—3 or 4 lb. rump roast
¼ tsp. garlic powder
¼ tsp. seasoned salt
⅛ tsp. salt
⅛ tsp. pepper
1 pkg. dry onion soup mix
2 Tbsps. Worcestershire
   sauce
1—10 oz. can cream of
   mushroom soup

SERVES 4–6
Put foil in a roaster pan and then set roast on the foil. Mix together the garlic powder, seasoned salt, salt, pepper, onion soup mix, Worcestershire sauce, and soup. Pour over roast. Seal foil and bake at 200° from 7:00 a.m. to 5:00 p.m. or for 10 hours. Dinner's ready when you get home!

STUFFED PEPPERS

6 large green bell peppers
5 cups boiling salted water
2 strips bacon
1 lb. ground beef
1 small onion, chopped
1 tsp. salt
⅛ tsp. garlic powder
1 cup rice, cooked
1—15 oz. can tomato sauce

SERVES 6
Cut thin slice from stem end of each pepper, then remove all seeds and membranes. Wash thoroughly, then cook peppers in boiling salted water 5 minutes. Drain. Cook bacon in a large skillet until crisp. Remove. Saute ground beef and chopped onion in bacon drippings until onion is tender. Drain off fat. Stir in seasonings, rice and 1 cup tomato sauce. Add finely chopped bacon. Heat through. Stuff each pepper with meat mixture and stand them upright in an ungreased baking dish. Pour remaining tomato sauce over peppers. Cover and bake 45 minutes at 350°. Uncover and bake 15 minutes longer.

SUMMIT MEAT LOAF

1—8 oz. can tomato sauce
¼ cup brown sugar
¼ cup vinegar
1 tsp. prepared mustard
1 egg, slightly beaten
1 med. onion, chopped
¼ cup cracker crumbs
2 lbs. ground beef
1½ tsp. salt
¼ tsp. pepper

SERVES 8
Combine tomato sauce, brown sugar, vinegar and mustard in a small bowl. Set aside. Combine egg, onion, cracker crumbs, ground beef, salt and pepper in mixing bowl. Add ½ cup of the tomato mixture and blend thoroughly. Turn into a loaf pan. Make a depression in top of loaf and pour remaining tomato sauce over top of meat. Cook, uncovered, 1 hour at 350°.

GERMAN CABBAGE BURGERS

1 lb. hamburger
⅓ onion, chopped
½ tsp. salt
Pepper
3 cups cabbage, shredded
1 loaf bread dough
Butter, melted

SERVES 6
Brown hamburger and onion in skillet. Add salt and pepper; drain grease. Cook cabbage until tender, drain. Roll bread dough ¼-inch thick and cut into 6–8-inch squares. Combine cabbage and hamburger. Spoon onto dough. Fold over and pinch edges together. Bake in 350° oven for 20–25 minutes or until golden brown. Brush top with butter. Good with your favorite mustard.

FOR A QUICK VARIATION:
Double ingredients. Roll one loaf bread dough out to fit a greased 9×13 pan. Sqread cooked filling on top. Roll second loaf & lay on top. Bake at 350° for 25 minutes or until golden brown. Cut in squares to serve. Serves 10–12.

 Onion odor may be removed from hands by rubbing them with dry salt.

MEATS

GREAT BEEF HOT POT

8 med. potatoes, thinly
    sliced
2 lbs. lean ground beef,
    browned
2 med. onions, thinly sliced
3 cups cabbage, thinly
    sliced
2 med. carrots, sliced
1 tsp. leaf marjoram,
    crumbled
2 tsp. salt
¼ tsp. pepper
2 Tbsp. butter
2 Tbsp. parsley, chopped
1½ cups beef broth

SERVES 6–8
Place one third of the potato slices in the bottom of a 9×12-inch casserole; top with even layers of half of the ground beef, onion slices, cabbage and carrot slices; sprinkle with part of the marjoram, salt and pepper. Repeat layers, ending with potato slices arranged in a pattern on top. Dot with butter and sprinkle with parsley. Pour beef broth over; cover casserole. Bake at 350° for 1½ hours, or until potatoes are tender.

MONDAY NIGHT HASH

Sunday's leftover roast,
    onions, potatoes, carrots
    & gravy
1–2 Tbsp. vegetable oil
Salt & pepper
Eggs

In food processor or meat grinder, coarsely grind meat, potatoes, carrots and onions. Mix with enough gravy to moisten well. Add oil to skillet and fry hash. Salt and pepper to taste. Fry until lightly browned, turn with spatula and brown on other side. Serve with a fried egg on top of each serving or with ketchup.

When baking a casserole, spray the inside sides of your dish lightly with non-stick vegetable spray coating for easier clean-up.

PORK TENDERLOIN IN NORMANDY SAUCE

2 lb. pork tenderloin
¼ cup seedless raspberry
or blackberry jelly
2 Tbsps. butter, melted

NORMANDY SAUCE:
6 Tbsps. butter
4 Golden Delicious apples,
pared and sliced thinly
3 Tbsps. flour
4 Tbsps. sugar
¾ cup apple juice
¾ cup whipping cream

SERVES 4
Place pork in shallow roasting pan. Spread jelly over the roast, then drizzle melted butter over it. Roast, uncovered, at 390° for 45 minutes. (Can use a meat thermometer to insure internal temperature of 160.) Slice pork into medallions. Serve Normandy Sauce separately.

NORMANDY SAUCE:
Melt butter in a large sauté pan. Sauté apples until tender. Sprinkle flour over apples and cook 3–5 minutes. Add sugar, apple juice, and cream. Cook until thickened.

BRANDIN' BEANS

1 lb. pinto beans
1 med. onion, chopped
1 lb. ground beef
1 Tbsp. chili powder
½ cup taco sauce
½ tsp. oregano
½ tsp. cumin seed
1—16 oz. can tomatoes,
chopped
1 clove garlic
2 jalapeno peppers, seeded
and chopped
1 Tbsp. oil

SERVES 12
Cover beans with water and cook 3–4 hours until tender. Saute onion in cooking oil and add to tender beans. Brown ground beef and add to beans. Add chili powder, taco sauce, oregano, cumin seed, tomatoes, garlic and jalapeno peppers to bean mixture. Cook all until thick, approximately 30 minutes. Serve over Navajo Fry Bread (see Index) for something special.

MEATS

WILD RICE AND SAUSAGE

2 Tbsp. butter
1 med. onion, chopped
1—4 oz. can mushrooms,
   drained
1 lb. smoked sausage,
   sliced thin
Dash of poultry seasoning
1—6 oz. box Uncle Ben's
   Long Grain and Wild Rice

SERVES 6
Melt butter in a large skillet. Add onions and mushrooms and saute until translucent and tender. Add sausage, and cook 10–15 minutes. Add poultry seasoning. Meanwhile, cook rice according to package directions. When done, add the sausage mixture. Toss and serve.

HOT POTATO AND WURST

8 med. potatoes
1 Tbsp. salad oil
1½ lbs. knackwurst and
   bratwurst in desired
   proportions
4 tsp. flour
4 tsp. sugar
1 tsp. salt
1 tsp. dry mustard
1 tsp. celery seed
⅔ cup chicken broth
⅓ cup white wine vinegar
¼ cup parsley, finely
   chopped
½ small red onion, sliced
   and separated into rings
½ cup sliced celery

SERVES 6
Cover potatoes with water and cook until tender when pierced; drain. Peel and slice; set aside. In skillet over medium heat, add oil and wurst and cook, stirring, until lightly browned. Remove from pan and set aside. Add flour, sugar, salt, mustard and celery seed to drippings in skillet. Mix well, stir in broth and vinegar and cook until dressing boils and thickens, stirring constantly. Gently stir in potatoes, wurst, parsley, onion and celery until coated and hot throughout.

 Use some of the water the potatoes have been cooking in when making your gravies. Can even be used in place of some milk when making chicken gravy and you won't know the difference.

ப ப ப ப ப ப ப ப ப ப ப ப ப ப ப ப ப ப ப

DESPERATION DINNER

1 lb. beef smoked sausage sliced (Hillshire Farms is good)
4—15 oz. cans butter beans or large lima beans (try Ellis)
2—16 oz. cans stewed tomatoes
2 onions, chopped

SERVES 4–6
In a large pot, brown the sliced sausage and onion. Open all the cans and add to the pot...don't drain. Cover and cook as long as you want. It is ready at about 20 minutes, but you can start it early in the morning and let it cook all day in the crockpot. This supper is the greatest when you need something in a jiffy, or when you'll be gone all day and want dinner ready when you get home.

RITA'S CHALUPA

1 lb. dry pinto beans
3 lbs. pork roast
7 cups water
½ cup onion, chopped
½ tsp. garlic powder
1 Tbsp. salt
2 Tbsp. chili powder
1 Tbsp. cumin
1 tsp. oregano
1—4 oz. can chopped green chilies
1 lb. Italian sausage (Polish, Chorizo, German can also be used)
½ lb. Monterey Jack cheese
½ lb. jalapeno pepper Monterey Jack cheese

SERVES AN ARMY
Place beans in large roasting pan and cover with water. Bring to boil and cook 1 minute; cover and remove from heat and let stand for one hour. Add remaining ingredients, except cheeses, to beans. Cover and cook in 325° oven for 5 hours, or until roast falls apart and beans are done. Remove any bone in the roast and skim off any fat. Add cheeses and heat until cheese melts. The amount of each cheese can be varied depending on the degree of hotness desired. This recipe can be varied as many was as you can think of and still be great. It freezes well, can be thickened and used as a dip, served over corn tortillas or in flour tortillas.

FAJITAS

1–2 lb. sirloin

MARINADE:
1—16 oz. bottle Bernstein's Italian dressing
½ cup Worcestershire sauce
⅛ tsp. garlic powder
Salt and pepper

1 dozen flour tortillas, warmed

GARNISHES:
Chopped tomato
Chopped lettuce
Grated Cheddar cheese
Sour cream
Guacamole, see Index
Picante sauce, see Index

SERVES 6

Trim all the fat from the steak and cut strips 3 inches by ½-inch. Do this while the steak is still slightly frozen. Mix marinade ingredients, saturate each piece, then lay in glass dish and pour remaining sauce over all. Cover with clear wrap and refrigerate 6–8 hours or overnight. Cook strips over a hot fire on the outdoor grill. Serve immediately rolled in a warm flour tortilla and garnished with your choice of tomatoes, lettuce, cheese, sour cream, guacamole, or hot sauce. Serve with Spanish Rice, refried beans and extra guacamole.

Fajita is a Spanish word meaning "little girdle or belt." Traditionally, fajitas are made from skirt steak, hence the name, but this cut of beef is not generally available. Round steak or flank steak work just as well. Purists will also cook fajitas over a mesquite fire which imparts a slightly sweet flavor to the meat. It is a fun dish to cook and serve, as it allows your guests to embellish their fajita to their own taste. Try it at a casual buffet supper.

 Put uncooked lasagna noodles in your lasagna casserole (just as though you had already cooked them) and bake the lasagna as you normally would. The noodles cook and you have cut preparation time in half!

PANCHO'S CASSEROLE

1 Tbsp. oil
1 med. onion, chopped
¼ tsp. garlic powder
1 lb. lean ground beef
1—28 oz. can stewed
   tomatoes
1 pkg. taco seasoning mix
1—4 oz. can diced green
   chilies
1—2½ oz. can black
   olives, chopped
1—¾ lb. bag tortilla chips,
   lightly crushed
½ lb. Mozzarella cheese,
   grated
1 pt. sour cream
½ cup Cheddar cheese,
   grated

SERVES 6-8
Saute onion in oil in a large skillet over medium heat. Add meat and garlic powder and cook beef until browned. Drain fat. Blend in tomatoes, taco seasoning, chilies and olives and simmer about 10 minutes. Grease a 9×13 inch Pyrex baking dish. Layer half of chips over bottom. Add all meat mixture, then Mozzarella, then sour cream. Top with remaining chips. Bake at 350° until heated through, about 30 minutes. Sprinkle with Cheddar cheese and continue baking until cheese melts. Let stand 5 minutes before serving.

MOM'S ITALIAN DELIGHT

2 lbs. ground beef
1 med. onion, chopped
1—6 oz. can tomato sauce
1—6 oz. can tomato paste
1—16 oz. can corn
1 small can ripe olives,
   sliced
1 small can mushrooms,
   sliced
1 tsp. oregano
1 tsp. basil
Salt and pepper
4 cups wide noodles
1 lb. Cheddar cheese,
   grated

SERVES 6-8
Brown meat and onion in skillet; drain fat. Add tomato sauce, tomato paste, corn, olives, mushrooms, oregano, basil, salt and pepper; mix well. Cook noodles and drain. Combine noodles and cheese with meat sauce and pour into large casserole. Bake 35 minutes at 350°.

MEATS

STUFFED PASTA SHELLS

2 Tbsp. vegetable oil
8 oz. fresh mushrooms,
  chopped
1 tomato, chopped
1 onion, chopped
¼ tsp. garlic powder
¼ cup fresh parsley,
  chopped
½ tsp. dried oregano leaves
½ tsp. dried basil leaves
Salt to taste
1—8 oz. box manicotti
  shells
1—16 oz. container Ricotta
  cheese
1—10 oz. box frozen
  spinach, thawed
1—15 oz. jar spaghetti
  sauce
½ cup grated Mozzarella
  cheese

SERVES 6–8
Saute mushrooms, onion, tomato, garlic, parsley, oregano, basil and salt in oil in deep skillet for 15 minutes or until vegetables are tender. Boil shells as directed on package. When vegetables in skillet are ready, stir in ricotta cheese and spinach. Drain shells; fill each with the spinach-cheese mixture. Pour spaghetti sauce into skillet; bring to boil over medium heat. Arrange stuffed shells in spaghetti sauce; sprinkle with mozzarella cheese. Reduce heat to low and simmer, covered, 10–15 minutes until cheese is melted and shells are heated through. A fancy meal that can be done in 30 minutes! (Browned hamburger can be added to spaghetti sauce.)

CAVATELLI

½ lb. ground beef
½ lb. ground pork
3 slices bacon, diced
½ cup mushrooms, diced
1 onion, chopped
1—16 oz. can Italian-style
  peeled tomatoes
1 bay leaf
¼ tsp. garlic powder
½ tsp. dried basil
1 tsp. salt
Pepper to taste
1—6 oz. can tomato paste
Cooked pasta
Parmesan cheese

SERVES 4
In a large skillet, brown ground beef, pork, bacon, mushrooms and onion. Add tomatoes, bay leaf, garlic, basil, salt and pepper. Simmer 1 hour, adding water if necessary. Add tomato paste and simmer an additional 15 minutes. Remove bay leaf. Pour sauce over cooked pasta and top with grated Parmesan cheese. This is best if prepared the day before, refrigerated overnight, and heated up the next day. This is a rich Italian sauce with a unique flavor ...different from the usual spaghetti and meatballs!

VEAL (OR MEATBALL) PARMIGIANA

SAUCE:
2 Tbsp. margarine
½ cup chopped onion
2—8 oz. cans tomato paste
1—12 oz. can tomatoes
2 tsp. dried basil
2 tsp. granulated sugar
1 tsp. oregano
1 tsp. salt
½ tsp. pepper
½ tsp. garlic powder
½ cup dry red wine
8 mushrooms, sliced
6 oz. spaghetti or noodles,
  cooked and drained

VEAL PATTIES:
1–1½ lbs. veal, ½″ thick
2 eggs, beaten
3 Tbsp. fine dry bread
  crumbs
2 Tbsp. butter
2 Tbsp. oil
8 oz. Mozzarella cheese
6 Tbsp. Parmesan cheese

STUFFED MEATBALLS:
1 lb. hamburger
1 cup dried bread crumbs
½ cup milk
2 Tbsp. minced onion
1 tsp. garlic powder
⅛ tsp. pepper
8 oz. Mozzarella cheese,
  cut into 12 cubes
3 Tbsp. flour
2 Tbsp. oil
6 Tbsp. Parmesan cheese

SERVES 4

To make sauce, saute onion in margarine. Whirl other ingredients, except mushrooms, in blender or food processor. Add mixture to onions along with the mushrooms. Simmer 15 minutes.

If using veal:
Pound veal slices, dip each in beaten egg, then bread crumbs. Heat butter and oil in skillet and lightly brown. Top cooked and drained spaghetti or noodles with half of the tomato sauce, then veal slices, half the cheeses, the remaining tomato sauce, and the remaining cheeses. Bake, covered, at 375° for 30–45 minutes.

If using meatballs:
Mix together hamburger, bread crumbs, milk, minced onion, garlic and pepper. Completely cover each cheese cube with meat. Roll in flour and brown on all sides. Add sauce, heat to boiling. Simmer 5–10 minutes. Serve over spaghetti or noodles (also good on rice). Top with Parmesan cheese.

MEATS

PENNSYLVANIA DUTCH PORK CHOPS

4 pork chops
1 Tbsp. oil or bacon
  drippings
1—8 oz. can applesauce or
  1 large apple, finely
  chopped
1—16 oz. can sauerkraut,
  undrained and chopped
¼ cup onion, finely
  chopped
2 Tbsp. brown sugar
½ tsp. caraway seed
Salt and pepper

SERVES 4
In skillet, heat bacon drippings or oil and brown pork chops on both sides. Combine applesauce, sauerkraut, onion, brown sugar and caraway seed. Spoon over chops. Season with salt and pepper. Cover and simmer until chops are tender, 35–45 minutes.

SCALLOPED POTATOES WITH PORK CHOPS

6 pork chops, ½" thick
1 Tbsp. fat
5 cups potatoes, sliced
6—1 oz. slices processed
  American cheese
1 tsp. salt
¼ tsp. pepper
¼ cup onion, chopped
¼ cup celery, chopped
1—10½ oz. can cream of
  chicken soup
1¼ cups milk

SERVES 4-6
Brown chops in hot fat. Place half of potatoes in greased 9×13 inch baking pan. Top with cheese slices. Add remaining potatoes. Place chops on potatoes. Sprinkle with salt and pepper. Saute onion and celery in drippings in skillet until tender. Add soup and milk to skillet, heat, and pour over chops. Cover and bake at 350° for one hour. Remove cover and bake 30 minutes longer.

 When making meat balls or patties wet your hands with cold water before shaping the meat and the grease won't stick to your hands as badly.

PAINT MINES PORK ROAST

Pork roast
Water
Onions
Salt and pepper

GRAVY:
3–4 Tbsp. cornstarch
½ cup cold water
Salt and pepper
1 tsp. Kitchen Bouquet

Place pork roast fat side up in roasting pan, and add 2 inches of water to pan. Quarter 1 or 2 onions and place in water. Generously salt and pepper roast. Cook, covered, at 325°, 20–30 minutes for every pound of roast or until meat thermometer reaches 170°. When done, remove roast and onions. Mix together 3–4 tablespoons cornstarch with ½ cup cold water. (May need more or less of this mixture depending on amount of water and drippings in your roaster.) Add to drippings and stir over medium-high heat until desired consistency. Season with salt, pepper and Kitchen Bouquet. Skim grease off gravy. Serve with mashed potatoes and green beans.

BARBECUED PORK ROAST: Pork roast is also good cooked in barbecue sauce (your favorite or see Index). The roast either can be sliced and served, or shredded, mixed with barbecue sauce, and served on buns.

PIKE'S PEAK PORK TENDERLOIN

16 strips bacon
8 pork tenderloins, cut
½″ thick
Salt
Pepper
Garlic powder
8 onion slices
8 tomato slices
16 fresh mushroom caps
2 Tbsp. butter

SERVES 6–8
On a broiling pan, criss-cross 2 uncooked bacon strips. Place tenderloin on top and sprinkle with seasoning. Cover with onion and tomato. Bring bacon strips together and overlap across top of pork. Repeat for other tenderloins. Bake, uncovered, for 50–60 minutes at 350°. Saute mushroom caps in butter. Just before serving insert toothpick through two mushrooms and stick in center of each tenderloin. A very easy and quick dinner after a busy day. Just serve with baked potato and Cauliflower Supreme (see Index).

MEATS

FLORENTINE CHOPS

6 pork chops
Vegetable oil
6 Tbsp. butter
6 Tbsp. flour
1¼ cups strong chicken
  stock
1¾ cups milk
Salt and pepper
Nutmeg to taste
2 egg yolks
1½ lbs. fresh spinach,
  chopped & lightly steamed
2 Tbsp. grated onion
1½ cups Swiss cheese,
  grated
5 Tbsp. Parmesan cheese
Cooked rice

SERVES 4–6

Brown chops in greased skillet; then cover and cook slowly for about 30 minutes. In saucepan, melt butter, stir in flour and cook over low heat for 3 minutes. Stir in chicken stock and milk and stir over medium-high heat until thickened. Add salt, pepper and nutmeg. Pour a little of the sauce into egg yolks, then return yolk mixture to the sauce. Stir until smooth and thick. In small bowl, mix together the grated onion, spinach and 2 cups of the sauce. Spread spinach mixture over bottom of a large, shallow, greased casserole. Arrange chops on top of spinach. Stir the Swiss cheese into the remaining sauce and stir over low heat until melted. Pour sauce over chops, sprinkle with Parmesan cheese and bake, uncovered, at 400° for 15 minutes or until bubbling and cheese is slightly browned. Serve with rice.

HOPPIN' JOHN

1 onion, chopped
4–6 slices bacon, chopped
2 cups ham, chopped
1 cup raw rice
1—16 oz. can black-eyed
  peas
1¾ cups water
Salt and pepper to taste

SERVES 4–6

Saute the chopped onion and bacon. Drain grease. Add remaining ingredients, pour into a 2 quart casserole, cover and bake at 350° for 40–50 minutes, or until rice is tender and liquid is absorbed. This delicious southern-style main dish is great served with a green salad and cornbread. Also, it is almost better as leftovers, as the flavors have had time to blend.

MRS. KIMSEY'S HAM LOAF
AND HORSERADISH SAUCE

2 lbs. fresh pork, ground
1 lb. smoked, cured ham,
ground
1 cup milk
1 cup cracker crumbs
2 eggs
Salt and pepper to taste

HORSERADISH SAUCE:
½ pint whipping cream,
whipped
1 tsp. sugar
1 Tbsp. vinegar
3 Tbsp. horseradish (vary
to taste)
¼ tsp. salt
Several dashes cayenne
pepper

SERVES 8
Have the butcher grind the fresh pork and the ham together. Mix with remaining ingredients. Put in a loaf pan and bake 1½ hours at 350°. Serve with Horseradish Sauce to make the entree complete.

To make sauce, blend all ingredients together and serve on ham loaf.

KATHLEEN'S LAMB STEW

1 lb. beef stew meat
1 lb. lamb stew meat
1 cup burgundy, or a
hearty red wine
1—10½ oz. can tomato soup
1 med. onion, chopped
3 large unpeeled potatoes,
cubed
6 large carrots, sliced
1 tsp. salt
¼ tsp. pepper
½ tsp. sweet basil
1½–2 cups water
½ lb. fresh mushrooms,
halved
1—10 oz. pkg. frozen peas

SERVES 6
Combine all ingredients except mushrooms and peas in crockpot or roasting pan. Cook on high in crockpot, or at 275° in oven for 6 hours. Check occasionally to see if stew needs more water. Ten minutes before serving add mushrooms and peas and simmer. Serve with All Bran Rolls (see Index) and a green salad. Even better the next day!

MEATS

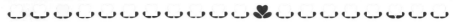

LEG O' LAMB

3–4 lb. leg of lamb
Salt
Pepper
Garlic powder, or slivers of
**   fresh garlic**
Mint jelly

SERVES 6
Season the lamb well with salt, pepper and garlic powder. Place in a roasting pan and cover. Bake at 350° for about 2 hours, or until the meat is tender when pierced with a fork. Serve with mint jelly. This is especially good with Parsleyed New Potatoes, Country-Style Green Beans and Sour Cream Lemon Pie for Sunday dinner.

FRANCES'S FAMOUS LAMB CHOPS

4 lamb chops
Salt
Pepper
4 slices onion
Sour cream

SERVES 4
Season the lamb chops with salt and pepper. Place in a shallow roasting pan. Lay a slice of onion (the whole slice, not just a ring) on each chop, then spoon a dollop of sour cream on top of the onion. Cover and bake at 350° for 1 hour.

These are also delicious when cooked in a Romertopf (clay) cooker. . .a nice change from chicken and beef.

RAY'S HERB BUTTER FOR CHOPS

1 pearl onion
1 large garlic clove
¼ tsp. salt
¼ tsp. ground rosemary
½ lb. butter or margarine
2 Tbsp. chopped parsley
1 tsp. whole thyme
2–5 drops Tabasco

Process onion and garlic in food processor with blade until well chopped. Let mixture rest (pour off any liquid if you wish). Chop parsley. In a bowl, cream together the butter, onion-garlic mixture, parsley and other herbs until well blended. Add Tabasco to taste. Spoon mixture into a butter mold or custard cup and refrigerate (will keep in fridge for 2 weeks). Serve over piping hot broiled meats. It's wonderful!

DONNIE'S ORIGINAL WILD GAME STEW

Venison or duck, cubed
Salt
Pepper
Garlic powder
Hot oil
2 Tbsp. butter
2 Tbsp. onion, grated
2 Tbsp. pimiento, chopped
1—10½ oz. can cream of
   mushroom soup
1 Tbsp. fresh parsley (or
   1 tsp. dried)
2 tsp. wine or sherry
1 tsp. Worcestershire
   sauce
¼ tsp. cayenne pepper (or
   less, to taste)
½ tsp. salt
1 cup mushrooms,
   chopped
Cooked rice or noodles

SERVES 4–6
Use your own judgment on how much game to use, depending on the number of people you have to feed and how much game you have on hand. Sprinkle game with salt, pepper and garlic powder. Saute in hot oil until browned on all sides. Remove meat from pan and dispose of oil. In a Dutch oven, melt butter. Add the rest of the ingredients except rice, adding water if necessary to thin the stew. Add browned meat and simmer for 40 minutes. Serve over rice or noodles.

This really is an original recipe from the hunter in the family. It is wonderful . . . makes an exceptional meal!

 Sprinkle a frying pan with salt before adding meat to prevent fat from splattering.

MEATS

ᒍ ᒍ ᒍ ᒍ ᒍ ᒍ ᒍ ᒍ ᒍ ᒍ ᒍ ᒍ ᒍ ᒍ ᒍ ᒍ ᒍ ᒍ

BAR-B-QUE SAUCE

2¼ cups ketchup
2¼ cups water
2 tsp. instant beef bouillon
    granules
1¼ tsp. dry mustard
1 Tbsp. chili powder (or
    less if you like mild)
¼ tsp. cayenne pepper
    (cut in half or omit if
    you prefer a milder
    flavor)
½ tsp. garlic powder
½ tsp. salt
2 tsp. Worcestershire
    sauce
2 shakes Tabasco sauce
3 Tbsp. brown sugar
½ tsp. Liquid Smoke
1 Tbsp. lemon juice

MAKES 1 QUART
Combine all ingredients in a saucepan and bring to a boil. Reduce heat and simmer, stirring occasionally, for 15 minutes. Cool to room temperature. Keeps well in the refrigerator for several weeks. This is a rather "hot" barbecue sauce, but one that is loaded with flavor. Keep some on hand at all times and use it with:

Baked Ham: Put sliced ham in a skillet, add some sauce and simmer almost dry.

Chicken: Good for grilling outside or spread on chicken pieces and roast in oven at 350°.

Steaks, Pork Chops, Ribs: Put on steaks and barbecue outside.

Sandwiches: Marinate shredded, cooked beef in sauce and pile on buns.
Take thin sliced German sausages simmered in sauce. Place on hot buttered onion buns, that have been toasted. Mmmm good!

CELEBRATION MUSTARD-GINGER GLAZE

½ cup Dijon mustard
2 Tbsp. soy sauce
2 garlic cloves, mashed
1 tsp. ground thyme
1 tsp. ground rosemary
½ tsp. powdered ginger
(or use fresh, chopped
finely, if you like ginger)
2 Tbsp. olive oil

Blend together the mustard, soy sauce, garlic, thyme, rosemary and ginger. With a wire whisk, beat in the olive oil a few drops at a time until the consistency of the mixture is creamy. Four hours before putting leg of lamb in the oven, brush mustard coating over entire surface and set on a rack in a roasting pan to marinate outside the oven. (If you didn't plan four hours ahead, don't worry—it just doesn't permeate the meat as deeply.) Cook roast to desired doneness. The coating browns nicely.

Keeps in a jar in the refrigerator for about a week, and you'll use the leftover glaze quickly. A marvelous coating for lamb when making dinner for company, but equally good on chicken for yourself. . . its piquant taste is so good you'll invent things to put it on!

PICANTE SAUCE

1—12 oz. can jalapeno
slices, mild variety,
drained
1—4 oz. can green chilies
2 med. onions, chopped
2—1 lb. cans tomatoes,
undrained
⅓ cup vinegar
¼ tsp. garlic powder
2 tsp. salt

MAKES ABOUT 6 CUPS
Place all ingredients in a food processor or blender and process until tomato is pureed. If this is too hot, add more tomatoes or reduce jalapenos. Refrigerate. Keeps well in the refrigerator.

Chicken
&
Fish

CHICKEN AND FISH

TEXAS PICNIC CHICKEN

1 fryer, cut up
½ cup flour
Shortening
½ onion, chopped finely
2 Tbsp. celery, chopped
¼ tsp. garlic powder
1½ tsp. sugar
1½ tsp. paprika
½ tsp. salt
¼ tsp. black pepper
¾ cup ketchup
3½ Tbsp. vinegar
¼ cup water
1 Tbsp. Worcestershire
   sauce
¼ cup butter

SERVES 4
Coat chicken with flour and brown in shortening. Combine remaining ingredients, heat until butter is melted. Place chicken in single layer in baking pan. Spoon sauce over all chicken. Cover with foil and bake at 350° for 1 hour 15 minutes.

AMAZING BARBECUED CHICKEN

1 chicken, cut up
1 cup flour
Shortening for frying
⅓ cup ketchup
1 can cola (your choice)

SERVES 4
Shake chicken and flour in plastic bag. Remove chicken and brown in shortening. Combine cola and ketchup in casserole dish. Add chicken pieces. Bake, uncovered, for 1 hour 15 minutes at 350°.

CHICKEN POT PIE

5 Tbsp. butter
$^1/_3$ cup flour
3 cups chicken broth
$^1/_8$ tsp. pepper
$^1/_8$ tsp. ground thyme
Salt to taste
4 cups cooked chicken, cut up
1—10 oz. pkg. frozen peas and carrots, cooked and drained
2–3 Tbsp. sherry (optional)
2½ cups Bisquick
$^2/_3$ cups milk

SERVES 4–6

Melt butter in a large pot. Stir in flour and cook over medium heat. Gradually add chicken broth, stirring constantly. Stir and simmer until it is gravy-thick. Add seasonings. Add chicken and vegetables and simmer until heated through. Stir in sherry. Pour into 2 quart casserole.

Stir together Bisquick and milk to make a manageable dough. Turn onto floured board and knead lightly until dough is smooth. Roll out to a circle large enough to cover the top of the chicken casserole. Set dough on top of chicken mixture. Bake at 450° until golden brown, about 10 minutes. This quick, easy one-pot dinner will be a fast favorite with the family!

CHICKEN AND FISH

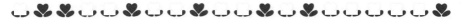

TERIYAKI CHICKEN

1—8 oz. can crushed
  pineapple, undrained
¼ cup teriyaki sauce
2 Tbsps. lemon juice
2 Tbsps. red wine vinegar
2 cloves garlic, minced
1 Tbsp. olive oil
¼ tsp. mesquite liquid
  smoke
6 chicken breast halves,
  skinned and boned

SERVES 6
Combine first 7 ingredients; place in a shallow container or a ziplock baggie. Add chicken; cover or seal and chill 1 to 2 hours, turning occasionally. Remove chicken from marinade. Grill chicken, covered over medium coals for 4 to 5 minutes on each side.

CHICKEN A LA KING

6 Tbsp. butter
¼ cup carrots, sliced
¼ cup celery, sliced
¼ cup onion, chopped
¼ cup flour
½ tsp. salt
1 cup chicken broth
1 cup half and half
2 cups chicken, cooked &
  cubed
1—3 oz. can sliced
  mushrooms, drained
2 Tbsp. pimiento, chopped
Toast triangles, or baked
  patty shells

SERVES 4
Melt butter in saucepan and saute carrots, celery and onion until tender. Stir in flour and salt. Add broth and half and half. Stir constantly over medium heat until mixture thickens and bubbles. Stir in chicken, mushrooms and pimiento. Serve over toast triangles or in patty shells. This is one of those recipes that is always good.

CHICKEN STIR-FRY

2 Tbsps. vegetable oil
**1 lb. chicken breast,
 boneless, skinless,
 cut-up**
**1 lb. pkg. frozen stir-fry
 vegetables**
Salt
Pepper
Garlic powder
Soy sauce
Cooked rice

SERVES 4

Heat oil in a large skillet. Sauté chicken until it is cooked through. Remove chicken. Add vegetables to skillet, season with salt, pepper, and garlic powder. Cover and cook 5 minutes until tender-crisp. Return chicken to pan, then add soy sauce and toss to coat. Serve immediately over cooked rice.

This is a super easy, delicious meal . . . ready in minutes!

CHICKEN AND FISH

CASTLE ROCK CHICKEN CASSEROLE

1—6 oz. pkg. long grain
and wild rice
3 cups cooked, diced
chicken
1 cup mayonnaise
1—10 oz. pkg. frozen
French-cut green beans,
thawed
1—10½ oz. can cream of
celery soup
1 small onion, chopped
1—8 oz. can water
chestnuts, sliced
(optional)
Salt and pepper to taste

SERVES 8
Cook rice according to package directions. Combine rice with other ingredients and bake for 45 minutes, covered, at 350°. Freezes well before baking. This is a delicious casserole, complete in itself.

KING RANCH CHICKEN

1 large fryer
2 tsp. salt
1 tsp. pepper
1 bay leaf
1—10½ oz. can cream of
chicken soup
1—10½ oz. can cream of
mushroom soup
1—10½ oz. can Rotel
tomatoes with green
chilies
½ cup chicken stock
Salt and pepper to taste
12 corn tortillas, torn in
small pieces
2 onions, finely chopped
3 cups sharp Cheddar
cheese, grated

SERVES 6–8
Cook chicken in water seasoned with
2 teaspoons salt, pepper and bay leaf.
Remove cooked chicken; reserve ½
cup of the chicken stock. Debone
chicken and cut into bite-sized pieces.
Set aside. Combine soups, tomatoes,
chicken stock, salt and pepper to taste.
Mix well. In a 3 quart casserole, make
3 layers in the following order: torn tortillas, chicken, soup mixture, chopped
onions, and grated cheese. Bake at
350° for about 45 minutes, or until
bubbly. The tomatoes add a unique
twist to this version of chicken enchiladas.

CHICKEN CHIMICHANGAS

¼ tsp. garlic powder
1 large onion, diced
2 tomatoes, diced
1 tsp. ground cumin
2 cups cooked chicken, diced
1—4 oz. can chopped green chilies
1 tsp. salt
8 to 10 flour tortillas
1½ cups Monterey Jack or Longhorn cheese, grated
Vegetable shortening for frying

SERVES 6
Combine garlic, onion, tomato and cumin. Heat 1 tablespoon oil in a frying pan, add tomato mixture and bring to a simmer over medium heat, uncovered. Lower heat and cook until onions are soft, straining off any liquid. Add chicken, chilies and salt. In the center of each tortilla, place 2 heaping tablespoons of chicken mixture, and a heaping tablespoon of cheese. Fold one side of tortilla to cover filling; fold in adjacent sides, then the final flap. Secure with a toothpick. Heat 2 inches vegetable shortening to 475° in a skillet. Place chimichangas, flap side down, in skillet and fry until golden brown. Turn and fry other side. Drain and keep warm in a low oven until all are done.

Serve with salsa, sour cream, guacamole, lettuce and tomato as accompaniments. These are also good unfried, as a chicken burrito. The chicken mixture is also good in tacos or enchiladas, a really versatile filler.

FRENCH ONION CHICKEN

1—10 oz. can cream of mushroom soup
1 soup can milk
¾ cup regular rice, uncooked
1—4 oz. can sliced mushrooms, undrained
1 packet dry onion soup mix
4 chicken breast halves

SERVES 4
Blend soup and milk; reserve ½ cup of the mixture. Stir together remaining soup mixture, rice, mushrooms and half the onion soup mix. Pour into an 11½ ×7½ inch baking dish. Arrange chicken breasts on the rice mixture. Pour ½ cup reserved soup mixture over chicken and sprinkle with remaining onion soup mix. Cover and bake 1 hour at 350°. Uncover and bake an additional 15 minutes.

CHICKEN AND FISH

CHICKEN TETRAZZINI

½ cup carrots, sliced
½ cup celery, sliced
1 large chicken
1—10 oz. pkg. broccoli,
  asparagus or peas

SAUCE:
¼ cup butter
¾ lb. mushrooms, sliced
¼ cup flour
½ tsp. salt
1½ cups chicken broth +
  ½ tsp. chicken bouillon
1½ cups cream
¼ cup dry white wine
½ cup Romano, Cheddar
  or Parmesan cheese

½ lb. or 2 cups spaghetti
  or linguine

SERVES 6

Cook chicken in water with chopped carrots and celery. Add salt and pepper to taste. Save broth and cut cooked chicken into bite-sized pieces. Cook broccoli according to package directions; drain and set aside.

To prepare sauce: in medium size saucepan, melt butter and saute mushrooms. Set aside half of the mushrooms. Blend flour and salt into remaining mushrooms and butter. Add 1½ cups chicken broth and cream and cook, stirring constantly, until thickened and bubbly. Stir in cheese and wine. (If using Parmesan cheese, wait and sprinkle on top of casserole.)

In separate bowl, combine half of the remaining mushrooms, cut-up chicken and ¾ cup of sauce; set aside. In greased 9×13-inch baking dish, combine remaining half of mushrooms with cooked, drained spaghetti and 1½ cups of sauce. Top spaghetti layer with a layer of the broccoli, then top with chicken. Cover with remaining sauce. Cook, covered, in 325° oven for 25 minutes or until bubbly.

When the sauce is too thick, stir in more liquid, a tablespoon at a time, until it reaches the desired consistency.

ADELE'S CHICKEN

4 chicken breasts, skinned
and deboned
4 slices Swiss cheese
1—10½ oz. can cream of
chicken soup, undiluted
¼ cup dry white wine
½ cup herb-seasoned
stuffing
¼ cup butter or margarine,
melted

SERVES 4
Arrange chicken in a lightly greased
9x13 inch baking dish. Top with cheese
slices. Combine soup and wine, stirring
well. Spoon evenly over chicken, sprinkle with stuffing mix. Drizzle butter over
crumbs. Bake, uncovered, at 350° for
45–55 minutes.

CHICKEN BREASTS MANDALAY

4 chicken breasts, halved
3 Tbsp. flour
½ tsp. curry powder
1½ tsp. salt
4 Tbsp. oil
2 Tbsp. brown sugar
2 chicken bouillon cubes
1—8¾ oz. can apricot
halves
½ medium onion, cut up
1 cup water
2 Tbsp. lemon juice
2 tsp. soy sauce
Cornstarch
2–3 tsp. water

SERVES 4
Shake chicken in mixture of flour, curry
powder and salt. Brown lightly in oil in
skillet. Remove chicken and place in
large baking dish. Stir together sugar,
bouillon, apricots, onion, water, lemon
juice and soy sauce. Pour over chicken.
Bake, covered, for 1 hour at 350° or until chicken is tender. Remove chicken
to serving dish. Add 2–3 teaspoons of
cornstarch, dissolved in cold water, to
sauce to reach desired thickness.

CHICKEN AND FISH

OVEN LEMON CHICKEN

1 chicken, cut into pieces
1 cup flour
2 tsp. salt
1 tsp. paprika
6 Tbsp. butter

BASTING SAUCE:
¼ cup lemon juice
1 Tbsp. salad oil
½ tsp. salt
½ tsp. pepper
½ tsp. thyme
½ tsp. garlic
½ tsp. onion salt

SERVES 4
Coat chicken pieces in a mixture of flour, salt and paprika. Melt butter in a baking pan, add chicken pieces, and coat with butter evenly. Arrange in a single layer. Bake, uncovered, at 375° for 30 minutes. Blend together ingredients for sauce. Turn chicken pieces and pour lemon sauce evenly over them. Continue baking until chicken is brown and tender, about 30 minutes. Garnish with lemon wedges.

CHICKEN BREASTS WITH SOUR CREAM

6 chicken breasts
1 cup sour cream
¼ tsp. garlic powder
1 tsp. celery salt
1 tsp. salt
2 Tbsp. lemon juice
1 tsp. Worcestershire
 sauce
Pepper
Paprika
Bread crumbs
½ cup butter

SERVES 6
Combine sour cream, garlic, celery salt, salt, lemon juice, Worcestershire sauce, pepper and paprika. Coat chicken breasts with mixture, lay in buttered baking dish, marinate overnight. Sprinkle with bread crumbs and place a pat of butter on each. Bake, uncovered, for 1 hour and 10 minutes at 350°.

CHICKEN AND FISH

CHICKEN CORDON BLEU

**6 chicken breast halves,
   boned
1 egg, beaten
1½ tsp. salt
½ tsp. pepper
4 Tbsp. flour
2 Tbsp. olive oil
2 Tbsp. butter
1—10½ oz. can cream of
   chicken soup
1—10½ oz. can cream of
   celery soup
Garlic
Salt and pepper to taste
1 cup dry white wine
6 slices ham
6 slices Swiss cheese**

SERVES 6

Dip chicken in egg, then in flour mixed with 1½ teaspoons salt and ½ teaspoon pepper. Lightly brown meat on both sides in skillet, in a mixture of olive oil and butter. Combine condensed soup, garlic, salt and pepper to taste, and wine; pour over chicken that has been placed in a 2 quart casserole. Bake, covered, at 325° for 1½–2 hours. Just before serving, top chicken with ham and cheese. Return to oven, uncovered, until cheese is melted. Serve with Home Seasoned Wild Rice (see Index).

ORANGE CHUTNEY CHICKEN

**3 lbs. chicken breasts
1 tsp. salt
¼ tsp. pepper
2 Tbsp. vegetable oil
½ cup orange juice
½ cup chutney, chopped
¼ cup sugar
2 Tbsp. lemon juice
2 oranges, peeled, cut into
   ½" slices
1 Tbsp. cornstarch
¼ cup cold water**

SERVES 6

Sprinkle chicken with salt and pepper; heat oil and brown lightly. Place chicken in 9x13 inch casserole. Add orange juice and bake for 30 minutes. Combine chutney, sugar and lemon juice. Place orange slices over chicken and top with chutney mixture. Continue baking, covered, for 15 minutes; remove cover and bake additional 15 minutes or until chicken is tender. Remove chicken to serving platter. Combine cornstarch and water. Place baking dish on stove and bring drippings to boil. Stir in cornstarch mixture; stir until thick. Pour over chicken and serve.

CHICKEN AND FISH

PARMESAN CHICKEN

½ cup bread crumbs,
  finely ground
⅓ cup grated Parmesan
  cheese
2 tsp. parsley flakes (or 2
  Tbsp. chopped fresh)
¼ tsp. garlic salt
¼ tsp. pepper
¼ cup Italian dressing
6 chicken breast halves

SERVES 6
Combine bread crumbs, Parmesan cheese, parsley and seasonings. Dip each chicken breast in Italian dressing, then dredge in breadcrumb mixture. Place in a baking pan. Bake uncovered at 350° for 45 minutes to 1 hour.

GOURMET CHICKEN BREASTS

1½ lbs. chicken fillets
⅓ cup flour
Salt and pepper
3 Tbsp. butter
2 Tbsp. onion, chopped
¼–½ lb. mushrooms,
  sliced
1½ cups cream
1—1 lb. pkg. frozen peas
½ cup carrots, sliced and
  cooked

SERVES 4
Cut chicken fillets into thin strips. Shake in flour seasoned with salt and pepper in a plastic bag. Heat 2 tablespoons butter in large skillet, add chicken and cook over medium heat until slightly golden. Set aside. Melt remaining butter in skillet. Add onions and mushrooms and cook until tender. Add cream, peas and carrots and bring to a boil, stirring continually. Put on low heat, add salt and pepper to taste and add chicken pieces. Good served with wild rice with almonds.

MANDARIN GAME HENS

2 Cornish game hens
2 Tbsp. vegetable oil
4 Tbsp. Kitchen Bouquet
⅔ cup orange juice
concentrate
Soy sauce to taste
Garlic powder to taste
4 Tbsp. orange marmalade
1—11 oz. can mandarin
oranges

RICE MIXTURE:
2 cups quick rice
4 tsp. grated orange rind
¾ cup raisins
2 cups boiling water
2 chicken bouillon cubes

SERVES 2
Split each game hen. Brush with vegetable oil, then with Kitchen Bouquet. Combine rice mixture ingredients and place in bottom of glass baking dish. Place hens, breast side down, on top of rice mixture. Cover and bake 30 minutes in 350° oven. Out of the oven, breast side up, baste with a marinade of the orange juice, soy sauce and garlic powder. Top each hen with a tablespoon of orange marmalade. Cover and bake another 30 minutes or until hens are tender. Garnish with mandarin oranges.

COOK HIS GOOSE

1 wild goose
1 large can sauerkraut
½ cup burgundy wine
Salt and pepper
2-3 Tbsp. cornstarch
⅓ cup cold water

SERVES 4
Place goose in large roasting pan. Add 1½ inches of water to bottom of pan. Add burgundy and arrange sauerkraut around goose with about ⅓ cup in body cavity. Season with salt and pepper. Cook, covered, at 325° for 2 hours, basting occasionally.

To make gravy, skim fat off pan juices. Leave sauerkraut in pan. Add cornstarch mixed in cold water and stir over medium high heat until thick. Add more cornstarch if necessary. Salt and pepper to taste. Serve over mashed potatoes.

CHICKEN AND FISH

BLUE CREEK DOVE

16 doves
Salt and pepper
Flour
8 slices bacon
⅛ tsp. Tabasco
4 Tbsp. Worcestershire
  sauce
½ cup beef bouillon
½ cup cooking burgundy
12 oz. mushrooms
2 Tbsp. butter
1 tsp. lemon juice
Chopped parsley, for garnish

SERVES 4

Dry doves and season with salt and pepper. Dust lightly with flour. In a large Dutch oven, cook bacon until crisp. Remove, and drain on a paper towel. Arrange birds in a single layer in Dutch oven and brown on all sides in hot bacon drippings. With breasts down, reduce heat to low, and add Tabasco, Worcestershire and liquids. Cover and cook for 20 minutes. Stir, turn birds up and continue cooking, covered, for another 20 minutes. Add more liquid if necessary. While birds are cooking, saute mushrooms in butter and lemon juice. Add mushrooms to doves for final 15 minutes of cooking. To serve, crumble bacon over top, garnish with parsley, and serve with rice. You can increase the cooking time on these to 1 hour total, but make sure the heat is on low. Any longer, and the meat will fall off the bone. This is a delicious way to prepare dove...it is good with chicken, too.

CHICKEN AND FISH

LOIS JEAN'S CRABMEAT AU GRATIN

1 cup onion, chopped fine
1 stalk celery, chopped fine
¼ cup butter or margarine
½ cup flour
1—13 oz. can evaporated milk
2 egg yolks, beaten
1 tsp. salt
¼ tsp. cayenne pepper
½ tsp. black pepper
1 lb. white crabmeat (fresh is preferable, canned is okay)
½ lb. Cheddar cheese, grated

SERVES 6
Saute onions and celery in butter until onions are wilted. Blend flour well with this mixture. Pour in the milk gradually, stirring constantly. Add egg yolks, salt and peppers. Cook for 5 minutes. Remove from heat and stir in crabmeat. Transfer to a lightly greased casserole and sprinkle with grated cheese. Bake at 375° for 10–15 minutes or until light brown. Can also be baked in individual shell dishes. Good and easy!

FRIED CATFISH

6 catfish fillets, skinned and pan-dressed
½ cup buttermilk
1½ cups yellow cornmeal
¼ tsp. salt
½ tsp. baking powder
⅛ tsp. black pepper
Vegetable oil for frying
Lemon wedges

SERVES 4
Place catfish in pie pan and add buttermilk. Turn fish until well coated. Combine cornmeal, salt, baking powder and pepper in plastic bag. Heat 3 inches of oil in large, heavy saucepan or skillet. Remove catfish one at a time from buttermilk, drop into plastic bag of cornmeal mixture and shake until well coated. Repeat to coat all catfish. When oil has reached 360°, fry catfish, several at a time, for 3–5 minutes or until golden on both sides. Drain well. Good served with Pan de Lote and Susie's Tomato and Onion Salad (see Index).

When using frozen shrimp, soak in ice-cold salted water for ten minutes. The shrimp will taste real close to fresh.

CHICKEN AND FISH

MICROWAVE FISH FILLETS

1 lb. firm fish fillets (sole, haddock or scallops)
½ tsp. salt
⅛ tsp. pepper
½ cup butter, melted
½ cup fresh parsley, chopped (or 3 tsp. dried)
1 Tbsp. lemon juice
½ cup buttery flavored cracker crumbs
½ tsp. paprika

SERVES 4
Place fish in glass baking dish, with thickest, meaty areas toward the outside edge of the dish. Sprinkle with salt and pepper. Mix parsley and lemon juice with butter. Pour over fish. Top with crumbs, then sprinkle with paprika. Microwave on high for 9 to 11 minutes, rotating dish ½ turn after 5 minutes. Serve with with brown or wild rice for a fast, easy and nutritious meal.

CRAB STUFFED FLOUNDER

¼ cup chopped onion
⅓ cup butter
1½ cup chopped fresh mushrooms
½ lb. crabmeat
½ cup coarse saltine cracker crumbs
2 Tbsp. parsley, chopped
½ tsp. salt
⅛ tsp. pepper
2 lbs. flounder fillets

SAUCE:
3 Tbsp. butter
3 Tbsp. flour
¼ tsp. salt
¾ cup half and half
⅓ cup dry white wine
1 cup Swiss cheese, grated
½ tsp. paprika

SERVES 8
In a skillet, saute onions and mushrooms in butter until tender. Stir in crab, cracker crumbs, parsley, salt and pepper. In lightly greased baking dish arrange half the pieces of flounder. Top each with stuffing mixture, then with another piece of flounder. Set aside and prepare sauce.

Melt butter in saucepan and blend in flour and salt. Add half and half and wine to flour mixture and cook, stirring constantly, until mixture thickens and bubbles. Pour over fillets and bake, covered, for 25 minutes at 325°. Sprinkle with cheese and paprika. Return to oven and bake, uncovered, 10 minutes longer or until fish flakes easily with a fork. Rich, but oh, so good!

BAKED HADDOCK

½ cup margarine, melted
Juice of 2 limes
Salt and pepper to taste
⅛ tsp. garlic powder
3 lbs. haddock fillets
½ cup Parmesan cheese
2—3 oz. cans fried onions,
   crushed

SERVES 6
Mix margarine, lime juice, salt, pepper and garlic powder. Spread on both sides of fish and marinate for 1 hour in a Pyrex baking dish. Sprinkle with Parmesan cheese and crushed onions, and bake at 400° for 15 minutes, or until fish flakes easily with a fork.

GRILLED SALMON WITH DILL SAUCE

Salmon steaks
Two parts butter
One part lemon juice

DILL SAUCE:
1 cup salad oil
½ tsp. garlic powder
1 Tbsp. dill weed
1 Tbsp. green onion
½ tsp. salt
1 tsp. dry mustard
2 Tbsp. wine vinegar
1 egg

Place salmon steaks on grill over a medium hot fire. Baste with butter-lemon mixture until done; about 5 minutes on each side.

To prepare sauce, mix ¼ cup of the oil and all other ingredients in a blender or food processor. Blend on low speed. Add remaining oil and blend for 5 seconds. Makes a creamy sauce.

SALMON SAUCE

½ lb. butter
1 clove garlic, minced
4 Tbsp. soy sauce
2 Tbsp. mustard
½ cup ketchup
Dash Worcestershire sauce

Heat all ingredients together in a saucepan. Cool. Use as basting sauce while grilling or broiling salmon. Use remaining sauce as garnish on cooked salmon.

CHICKEN AND FISH

SANDY HOOK SCALLOPS

⅔ stick butter, melted
2 tsp. minced parsley
2 tsp. minced chives
Dash garlic powder
⅔ cup herb-seasoned
    stuffing
1 lb. scallops
Lemon wedges

SERVES 4
Combine butter, parsley, chives, garlic powder and stuffing. Spread some of the crumb mixture in the bottom of a buttered pie plate, top with scallops, and sprinkle with remaining crumb mixture. (Can also use 4 individual baking shells—be sure to bake on a cookie sheet.) Bake at 350° for 25–30 minutes. Serve with lemon wedges.

SHRIMP TEMPURA

1 lb. shrimp, large or
    jumbo

BATTER:
2 eggs
1 cup cold water
¾ cup flour
Dash of salt
OR: Try one of the Tempura mixes available in your supermarket. They are very good.

VEGETABLES:
Carrot slices
Eggplant slices
Cauliflower flowerettes
Sweet potatoes, sliced
Turnips, sliced
Broccoli flowerettes
Zucchini, sliced thick
Mushrooms, whole

SERVES 2
Combine eggs and cold water; beat until frothy. Add flour and salt and beat until well blended. Set bowl in ice cubes or refrigerate until ready to use.

Dip shrimp into batter and, one at a time, add to preheated (350°) oil. When golden brown, remove to heated serving dish.

Vegetables also can be dipped in batter and deep fried. Serve with the shrimp, making it a complete meal.

Fried shrimp and vegetables can be dipped in tempura sauce which can be purchased with tempura mix. Sweet and sour, hot mustard or cocktail sauces are also good.

❧ ❧

CAJUN SHRIMP
(Shrimp Etouffee)

2 lbs. fresh shrimp, peeled
Salt and pepper
Cayenne pepper
¼ lb. butter
1 cup onion, chopped
½ cup celery, chopped
½ cup green pepper,
  chopped
3 cloves garlic, pressed
1 Tbsp. cornstarch
1½ cups water
Cooked rice

SERVES 4
Split shrimp and season with salt, pepper and cayenne to taste. Set aside. Melt butter in saucepan and add onions, celery, peppers and garlic. Cook slowly, uncovered, until onions are limp. Add seasoned shrimp and simmer, stirring occasionally, for 20 minutes. Dissolve cornstarch in water and add to mixture. Cook another 10–15 minutes, stirring occasionally. Serve over cooked rice.

This delicious smothered shrimp (*etouffee* is a Cajun derivative of the French verb *etoufer*, to smother) is a great company entree.

SHRIMP CASSEROLE

1—6 oz. pkg. Uncle Ben's
  Wild Rice
1 Tbsp. butter
½ cup onion, chopped
2 cups cooked shrimp
1—10 oz. can cream of
  shrimp soup
1—8 oz. container sour
  cream
½ tsp. curry powder
  (optional)

SERVES 6
Cook rice as directed on box. Saute onions in butter. Combine cooked rice and onions with remaining ingredients in a 2½ quart casserole dish. Bake at 300°, uncovered, for 25 minutes or until heated through. Can use this same recipe substituting chicken and one can cream of chicken soup for the shrimp and shrimp soup. Good with Sauteed Snowpeas and Mushrooms (see Index), or a tossed green salad.

CHICKEN AND FISH

❧❧❧❧❧❧⌣❧⌣⌣❧❧⌣❧⌣❧⌣⌣⌣⌣⌣⌣⌣⌣

GRILLED TROUT FILLETS
WITH TOMATO BUTTER

Trout fillets (or any other firm-fleshed white fish fillets)
Lemon pepper
Melted butter

TOMATO BUTTER:
¼ lb. unsalted butter
2 Tbsp. tomato paste
½ tsp. salt
¼ tsp. sugar

For the best flavor, soak several handfuls of mesquite wood chips in water. Prepare a moderately hot charcoal fire. When the coals are covered with light ash, remove the chips from the water and spread over the coals. Start cooking the fish immediately.

Place one-inch thick fillets, brushed with mixture of lemon pepper and butter, on the grill. Cook for 5–8 minutes on each side, basting often, until fish flakes. Serve immediately with Tomato Butter.

To make tomato butter, cream all ingredients in a food processor until light and fluffy. Chill, and serve with trout fillets.

This is the fisherman's way to eat fish!

GOOD OL' TUNA CASSEROLE

1—7 oz. can flaked tuna
1 can cream of mushroom soup
3 cups cooked noodles
1—5 oz. pkg. frozen peas or ½ cup chopped celery
¾ cup American processed cheese, grated
½ cup crushed potato chips

SERVES 4
In a buttered casserole, combine all ingredients except potato chips, and mix well. Top with crushed potato chips. Bake at 325° for 30 minutes or until bubbly.

CHICKEN AND FISH

JUDY'S TUNA ISLANDS

1—7 oz. can tuna, flaked
2 eggs, beaten
1—14 oz. can evaporated
  milk
¼ tsp. salt
½ cup Cheddar cheese,
  grated

CREAMED PEAS:
1—10 oz. pkg. peas
4 Tbsp. butter
2 Tbsp. flour
1 cup half and half
½ tsp. sugar
Salt to taste

Combine tuna, eggs, evaporated milk, ¼ tsp. salt and Cheddar cheese in bowl. Using a small measuring cup, pour into greased muffin cups, filling almost to the top. Bake 30 minutes at 350°. Serve hot with creamed peas over top. Can sprinkle with crushed potato chips if desired.

To prepare creamed peas, cook peas for 3 minutes and drain. Melt butter over medium heat and stir in flour. Gradually add half and half, stirring constantly, until thick and creamy. Add more milk if necessary to get right consistency.

Need a hot meal at lunchtime? This one would fill the bill. Fast, easy, no mess—remember this next time you have drop-in guests at lunch.

Vegetables, Rice & Pasta

VEGETABLES, RICE & PASTA

ASPARAGUS AMANDINE

1—10½ oz. can cream of
   chicken soup
¼ cup milk
3 hard-cooked eggs, sliced
1 cup American cheese,
   cubed
2—10 oz. pkgs. frozen cut
   asparagus, cooked
1 cup sliced almonds
½ cup bread crumbs
2 Tbsp. butter

SERVES 6
Combine milk and soup. Stir in eggs, cheese and asparagus. Pour mixture into buttered casserole. Cover with almonds and crumbs. Dot with butter. Bake at 350° for 30–40 minutes, until bubbly and slightly brown on top.

TANGY ASPARAGUS - TOMATO

3 slices bacon
¼ cup sliced green onion
3 Tbsp. vinegar
1 Tbsp. water
2 tsp. sugar
¼ tsp. salt
1½ lb. fresh asparagus
2 med. tomatoes, cut in
   wedges

SERVES 4
Cook bacon until crisp. Drain, and re-serve drippings. Crumble bacon and set aside. Add onion to reserved drip-pings; saute until tender. Add crumbled bacon, vinegar, water, sugar and salt. Bring to boil; add asparagus. Cover and cook 5 minutes. Add tomato wedges. Cover and cook until heated through, about 3 minutes. Spoon liq-uid over frequently.

ASPARAGUS VINAIGRETTE

3—10 oz. pkgs. frozen
   asparagus spears (or
   comparable fresh
   amount), blanched
⅓ cup cider vinegar
¾ cup vegetable oil
½ tsp. salt
⅛ tsp. pepper
1 Tbsp. finely chopped
   pimiento

SERVES 10-12
Cook asparagus according to package directions. Do not overcook. Drain thor-oughly. Place in a shallow dish. Com-bine remaining ingredients and blend well. Pour over asparagus. Cover and refrigerate 2-3 hours. To serve, drain vinaigrette and arrange asparagus on a serving platter. Garnish with pimiento.

VEGETABLES, RICE & PASTA

GREEN BEANS PROVENCAL

1 lb. fresh green beans
1 onion, coarsely chopped
4 cloves garlic, minced
2 Tbsps. olive oil
4 large tomatoes, peeled,
    seeded, and coarsely
    chopped
½ cup dry white wine
1–2¼ oz. can sliced ripe
    olives
1 Tbsp. lemon juice
¼ tsp. coarsely ground
    black pepper

SERVES 6
Wash green beans; trim ends, and remove strings. Bring ½ cup water to a boil in a large saucepan; add beans. Cover, reduce heat to medium, and cook 10 minutes or until tender. Drain beans. Set aside; and keep warm.

Sauté onion and garlic in olive oil in a skillet over high heat 5 minutes or until crisp tender. Stir in tomatoes and wine; bring to a boil. Reduce heat, and simmer, uncovered, 20 minutes stirring occasionally. Stir in olives. Spoon sauce over green beans. Pour lemon juice over sauce; sprinkle with pepper.

GREEN BEANS ORIENTAL

2 Tbsps. sliced almonds
2 tsp. butter, melted
1¼ lb. green beans
2 Tbsps. butter
½ cup chicken broth
¼ tsp. salt
¼ tsp. pepper
1 tsp. cornstarch
1 Tbsp. water
1½ tsp. lemon juice

SERVES 5
Sauté almonds in 2 tsp. butter in a small skillet until lightly browned. Set aside.

Wash green beans and trim ends. Cut beans into French-style strips. Melt 2 Tbsps. butter in a large skillet; add green beans, and cook over high heat, stirring constantly, 5 minutes.

Add chicken broth, salt, and pepper; bring to a boil. Reduce heat; cover and simmer 8–10 minutes. Combine cornstarch and water; stir into beans. Cook 1 minute, stirring constantly. Stir in lemon juice. Sprinkle sautéed almonds over green beans.

VEGETABLES, RICE & PASTA

LONG'S PEAK BAKED BEANS

½ lb. hamburger
5 slices bacon, chopped
1 small onion, chopped
⅓ cup brown sugar
½ cup ketchup
2 Tbsp. prepared mustard
¼ tsp. pepper
⅓ cup sugar
⅓ cup barbecue sauce
2 Tbsp. molasses
½ tsp. salt
½ tsp. chili powder
1—46–54 oz. can pork and
   beans, drained
1—15 oz. can black-eyed
   peas, drained
1—15 oz. can red kidney
beans, drained and rinsed

SERVES 10–12
In a skillet, brown hamburger, bacon and onion. Drain well. Combine remaining ingredients, except beans, and mix well. Mix in beans. Cover and bake at 350° for 1 hour. Best if left in refrigerator for 3 or 4 hours before baking.

Baked beans have never tasted so good!

PICNIC BEANS

¼ lb. bacon, chopped
1 small onion, chopped
1—1 lb. can butter beans
   and juice
¼ cup brown sugar
8 oz. chili sauce
Salt and pepper to taste

SERVES 4
Brown bacon with the onion in a skillet. In a 1-quart casserole combine bacon, onion and bacon drippings with beans, brown sugar, chili sauce, salt and pepper. Cover and bake at 350° for 1 hour.

 For a flavor variation, cook vegetables in chicken stock, beef stock, or consomme.

VEGETABLES, RICE & PASTA

ORANGE GLAZED BEETS

1—10 oz. pkg. frozen beets
1 Tbsp. sugar
1 Tbsp. cornstarch
¼ tsp. caraway seed
¼ tsp. salt
¼ cup orange juice
2 Tbsp. butter

SERVES 2–4
Cook beets according to package directions. Drain beets, reserving $\frac{1}{3}$ cup liquid. In saucepan, combine all ingredients except beets and mix well. Cook over medium-high heat, stirring constantly, until mixture is thickened and clear. Add beets; heat through.

BROCCOLI SWISS BAKE

1½ cups summer squash, cut into ½ inch pieces
3 cups fresh broccoli, cut up
½ cup butter
1 egg, beaten
½ cup Swiss cheese, grated
¼ cup milk
¼ tsp. dry mustard
1 tsp. salt
Pepper and cayenne to taste
½ cup parmesan cheese
2 Tbsps. toasted sesame seeds

SERVES 6
Steam squash and broccoli until they are tender-crisp. Layer in a 9×13 casserole dish. Melt butter and mix with egg, Swiss cheese, milk, and seasonings. Pour over broccoli and squash. Top with parmesan cheese and sesame seeds. Bake at 350° for 20 minutes.

 Because atmospheric pressure is less at higher altitudes, the temperature required for water to boil is lower. Therefore, cooking food in water boiling at this lower temperature takes longer.

VEGETABLES, RICE & PASTA

BROCCOLI DELIGHT

1—14 oz. can artichoke
  hearts, drained and
  quartered
3 carrots, sliced
1—10 oz. pkg. frozen or
  fresh chopped broccoli
¾ can cream of mushroom
  soup
¼ cup mayonnaise
2 eggs, slightly beaten
1 tsp. lemon juice
¼ tsp. garlic salt
1 cup Cheddar cheese,
  grated
¼ cup butter, melted
¾ cup bread crumbs

SERVES 6
Place artichokes in an 8×8 inch casserole. Cook carrots and broccoli separately until tender; drain and add to artichokes. Combine soup, mayonnaise, eggs, lemon juice and garlic salt; pour over vegetables. Sprinkle with cheese, and bread crumbs that have been tossed in the melted butter. Bake for 25 minutes at 325°. Serve hot.

BROCCOLI-MUSHROOM SOUFFLE

¾ cup mushrooms, sliced
½ cup butter
¾ cup broccoli, cooked
  and chopped
1 tsp. minced fresh onion
3 Tbsp. flour
1 cup half and half
4 egg yolks
½ tsp. salt
¼ tsp. pepper
⅛ tsp. nutmeg
4 egg whites

SERVES 4–6
Saute mushrooms in 2 tablespoons butter until tender. Stir in cooked broccoli and onion, and stir-fry for 2–3 minutes. Remove from skillet and reserve. Melt remaining 2 tablespoons butter and stir in flour with whisk. Gradually add half and half, stirring constantly until thick and smooth. Remove from heat and add yolks, one at a time, beating after each addition. Blend in salt and pepper; add mushrooms and broccoli. Beat egg whites until stiff and fold into vegetable mixture. Pour into greased 1-quart casserole or souffle dish. Bake at 375° for 30–40 minutes. Good by itself or with Hollandaise Sauce (see Index).

VEGETABLES, RICE & PASTA

❧❧❧❧❧❧❧❧❧❧❧❧❧❧❧❧❧❧❧❧❧

RED CABBAGE WITH APPLES

1 med. red cabbage
3 tart apples
5 Tbsp. butter
¾ cup apple juice
4 Tbsp. red wine vinegar
3 Tbsp. brown sugar
½ tsp. salt
½ tsp. pepper
3 cloves
1 bay leaf
Juice of ½ lemon

SERVES 6
Wash cabbage, drain and cut as for slaw. Wash and core apples; peel and cut into small pieces. Saute cabbage and apples in butter for 3–4 minutes. Add apple juice, vinegar, sugar, salt, pepper, cloves and bay leaf. Stir, bringing to a boil. Cover and let simmer for 45 minutes or until tender.

APRICOT-GLAZED CARROTS

2 lbs. carrots, peeled and
  sliced
3 Tbsp. butter or
  margarine
⅓ cup apricot-pineapple
  preserves
¼ tsp. ground nutmeg
¼ tsp. salt
½ tsp. freshly grated
  orange peel
2 tsp. fresh lemon juice
Parsley

SERVES 4–6
Peel carrots and slice. Cook in salted water until tender, but not mushy. Drain. Dot with butter and let it melt. Stir in preserves until blended. Add spices and lemon juice. Toss well until coated. Garnish with parsley and serve immediately.

SUSIE'S TARRAGON CARROTS

5–6 med. carrots, peeled
  and cut in julienne strips
2 tsp. butter
Dried leaf tarragon

SERVES 4
Saute carrots in butter until tender but not limp. Sprinkle with tarragon and serve immediately.

❤ *For that very special dinner serve cooked carrots whole and after glazing push a sprig of parsley in the end.*

VEGETABLES, RICE & PASTA

CAULIFLOWER SUPREME

1 med. head of cauliflower
Salt and pepper to taste
1 cup dairy sour cream
1 cup sharp American
 cheese, grated
1 tsp. toasted sesame seeds

SERVES 4–6
Break cauliflower into flowerets. Cook 10–15 minutes. Drain well. Place half of cauliflower in quart casserole. Season with salt and pepper. Spread with ½ cup sour cream and sprinkle with half of the cheese. Top with 1 teaspoon toasted sesame seeds. Repeat layer. Bake at 350° until cheese melts and sour cream is heated through, about 10 minutes.

KIKA'S SUNSHINE VEGETABLES
(Porotos Granados)

1—10 oz. pkg. frozen cut
 corn
2 small yellow crookneck
 squash, cut up
1½–2 cups cooked pinto
 beans
1 onion, chopped
Bacon drippings
½ tsp. chili powder (or
 more to taste)

SERVES 4–6
Cook corn and squash in a small amount of water. Drain when tender. Stir in pinto beans. Saute onion in bacon drippings until transparent. Stir onion, drippings and all, into vegetables. Season with chili powder and stir to blend. Serve immediately. This recipe came to Kitchen Keepsakes by way of Chile. It is a delicious combination of vegetables that our kids enjoy. Makes an excellent accompaniment to most any entree.

CORN FRITTERS

2 eggs, separated
1—8½ oz. can cream-style
 corn
1¼ cups pancake mix (dry)

MAKES 2 DOZEN
Beat egg yolks slightly. Stir in corn and pancake mix. Beat egg whites until stiff. Fold into mixture. Drop by heaping teaspoonfuls into 375° deep fat. Cook until golden brown. Drain on paper towels and serve hot. Good with ham.

STUFFED EGGPLANT

1 eggplant
¼ cup onion, chopped
¾ cup mushrooms, sliced
4 Tbsp. butter
4 Tbsp. flour
2 cups milk
¼ cup butter, melted
1 cup bread crumbs
Salt
Pepper
Garlic salt

SERVES 2
Cut a thick slice off the side of the eggplant. Cook both pieces in salted boiling water until tender, about 15 minutes. Scoop out pulp, leaving shell ¼ inch thick. Saute onion and mushrooms in melted butter. Blend in flour and milk. Cook, stirring constantly, until it boils. Simmer 1 minute. Add cut up eggplant pulp. Season with salt, pepper and garlic. Pour into shell or greased baking dish. Top with buttered bread crumbs. Bake 20 minutes in 350° oven.

EGGPLANT REGINA

1 eggplant, pared and
sliced
3–4 Tbsp. vegetable oil
2 large tomatoes, sliced
Ground marjoram
Salt
Onion powder
¼ lb. Cheddar cheese,
grated

SERVES 4
Lightly brown eggplant in hot oil. Place a layer of eggplant sices in a 1½ quart casserole dish. Add a layer of sliced tomatoes. Sprinkle a little marjoram, salt and onion powder on the tomatoes, then cover with half the cheese. Repeat with another layer of eggplant, tomato, spices and cheese. Bake uncovered at 350° for 20–30 minutes.

 Vegetables that grow underground should be cooked covered, those that grow above ground should be cooked uncovered.

VEGETABLES, RICE & PASTA

FRIED OKRA AND TOMATOES

½ cup cornmeal
¾ tsp. salt
1—10 oz. pkg. frozen cut
   okra
3 slices bacon, cut into
   pieces
½ small onion, chopped
1½ med. tomatoes,
   chopped
1 tsp. finely chopped fresh
   hot red chili

SERVES 3
Shake thawed okra in plastic bag with cornmeal and salt. Fry bacon in skillet until crisp; remove and set aside. Add okra and onion to bacon drippings. Saute, stirring frequently, until onion is tender and okra is lightly browned. Add tomatoes, chili and bacon and cook for 15 minutes or until tomatoes are soft. Salt to taste.

PINEAPPLE CASSEROLE

2 Tbsp. flour
½ cup sugar
1—15 oz. can pineapple
   tidbits with juice
3 slices bread
3 eggs, slightly beaten
6 Tbsp. butter, melted

SERVES 6
In a 2½ quart souffle dish, mix flour and sugar. Add pineapple and juice. Tear 2 slices of bread into pieces and add to the mixture. Add beaten eggs and mix well. Top with 1 more slice of broken bread, but *do not stir.* Pour melted butter over all and bake at 350° until bread is toasted, about 30–45 minutes. This is good with ham or pork...an interesting and different accompaniment.

POTATO CAKES

2 cups mashed potatoes
1/3 cup Cheddar cheese,
  grated
1/4 cup cracker crumbs
1 egg
2 Tbsp. parsley, chopped
1 tsp. onion, finely
  chopped
1/2 tsp. Lawry's Pinch of
  Herbs
1/4 tsp. salt
1 Tbsp. vegetable oil

SERVES 4

Mix mashed potatoes, cheese, crumbs, egg, parsley, onion, herbs and salt. Heat oil in skillet. Drop potato mixture by rounded tablespoonfuls into skillet. Flatten with spatula. Cook over medium heat until light brown, about 3 minutes on each side. Good with Zesty Beef 'N Zucchini (see Index).

CRUSTY NEW POTATOES

8 small new red potatoes
1/4 cup butter
1/2 tsp. seasoned salt
1 cup cornflakes, crushed

SERVES 4

Preheat oven to 400°. Boil unpeeled potatoes until tender when pierced with a fork; drain and peel. Melt butter and add seasoned salt. Roll each potato in seasoned butter, then in crushed cornflakes. Place in a glass baking dish. Repeat with each potato. Bake for 25 minutes.

An easy recipe that is an elegant accompaniment for steak or chicken.

Many things can be added to butter to help season hot cooked vegetables. Here are just a few that can be added to 1/4 cup of butter:

1 Tbsp. horseradish	2 Tbsp. sliced scallions
2 Tbsp. grated Swiss cheese	2 Tbsp. Parmesan cheese
1 tsp. celery seed	1/4 tsp. garlic powder
2 Tbsp. lemon juice + 1 tsp. grated lemon rind	1 Tbsp. minced chives in lemon butter

VEGETABLES, RICE & PASTA

GRANDE POTATOES

4–5 potatoes
⅓ cup margarine or butter
½ red bell pepper,
  coarsely chopped
½ onion, coarsely chopped
1—10½ oz. can cream of
  celery soup
½ cup milk
4 oz. Cheddar cheese,
  grated
2 drops hot pepper sauce
1—4 oz. can chopped
  green chilies, drained
½ tsp. salt
¼ cup Cheddar cheese,
  grated

SERVES 6–8
Boil potatoes, with skins on, until done. Drain and let cool. Thinly slice the unpeeled potatoes. In skillet, melt butter and saute pepper and onion until tender. Add soup, milk and 4 ounces cheese and stir over low heat until cheese is melted. Stir in hot pepper sauce, green chilies and salt. Add potatoes and toss gently. Pour into buttered casserole and top with ¼ cup grated cheese. Cover and bake at 350° for 30 minutes or until bubbly.

"PRETTY" STUFFED POTATOES

4 baked potatoes
½ cup carrots, sliced and
  cooked
4 Tbsp. butter
¼ cup sour cream
½ tsp. salt
½ cup Cheddar cheese,
  grated
½ cup peas, cooked for 2
  minutes
1 Tbsp. diced pimientos
1 cup buttered bread
  crumbs
3 slices bacon, fried and
  crumbled

SERVES 6–8
Cut baked potatoes lengthwise and scoop out inside, saving the skin. Mash potatoes and carrots, along with butter, sour cream and salt. Fold in cheese, peas and pimientos. Heap mixture into potato shells. Top with buttered bread crumbs and crumbled bacon. Return to oven and bake for 15 minutes at 350°.

 For fluffier mashed potatoes, add a pinch of baking soda along with the milk and butter.

VEGETABLES, RICE & PASTA

❦ ❦ ❦ ❦ ❦ ❦ ❦ ❦ ❦ ❦ ❦ ❦ ❦ ❦ ❦ ❦ ❦ ❦ ❦

PRAIRIE SCHOONERS

4 large baked potatoes
1—15 oz. can ranch style
  beans
1 cup sour cream
1 stick butter, softened
Salt, pepper, and chili
  powder to taste
2 Tbsp. chopped green
  pepper
2 Tbsp. chopped onion
1 Tbsp. butter or margarine
1 cup Cheddar cheese,
  grated

SERVES 4

Slice off top one-third of baked potato lengthwise. Scoop out potato leaving ¼ inch around potato skin. Mash potato until free of lumps. Drain beans thoroughly, reserving juice. Mash beans. Whip sour cream, butter, mashed beans, salt, pepper, and chili powder. Add to mashed potatoes, adding enough bean juice to moisten. Spoon mixture into potato shells. Saute green pepper and onion in margarine. Top each potato with grated cheese, onion, and green pepper. Bake at 425° about 10 minutes or until browned.

CRAB STUFFED POTATOES

4 medium to large baking
  potatoes
½ cup butter
½ cup milk
1 tsp. salt
Pepper
1 tsp. dried, minced onion
1 cup Longhorn cheese,
  grated
1—6½ oz. can crab meat
Paprika

SERVES 6–8

Wash and dry potatoes. Bake at 350° for 1 hour, or until you can pierce with a fork. (Do not wrap potatoes in foil to bake, as the skins will not crisp.) Cut the baked potatoes lengthwise and scoop out the insides. Whip potato with butter, milk, salt and pepper, onion and cheese. Stir in drained crabmeat, and refill the potato shells. Place on a baking sheet, sprinkle with paprika, and reheat at 400° for about 15 minutes. These can be made ahead and frozen before baking.

VEGETABLES, RICE & PASTA

PARSLEY POTATOES

3 large potatoes
¾ cup water
2½ Tbsp. butter
⅛ tsp. garlic powder
1 tsp. dried parsley, or
   1 Tbsp. fresh, chopped
¼ tsp. salt

SERVES 6

Wash the potatoes well. Cut into ¼-inch thick slices. In a jelly-roll pan, place sliced potatoes in a single layer. Add water. Bake 10 minutes at 375°. Increase cooking temperature to 450° to brown, cook about 5–7 more minutes. Meanwhile, in a small saucepan over medium heat, melt butter. Add garlic and cook 2 minutes, stirring until golden. Pour over potatoes, add parsley and salt, and toss to coat. Good with Stock Show Steak (see Index).

PERFECT POTATOES

1 cup hot water
1 packet dry onion soup
   mix
½ cup butter, melted
¼ tsp. pepper
8 med. or small potatoes,
unpeeled, cut in 1″ cubes
Parsley flakes

SERVES 6

Combine water, soup mix, butter and pepper in a greased 2 quart casserole. Add potatoes. Bake, covered, at 350° about 1½ hours or until potatoes are tender. Uncover during the last 30 minutes cooking time. Sprinkle with parsley flakes to serve. These delicious potatoes are the perfect accompaniment...from hamburgers to steak.

 When peeling potatoes, keep parings thin—the minerals lie close to the skin.

VEGETABLES, RICE & PASTA

❧ ❧ ❧ ❧ ❧ ❧ ❧ ❧ ❧ ❧ ❧ ❧ ❧ ❧ ❧ ❧ ❧ ❧ ❧

SWEET POTATOES AND MARSHMALLOWS

1 cup milk
1 tsp. vanilla
3 Tbsp. sugar
½ stick butter
2—29 oz. cans sweet
  potatoes, drained and
  mashed
¼ tsp. cinnamon
Few dashes nutmeg
1 Tbsp. orange juice
Miniature marshmallows

SERVES 6–8
Scald milk and add vanilla, sugar and butter. To mashed potatoes, add cinnamon, nutmeg and orange juice. Mix well. Stir in milk mixture and beat until smooth, light and fluffy. Put half the potato mixture in a lightly greased 2 quart casserole. Add a layer of marshmallows. Top with remaining potatoes and bake at 350° until very hot (about 20–30 minutes). Add a top layer of marshmallows and brown.

SAUTEED SNOWPEAS AND MUSHROOMS

1 Tbsp. butter
¾ lb. fresh mushrooms,
  sliced
1—8 oz. can water
  chestnuts, sliced and
  drained
¾ lb. fresh snowpeas

SERVES 6–8
In a heavy skillet, melt butter over medium heat. Saute mushrooms and water chestnuts until barely tender. Add snowpeas and saute until peas turn bright green. Do not overcook. Serve immediately.

SPINACH SOUFFLE

2 cups cottage cheese
3 eggs, beaten
¼ cup melted butter
3 Tbsp. flour
¼ lb. Longhorn cheddar
  cheese, cubed
1—10 oz. pkg. frozen chopped spinach, partially
  defrosted

SERVES 6–8
Combine cottage cheese, eggs, butter, flour and cheddar cheese. Stir in spinach, making sure it is thoroughly mixed. Pour into a 3 quart greased casserole and bake at 350° for 1 hour or until browned. This is **delicious**...a great way to serve spinach to those who don't normally like it.

VEGETABLES, RICE & PASTA

COUNTRY QUICHE

1—2 lb. bag frozen French
　fries
1 large yellow onion,
　minced
2 sticks butter
1—10 oz. pkg. frozen
　mustard greens, spinach
　or broccoli
12 eggs
2 cups whipping cream
1 lb. Swiss cheese, grated
Salt
Pepper
Nutmeg

SERVES 10–12

Saute frozen French fries and onion in butter until light brown, turning frequently. Drain well. Grease a large 3-quart casserole. Parboil greens, drain and set aside. Beat together eggs and cream. Layer half of the potatoes and onions in casserole, top with the greens and half the cheese, season with salt, pepper and nutmeg to taste. Pour a third of the egg and cream mixture over top. Add remaining potatoes, then cheese. Pour all of the egg and cream mixture over top. Bake at 350° for 1 hour. Serve with ham and tossed salad.

VEGETABLE SURPRISE

2—3 cups yellow squash,
　sliced and cooked
1 onion, chopped
2 carrots, peeled and
　grated
1 egg, slightly beaten
4 Tbsp. butter, sliced
½ cup mayonnaise
1 Tbsp. sugar
1 cup sharp Cheddar
　cheese, grated and
　divided
1 to 1½ cups Ritz crackers,
　crumbled and divided
Dash cayenne pepper
Salt and pepper
Oregano

SERVES 6

Place well-drained, hot squash in large mixing bowl. Add onion, carrots, egg, butter, mayonnaise, sugar, half of the cheese, and half of cracker crumbs. Season with cayenne, salt, pepper, and oregano. Mix all ingredients well; place into a buttered 1½ qt. casserole. Top with remaining cheese and crumbs. Bake at 350° for 20 min.

Surprise! Kids love this!

VEGETABLES, RICE & PASTA

ACORN SQUASH

**2 acorn squash, halved,
  seeds removed
1 stick butter
1⅓ cups brown sugar**

**OTHER ADDITIONS:
Pineapple tidbits
Pecans**

SERVES 4
Set squash halves on cookie sheet for baking. Place 2 tablespoons of butter in each and ⅓ cup brown sugar. Add pineapple or pecans if desired. Bake in 325° oven for 2 hours or until very tender and most of the butter and brown sugar have cooked into the squash. To shorten cooking time, put halved squash in microwave on high for 5–10 minutes before oven baking.

SQUASH FLUFF

**1 cup mushrooms, chopped
1 med. onion, chopped
1 large garlic clove, chopped
1 Tbsp. oil or butter
2 med. zucchini
4 med. summer squash
3 med. crookneck squash
2 ears corn, shucked
1 cup whole wheat bread
  crumbs
Parsley, chervil (optional)
6 eggs, separated
Salt**

**SAUCE:
1 Tbsp. butter
1 Tbsp. whole wheat flour
1 cup milk, scalded
1 med. tomato, chopped
  finely
¼ cup grated sharp
  Cheddar cheese
Fennel seed (or coriander
  or caraway)
Salt**

SERVES 4–6
Saute mushrooms, onion and garlic in oil or butter. Grate squashes finely, mix with ¾ cup of bread crumbs. Add mushroom mixture to squashes with a couple of tablespoons of egg yolks (to bind mixture), the corn, salt (parsley and chervil). Beat egg whites until stiff, then fold into vegetable mixture. Bake in bread crumb-lined 8×8-inch dish (first coat dish with oil, then circulate crumbs until sides and bottom are coated) in 350–375° oven for about 30 minutes. Add remaining bread crumbs to top while baking.

To make sauce, melt butter, whisk in flour (avoid lumps!). Add ½ cup of scalded milk, beating vigorously with wire whisk. After 5 minutes, add remaining scalded milk and remaining ingredients. Cook 20–30 minutes, stirring occasionally. Serve on individual cut portions of squash loaf.

VEGETABLES, RICE & PASTA

BROILED ITALIAN TOMATOES

3 tomatoes, halved
2 Tbsp. Italian oil and
vinegar dressing
2 Tbsp. butter, melted
6 rounded Tbsp. bread
crumbs
2 Tbsp. Parmesan cheese
Garlic salt

SERVES 4–6
Place tomato halves in shallow baking dish with ½-inch water in the bottom of dish. Pour 1 teaspoon Italian dressing on each. Combine melted butter, bread crumbs, cheese and garlic, mixing thoroughly. Pile bread crumb mixture on each tomato half. Bake 20 minutes at 350° or until just brown under the broiler. Serve immediately.

MUSHROOM STUFFED TOMATOES

4 firm tomatoes
Water
⅓ cup butter
3 Tbsp. green onion,
chopped
¼ cup parsley, chopped
½ lb. fresh mushrooms,
sliced
⅛ tsp. nutmeg
Salt
Pepper
⅓ cup seasoned bread
crumbs or Pepperidge
Farm stuffing
6 tsp. Parmesan cheese

SERVES 4
Wash tomatoes and cut off stem end. Scrape out pulp and reserve. Place shells in a shallow baking dish with ½ inch water in the bottom. Melt butter in a skillet and add green onions, parsley, mushrooms, nutmeg, salt and pepper. Simmer until onion and mushrooms are tender. Add tomato pulp and cook 3 minutes. Add bread crumbs and cook until mixture is just moist. Fill tomatoes and sprinkle each with 1½ teaspoons Parmesan cheese. Bake 20–25 minutes at 350°; do not overcook.

VEGETABLES, RICE & PASTA

TOMATOES ROCKEFELLER

1—10 oz. pkg. frozen
  chopped spinach
⅛ tsp. garlic powder
¼ cup onion, chopped
  fine
½ cup butter
1 cup bread crumbs
¼ cup Parmesan cheese
¼ tsp. cayenne pepper
¼ tsp. thyme
½ tsp. black pepper
2 eggs, beaten
6 large, fresh tomatoes,
  sliced ½" thick

SERVES 8
Cook spinach according to package directions. Drain. Add garlic powder, onion and butter to hot spinach. Stir in next six ingredients, cool, then add eggs. Heap spinach atop tomato slices and bake on lightly greased cookie sheet at 325° for 20 minutes. Excellent with steaks or prime rib!

ZUCCHINI CASSEROLE

2 lbs. zucchini squash
¼ cup onion, chopped
1 cup sour cream
1—10½ oz. can cream of
  chicken soup
1 cup grated carrots
½ cup melted butter
2 cups Pepperidge Farm
  stuffing

SERVES 4–6
Cook together the squash and onion. Drain and add sour cream, cream of chicken soup and grated carrots. Pour into casserole dish, top with stuffing that has been mixed with melted butter. Bake at 350° until bubbly, about 20 minutes.

When cutting corn off the cob for freezing, put the ear in the tube center of an angel food pan for support. Cut the corn off the cob so it falls right into the pan.

VEGETABLES, RICE & PASTA

🌿🌿🌿🌿🌿🌿🌿🌿🌿🌿🌿🌿🌿🌿🌿🌿🌿🌿🌿

ZUCCHINI PUFF

3 cups zucchini, thinly
   sliced and pared (about
   4 small squashes)
1 cup Bisquick
½ cup onion, chopped
¾ cup Parmesan cheese,
   grated
2 tsp. dried parsley
½ tsp. seasoned salt
½ tsp. oregano
⅛ tsp. pepper
½ tsp. garlic powder
Scant ½ cup vegetable oil
4 eggs, beaten

SERVES 12
Mix all ingredients in a large mixing bowl. Pour into a lightly greased 9×13 inch pan. Bake at 350° for 25 minutes. Should be golden brown. Serve as a vegetable side dish by cutting into 2-inch squares (or larger). Also good as an appetizer if cut into bite-sized squares. Freezes well.

HOME-SEASONED WILD RICE

¼ cup onion, chopped
½ cup fresh mushrooms,
   sliced
½ cup butter
2 cups wild rice
1 tsp. salt
2 cups consomme
2 cups water
¾ cup pimientos, chopped
   (optional)
½ cup fresh parsley, chopped or 1 Tbsp. dried
   (optional)

SERVES 8
Lightly saute the onions and mushrooms in butter. Stir in rice and salt. Add consomme and water. Simmer, covered, for 1 hour. Remove from heat and stir in pimientos and parsley, if desired. They add to the flavor and visual appeal of the dish, but it certainly is tasty without them.

VEGETABLES, RICE & PASTA

SPANISH RICE

1 cup rice
2 Tbsp. bacon drippings
1 med. onion, chopped
¼ tsp. garlic powder
1—16 oz. can stewed
  tomatoes
½ tsp. black pepper (more
  if you desire)
1 tsp. salt
1½ cups water

SERVES 4–6
Fry rice in bacon drippings until brown-ed. Add onion and garlic and saute for a minute. Add remaining ingredients, cover and simmer until tender, about 20 minutes. Excellent with Mexican food or pork chops.

WHEAT PILAF

1 stick butter or
  margarine, melted
1¼ cups bulgur wheat
1—10½ oz. can beef
  bouillon
1—10½ oz. can French
  onion soup
1—4½ oz. can sliced
  mushrooms (with liquid)

SERVES 6
Combine ingredients in a 2½–3 quart casserole. Cover tightly and bake at 350° for 45 minutes. Nice change from rice and potatoes.

VEGETABLES, RICE & PASTA

SOUR CREAM NOODLES

8 oz. medium-fine noodles
1 pint sour cream
½ cup small curd cottage
   cheese
1 tsp. garlic powder
1 Tbsp. Worcestershire
   sauce
½ Tbsp. minced parsley
1 tsp. salt
¼ cup green onions,
   sliced
Generous dash Tabasco
   sauce

SERVES 6
Cook noodles as directed; drain. Mix all other ingredients and toss with noodles. Bake, uncovered, at 350° for 25–30 minutes.

POPPY SEED NOODLE CASSEROLE

2—10½ oz. cans beef broth
2—10½ oz. cans water
2—8 oz. pkgs. thin egg
   noodles
¼–½ cup vegetable oil
3 Tbsp. poppy seeds
2¾ oz. pkg. sliced
   almonds, roasted

SERVES 10
Bring broth and water to a boil in large saucepan. Add noodles. Cover and simmer until liquid is absorbed. Toss with poppy seeds and oil. Pour into a buttered 1-quart casserole. Sprinkle with almonds and serve warm.

When cooking noodles or macaroni, first bring your water to boiling point, add noodles, stir, bring to a second boil, turn off and cover. Let set until tender. Works like a charm.

PASTA PRIMAVERA

1 lb. ground Italian sausage
1 cup sliced fresh
  mushrooms
3 Tbsp. butter
3 Tbsp. olive oil
¼ tsp. garlic powder
⅓ cup green onions,
  sliced (tops and all)
1 zucchini, chopped
1 green pepper, seeded
  and chopped
1 tsp. dried parsley (or 1
  Tbsp. fresh)
½ tsp. basil
½ tsp. oregano
12 oz. fettucini noodles
  (can use spaghetti)
3 Tbsp. butter
1 cup whipping cream
⅔ cup Parmesan cheese

SERVES 6

Cook sausage in a skillet until browned and done. Drain and set aside in a bowl. In the same skillet, saute mushrooms in 3 tablespoons butter. Put mushrooms in bowl with sausage. Add olive oil to skillet and saute garlic and onions lightly. Stir in zucchini, green pepper, parsley, basil and oregano. Cook until vegetables are tender-crisp. Stir in sausage and mushrooms. While vegetables are cooking, cook fettucini in boiling salted water until tender but not mushy. Drain. In a large saucepan, heat 3 tablespoons butter with whipping cream. When slightly thickened, stir in cooked fettucini and grated Parmesan. Pour onto large platter and top with vegetables and sausage mixture. Serve immediately!

Try this for an Italian-type dish that is different from spaghetti and meatballs. It truly is a meal in itself!

Desserts

DESSERTS

PLUM CREEK APPLESAUCE CAKE

½ **cup butter or margarine**
1 **cup sugar**
1 **egg**
1¼ **cups flour**
1 **tsp. soda**
1 **tsp. cinnamon**
½ **tsp. salt**
¼ **tsp. ground cloves**
¾ **cup raisins**
¾ **cup walnuts or pecans,**
  chopped
1 **cup applesauce**

FROSTING:
¼ **cup butter**
½ **cup brown sugar**
3 **Tbsp. milk**
¾ **cup powdered sugar**
½ **tsp. vanilla**

Cream butter and sugar; add egg and mix well. Sift together flour, soda, cinnamon, salt and cloves. Stir dry ingredients into batter. Fold in raisins, nuts and applesauce. Spread batter into 9×13 inch greased pan. Bake at 350° for 30 minutes or until toothpick inserted in center comes out clean.

To make frosting, melt butter in small saucepan. Remove from heat; add brown sugar and stir until smooth. Bring to boil over low heat, stirring constantly; boil 1 minute. Remove from heat and add milk. Stir in powdered sugar and add vanilla. Frost while cake slightly warm.

There is a saying — trite but true —
"Kissin' don't last, but cooking do."
An art that will not lose its worth
As long as men live on this earth.
'Tis nice, of course, to sing and play,
To paint, to draw, to dance ballet;
But these all fail man's needs to meet —
Each day, three meals he wants to eat.
So, she who roasts and broils and bakes
Pies and cakes and cookies makes
Will find that cooking is an art
That gives a shortcut to the heart.

BETSY'S BANANA CAKE

2 sticks butter
¾ cup sugar
2 eggs
1 cup ripe bananas,
  mashed
1 tsp. vanilla
2 cups flour
½ tsp. salt
½ tsp. baking soda
6 Tbsp. buttermilk

**CREAM CHEESE
  FROSTING:**
8 oz. cream cheese
6 Tbsp. butter
3 cups powdered sugar
1 tsp. vanilla

GARNISH:
1½–2 med. firm-but-ripe
  bananas, sliced
1½ cups chopped walnuts
Powdered sugar

Cream together butter and sugar until light and fluffy. Add eggs, one at a time, beating well after each addition. Add mashed bananas and vanilla, mixing thoroughly. Sift together dry ingredients and add to butter mixture. Stir until flour is mixed in. Add buttermilk. Mix for one minute. Pour batter into two greased and floured 9-inch layer cake pans. Bake at 350° for 25–30 minutes. Cool in pans on a rack for 10 minutes, remove from pans, and cool on rack for 1 hour. When cooled, place one layer on a serving plate. Frost with cream cheese frosting. Arrange slices of banana over frosting, cover with second cake layer and frost top and sides of cake. Cover sides of cake with chopped nuts, holding nuts in palm and pressing firmly to sides of cake. Dust top of cake with powdered sugar if desired.

To prepare frosting, cream together cream cheese and butter that are room temperature. Sift in powdered sugar and beat until smooth. Stir in vanilla.

This cake can also be baked in a 9×13 inch pan for 35–40 minutes. Frost cake with half of frosting, top with sliced bananas and top with remaining frosting. Sprinkle with chopped nuts and dust with powdered sugar.

DESSERTS

CARROT CAKE

1½ cups oil
4 eggs
2 cups sugar
2 cups flour
2 tsp. baking soda
2 tsp. cinnamon
1 tsp. salt
2 cups carrots, grated
1—8 oz. can crushed
   pineapple
1 cup nuts, chopped

FROSTING:
12 oz. cream cheese
¹/₃ cup butter
½ tsp. vanilla
2 cups powdered sugar
2 Tbsp. milk
½ cup coconut
¼ cup currants or
   chopped raisins
¼ cup walnuts

Combine oil, eggs and sugar. Beat well. Add dry ingredients and mix at low speed until well blended. Stir in pineapple and grated carrots; fold in nuts. Pour into greased and floured 9×13 inch pan. Bake at 350° for 60 minutes.

To make frosting, cream together cream cheese and butter, blend in powdered sugar and vanilla. Add enough milk to make smooth. Stir in coconut, currants and walnuts.

CHOCOLATE CHERRY COFFEE CAKE

1 pkg. fudge cake mix
1—21 oz. can cherry pie filling
2 eggs, beaten

FROSTING:
½ cup buttermilk
½ cup margarine
¼ cup cocoa
1 heaping tsp. instant coffee powder dissolved in a few drops very hot water
4 cups powdered sugar
1 cup small marshmallows
1 cup pecans, chopped

SERVES 15

Mix batter ingredients well. Pour into a greased jelly roll pan and bake at 350° for 25–30 minutes.

To make frosting, combine buttermilk, margarine, cocoa and coffee in a saucepan. Bring to a boil, remove from heat and stir in powdered sugar, marshmallows and pecans. Spread on cake immediately after removing from oven. Good, fast dessert!

 Do not assume that your sea level recipe will fail at high altitude. Try it first. It may need little or no modification. If you have questions, contact your local county extension agent.

Cake Recipe Adjustment Guide for High Altitudes—Customary Measurements

Adjustment	3,000 ft.	5,000 ft.	7,000 ft
Reduce baking powder, for each tsp. decrease	⅛ tsp.	⅛–¼ tsp.	¼ tsp.
Reduce sugar, for each cup, decrease	0-1 Tbsp.	0-2 Tbsp.	1-3 Tbsp.
Increase liquid, for each cup, add	1-2 Tbsp.	2-4 Tbsp.	3-4 Tbsp.

CHOCOLATE-MACAROON CAKE

MACAROON FILLING:
4 egg whites
½ cup +2 Tbsp. sugar
1 tsp. vanilla extract
⅓ cup sugar
2 cups grated coconut
1 Tbsp. flour

CAKE:
1¼ cup sugar
½ cup shortening
3 egg yolks
1 tsp. salt
1 tsp. vanilla
½ cup cocoa
¾ cup hot coffee
2 cups sifted flour
1 tsp. soda
½ cup sour cream

CHOCOLATE CREAM
FROSTING:
1 cup semi-sweet
chocolate pieces,
melted
2 Tbsp. butter
1 egg yolk
1½ cup powdered sugar
¼ cup milk

Beat all 4 egg whites until soft mounds form. Add ½ cup plus 2 tablespoons sugar gradually; beat until stiff. Pour ¼ of the beaten egg whites into separate bowl. To this, gradually add ⅓ cup more sugar, beating until stiff. Add 1 teaspoon vanilla and stir in coconut and 1 tablespoon flour; set aside.

To prepare cake batter, cream sugar, shortening, yolks, salt, vanilla, cocoa and coffee. Beat until light, about 4 minutes. Blend in flour, sour cream and soda. Fold in remaining ¾ of the beaten egg whites. Turn ½ of the chocolate cake batter into a 10-inch tube pan which has been greased on bottom. Pour coconut mixture on top. Cover with other half of chocolate batter. Bake at 350° for 45–55 minutes. Do not invert pan. Cool completely; remove from pan. Frost with chocolate cream frosting.

To make frosting, combine ingredients and beat until smooth and a spreadable consistency.

SUZIE'S CHOCOLATE SOUR CREAM CAKE

1½ cups sugar
1 rounded Tbsp. butter
2 eggs
1 cup sour cream
2 cups flour
3 Tbsp. cocoa
1 tsp. salt
2 tsp. soda
1 cup brewed coffee
1 tsp. vanilla

Cream sugar and butter. Add eggs, sour cream, flour, cocoa, salt, soda, coffee and vanilla. Blend well. Pour into greased and floured 9×13-inch pan, and bake at 350° for 20–30 minutes. Frost with Never-Fail Chocolate Frosting when cooled. This flavorful, moist chocolate cake is also good without frosting. Either way, it won't last long!

NEVER-FAIL CHOCOLATE FROSTING

¼ cup margarine, melted
  (can use Crisco or butter)
½ cup cocoa
¼ tsp. salt
⅓ cup milk
1½ tsp. vanilla
3½ cups confectioners
  sugar

Combine melted margarine, cocoa and salt; then add milk and vanilla. Mix in sugar in 3 parts. Mix until smooth and creamy. Add more sugar to thicken, or milk to thin to make it a good spreading consistency.

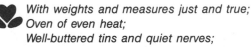

With weights and measures just and true;
Oven of even heat;
Well-buttered tins and quiet nerves;
Success will be complete.

DESSERTS

COOKIES 'N CREAM CAKE

1 pkg. white cake with
  pudding mix
1¼ cups water
3 egg whites
1½ cups coarsely
  crushed, chocolate,
  creme-filled sandwich
  cookies

FROSTING:
2½ cups powdered sugar
¾ cup butter
½ tsp. vanilla
1 egg white
1½ Tbsp. milk
5 cookies, cut in half

In bowl, combine cake mix, water and egg whites; beat for 2 minutes. Gently stir in coarsely crushed cookies. Pour into greased 9×13 inch pan and bake at 325° for 30–35 minutes or until done.

To prepare frosting, combine powdered sugar, butter, vanilla and egg white; beat until smooth. Frost cake and place cookies, which have been cut in half, upright around cake.

CHRISTMAS FRUITCAKE

2 eggs
2 cups water
2 pkgs. Pillsbury Date
  Quick Bread mix
2 cups pecans (halves or
  chopped)
2 cups raisins
2 cups candied cherries
1 cup candied pineapple,
  cut up (may substitute 2
  lbs. [4 cups] candied
  mixed fruit for the cherries and pineapple)

**MAKES 1 LARGE TUBE CAKE
OR 2 LOAVES**
In a large bowl, combine eggs and water. Add remaining ingredients, stir by hand until well mixed. Pour into greased and floured tube pan, or 2 loaf pans. Bake at 350° for 75–85 minutes or until tested done with a toothpick. Cool; then remove from pan. Store tightly wrapped in refrigerator. Glaze with warm corn syrup if desired.

Note: At altitudes above 3500 feet, add 2 tablespoons flour to breadmix and bake at 375° for 60–70 minutes.

ROME APPLE CAKE

1½ cups sugar
¾ cup cream cheese
½ cup butter, softened
1 tsp. vanilla
2 eggs
1½ cups flour
1½ tsp. baking powder
¼ tsp. salt
3 cups Rome apples,
   peeled and chopped
2 tsp. cinnamon
¼ cup sugar

SERVES 12–15
Beat together the sugar, cream cheese, butter, and vanilla until fluffy. Add eggs one at a time, beating after each addition. Add dry ingredients and blend well. Combine the cinnamon and sugar in a separate bowl. Sprinkle 2 teaspoons cinnamon/sugar mixture over apples and stir to coat. Add apples to cake batter. Pour into a greased and floured Bundt pan, or 9×13 inch layer pan. Sprinkle remaining cinnamon/sugar on top of batter. Bake at 350° for about 45 minutes or until cake tests done.

CHARLOTTE'S NUT CAKE

1 cup sugar
1 cup brown sugar
1 cup vegetable oil
3 eggs, slightly beaten
2½ cups flour
1 tsp. cinnamon
1 tsp. ground cloves
1 tsp. nutmeg
1 tsp. salt
1 tsp. soda
1 tsp. baking powder
1⅓ cup buttermilk
2 tsp. almond extract
1 cup nuts, chopped

GLAZE:
1 cup sugar
⅓ cup water

SERVES 15
Cream sugars and oil. Add eggs. Mix together the dry ingredients and add alternately with buttermilk, beginning and ending with flour mixture. Mix well. Stir in extract and nuts. Pour into a greased and floured 9×13 inch pan and bake at 350° for 35 minutes or until cake tests done.

If you like, boil together the glaze ingredients and pour over warm cake. It makes a nice finishing touch, but the cake is delicious without it.

DESERTS

MANDARIN ORANGE CAKE

1 lemon cake mix
4 eggs
½ cup oil
1—11 oz. can mandarin
   oranges, undrained

TOPPING:
13½ oz. carton Cool Whip
1—20 oz. can crushed
   pineapple, undrained
1 small pkg. instant vanilla
   pudding

Combine first 4 ingredients in mixing bowl and beat 4 minutes. Pour into greased and floured 9×13-inch pan or three round pans. Bake until golden brown, 15–20 minutes if in small pans, 30 minutes for single larger pan.

To prepare topping, mix all ingredients until dissolved. Frost and refrigerate cake.

PEANUT BUTTER CUPCAKES

½ cup peanut butter
⅓ cup shortening
1½ cups brown sugar
2 eggs
2 cups flour
2 tsp. baking powder
½ tsp. ground cinnamon
½ tsp. salt
1 cup milk

TOPPING:
½ cup brown sugar
½ cup flour
¼ cup peanut butter
2 Tbsp. margarine, melted
½ tsp. cinnamon

MAKES 18
Cream ½ cup peanut butter and shortening. Slowly beat in brown sugar. Add eggs, beating until fluffy. Sift together flour, baking powder, cinnamon and salt; add alternately with milk, beating after every addition. Fill paper baking cups in muffin tins half full. Combine topping ingredients and mix until crumbly. Top batter with a full tablespoon of topping. Bake at 375° for 18 to 20 minutes.

 To keep brown sugar soft, add a piece of bread to the bag.

WESTERN SLOPE PEAR CAKE

1 cup butter
1 cup sugar
1 cup brown sugar
2 eggs, beaten
1 tsp. vanilla
2½ cups flour
2 tsp. baking powder
1 tsp. baking soda
½ tsp. salt
2 tsp. ground cinnamon
½ cup reserved pear
   syrup
1—16 oz. can pears, diced
1 cup raisins
1 cup walnuts, chopped

CARAMEL GLAZE:
⅓ cup brown sugar
1½ Tbsp. butter
3 Tbsp. reserved pear
   syrup
¾ cup powdered sugar

Cream together butter and sugars. Blend in eggs and vanilla. Sift together dry ingredients and add to butter mixture, alternating with pear syrup. Stir in pears, raisins and nuts. Pour into a greased 9×13 inch pan; bake at 400° for 25 minutes or until done. While warm, spread with caramel glaze.

To prepare glaze, bring sugar, butter and syrup to a boil. Stir in powdered sugar and spread on warm cake.

It is a good idea to keep your words soft and sweet. You never know when you may have to eat them.

DESSERTS

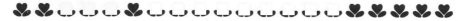

APRICOT NECTAR CAKE

CAKE:
1—18½ oz. box yellow
  cake mix
4 eggs
¾ cup oil
¾ cup apricot nectar
3 tsp. lemon extract

LEMON GLAZE:
1½ cups powdered sugar
Juice of 2 lemons, and
  grated rind

SERVES 12

In a medium mixing bowl, combine cake mix, eggs, oil, apricot nectar, and lemon extract. Beat at medium speed for 4 minutes. Pour into a greased and floured Bundt pan. Bake at 325° for 55 minutes. Let stand 5 minutes; turn out onto a serving dish. Combine glaze ingredients. Prick holes in cake with fork and pour glaze over warm cake.

Note: If baking this cake at an altitude above 5000', stir 2 Tbsps. flour into mix.

PINEAPPLE PUDDING CAKE

1 yellow cake mix
2²/₃ cups flaked coconut
1—8 oz. pkg. cream cheese
2 cups milk
1—3 oz. pkg. vanilla
  instant pudding
1—20 oz. can crushed
  pineapple, well drained
1—8 oz. container Cool
  Whip

Prepare cake mix as directed on package. Add 1¹/₃ cups coconut after beating. Bake in greased and floured 9x13-inch cake pan for 30–35 minutes or until done. Beat cream cheese to soften; gradually blend in milk. Add pudding mix; beat at low speed for 2 minutes. Spread evenly over cool cake. Spoon pineapple over pudding. Spread whipped topping over pineapple; sprinkle with remaining coconut. Chill.

PARK SPRINGS POUND CAKE

1 lb. butter (4 sticks)
2 cups sugar
4 cups flour, sifted
1 dozen eggs, separated
⅛ tsp. salt
2 tsp. vanilla
2 tsp. lemon extract

Cream butter and sugar. Gradually add beaten egg yolks, mixing well. Add flour and **unbeaten** egg whites alternately until smooth. Add salt and extracts and mix well. Pour into a well-greased Bundt or tube pan. Bake at 325° for 1½ hours, or until tested done with a wooden pick. This makes a very fine-textured cake. . .one that is excellent for gift-giving. It slices beautifully, and is delicious plain or topped with fresh fruit or ice cream. The secret to good pound cake is making sure you beat it well.

GEORGIA'S RUM CAKE

1 cup pecans, chopped
1 yellow cake mix with pudding
3 eggs
⅓ cup oil
½ cup cold water
½ cup rum

GLAZE:
1 stick butter
¼ cup water
1 cup sugar
½ cup rum

Grease a Bundt or tube pan. Place chopped nuts on bottom of pan. Combine cake mix with eggs, oil, water and rum. Pour batter over nuts and bake at 325° for 1 hour. Cool. Loosen cake from pan and invert on a plate. Pierce top of cake with a utility fork and drizzle glaze over, letting it soak in.

To prepare glaze, melt butter in a saucepan. Stir in water and sugar and boil 5 minutes. Stir in rum.

DESSERTS

STRAWBERRY ANGEL FOOD CAKE

1 box angel food cake mix
1 pint fresh strawberries,
   washed, hulled, halved
   (save some for garnish)
2 Tbsp. sugar
1—12 oz. carton Cool Whip

(May substitute 1—10 oz.
   pkg. frozen strawberries,
   thawed, for fresh. Omit
   sugar.)

Prepare cake mix as directed on package. Cool. Invert on a serving plate. Sprinkle fresh strawberries with a couple of tablespoons of sugar and let set out while cake is cooking and cooling. When ready to ice, thoroughly mash berries in their own juice. Stir into the Cool Whip and frost cake. Garnish with whole strawberries. This is a pretty cake, easy to make and delicious to eat. Good for birthday parties, summer desserts, or Valentine's Day. Store in the refrigerator.

TRADITIONAL SPICE CAKE

1½ cups sugar
½ cup Crisco
3 eggs
1 tsp. vanilla
1 cup buttermilk
2 cups flour
1 tsp. baking powder
1 tsp. soda
1 tsp. cinnamon
½ tsp. allspice
½ tsp. ground cloves
1 cup nuts, chopped
   (optional)
½ cup raisins (optional)

SERVES 12–15
Cream sugar and shortening until light and fluffy. Add eggs one at a time, beating well after each addition. Mix vanilla and buttermilk. Mix together the dry ingredients. At low speed, add dry ingredients alternately with buttermilk, beginning and ending with dry ingredients. Blend well. Stir in nuts and raisins if desired. Pour into greased and floured 9×13-inch pan and bake at 350° for 35–40 minutes or until tested done. When cake is cooled, frost with Caramel Icing (recipe on following page).

(For altitudes above 4,000 feet, decrease baking powder to ¾ teaspoon, sugar to 1⅓ cups, and add ¼ cup more to the buttermilk.)

CARAMEL ICING

⅓ cup butter
1 cup brown sugar, packed
¼ cup milk
⅛ tsp. salt
½ tsp. vanilla
1¼ cups powdered sugar

Melt butter in a saucepan. Stir in brown sugar and cook over low heat for 2 minutes, stirring constantly. Add milk and salt and continue stirring to a boil. Boil for 3 minutes; remove from heat and cool. Add vanilla and stir well. Beat in powdered sugar until icing is a good spreading consistency.

SNOW-CAPPED ICING

2¼ cups sugar
½ cup water
3 Tbsp. white Karo syrup
3 egg whites, beaten stiff
3 Tbsp. powdered sugar

**GENEROUSLY FROSTS
1 LARGE TUBE CAKE**
In a saucepan, mix sugar, water and Karo syrup. Cook to soft ball stage, 238° on your candy thermometer. Slowly add in a thin stream to beaten egg whites, beating all the while. Continue beating until the icing is like cream. Add powdered sugar and mix until it reaches spreading consistency.

This soft-on-the-inside, crusty-on-the-outside icing is wonderful on **any** kind of cake. With chocolate cake, garnish the icing with melted semi-sweet chocolate drizzled over it. Sprinkle toasted coconut on it when icing a yellow cake. Dust it with slivered, toasted almonds for an angel food cake. It is so versatile, reliable, and — unbeatable!

Prevent icing from running off a cake by dusting the surface with a little cornstarch before icing.

DESSERTS

CREME WAFERS

1 cup softened butter
1/3 cup whipping cream
2 cups sifted flour

FILLING:
1/4 cup softened butter
3/4 cup powdered sugar
1 egg yolk
1 tsp. vanilla

MAKES 5 DOZEN DOUBLE COOKIES
Blend together the butter, cream and flour. Mix well and chill. Roll 1/3 of the dough at a time, keeping the remainder refrigerated. Roll out dough to 1/8" thickness on a floured board. Cut 1½-inch rounds. Put about ½ cup granulated sugar on a piece of waxed paper. Coat each round (both sides) with sugar. Place on ungreased baking sheet and prick with a fork. Bake at 375° for 7–9 minutes. Cool. Spread one cookie with filling, then top with another cookie.

To make filling, blend ingredients in the order listed. Tint with food coloring if desired.

These rich cookies make wonderful party treats; or when served with fruit or ice cream, make dessert a special occasion.

LEMON-BUTTER COOKIES

½ cup butter
1—3 oz. pkg. cream cheese
½ cup sugar
1 tsp. grated lemon rind
¼ tsp. lemon extract
1 cup sifted flour
2 tsp. baking powder
¼ tsp. salt
1¼ cup coarsely crumbled
   corn flakes

MAKES 3 DOZEN

Cream together butter, cream cheese and sugar until light and fluffy. Blend in lemon rind and lemon extract. Sift together flour, baking powder and salt. Gradually add dry ingredients and cornflakes to creamed mixture; mix well. Chill dough in refrigerator about 1 hour. Shape dough into 1-inch balls. Flatten slightly with bottom of glass dipped in sugar. Bake in 350° oven for 12–15 minutes or until done.

MOLASSES COOKIES

¾ cup shortening
1 cup sugar
¼ cup molasses
1 egg
2 cups flour, sifted
2 tsp. baking soda
½ tsp. ground cloves
½ tsp. ginger
½ tsp. salt
½ tsp. cinnamon
Granulated sugar

MAKES 4 DOZEN

Melt shortening, then let cool. Add sugar, molasses, and egg. Beat well. Sift together the dry ingredients, then add to the first mixture. Mix well then chill. Form into 1-inch balls, and roll in granulated sugar. Place on a greased cookie sheet about 2 inches apart. Bake at 375° for 8 minutes. Cookies should be chewy. . . not quite done in the middle. If you like spice-type cookies, these surely will be a favorite.

 Dust greased cookie sheets with a little flour. This will keep the cookies from spreading during baking.

DESSERTS

MONSTER COOKIES

½ cup margarine, melted
1 cup plus 2 Tbsp. brown
  sugar, packed
1 cup white sugar
3 eggs
¾ tsp. vanilla
¾ tsp. dark Karo syrup
1 heaping cup crunchy
  peanut butter
4½ cups oatmeal
2 tsp. baking soda
3 oz. chocolate chips
3 oz. plain M&Ms

MAKES 3 DOZEN
Cream together shortening and sugars until creamy. Add eggs and beat well. Beat in vanilla, syrup, and peanut butter. Add dry ingredients and mix well. Mix in M&Ms and chocolate chips. Drop by heaping tablespoonfuls onto cookie sheet. Bake at 375° for 11 minutes. Watch carefully, do not overcook.

OATMEAL DATE COOKIES

1 cup shortening
1 cup brown sugar
1 cup white sugar
3 eggs
1 tsp. vanilla
2 cups sifted flour
1 tsp. baking powder
¾ tsp. baking soda
½ tsp. salt
2 cups quick-cooking
  oatmeal
½ cup chopped walnuts
  or pecans
1 cup dates, chopped
1 cup flaked coconut

MAKES 3–4 DOZEN
Cream together shortening and sugars until light and fluffy. Add eggs, one at a time, beating well after each addition. Blend in vanilla. Sift together flour, baking powder, baking soda and salt. Add to creamed mixture, mixing well. Stir in oats, walnuts, dates and coconut. Drop by teaspoonfuls onto greased baking sheets. Flatten with bottom of drinking glass dipped in sugar. Bake at 375° for 7–8 minutes or until lightly browned.

CHEWY OATMEAL-RAISIN COOKIES

1¼ cup butter-flavored
  Crisco (can use
  margarine or butter)
1 cup brown sugar
1 cup white sugar
2 eggs
1 tsp. vanilla
½ tsp. salt
1 tsp. nutmeg
2½ cups rolled oats
  (quick-cooking is okay)
1 tsp. baking soda
1¼ cups flour
1 cup raisins

MAKES 4 DOZEN BIG COOKIES
Cream shortening and sugars. Add eggs and beat well. Stir in vanilla, salt and nutmeg. Blend in the oats. Add soda and raisins to flour, then stir into the dough. Drop by the teaspoonful onto a lightly greased cookie sheet and bake at 350° until lightly browned, about 15 minutes. These are good, old-fashioned oatmeal raisin cookies!

PEPPERNUTS (PFEFFERNUSSE)

½ cup shortening
¾ cup sugar
1 egg, well beaten
1 tsp. vanilla
½ tsp. cinnamon
¼ tsp. cloves
1 Tbsp. anise seed
¾ tsp. salt
½ tsp. baking soda
3 Tbsp. water
Scant ½ cup light corn
  syrup
⅛ cup molasses
3¼ cups flour

MAKES 4 DOZEN
Cream shortening and sugar until light and fluffy. Add egg, spices, vanilla and salt. Combine soda, water, corn syrup and molasses, add to creamed mixture. Add flour and chill 2–3 hours. Roll dough into ropes about ½-inch in diameter. Cut ropes into 1-inch pieces and place 1 inch apart on an ungreased cookie sheet. Bake at 375° for 15 minutes.

This traditional German Christmas cookie is fun to have on hand during the holiday season. A friend makes a batch of these and sets a basket of them out for munching. They freeze well.

DESSERTS

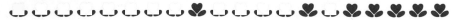

SANDTARTS

1 lb. butter, softened
3½ cups flour, sifted
6 Tbsp. sugar
2 cups pecans, chopped
2 tsp. vanilla
Powdered sugar

MAKES 4 DOZEN

Cream together softened butter, flour and sugar until blended. Add nuts and vanilla and mix well. Chill 1 hour. Shape into small rounds. Bake for 6–8 minutes at 350° on ungreased cookie sheets. Cool, then roll in powdered sugar. Sometimes called Mexican wedding cookies, these rich cookies are always a favorite at Christmas.

EASY APPLE RAISIN BARS

CRUMB MIXTURE:
2 cups flour
1½ cups sugar
2 cups quick-cooking oats
1¼ cups melted butter
1 tsp. baking soda

FILLING:
½ cup raisins
1—20 oz. can apple pie
  filling
½ cup chopped nuts
½ tsp. cinnamon
½ tsp. nutmeg

MAKES 2½ DOZEN

Combine flour, sugar, oats, butter and soda. Mix well. Reserve 1½ cups of mixture. Press remaining mixture into ungreased 9×13-inch pan. Bake at 350° for 15–20 minutes. Combine raisins, pie filling, nuts, cinnamon and nutmeg. Mix well. Spread evenly over hot crust. Sprinkle with reserved crumb mixture. Bake for another 30 minutes. Cool completely before cutting into bars.

This is a delicious, nutritious after-school snack.

O weary mothers mixing dough
Don't you wish that food would grow?
A smile would come, I know, to see,
A cookie bush or a donut tree!

HARVEST SQUARES

FIRST LAYER:
1 yellow cake mix, reserve
  1 cup for topping
1 cup butter, melted
1 egg

SECOND LAYER:
1—1 lb. can pumpkin
$^2/_3$ cup milk
½ cup brown sugar
2 eggs
$^1/_3$ cup white sugar
1½ tsp. cinnamon
½ tsp. allspice
½ tsp. nutmeg

TOPPING:
1 cup reserved cake mix
½ cup sugar
1 tsp. cinnamon
¼ cup melted butter

MAKES 30 SQUARES

Mix cake mix (minus 1 cup) with melted butter and egg. Spread on bottom of 9×13-inch pan.

To prepare second layer, combine all ingredients and mix well. Spread over bottom layer.

Mix together topping ingredients and sprinkle on top of the other two layers. Bake at 350° for 50–60 minutes.

Try this delicious bar cookie after a busy day of raking leaves or chopping firewood. Top with a dollop of whipped cream or vanilla ice cream for a few extra calories!

CARAMEL BROWNIES

1—14 oz. pkg. caramels
$^1/_3$ cup evaporated milk
1 box German Chocolate
  cake mix
$^1/_3$ cup evaporated milk
¾ cup margarine, melted
1 cup pecans, chopped
1 cup chocolate chips

MAKES 4 DOZEN

Melt caramels with ½ cup evaporated milk in a saucepan over low heat. In a mixing bowl, combine cake mix, $^1/_3$ cup evaporated milk and melted margarine. Stir in nuts. Mix well. Spread half the dough in a greased 9×13-inch pan. Bake at 350° for 8 minutes.

Remove from oven and sprinkle chocolate chips over baked mixture. Pour caramel mixture over this. Using a kitchen knife. spread and press the remaining dough (it will be thick) over caramel mixture. It will not cover completely. Return to oven and bake another 18 minutes. Cool; then refrigerate to set the caramel layer. Cut into small squares as this is a rich and delicious brownie variation.

* Can be prepared with caramel dip instead of caramel mixture.

DESERTS

CREAM CHEESE BROWNIES

CREAM CHEESE LAYER:
1—3 oz. pkg. cream cheese
2 Tbsp. butter
¼ cup sugar
1 egg
1 Tbsp. flour
½ tsp. vanilla

BROWNIE LAYER:
1—4 oz. pkg. German
  sweet chocolate
3 Tbsp. butter
2 eggs
¾ cup sugar
½ tsp. baking powder
¼ tsp. salt
½ cup flour
1 tsp. vanilla
¼ tsp. almond extract
½ cup nuts, chopped

**CREAM CHEESE
  FROSTING:**
4 oz. cream cheese
½ lb. powdered sugar
¼ cup butter
Milk
1 tsp. vanilla

SERVES 6–9
Melt sweet chocolate and 3 table-spoons butter over very low heat. Stir and let cool. While cooling, prepare cream cheese layer. Cream the cream cheese with 2 tablespoons butter. Add sugar, egg, flour and vanilla and mix well. In separate bowl, beat two eggs until lemon-colored, add sugar and beat well. Add baking powder, salt and flour. Blend in cooled chocolate mixture, 1 teaspoon vanilla, almond extract and chopped nuts. Spread half the chocolate batter in a 9-inch pan. Cover with cheese mixture. Spoon remaining chocolate batter over top. Bake at 350° for 35–40 minutes. Cool and frost.

To make frosting, cream together cream cheese and butter, then blend in powdered sugar and vanilla. Add enough milk to make smooth.

CHOCOLATE BUTTER-CREAM BARS

FIRST LAYER:
½ cup butter
½ cup sugar
⅓ cup cocoa
1 tsp. vanilla
1 egg
2 cups graham cracker
   crumbs (1 cellophane
   pkg.), crushed
1 cup flaked coconut
½ cup pecans, chopped

SECOND LAYER:
½ cup butter, softened
2 cups powdered sugar
2 Tbsp. instant vanilla
   pudding
3 Tbsp. milk

THIRD LAYER:
1—6 oz. pkg. chocolate
   chips
2 Tbsp. butter
Milk

MAKES 4 DOZEN
Combine butter, sugar, cocoa and vanilla in a saucepan. Cook over low heat to melt butter. Add egg and cook 5 minutes, stirring constantly. Stir in crumbs, coconut and nuts. Press mixture in a 9×13-inch pan and chill for 15 minutes.

Meanwhile, cream butter and sugar. Add pudding and milk and beat until smooth. Spread over first layer and chill another 15 minutes.

For third layer, melt chocolate chips with butter. Add milk until mixture is thin enough to spread. Frost bars and chill. Cut into small squares.

A bite or two of this confection will satisfy a sweet tooth and a chocolate craving all at once!

DESSERTS

KRISPIE BARS

1—6 oz. pkg. butterscotch
  chips
½ cup crunchy peanut
  butter
4 cups Rice Krispies
  cereal

CHOCOLATE LAYER:
1—6 oz. pkg. semi-sweet
  chocolate chips
½ cup powdered sugar
2 Tbsp. butter
1 Tbsp. water

MAKES 16
Melt butterscotch chips and peanut butter over low heat, stirring constantly until smooth. Remove from heat and add cereal and stir until well coated. Press half of the mixture into a buttered 8-inch pan. Chill while preparing fudge chocolate mixture.

Melt chocolate chips, powdered sugar, butter and water over hot water; stir until smooth. Spread chocolate over chilled cereal mixture. Spread remaining cereal mixture evenly over top. Press gently and refrigerate until firm. Cut into squares.

FRUIT BARS

2 sticks butter or
  margarine
1¾ cup sugar
4 eggs
1 tsp. vanilla
3 cups flour, sifted
1½ tsp. baking powder
½ tsp. salt
1—30 oz. can cherry pie
  filling (can use blueberry
  or apple)

GLAZE:
¾ cup powdered sugar
2 Tbsp. lemon juice

MAKES 2 DOZEN BARS
Cream together the butter and sugar. Add eggs one at a time beating well after each addition. Stir in vanilla. Add dry ingredients and blend well. Spread ¾ of the batter on a greased 11×15 jelly roll pan. Cover with pie filling. Spread the remaining batter over top (it won't quite cover completely).

Bake at 350° for 40–45 minutes. Mix glaze ingredients and drizzle over warm bars.

TOFFEE PECAN BARS

1½ cups flour
¾ cup brown sugar
¾ cup butter or margarine
2 eggs
1½ cups brown sugar
1½ tsp. vanilla
3 Tbsp. flour
1½ tsp. baking powder
¾ tsp. salt
1⅓ cups flaked coconut
1½ cups pecans, chopped

MAKES 2 DOZEN
Combine 1½ cups flour and ¾ cup brown sugar in bowl. Cut in butter until mixture is crumbly. Press crumb mixture into greased 9×13-inch pan. Bake in 350° oven 15 minutes. Beat eggs well and add brown sugar and vanilla, mixing well. Add flour, baking powder and salt and blend well. Stir in coconut and pecans. Spread topping over baked layer. Bake in 350° oven 30 minutes or until topping is brown. While warm, cut into 3×1½-inch bars. These will be a big hit in any household!

FLAKY PIE CRUST

PER CRUST:
1⅓ cups flour
½ tsp. salt
½ cup Crisco
About 3–4 Tbsp. ice water

MAKES ONE 9 INCH CRUST
Mix salt and flour with one hand. Add Crisco and break up shortening in flour until pieces are pea size. Sprinkle cold water over mixture and toss around with hand. Add enough water until dough holds together when gathered as if making a snowball. Avoid working the dough too much.

To make dough in a food processor, combine flour, salt and Crisco in processor. Blend until mealy. Add ice water, a tablespoon at a time with machine running, until dough makes a ball.

Flatten dough on floured surface and roll about an inch larger than pan. Put in pan and trim edges. For a baked pie shell, bake at 450° for 8–10 minutes. (Be sure to prick the bottom and sides.)

DESERTS

BUTTERY PIE CRUST

3 cups flour
1¾ cups butter, or ½ cup
butter + ¾ cup Crisco
1 egg, slightly beaten
1 heaping tsp. salt
5 Tbsp. cold water
1 Tbsp. vinegar

MAKES 2 DOUBLE 9" CRUSTS
Cut butter into flour until mixture resembles crumbs. (Do this in a food processor if you have one.) Combine egg, salt, water and vinegar and sprinkle over crumbs until mixture holds together (or forms a ball in the food processor.) Chill for 30 minutes. Divide into 4 equal balls, roll each out and place in pie pans. Flute edges. Use what you need and freeze the rest. Pie crusts can be frozen up to 1 month. (Can freeze dough before shaping, but if you've got 4 pie pans, you might as well shape them all at once while you've got the rolling pin out!)

RHUBARB CUSTARD PIE

2 eggs
2²/₃ Tbsps. milk
2 cups sugar
4 Tbsps. flour
¾ tsp. nutmeg
4 cup pink rhubarb, cut up
2 Tbsp. butter
Pastry for 9-inch two-crust
pie

SERVES 6
Beat eggs. Add milk, sugar, flour, and nutmeg and beat well. Mix in rhubarb. Pour into prepared 9-inch pie pan. Dot with butter and top with second crust. Crimp edges; place pie in center of pre-heated oven and bake at 400° for 55–60 minutes.

Roll the circle of your pastry dough so that it will be large enough to extend 2 inches all around the edge of an inverted pie pan. Transfer the pastry to the pan by rolling it around the rolling pin.

SOUR CREAM APPLE PIE

4 cups apples, peeled and
    sliced
½ pint sour cream
4 Tbsp. flour
¾ cup sugar
1 tsp. cinnamon
½ cup brown sugar
1—9" pie shell, unbaked

TOPPING:
¼ cup butter
1 tsp. cinnamon
⅓ cup sugar
⅓ cup flour

SERVES 6–8
Combine apples, sour cream, flour, sugar, cinnamon and brown sugar in bowl; mix well. Pour into pie shell. Combine topping ingredients and sprinkle over apple mixture. Bake at 425° for 15 minutes. Reduce heat and bake for 50 minutes at 350°.

BLUEBERRY CREAM PIE

1—8" pie crust, baked
½ cup sugar
3 Tbsp. cornstarch
¼ tsp. salt
½ cup water
1 Tbsp. lemon juice
2 Tbsp. butter
3 cups blueberries
2 cups whipping cream
2 Tbsp. powdered sugar
½ tsp. vanilla

SERVES 6–8
In medium saucepan, combine sugar, cornstarch and salt. Stir in water and lemon juice; blend well. Cook over medium heat until mixture boils and thickens. Remove from heat and stir in butter, then blueberries. Cool. In separate bowl, beat cream until soft peaks form. Blend in powdered sugar and vanilla; beat until stiff peaks form. Spoon half of whipped cream mixture into cooled, baked crust. Top with blueberry mixture; top with remaining whipped cream. Refrigerate at least 2 hours or until set.

DESERTS

CARAMEL APPLE PIE

CRUST:
3 cups sifted flour
¼ cup sugar
1½ tsp. salt
6 Tbsp. butter
¼ cup oil
1 egg
¼ cup cold water
¼ cup walnuts, chopped

APPLE FILLING:
1 cup sugar
⅓ cup flour
2 tsp. grated lemon peel
¼ cup lemon juice
6 cups pared, sliced apples

CARAMEL SAUCE:
½ lb. (about 28) light colored candy caramels
½ cup evaporated milk or half and half

TOPPING:
1—8 oz. pkg. cream cheese
⅓ cup sugar
1 egg

MAKES 20–24 SERVINGS

To prepare crust, sift flour with sugar and salt. Cut in butter until particles are fine. Blend oil with egg and water. Add to dry ingredients; stir with fork until mixture holds together in a ball. Pat or roll out to cover ungreased jelly roll pan.

To prepare filling, combine ingredients in a saucepan and cook over medium heat, stirring constantly, until thickened. Spread apple filling over pastry.

To prepare caramel sauce, melt caramels with milk over boiling water or in microwave. Drizzle sauce over apples.

To prepare topping, whip ingredients together until light and smooth. Spread cream cheese topping between strips of caramel sauce. Sprinkle with nuts. Bake at 375° for 30–35 minutes. Serve hot or cold.

When separating the yolk from the white of an egg, if you drop a portion of egg yolk into the whites, moisten a cloth with cold water, touch it to the yolk and it will adhere to the cloth.

FRENCH CHOCOLATE PIE

½ cup butter
¾ cup sugar
6–8 Tbsp. cocoa
2 eggs
2 cups Cool Whip
9″ pie shell, baked
Cool Whip to garnish

SERVES 6
Cream butter with sugar. Add cocoa and stir well. Add eggs, one at a time, beating 5 minutes after each addition at high speed. Fold in Cool Whip. Pour into cooled pie shell, and chill until firm, about 2 hours. Serve each slice with a dollop of Cool Whip. Easy and delicious!

SOUR CREAM LEMON PIE

1 cup sugar
¼ cup freshly squeezed lemon juice
Finely grated rind of 1 lemon
3 Tbsp. cornstarch
1 cup milk
3 eggs, separated
1 cup sour cream
1—9″ pie crust, baked
½ cup sugar

SERVES 6–8
Combine 1 cup sugar, lemon juice, grated rind, cornstarch, milk and egg yolks. Cook in a saucepan over medium heat, stirring constantly, until thick. Let mixture cool completely. When cold, stir in sour cream and pour into cooled pie shell. Beat egg whites with ½ cup sugar to stiff peaks. Spread over filling and bake for 10 minutes at 350° until meringue browns. If you like lemon pie, you'll wonder where this recipe has been hiding all your life.

When separating the yolk from the white of an egg, break it into a funnel over a glass. The white will pass through and the yolk will remain in the funnel.

DESERTS

EASY LIVIN' PIE

Graham cracker crust (see
   Index)
1 cup Eagle Brand milk
1—8 oz. container Cool
   Whip
1 small can frozen
   lemonade concentrate

SERVES 6–8
Mix all ingredients and beat well. Pour into prepared graham cracker crust and refrigerate. This is a refreshing light summertime dessert. Vary this by making small individual pies in miniature muffin tins, and serve at a party or luncheon. (Use a regular pastry crust if making individual pies.)

GRANDMA COOK'S PEACHES AND CREAM PIE

1—9″ pie crust, unbaked
5 cups fresh peaches, sliced
¾ cup sugar (or more, if
   peaches not ripe & sweet)
4 Tbsp. flour
¼ tsp. salt
½ tsp. cinnamon
1 cup cream

Place peaches in unbaked pie crust. Mix together sugar, flour, salt, cinnamon and cream. Pour over peaches. Bake in 400° oven for 40 minutes.

PEAR CRISP PIE

6–8 pears, peeled, cored
   and sliced
½ cup sugar
1 tsp. grated lemon peel
3 Tbsp. lemon juice
1—9″ pie shell, unbaked

TOPPING:
½ cup flour
½ cup sugar
½ tsp. ginger
½ tsp. cinnamon
⅓ cup butter

SERVES 6–8
Toss pears with sugar, lemon peel and lemon juice. Turn into pie shell. Combine flour, sugar and spices in a bowl. Cut in butter until mixture resembles crumbs. (Do this in the food processor.) Sprinkle mixture over pears. Bake at 400° for about 45 minutes or until pears are tender. May serve with a dollop of whipped cream on each slice. Vanilla ice cream is good, too. This is a nice change from apple pie.

PINEAPPLE MILLIONAIRE PIE

1—9" graham cracker crust
½ cup powdered sugar
1 stick margarine, softened
1 large egg
¼ tsp. salt
1 tsp. vanilla
1 cup whipping cream
½ cup powdered sugar
1 cup crushed pineapple, drained (can also use apricots)
½ cup nuts, chopped

SERVES 8
Cream sugar and margarine. Add egg, salt and vanilla. Mix until fluffy. Spoon mixture evenly into pie crust. Chill. Whip cream until stiff. Add powdered sugar, pineapple (or apricots) and nuts. Spoon over first layer and chill.

LEONA'S PUMPKIN PIE

9" pie crust, unbaked
1½ cups Libby canned pumpkin
1 cup milk or half and half
1 cup sugar
¼ tsp. Salt
¼ tsp. nutmeg
¼ tsp. cinnamon
2 eggs, beaten
1 Tbsp. butter, melted

SERVES 6–8
Combine all ingredients in medium size mixing bowl and mix well. Pour into pie shell and bake at 375° for 45–60 minutes or until knife inserted in center comes out clean. Serve with sweetened whipped cream.

DESERTS

RASPBERRY CHIFFON PIE

GRAHAM CRACKER CRUST:
1 cellophane-wrapped pkg.
graham crackers (about
20 crackers)
¼ cup sugar
⅓ cup butter, softened

FILLING:
2—10 oz. pkgs. frozen
raspberries (can also
substitute 1 can frozen
raspberry juice concen-
trate, but add an extra
Tbsp. gelatin)
2 Tbsp. lemon juice
1 Tbsp. unflavored gelatin
4 large egg yolks
4–5 large egg whites
6 Tbsp. sugar
1 cup whipping cream

**Whipped cream for
garnish**

SERVES 6–8

Crush graham crackers in a food processor, or place in a plastic bag and
crush finely with a rolling pin. Combine
crumbs, sugar and butter and blend
well. Press crumb mixture into 9-inch
pie plate, covering bottom and sides
evenly. Bake at 375° for 8 minutes and
cool.

To make filling, purée raspberries in
blender or food processor. Pour into
saucepan and add lemon juice. Sprinkle gelatin over the surface and mix
well. Cook mixture over medium heat
until it thickens; about 1 minute after
it starts boiling. Spoon ½ cup of mixture
into egg yolks. Blend well. Return mixture to pan and bring to boil.

Beat egg whites until they form soft
peaks. Add sugar and mix well. In separate bowl beat whipping cream until
it forms peaks. Fold in raspberry mixture and egg whites. Pour into crust.
Refrigerate. Garnish with extra whipped cream.

STRAWBERRY RHUBARB PIE

**Pastry for a 9″ double pie
crust**
3½ cups rhubarb, cut up
1½ cups strawberries,
sliced
1½ cups sugar
⅓ cup flour
1½ Tbsp. butter

SERVES 6

In large bowl, combine rhubarb, straw-
berries, sugar and flour. Mix together.
Pour into uncooked pastry-lined pan.
Dot with butter. Cover top with crust.
Sprinkle with sugar. Bake at 425° for
40–50 minutes.

MRS. Z's STRAWBERRY DELITE

CRUST:
3 egg whites
1 cup sugar
1 tsp. vanilla
18 crushed soda crackers
1 tsp. baking powder
½ cup chopped pecans or walnuts

FILLING:
2 cups Cool Whip
1 box frozen strawberries, drained

SERVES 6
Beat egg whites until stiff, gradually add sugar, then the vanilla. Fold in dry ingredients. Spread in 9-inch pie pan. Bake at 350° for 30 minutes.

Combine Cool Whip and strawberries. Spread over cool crust. Refrigerate 4 hours or more before serving.

APPLE DUMPLINGS

2–2½ cups flour
2 tsp. baking powder
1 tsp. salt
¾ cup shortening
½ cup milk
4–6 Granny Smith apples, peeled, cored and cut into eighths
Sugar, Cinnamon, Nutmeg
Butter

SYRUP:
2 cups sugar
¼ tsp. cinnamon
¼ tsp. nutmeg
2 cups hot water
¼ cup melted butter
Cream

MAKES 12
In a food processor, if you have one, combine flour, baking powder and salt. Cut in shortening until mixture resembles crumbs. Gradually add milk, to make a soft dough. Roll dough into a ⅛-inch thick rectangle. Cut into 5-inch squares. Place 2–4 pieces of apple on each square. Sprinkle each with sugar, cinnamon and nutmeg. Dot each with butter. Moisten edges of dumpling with water, bring corners to center and pinch edges to seal. Place dumplings in a 9×13-inch baking dish which has been lightly greased.

Stir syrup ingredients together to dissolve sugar. Pour syrup over dumplings and bake at 375° for 35–45 minutes or until golden. Serve with cream, if desired.

DESSERTS

BREAD PUDDING

4 eggs
¾ cup sugar
1 tsp. vanilla
2 cups milk
½ cup raisins
½ cup water
8 slices white bread
½ cup sugar
1 tsp. cinnamon

SAUCE:
½ cup butter
1 cup sugar
½ cup + 2 Tbsp. heavy
cream

SERVES 6–8

In a bowl, beat eggs well. Add sugar, vanilla, and milk and beat until well blended. In another bowl, soak the raisins in the water for about 10 minutes. Drain any excess liquid. Add drained raisins to egg/milk mixture. Arrange bread slices in a greased 9×13 pan. Don't worry about making them fit. . . squeeze them in or overlap. Cover bread with egg/milk/raisin mixture. Let set a few minutes for bread to soak up the liquid. Mix sugar and cinnamon and sprinkle on top. Bake at 350° for 30 minutes.

While pudding is cooking, prepare the sauce by combining butter and sugar in a saucepan. Bring to a boil and cook for 10 minutes, stirring constantly. Add cream and return to stove. Simmer 8–10 minutes, stirring frequently.

Cut pudding in squares to serve and ladle warm sauce over each serving.

To prevent soggy pie crust in an unbaked pie shell, brush the crust with a thin coating of egg white. Especially good for fruit pies.

SARAH'S APPLE STRUDEL

1 cup sugar
⅓ cup water
8 tart apples, peeled,
  cored, thinly sliced
½ cup slivered almonds,
  toasted (optional)
½ cup currants or raisins
1 Tbsp. lemon juice
1½ tsp. ground cinnamon
Pinch ground cloves
½ tsp. allspice
Pinch nutmeg
24 sheets phyllo dough,
  thawed
1¼ cups butter, melted

GLAZE:
3 Tbsp. butter, melted
1 cup powdered sugar
Milk

Combine water and sugar in saucepan, bring to a boil, add apples and simmer 10 minutes. Combine apples, ½ cup almonds, currants, lemon juice, cinnamon, cloves, allspice and nutmeg in large bowl and mix well. Place the 24 sheets of phyllo between 2 pieces of wax paper. Cover with damp tea towel. Place one sheet of phyllo on your work area and brush with butter. Fold in half lengthwise and spread 1 heaping tablespoon of the apple filling along short end about 1½ inches from the edge. Fold side edges ½ inch over filling. Roll up strudel, tucking in edges as you roll. Place seam side down on buttered jelly roll pan. Repeat with other 23 sheets of phyllo. Brush top and sides with melted butter. Bake until golden brown, in 350° oven for about 20–25 minutes. Sprinkle with powdered sugar or drizzle with glaze while still slightly warm. Can be served with ice cream or whipped cream.

To prepare glaze, combine butter and powdered sugar in small bowl; add enough milk to make a glaze consistency.

DESSERTS

CHOCOLATE CHEESECAKE

**CHOCOLATE CRUMB
    CRUST:**
8½ oz. chocolate wafer
    cookies, finely ground
Pinch salt
Pinch ground cinnamon
⅓ cup butter, melted

CHEESECAKE:
12 oz. semisweet
    chocolate
2 Tbsp. butter
1½ lbs. cream cheese, at
    room temperature
1½ cups whipping cream
1 tsp. vanilla
1 cup sugar
3 large eggs
2 Tbsp. cocoa powder
Powdered sugar

**Fresh strawberries to gar-
    nish, if desired**

SERVES 6–8
Mix cookie crumbs, salt and cinnamon in medium bowl. Drizzle melted butter over crumb mixture and toss with fork until darkened and uniform. Press crumb mixture evenly on sides and bottom of buttered springform pan or pie dish. Refrigerate 30 minutes before adding cheesecake.

Melt chocolate and butter in double boiler or microwave. Stir until smooth. In separate bowl, beat softened cream cheese until smooth. Gradually beat in chocolate mixture; continue to beat until smooth and uniform in color. Continue beating, adding cream, vanilla and sugar. Add eggs, beating well after each. Sprinkle cocoa powder over batter and beat in at low speed. Pour batter into cold crumb crust; spread smooth. Bake at 350° for 30 minutes, reduce temperature to 325° and continue baking 30 minutes longer. Turn oven off. Let cake stand in oven with door ajar 30 minutes. Completely cool before removing from springform pan. Refrigerate cake, uncovered, overnight or at least 8 hours. Cover loosely with plastic wrap and refrigerate until ready to serve. Before serving, dust powdered sugar lightly over cake. Garnish with strawberries, if desired.

NEW YORK CHEESECAKE

CRUST:
1 cup flour
¼ cup sugar
1 tsp. grated lemon peel
½ tsp. vanilla
1 egg yolk
¼ cup butter, softened

FILLING:
5—8 oz. pkgs. cream
  cheese, softened
1¾ cups sugar
3 Tbsp. flour
2 tsp. grated lemon peel
1½ tsp. grated orange
  peel
¼ tsp. vanilla extract
5 eggs
2 egg yolks
¼ cup cream

PINEAPPLE GLAZE:
2 Tbsp. sugar
4 tsp. cornstarch
2—8¼ oz. cans crushed
  pineapple
2 Tbsp. lemon juice
2 drops yellow food color

SERVES 15–20

In medium bowl, combine flour, sugar, lemon peel and vanilla. Blend in yolk and butter. Mix with fingers until smooth. Dough can be rolled to cover bottom and sides of springform pan or 9×13-inch pan. Bake in 400° oven for 6–8 minutes or until golden. Cool.

To prepare filling, blend cheese, sugar, flour, peels and vanilla at high speed in large mixer bowl. Beat in eggs and yolks, one at a time, until smooth. Beat in cream. Pour into pan. Bake at 500° for 10 minutes; lower oven temperature to 250° and bake 1 hour longer. Remove to rack to cool for two hours.

To make glaze, combine sugar and cornstarch in small saucepan. Stir in remaining ingredients. Boil 1 minute or until thickened. Cool. Spread surface of cheese cake with glaze; refrigerate until well chilled—3 hours or overnight.

Other fruit glazes can be made using blueberries or strawberries. Cut in half the amount of lemon peel and orange peel in the cheese cake if using other toppings.

Also good glazed with 1½ cups of sour cream mixed with 3 tablespoons of sugar and ½ teaspoon vanilla.

DESSERTS

ELLEN'S CHERRY COBBLER

¼ cup butter
1 cup sugar
1 cup flour
2 tsp. baking powder
$^1/_8$ tsp. salt
½ cup milk
1 can sour red cherries
  with juice

SERVES 4–6

Cream ½ cup sugar with the butter. Blend in flour, baking powder and salt. Add milk and mix well. Spread in greased 8×8-inch pan. Evenly place cherries over top and pour juice over cherries and batter. Sprinkle with ½ cup sugar. Bake at 375° for 45 minutes or until brown. Great warm with ice cream!

CREAM PUFF DESSERT

1 stick margarine
1 cup water
1 cup flour
4 eggs
1 large box instant vanilla
  pudding
3 cups milk
1—8 oz. pkg. cream
  cheese, softened
1—8 oz. carton Cool Whip
Chocolate syrup

SERVES 12

Boil together the margarine and water. Add flour and mix well. Cool slightly and stir in eggs, 1 at a time. Mix well and spread into a 9×13-inch greased pan. Bake at 400° for 30 minutes. Cool completely.

In a large bowl, mix pudding, milk and cream cheese. Beat until lumps disappear. Pour into cream puff crust. Spread Cool Whip on top of pudding and drizzle syrup on top. Refrigerate. This keeps well for days.

FOUR FRUIT PIE

CRUST:
1 cup flour
½ cup nuts, chopped
½ cup butter

TOPPING:
8 oz. cream cheese
¼ cup sugar
1 Tbsp. milk

FRUIT:
1 can cherry pie filling
2–3 bananas
1 can mandarin oranges,
    drained, reserve juice
1 can pineapple chunks,
    drained, reserve juice

GLAZE:
½ cup sugar
2 Tbsp. cornstarch
½ cup orange juice
¼ cup juice from fruit
¼ cup lemon juice

SERVES 6–8

Mix crust ingredients and spread in a 12-inch pizza pan. Bake 15 minutes at 350°.

Mix together topping ingredients and beat until creamy. Spread on cooled crust.

Starting on the outside edge of the prepared crust, make a ring of cherry pie filling, then add a ring of each fruit, finishing with cherry pie filling in the middle.

In a saucepan, combine the glaze ingredients and cook until thick and smooth. Cool; pour over all fruit except cherry pie filling.

Chill at least two hours before serving. This is a **beautiful** dessert. . .almost too pretty to eat. You'll be delighted that it tastes as good as it looks!

Try microwaving puddings, rather than cooking them in the double boiler. Microwave on high for 2 minutes, turn dish and stir, microwave another 2 minutes. Turn dish and stir. Microwave 1–3 more minutes, depending on your microwave.

DESSERTS

SUMMERTIME LEMON DESSERT

CRUST:
15–20 graham crackers
½ cup butter

FILLING:
2—13 oz. cans sweetened
  condensed milk
Juice of 4 lemons
Couple drops yellow food
  coloring

TOPPING:
½ pint whipping cream,
  whipped
¼ cup granulated sugar
¼ tsp. almond extract
½ tsp. vanilla
1 cup pecans, chopped

SERVES 12

To make crust, roll graham crackers until fine. Combine cracker crumbs with melted butter and press into a 9×13-inch pan.

To make filling, combine condensed milk with the lemon juice and food coloring. Spread mixture over crust.

To prepare topping, beat together whipping cream, sugar, almond extract and vanilla. Spread over filling. Sprinkle with pecans. Refrigerate 24 hours.

LEMON FLUFF

4 eggs, separated
⅔ cup sugar
1 Tbsp. lemon rind, grated
¼ cup lemon juice (fresh
  if possible)
⅛ tsp. salt
1 cup whipping cream,
  whipped
1 cup vanilla wafers,
  crushed

SERVES 6–8

Beat egg yolks until thick and lemon-colored. Gradually add sugar, beating well after each addition. Add rind, juice and salt; blend well. Cook in a double boiler over hot water, stirring constantly until thickened. Remove from heat and cool. Beat egg whites until stiff, then fold into lemon mixture. Fold in whipped cream. Spread ¾ cup crumbs in bottom of an 8-inch square dish. Spoon lemon mixture on top; sprinkle with remaining crumbs. Freeze until firm.

PEACH-BLUEBERRY SHORTCAKE

¼ cup sugar
1 tsp. cinnamon
1—10 oz. can refrigerated flaky biscuits
2 Tbsp. butter, melted
4 peaches, sliced
1 cup fresh blueberries
½ cup sugar
1—8 oz. container whipped topping

SERVES 4–6

In small bowl, combine ¼ cup sugar and cinnamon. Separate each biscuit into 2 layers. Dip one side in melted butter then in the sugar-cinnamon mixture. On greased cookie sheet arrange biscuit pieces with sugared side up, overlapping edges to form a ring, placing one biscuit in center. Repeat with remaining biscuits to form another circle. Bake at 375° for 12–14 minutes or until biscuits are golden brown. While biscuits are baking, combine peaches, blueberries and ½ cup sugar. To assemble shortcake, place 1 biscuit circle on serving plate; spoon half of peach-berry mixture over biscuit layer. Top with half of the whipped topping. Repeat with remaining biscuit circle, fruit and whipped topping.

QUICK PEACH COBBLER

6 Tbsp. butter
1 cup sugar
¾ cup flour
1 tsp. baking powder
⅛ tsp. salt
¾ cup milk
4 cups sliced peaches
1-1½ cups sugar

SERVES 4–6

Melt 6 tablespoons butter in a 9x13-inch casserole. Combine sugar, flour, baking powder and salt. Stir in milk and mix well. Pour batter over butter in casserole, but do not mix together. Combine peaches and sugar, then spoon them over the batter and bake at 350° for 1 hour. You can't beat this for a fast and easy dessert.

DESSERTS

PETITE CHEESECAKES

2—8 oz. pkgs. cream
cheese, softened
¾ cup sugar
2 eggs
2 Tbsp. lemon juice
1 tsp. vanilla
24 vanilla wafers
1—12 oz. can cherry pie
filling

MAKES 2 DOZEN
Beat cream cheese, sugar, eggs, lemon juice and vanilla until light. Line muffin tins with paper liners. Place a vanilla wafer in bottom of each liner, then fill ⅔ full with cream cheese mixture. Bake at 375° for 15–20 minutes. Cool. Top each with a dollop of cherry pie filling and chill. Baked cheesecakes can be frozen before adding the cherry pie filling. This is a really pretty dessert, just right for a Christmas coffee or large dinner party.

RASPBERRIES VICTOR

2 pints fresh raspberries
(strawberries will work
too)
1 quart half and half
1—1" piece vanilla bean
(may substitute 1 tsp.
vanilla extract)
½ cup sugar
5 egg yolks

SERVES 6–8
In top of double boiler, combine half and half, vanilla bean (split, do not scrape) and sugar. Heat to boiling, then remove from heat. Remove vanilla bean. In a mixing bowl, beat egg yolks until they are thick and lemon-colored. Spoon ¼–½ cup hot milk mixture into the yolks, blending well. Then return egg yolks to hot milk. Stir to blend. Return mixture to double boiler, cooking and stirring to thicken, about 5 minutes. When thick, cool and refrigerate. (If using vanilla extract, add 1 teaspoon here.) Just before serving, divide fresh berries among 6–8 sherbet glasses. Cover with sauce. An easy and elegant dessert!

PINE CLIFF STRAWBERRIES

¾ cup sugar
½ cup whipping cream
¼ cup light corn syrup
2 Tbsp. butter
½ cup chopped Heath candy bars (about 1—1⅛ oz. double bar)
1 quart fresh strawberries, washed, hulled, and halved if too big
1 cup sour cream

SERVES 6

In a saucepan, combine sugar, cream, corn syrup and butter. Bring to a boil and cook for 3 minutes, stirring occasionally. Remove from heat and add candy. Stir until most of the candy is dissolved. (Be sure to chop the candy well. If you don't, there will be big pieces of unmelted toffee in the mixture.) Serve strawberries in sherbet glasses, topped with a dollop of sour cream, and drizzled with warm sauce. This is a heavenly way to eat strawberries. . .easy, elegant, delectable!

PINOCHLE CLUB STRAWBERRY DESSERT

CRUST:
1½ cups graham cracker crumbs
⅓ cup butter
¼ cup sugar

FILLING:
3 cups miniature marshmallows
½ cup orange juice
2 cups whipping cream, whipped
¼ cup sugar
¼ tsp. almond extract
1 quart strawberries, sliced

SERVES 12

Combine crust ingredients in small bowl. Press in bottom of 9×13-inch pan; refrigerate. In medium saucepan, combine marshmallows and orange juice; cook over low heat until marshmallows are melted, stirring constantly. Cool. Whip cream and add sugar and almond extract. Fold in marshmallow mixture. Spoon half of whipped cream mixture over crust. Spoon strawberries evenly over whipped cream mixture; top with remaining whipped cream. Refrigerate several hours before serving. Cut into squares to serve; garnish with whole berries.

DESSERTS

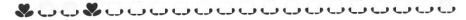

SWEET TEMPTATION

1½ cups graham cracker
crumbs
¼ cup sugar
⅓ cup butter, melted
1—8 oz. pkg. cream
cheese, softened
¼ cup sugar
2 Tbsp. milk
1½ cups Cool Whip
2 pints fresh strawberries,
washed and halved or
4 bananas, sliced
2—3⅛ oz. pkgs. vanilla
flavor instant pudding
and pie filling
3½ cups cold milk
2 cups Cool Whip

SERVES 12–15
Combine crumbs, sugar and melted
butter. Press firmly into a 9×13-inch
pan. Chill. Beat cream cheese with
sugar and milk until smooth. Stir in 1½
cups Cool Whip. Spread over crust. Arrange fruit over cream cheese layer.
Add cold milk to pudding mix and prepare as directed on the package. Pour
over fruit. Chill several hours or overnight. Before serving, spread remaining Cool Whip on top. Garnish with extra strawberries. This is another one of
those good desserts that is easy to
make and will feed a crowd.

SWEDISH CREAM

1 envelope unflavored
gelatin
1 cup whipping cream
1 cup sugar
1 cup sour cream
½ tsp. vanilla
Strawberries or raspberries, slightly sweetened

SERVES 6
In a saucepan, sprinkle gelatin on
whipping cream to soften; add sugar.
Stir over low heat until sugar and gelatin are dissolved. Remove from heat
and chill until mixture starts to thicken.
Add sour cream and vanilla, blending
well. Pour into sherbet glasses and
chill until set. Serve topped with slightly sweetened fresh fruit. This is an
easy, elegant dessert.

ALMOND ROCA

4½ cups blanched
   almonds, finely chopped
1¾ cups sugar
⅓ cup light corn syrup
¼ cup water
1 cup butter

CHOCOLATE GLAZE:
3 oz. semi sweet
   chocolate
3 oz. unsweetened
   chocolate
6 Tbsp. butter
4½ tsp. light corn syrup

MAKES 12 DOZEN PIECES
In 375° oven toast chopped almonds on a jelly-roll pan until lightly browned, about 30 minutes, stirring occasionally. Watch carefully to avoid burning.

In heavy 2-quart saucepan, over medium heat, combine sugar, corn syrup and water. Bring to a boil. Stir in butter. Continue to simmer, stirring frequently, until temperature on candy thermometer reaches 300° or hard-crack stage (when small amount of mixture dropped into ice water forms hard ball); about 20 minutes.

Remove from heat; stir in 1½ cups chopped and toasted almonds. Immediately pour mixture evenly onto ungreased jelly-roll pan. Cool slightly; about 3 minutes. Cut into 1x1½-inch pieces. Cool candy completely; remove from pan, then break into squares along cut lines.

To prepare chocolate glaze: melt all ingredients in small saucepan on stove or in bowl in the microwave. With wooden spoon beat mixture until cool—about 1½ minutes.

Dip each candy piece in chocolate mixture to coat; scrape excess. Roll in chopped almonds. Lay on wax paper in single layer. Refrigerate until chocolate is set.

 Lime deposits can be removed from your teakettle by heating vinegar in it and letting it stand overnight. Rinse the next day.

DESSERTS

PARTY TIME BANANA SPLIT

CHOCOLATE SAUCE:
2 cups powdered sugar
1—12 oz. can evaporated milk
½ cup butter
¾ cup semi-sweet chocolate chips

24 creme-filled chocolate sandwich cookies, finely crushed
¼ cup margarine
3 bananas, sliced
½ gallon vanilla ice cream
1—8 oz. can crushed pineapple, drained
Whipped cream
Pecans, chopped
Maraschino cherries

Combine all sauce ingredients in a saucepan. Bring to boil and cook 8 minutes, stirring constantly. Cool.

Combine cookie crumb and margarine and mix well. Press into a 9×13-inch glass dish. Arrange sliced bananas over crumbs. Spoon half of the ice cream over bananas. Pour half of cooled chocolate sauce over ice cream layer; freeze until firm. Spoon remaining ice cream over sauce layer, then cover with pineapple. Sprinkle with pecan pieces, and marschino cherry halves. Cover and freeze until firm. Take out of the freezer a little before serving. Cut into squares. Serve with some whipped cream and additional chocolate sauce on top.

An easy dessert for children's party that can be done ahead of time.

CARAMEL ICE BOX PIE

1—9″ graham cracker crust (see Index)
1—14 oz. can sweetened, condensed milk
1 large banana, peeled and sliced
1—9 oz. carton frozen whipped topping
2 Heath bars, chilled and crushed

SERVES 6
Pour condensed milk into large bowl and microwave on high until caramelized, about 5–8 minutes (depending on your microwave), stirring after three minutes. Can also simmer opened can in a pan of water on stove top for 2–3 hours. Cool. Place sliced bananas in pie crust. Spread caramelized milk over bananas. Spoon whipped topping on top, and sprinkle crushed Heath bars over top. Refrigerate until ready to serve.

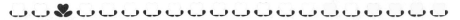

CHARLIE'S CHRISTMAS DATE CANDY

2 cups sugar
1 cup milk
3 Tbsp. butter
1 cup chopped dates
1 cup pecan halves

Cook sugar, milk and butter in a saucepan to the soft ball stage, 238° on your candy thermometer, stirring to prevent scorching. Add dates and cook over low heat until the dates dissolve, stirring constantly. Remove from heat, and beat until creamy. Pour into a buttered pan and cut into squares when cool.

Charlie has made this candy every Christmas for years, and now that he can count grandkids among his biggest fans he has to double the recipe!

PECAN CLUSTERS

1—7 oz. jar marshmallow
   creme
1½ pounds Hershey's milk
   chocolate kisses
5 cups sugar
1—13 oz. can evaporated
   milk
½ cup butter
6 cups pecans, chopped

MAKES 12 DOZEN CLUSTERS
Place marshmallow creme and kisses in a large bowl; set aside. Combine sugar, milk and butter in a saucepan. Boil mixture to a high point; let boil 8 minutes or to soft ball stage. Pour over marshmallow creme and kisses; blend well. Add pecans and mix. Drop by teaspoonful on waxed paper.

DESSERTS

MEXICAN FLAN

½ cup sugar
6 eggs
6 Tbsp. sugar
2 cups milk
1 tsp. vanilla
½ tsp. salt
Boiling water

SERVES 6–8
Place ½ cup sugar in a heavy skillet; cook over medium heat until sugar melts and forms a light brown caramel syrup. Stir well. Immediately pour syrup into a warm 8-inch round baking pan or dish. Rotate dish quickly to cover the bottom with syrup. (Pan can be warmed by setting it in warm water while making caramel.) Set aside.

In a mixing bowl, beat eggs with sugar. Add milk, vanilla and salt, blending well. Pour mixture into prepared pan, then set it in a shallow pan. Pour boiling water into outside pan to the depth of ½ inch. Bake at 350° for 35–45 minutes, or until sharp knife inserted in center comes out clean. Let custard cool, then refrigerate.

To serve, loosen the custard by running a knife around the outside edge of dish. Invert on a round serving plate, shaking gently to release. Cut custard in wedges, spooning caramel sauce on top. This light dessert is really easy to prepare. . .the perfect finishing touch to a Mexican food dinner.

MICROWAVE FUDGE

1 lb. confectioners sugar
½ cup cocoa
¼ cup milk
½ cup butter, melted
1 Tbsp. vanilla
½ cup pecans, chopped

Blend sugar and cocoa in 3-quart bowl. Add milk and butter. DO NOT STIR. Microwave at High setting for 2 minutes; then stir well. Add vanilla and nuts. Stir until blended. Pour into a buttered 8×8-inch dish. Refrigerate until set, then cut into squares.

ᵕ ᵕ

QUICK NUT CANDIES

1—6 oz. pkg. chocolate
   chips
1—12 oz. pkg. butter-
   scotch chips
1 cup salted peanuts
   (½ lb.)

MAKES 2 DOZEN
Combine chocolate and butterscotch chips in a 2-quart dish. Microwave on High 3–4 minutes. Stir to blend. (Can also melt chips in a saucepan over medium-low heat.) Stir in nuts. Drop on waxed paper by teaspoon. Let harden.

CHOCOLATE-PEANUT BUTTER TREATS

1 cellophane pkg. graham
   crackers, crushed
   (2 cups)
2 sticks butter, softened
1 lb. powdered sugar
1 cup peanut butter
10 plain Hershey bars,
   melted

Mix first four ingredients. A food processor works well for this. Press into a 9×13-inch pan. Pour melted Hershey bars over top, spreading evenly with a knife. Put in refrigerator until set, then cut into bite-sized pieces.

CANDIED POPCORN

4 quarts popcorn, popped
2 cups dry roasted nuts
1¼ cups sugar
⅔ cup margarine
⅔ cup dark Karo syrup
1 tsp. vanilla
½ tsp. soda

Melt margarine, sugar and Karo in a saucepan. Bring to a boil over medium heat, and boil for 5 minutes. Remove from heat and stir in vanilla and soda. Have popcorn and nuts spread out on a jelly-roll pan. Pour hot mixture over popcorn and nuts and bake for 1 hour at 250°. Stir every 10–15 minutes so that everything gets coated evenly. Stir again when you remove it from the oven.

DESSERTS

PEANUT BUTTER POPCORN BALLS

10 cups popped popcorn
12 caramels
3 Tbsp. butter
24 large marshmallows
⅓ cup peanut butter

MAKES 15 BALLS

Unwrap caramels; place in glass bowl and add butter. Microwave on High, uncovered, 1½ minutes or until caramels are melted, stirring once. Add marshmallows. Microwave on High 60 seconds or until melted, stirring once. Microwave a little longer if necessary. (This can be done in a saucepan on the stove.) Stir in peanut butter. Pour over popped corn and mix lightly until evenly coated. With buttered hands, form into balls.

GRAND MARNIER

¾ cup water
¾ cup sugar
8 egg yolks
⅓ cup Grand Marnier
  liqueur
1 cup whipping cream

Combine water and sugar in small saucepan. Bring to boil without stirring for exactly 5 minutes. Meanwhile beat egg yolks in bowl until thick. While continuing to beat, slowly drizzle hot syrup into yolks. Beat until cool. Add Grand Marnier. Beat whipping cream until thick but not stiff. Fold into egg and syrup mixture. Pour into dessert glasses; freeze. Take out of freezer 10 minutes before serving. A fun dessert for a special occasion.

BARBARA'S VANILLA ICE CREAM

3 eggs
2 cups sugar
4 cups heavy cream
2–3 Tbsp. vanilla
¼ tsp. salt
5–6 cups milk

MAKES 1 GALLON

Beat eggs, add sugar and beat 3–4 minutes. Add cream, vanilla, and salt. Mix well. Pour into freezer can and add milk to the fill line. Mix well, then proceed with the freezing process.

ပပပပပပပပပပပပပပပပပပပပပပ

EILEEN'S FAMOUS CHOCOLATE ICE CREAM

6 junket tablets
¼ cup cold water
2⅔ cups sugar
¾ cup cocoa
2 quarts fresh milk (not evaporated)
2⅔ cups whipping cream

MAKES 1 GALLON
Dissolve junket tablets in water. In a large saucepan, combine sugar and cocoa. Add milk slowly to make a smooth paste (you don't want any lumps). Add whipping cream and heat ingredients to 110°. Stir in dissolved junket quickly. Pour into ice cream freezer container and **let stand undisturbed for 10 minutes**. (This is a good time to pack ice and salt around the freezer container.) Proceed with the freezing process. This is an old recipe, and though it takes a little bit of extra time and effort, the results will make you as famous as Eileen for her homemade chocolate ice cream.

APRICOT-LEMON SHERBET

1—3 oz. pkg. lemon gelatin
2 cups boiling water
1 cup sugar
1—17 oz. can apricot halves
1 cup whipping cream

SERVES 8–10
Dissolve gelatin in boiling water. Add sugar and stir to dissolve. Cool. Puree apricots (with juice) in a food processor or blender. Add to gelatin mixture. Stir in whipping cream and combine well. Pour into an 8-inch square pan and freeze until nearly firm. Turn mixture into a bowl and beat with mixer (or in a food processor) until fluffy and smooth. DO NOT LET MIXTURE MELT. Return to pan and freeze until firm. Serve in sherbet glasses, garnished with a sprig of fresh mint. This light, refreshing dessert is perfect in the summer.

DESSERTS

PEPPERMINT ICE CREAM

6 eggs, beaten until foamy
1—14 oz. can Eagle Brand
   milk
1½ cups sugar
2 quarts half and half
1 tsp. vanilla
1½ cups crushed pepper-
   mint candies

MAKES 1 GALLON
Mix together all ingredients except peppermint candies. Proceed with freezing process until half frozen, then add peppermint. Continue freezing until hard.

JAN'S STRAWBERRY ICE CREAM

2—6 oz. pkgs. strawberry
   jello (or flavor to match
   fruit being used)
2 cups boiling water
2⅓ cups sugar
4 eggs
3 cups cream and 3 cups
   milk OR 6 cups half and
   half
2 tsp. vanilla
¼ tsp. salt
3–4 cups fresh straw-
   berries, crushed (or
   other fruit)

MAKES 1 GALLON
Add jello to boiling water and stir to dissolve. Add sugar and stir well. Combine all ingredients in 4-quart ice cream freezer container. Proceed to freeze.

MEXICAN CHOCOLATE ICE CREAM

3 eggs
1 cup sugar
2 quarts half-and-half
1—16 oz. can chocolate
   syrup
½ tsp. ground cinnamon
1 Tbsp. vanilla
¼ tsp. almond extract

MAKES 1 GALLON
Beat eggs at medium speed until frothy. Gradually add sugar, beating until thick. Heat half and half in a 3-qt. saucepan over low heat until hot. Gradually stir about one-fourth of hot mixture into eggs; add to remaining hot mixture, stirring constantly. Cook over low heat until mixture is slightly thickened and reaches 165°, stirring constantly. Remove from heat, and stir in chocolate syrup and remaining ingredients. Cool in refrigerator. Pour into freezer can and proceed with the freezing process.

Kids' Food

KIDS' FOOD

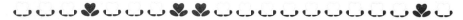

SUNRISE JUICE

Apricot juice
Cranberry juice

Fill a tall glass ⅓ full of apricot juice. Tilt glass and slowly add cranberry juice.

A BERRY GOOD COOLER

1¼ cups milk
1 Tbsp. sugar or honey
½ cup strawberries, raspberries, or blueberries
¼ cup dry milk powder or 2 Tbsp. powdered cream

SERVES 2
Blend all ingredients in blender or food processor until smooth. If using a blender add a few ice cubes for a coo-o-o-l drink.

APE SHAKE

1 cup milk
½ cup banana or strawberry yogurt
1 Tbsp. honey
1 banana, cut into chunks

MAKES 1 LARGE SHAKE
Blend all ingredients in blender or food processor until smooth. You'll go ape.

MATT'S PEANUTTY SHAKE

1 pint vanilla ice cream
½ cup creamy peanut butter
2 cups milk
1½ tsp. vanilla or ¼ cup chocolate syrup

SERVES 2
Blend all ingredients together in blender or food processor. Great when the gang drops in.

SHERBET COOLERS

1 pint sherbet, any flavor
1 quart milk
¼ tsp. vanilla

SERVES 6
Combine all ingredients in blender and whirl until smooth. Use green (lime) sherbet for St. Patrick's day and call them Shamrock Shakes.

D & J JUICE

½ cup orange juice concentrate
3 cups milk
2–3 Tbsp. sugar
1–2 eggs
5–8 ice cubes

MAKES 4 GLASSES
Mix all ingredients in a blender and serve. Yummy!

ANDY'S FAVORITE BREAKFAST DRINK

1—6 oz. can frozen orange juice concentrate
1—10 oz. pkg. frozen strawberries
¾ cup water
1 tsp. lemon juice
2–3 ice cubes

MAKES 4 SERVINGS
Blend all ingredients in blender or food processor until slushy. Loaded with Vitamin C!!

PINEAPPLE UPSIDE DOWN SHAKE

2 scoops vanilla ice cream
½ cup milk
1 small can pineapple chunks and juice
¼ tsp. cinnamon
Maraschino cherry

SERVES 2
Place all ingredients except the cherry in a blender. Cover and blend on medium speed until well blended. Pour into glasses and top with cherry.

KIDS' FOOD

STATE FAIR FROZEN CHOCOLATE BANANAS

⅓ cup chopped peanuts
  or granola
½ cup chocolate chips
1 large banana

Melt chocolate chips in a bowl in the microwave or in a small saucepan over low heat. Cut the banana into thirds and push a wooden stick into the end of each piece. Roll the banana in the melted chocolate or frost it with a knife. Roll in peanuts or granola and place on wax paper. Freeze. Wrap in foil to keep longer.

JENNA'S MAGIC SQUARES

2 pkgs. unflavored gelatin
1—6 oz. pkg. jello, any
  flavor
2½ cups water
¼ cup sugar or use arti-
  ficial sweetener

Dissolve unflavored gelatin in 1 cup of **cold** water. Set aside. In a saucepan, bring 1 cup of water to a boil and add jello and sugar. After bringing to a boil, remove from heat immediately. Add the gelatin and cold water mixture. Stir and add ½ cup cold water. Pour into a greased pan and set in the refrigerator until solid—about 2 hours. Cut into squares or use cookie cutters for special shapes. Store in an airtight container in the refrigerator. Great snack or birthday treat!

MELON BOAT

Half of a cantaloupe
Vanilla ice cream

Clean out half of a cantaloupe and fill with a couple of scoops of ice cream. Mom and Dad love this, too!

PEANUT BUTTER TOAST

Peanut butter
Bread

Toast a piece of bread and immediately spread with peanut butter. Mmmm good!

ROASTED PUMPKIN SEEDS

2 cups pumpkin seeds,
**   pull off the strands but**
**   do not wash**
1½ Tbsp. oil
1½ tsp. salt

Mix all ingredients well in a bowl and spread over a cookie sheet. Bake at 250° for 45–60 minutes. Stir occasionally. Eat with hot cider after a hard night of trick or treating.

STUFFED APPLE

Apple
Peanut butter
Raisins

Core a washed apple. Mix peanut butter with raisins and stuff the apple with the peanut butter mixture. Can slice the apple and serve, or eat it whole. Enjoy!

BABOON BUTTER

½ cup peanut butter
1 large banana
¼ tsp. cinnamon
1 Tbsp. shredded coconut
¼–½ cup raisins, currants
**   or chopped dates**

Mash together the peanut butter and bananas in a bowl with a fork. Add cinnamon, dried fruit and coconut. Stir to blend. Spread on graham crackers or your favorite bread.

 Use Lifesaver candies for candle holders for the birthday cake at a children's party.

KIDS' FOOD

A RITZY CRACKER

Ritz crackers
Cheese Whiz spread
Raisins
Celery, chopped fine
Carrots, chopped fine

Spread crackers with cheese. Top with raisins, celery and carrots.

THE COOKBOOK KIDS' SNACK

Bread
Cool Whip
Slices of processed
American cheese

Spread a slice of bread generously with Cool Whip. Top with 1½ slices of cheese.

RAISIN PEANUT BUTTER SPREAD

½ cup peanut butter
½ cup cream cheese
1 Tbsp. honey
¼ cup raisins
1 Tbsp. orange juice

With fork, mash peanut butter and cream cheese together in mixing bowl. Add honey, raisins, and orange juice. Mix well. Good spread on graham crackers, raisin bread, banana bread or whole wheat bread.

WILLIE'S MONKEY BUSINESS

1 banana
2 Tbsp. peanut butter

In a bowl, mash the banana with the peanut butter. Spread on bread or crackers. So good and nutritious.

 Wash out lunchboxes with a vinegar-water solution to prevent mold from forming, and to freshen the interior.

MOTHER'S DAY SURPRISE MUFFINS

1¾ cups flour
¼ cup sugar
2½ tsp. baking powder
¾ tsp. salt
1 egg
¾ tsp. salt
1 egg
¾ cup milk
⅓ cup cooking oil
Favorite jelly or jam

Preheat oven to 400°. Grease 12 muffin cups or line with paper baking cups. Combine flour, sugar, baking powder and salt in a medium mixing bowl. Stir well with spoon to mix. In a separate bowl or jar combine egg, milk and oil. Beat with fork until well mixed. Pour the milk mixture over the flour and mix with spoon just until all the flour is wet. Don't overmix. Fill each cup ⅓ full with batter. Top with heaping teaspoon of jelly or jam. Add enough batter to make cup ⅔ full. Bake until golden, about 20 minutes. Surprise mom with these!

ERIN'S QUIKSCUITS

3 cups flour
2 Tbsp. baking powder
1 tsp. ground coriander
1 tsp. salt
⅓ cup butter-flavor Crisco
1½ cups milk
⅓ cup honey
1 Tbsp. vanilla

MAKES 1 DOZEN LARGE BISCUITS
Mix together the dry ingredients. Cut in Crisco until mixture resembles crumbs. Slowly add milk, honey and vanilla. Mix to a soft dough. Drop by heaping teaspoonfuls on a lightly greased cookie sheet. Bake at 425° for about 12 minutes or until lightly browned. These biscuits are easy for kids to mix, and their slightly sweet taste makes them a natural hit with kids. For a variation, increase honey to ½ cup, sprinkle with cinnamon and sugar, and use for a fruit cobbler topping. Also, you can use this recipe to top leftover meat and vegetables for pot pie simply by decreasing the honey to ¼ cup.

Use a divider from an ice tray to cut biscuits in a hurry. Shape dough to conform with size of divider and cut. After baking, biscuits will separate at dividing lines.

249

KIDS' FOOD

SUNSHINE SALAD

1—3 oz. pkg. orange Jello
1 small can crushed
  pineapple
2 carrots, grated

SERVES 4–6
Drain pineapple well and save the juice. Make Jello according to package directions, using reserved pineapple juice as a part of the water. Stir in crushed pineapple and grated carrots. Chill until firm. Serve on a bed of lettuce.

WESLEY RABBIT SALAD

1—3 oz. pkg, cream cheese
⅓ cup grated carrot
3 parsley sprigs
Spinach leaves
1—8 oz. can pineapple tidbits, drained

SERVES 3
Grate carrot directly onto a paper towel, and pat dry with another paper towel. Divide cream cheese into three parts. With hands, shape each part to resemble a carrot, 3 inches long. Roll in grated carrot, coating completely. Insert a parsley sprig in top of each. Serve on spinach leaves and garnish with pineapple tidbits. Easy, fun, delicious!

TANYA'S PIZZAS

1 pkg. refrigerator
  biscuits, flaky are good
Pizza sauce
Mozzarella cheese, grated
Favorite topping: Pepperoni, Italian sausage, Hamburger, Mushrooms, Green pepper, Sliced olives

Preheat oven to 425° and grease a cookie sheet. Roll out each biscuit on a floured surface to make a 4-inch circle. Place on baking sheet. Spoon 1½ tablespoons of sauce onto each biscuit and spread to cover biscuit. Sprinkle with cheese. Add favorite topping. Bake for about 10 minutes.

BABYSITTER'S CHICKEN CASSEROLE

1—7 oz. pkg. uncooked
  macaroni
2 cans cream of
  mushroom soup
1 small onion, grated
2 cups cooked chicken,
  diced
2 cups cream or chicken
  broth
½ lb. diced Velveeta
  cheese
Salt & pepper

SERVES 4
Combine all ingredients in bowl and refrigerate overnight. Bake, uncovered, at 350° for 1 hour. Let stand 20 minutes before serving. As the name implies, babysitters love this casserole because all they have to do is put it in the oven!

TUNA BURGERS

⅓ cup butter
6 hamburger buns, split
1—7 oz. can tuna, drained
1 cup celery, chopped
¼ cup diced process
  yellow cheese
2 Tbsp. onion, minced
¼ cup mayonnaise
Salt and pepper to taste

SERVES 6
Split and butter hamburger buns. Combine other ingredients in bowl and spread mixture on half of the bun halves. Top with other halves. Place on cookie sheet and cover tightly with foil. Bake at 350° for 15 minutes.

CHILI CHEESY FRANKS

8 oz. Cheddar cheese,
  grated
¼ cup chili sauce
¼ cup pickle relish
8 hot dogs
8 hot dog buns

SERVES 8
Combine first three ingredients in a bowl, mix well. Split hot dogs lengthwise and fill with mixture. Place in bun. Place on foil rectangles, seal and heat at 400° for 15 minutes. Have 'em ready for the soccer team.

KIDS' FOOD

CHILI IN A CUP

1 lb. ground beef
1 small onion, chopped
2 tsp. chili powder
1 tsp. cumin
½ tsp. salt
¼ tsp. garlic powder
1—15 oz. can tomato
   sauce
1—10 oz. can refrigerated
   biscuits
10 slices American cheese

MAKES 10
Brown beef and onion in a frying pan. Drain grease. Add seasonings and stir well. Blend in tomato sauce. Cook over low heat for about 20 minutes, stirring occasionally. In the meantime, roll out each biscuit on a lightly floured surface to make a 4-inch circle. Turn a muffin tin upside down and grease the outside of each cup. Mold a biscuit circle over each cup. Bake at 400° about 10 minutes or until browned. Remove biscuit cups immediately and turn right side up on a cookie sheet. Cut cheese slices into 3-inch circles; add cheese trimmings to meat mix, stirring until melted. Spoon meat into biscuit cups and top with cheese circles. Bake 3–5 minutes until cheese melts.

VEGETABLE SURPRISE

1 medium potato, washed,
   peeled and quartered
1 carrot, peeled and
   quartered
1 onion, sliced
1 green pepper, seeded
   and sliced
1 tomato, cut in wedges
2 Tbsp. butter
Salt and pepper to taste

SERVES 2
Place vegetables on a sheet of heavy foil. Add butter, salt and pepper. Wrap foil around vegetables tightly. Bake at 400° for 1 hour. Good with steak or chicken.

 Select a jar lid the proper size for hamburgers. Remove liner and wash lid well. Fill with meat and smooth top with knife or spatula; turn over and tap.

COURTNEY'S FAVORITE SQUASH CASSEROLE

3 lbs. yellow crookneck
   squash, sliced, cooked
   in salted water, drained
1 small jar chopped
   pimientos
2 eggs, beaten
1 cup sour cream
1—10½ oz. can cream of
   chicken soup
1 small onion, chopped
1 stick butter or margarine
3 cups Pepperidge Farm
   Cornbread Stuffing mix

SERVES 10
Lightly grease a 9×13-inch pan. Sprinkle bottom of pan with 1 cup of the stuffing mixture. Combine squash, pimientos, eggs, sour cream, soup and onion. Spread in pan. Melt butter and stir in remaining 2 cups of stuffing. Spread over top of squash mixture. Bake at 350° for 45 minutes. They'll never know they're eating squash!

WATERMELON SURPRISE

½ gallon lime sherbet
½ gallon raspberry
   sherbet
6 oz. chocolate chips

Line a bowl with softened lime sherbet, about 1 inch thick. Fold chocolate chips into softened raspberry sherbet and pour into bowl over lime layer. Freeze 24 hours. Unmold and slice.

AVERY'S BANANA BOATS

1 banana per person
Hershey's plain milk
   chocolate bars
Miniature marshmallows

With a paring knife, cut a slit in the banana, from end to end, forming a pocket. Stuff the pocket with squares of milk chocolate and marshmallows. Wrap the banana in foil. Place the packages on the grill over glowing coals, or bake in the oven at 400° for 10 minutes. Remove foil and eat contents wtih a spoon, scooping out warmed banana with melted chocolate and marshmallow. What a treat!

KIDS' FOOD

BOB'S BREAD PUDDING

2 eggs
½ cup sugar
1 tsp. vanilla
2 cups milk
4 slices white bread
2 Tbsp. raisins
Cinnamon

SAUCE:
½ cup butter
1 cup sugar
½ cup heavy cream

SERVES 4

Break eggs in a 1-quart Pyrex baking dish. Beat until frothy. Add sugar and vanilla. Beat again. Add milk, slowly, beating until well blended. Break bread apart into 8–10 pieces and press them into the egg mixture with a fork. Let them soak for a little bit. Stir in raisins. Sprinkle mixture lightly with cinnamon. Bake at 350° in the center of the oven for 30 minutes. It should be puffy and golden.

Simmer the butter and sugar for 10 minutes. Add the cream and simmer for 8 minutes. Spoon over a serving of pudding. Eat it while warm. Delicious and easy for kids to make!

LINDA'S CARAMEL CORN

16 cups popped popcorn
1 cup brown sugar
½ tsp. salt
½ cup butter
¼ cup light Karo syrup
1 tsp. vanilla
½ tsp. soda

Pop popcorn and put in brown paper bag. Mix together brown sugar, salt, butter and Karo syrup in bowl. Microwave on high for 2 minutes; stir; microwave 3 additional minutes, stirring after each minute. Add vanilla and soda and stir. Pour over popcorn, shake, microwave 1 minute; shake; microwave 1 minute; shake; microwave 30 seconds; shake; microwave 30 more seconds. Pour out onto wax paper. Kids have lots of fun making this.

To remove chewing gum from fabrics, rub with ice and gum will roll off and leave no marks.

BANANA SPLIT POPSICLE

Maraschino cherries
Chocolate chips
3 ripe bananas
1 cup half and half

MAKES 12
Whip half and half in blender or food processor until very thick. Peel and break the bananas into chunks. Blend until smooth. Add ½ cup chocolate chips and whirl again until chocolate is broken into pieces. Place a cherry in the bottom of each popsicle container. Pour in banana mixture and freeze.

PEANUT PARFAIT

10 peanut butter sandwich
cookies
1—3 oz. pkg. instant vanilla
pudding mix
¼ cup smooth peanut
butter
¾ cup fudge sauce

SERVES 4
Crush 6 cookies and set aside. Prepare pudding according to package directions. Add peanut butter, stirring until smooth. Layer half of pudding evenly into 4 parfait glasses; add half of crushed cookies and half of fudge sauce. Repeat layers with remaining pudding, crushed cookies, and fudge sauce. Arrange whole cookie on side of each glass. Cover and chill until ready to serve.

KIDS' FOOD

CHOCOLATE POPCORN SQUARES

6 cups unsalted popped
  popcorn
1—12 oz. pkg. chocolate
  chips
¼ cup light corn syrup
1—7 oz. jar marshmallow
  cream

MAKES 2 DOZEN
Mix marshmallow cream, chocolate chips and corn syrup in a saucepan over low heat until melted and well blended. Pour over popcorn and mix well. Press into an 8-inch square buttered pan. Cool and cut into squares.

SHERRI'S MONSTER MUNCH

1 cup semi-sweet
  chocolate chips, melted
1 cup Shredded Wheat
  cereal, crushed
1 cup coconut
½ cup peanuts

MAKES 30 BALLS
Mix ingredients together. Form into little balls and freeze.

ICE CREAM SANDWICHES

12–16 large chocolate
  cookies
½ pint ice cream (your
  choice of flavors: try
  chocolate chip, vanilla,
  or chocolate mint)

6–8 SANDWICHES
Empty the ice cream into a bowl and stir until it softens just a little. With a butter knife, spread the softened ice cream on a cookie. Cover it quickly with another cookie. Wrap the sandwich in a square of foil and freeze immediately. Freeze at least 24 hours. Try other combinations. . .your imagination is your only limitation!

 Chocolate stains can be removed with a paste of borax and water.

❧ ❧ ❧ ❧ ❧ ❧ ❧ ❧ ❧ ❧ ❧ ❧ ❧ ❧ ❧ ❧ ❧ ❧ ❧

MEREDITH'S CRAZY CAKE

3 cups flour
2 cups sugar
1 tsp. salt
½ cup cocoa
2 tsp. soda
1 cup oil
2 Tbsp. vinegar
2 tsp. vanilla
2 cups water

Mix all the dry ingredients together in a 9×13-inch pan. With a spoon, make three depressions in the mixture. In the first hole, add the oil. In the second hole, add the vinegar. In third, add the vanilla. Pour the water over all. Mix well with a fork and bake at 350° for 40–45 minutes. Can also be mixed with a mixer and baked in a Bundt pan, but it is fun for kids to make in the 9×13-inch pan. Makes a moist cake that doesn't really need frosting.

OSCAR MOUSE COOKIES

1 cup crushed vanilla wafers
1 cup powdered sugar
1 cup nuts, finely chopped
2 Tbsp. light corn syrup
2–3 Tbsp. milk
Raisins
Licorice strips

MAKES 18
Combine all but last two ingredients and mix well. Form each mouse by rolling into 1-inch ball. Decorate balls with raisins for ears and licorice strips for tail and whiskers.

POMANDER BALL

1 orange
Whole cloves

Pierce the entire surface of the orange with a fork. Stick a clove into each hole, making sure that the surface is covered and no fruit is showing. Wrap the fruit in a veil of netting, tying a ribbon or bow to the top. Hang where air can circulate freely around the fruit, drying it out completely. When dried (in 2–3 days), hang pomander ball in your closet, dresser drawer, or in the bathroom.

KIDS' FOOD

PINE CONE BIRD FEEDERS

Pine cones
String or yarn
Peanut butter
Bird seed

Tie a length of string or yarn around a pine cone. Smear peanut butter around the pine cone, using a butter knife. Roll the pine cone in bird seed. Hang outside on a tree and watch the birds enjoy the treat!

SUGAR EASTER EGGS

4 cups sugar
3–4 Tbsp. water
Royal icing (see Index)
Miniature Easter decora-
tions: Animals, Bunnies,
Ducks, Baskets,
Flowers, Butterflies

In a large bowl, sprinkle sugar with water. While stirring constantly, fluff it around to get all the sugar slightly damp (if too wet will melt, and if not wet enough won't stick together). Pack into plastic egg molds (these can be purchased at any cake decorating store). Use a knife or spatula to run across top making it smooth. Invert the molded sugar onto wax paper. Cut through each egg about 1½ inches from end. Let dry for about 3 hours or until the outer ⅜ inch of sugar is hard and dry. Carefully scoop out the inside sugar, leaving a hollow shell. Take the bottom half of the shell and create an Easter scene. Use different colored frosting, make ponds for ducks, fill little baskets with candy, scatter flowers and butterflies around.

Lots of cute miniature animals and plants can be found at hobby stores for making the scenes. Frost the edge of the bottom half using Royal Icing for "glue." Place the top half on the bottom half and decorate around the opening and on the seam. Make a cluster of flowers or other decoration on top. These make fun gifts for teachers and friends at Easter time.

 To tint coconut, put desired amount of coconut in a jar. Squeeze in a few drops of food coloring, then several drops of water. Close lid on jar, and shake well. Green tinted coconut makes nifty "grass" when decorating Sugar Easter Eggs.

GINGERBREAD HOUSE

WALLS & ROOF:
Use graham crackers or

OR

GINGERBREAD DOUGH:
¾ cup shortening
1 cup brown sugar
1 egg
¼ cup molasses
2¼ cups flour
2 tsp. soda
1 tsp. cinnamon
1 tsp. ginger
½ tsp. ground cloves
¼ tsp. salt

ROYAL ICING:
3 egg whites, room
   temperature
1 lb. powdered sugar
½ tsp. cream of tartar

**IDEAS FOR CANDIES
YOU CAN USE:**
Flat mints, colored
   Christmas hard candies,
   licorice & cherry twists
   & ropes, gumdrops,
   colored miniature mar-
   shmallows, candy canes,
   peppermint candies,
   M&Ms, gum balls, cin-
   namon candies, jelly-
   beans, silver argees,
   multicolored nonpareils,
   sugar ice cream cones,
   Lifesavers

To make gingerbread, cream together the shortening, brown sugar, egg and molasses. Blend in remaining ingredients. Spread evenly on greased cookie sheet and bake at 375° for 10–15 minutes or just until set. Lay the box (see below) on the warm dough and with a sharp knife cut around the box edge for the walls. Let cut dough cool completely before removing from pan.

To make frosting, beat egg whites and cream of tartar until foamy. Add powdered sugar and continue beating 8–10 minutes. The consistency can be changed for different effects: thinner, you can frost the roof and pull some down to form icicles; it may need to be thicker to hold its shape in a cake decorator. This frosting dries very hard and will hold all the pieces in place.

To assemble Gingerbread House: start with a cardboard box and roof. You can use anything from a small, ½- pint milk carton to a bigger box. If using large milk carton, cut the bottom off to get the desired shape and height of house. If using a box, bend another piece of cardboard in the center for the peak of the roof. Measure for desired pitch of roof and cut to fit. Cut two pieces for the gable ends, glue in place. Don't worry about gaps—the frosting and candy will cover everything. On a paper plate, cover your box house with graham crackers or gingerbread, using frosting as your "glue." It works better to assemble the house and cover one day and decorate the next, because if house isn't dry, the weight of the candies might collapse it.

259

(more on next page)

❧ ❧ ❧ ❧ ❧ ❧ ❧ ❧ ❧ ❧ ❧ ❧ ❧ ❧ ❧ ❧ ❧ ❧ ❧ ❧

GINGERBREAD HOUSE, Continued

The roof can be frosted (a red-tinted roof is pretty) and left snowy looking or sprinkled with sugar or crystal glitter. It can be frosted and decorated with candies or cookies. A shingle effect can be made with cookies, sliced almonds, mint wafers, etc. The roof also can be covered with gingerbread then left plain or decorated.

The corners of the house can be filled with frosting and topped with candy. Fancy doors and windows can be made, snowmen and Christmas trees made with frosting and then decorated. Wreaths, a chimney, garland, and Santas are just a few of the things that can be made to decorate the walls.

Inverted ice cream cones can be frosted and decorated like Christmas trees and arranged around the house. "Merry Christmas from the Jones" (substitute your name for Jones) can be written across the back wall with a cake decorator.

We have made these with kids as young as 3 years old. The gingerbread houses are easy to assemble, and with a little help, any child can decorate a house that literally looks "good enough to eat." The pride he takes in his creation will far outweigh the small mess he makes. This is what memories are made of!

BREAKFAST

CAMPFIRE BREAKFAST
Silver Dollar Pancakes, Butter & Syrup, p. 32
Bacon and Fried Eggs, p. 26
Coffee, Orange Juice

FIRST DAY OF SCHOOL
Dutch Babies, p. 69
Sausage & Scrambled Eggs, p. 26
Sunrise Juice, p. 244
Coffee

SNOWY SUNDAY
Longhorn Brunch Casserole, p. 29
Apple Muffins, p. 66
Grapefruit Halves
Coffee

MOTHER'S DAY BY DAD AND KIDS
Quick & Easy Quiche, p. 30
Crunchy Granola Coffee Cake, p. 77
Cantaloupe Wedge
Coffee and Juice

SPECIAL OVERNIGHT GUESTS
Blueberry Lemon Pancakes, p. 35
Country Style Sausage & Soft Boiled Eggs
Tomato Juice, Coffee

FEEDING THE CREW
Scrambled Eggs, p. 26
Biscuits & Gravy, p. 27
Bacon
Orange Juice, Coffee

MENUS

BREAKFAST, Continued

BREAKFAST ON THE PATIO
Swiss Bacon & Tomato Stacks, p. 29
Caramel Sticky Buns, p. 76
Honeydew & Cantaloupe Wedges
Coffee

BRUNCHES & LUNCHEONS

WEDDING DAY BRUNCH
Gazpacho, p. 45
Chicken Cordon Bleu, p. 153
Fruit Salad with Poppy Seed Dressing, p. 99
Lemon Bread, p. 64   Poppy Seed Bread, p. 65
Petite Cheesecakes, p. 230
Cream Cheese Brownies, p. 210
Lemon Bars, p. 212
Champagne Punch, p. 22
Coffee or Tea

HIDEAWAY BRUNCH
Old South Shortcake, p. 31
Pineapple & Strawberries with Fruit Dip, p. 7
Bijou Springs Coffee Cake, p. 70
Champagne
Coffee or Tea

EASTER BRUNCH
Brunch Sandwich, p. 33
Sausage & Cheese Grits, p. 32
Wined Fruit Medley, p. 100
Victorian Coffee Cake, p. 72
Caramel Sticky Buns, p. 76
Apple Strudel, p. 223
Champagne, p. 23
Coffee or Tea

BRUNCHES & LUNCHEONS, Continued

SUMMERTIME SALAD LUNCHEON
Front Range Apple Salad, p. 96
Cashew Chicken Salad with Dijon Dressing, p. 110
Applewood Spinach Salad, p. 109
Divine Raspberry Salad, p. 112
Crab Salad Stuffed Avocado Salad, p. 112
Delicious Fruit 'n Cheese Spread, p. 10
Strawberry Bread, p. 65
Raisin Bread, p. 87
Blueberry Lemon Bread, p. 62
Grand Marnier, p. 238
Texas Tea, p. 20

BACK TO SCHOOL LUNCHEON
(For Moms Only!)
Ham 'n Avocado Crescents, p. 55
Sesame Seed Salad, p. 114
Stuffed Cinnamon Apples, p. 97
Pumpkin Muffins, p. 68
Apple Raisin Bars, p. 208
Coffee

BRIDGE CLUB LUNCHEON
Marco Polos, p. 57
Molded Peach Melba, p. 95
Carrot Cake, p. 192

DINNERS & SUPPERS

HUNTER'S DINNER
Wild Game Stew, p. 139
Barn-Raising Salad, p. 106
Harvest Batter Bread, p. 84
Sour Cream Lemon Pie, p. 217

MENUS

❧❧❧❧❧❧❧❧❧❧❧❧❧❧❧❧❧❧❧❧

DINNERS & SUPPERS, Continued

SEAFOOD DINNER
Bountiful Layers, p. 2
Grilled Trout with Tomato Butter, p. 159
or
Grilled Salmon, p. 162
Sandy Hook Scallops, p. 160
Tomato & Onion Salad, p. 108
Wheat Pilaf, p. 185
Crusty French Bread, p. 86
Four Fruit Pie, p. 227

CATTLEMEN'S DINNER
Calf Fries, p. 11
Stock Show Steak, p. 120
Parsley Potatoes, p. 178
Spinach Salad, p. 106
Potato Rolls, p. 84
Chocolate Cheesecake, p. 224

BUFFET DINNER
Oysters Florentine, p. 11
Orange Chutney Chicken, p. 153
Saucy Salad, p. 105
Sauteed Snowpeas & Mushrooms, p. 179
Crusty French Rolls, p. 86
Pinecliff Strawberries, p. 231

DO-AHEAD DINNER
Crabbies, p. 13
Lindy's Brisket, p. 118
Company Salad, p. 101
Country Potatoes, p. 175
Heavenly Biscuits, p. 77
Dessert Delight, p. 226

DINNERS & SUPPERS, Continued

SUNDAY DINNER
Ray's Herb Butter, p. 138
Leg o' Lamb, p. 138
Home Seasoned Wild Rice, p. 184
Asparagus Amandine, p. 166
All Bran Rolls, p. 83
Family Fruit Salad, p. 98
French Chocolate Pie, p. 217

MEXICAN DINNER
Chimichangas, p. 149
Rio Grande Bean Dip, p. 5
Spanish Rice, p. 185
Tossed Salad
Beer
Apricot-Lemon Sherbet, p. 239

MEXICAN BUFFET
Hot Nacho Dip, p. 6
Fajitas, p. 130
Picante Sauce, p. 141
Easy Guacamole, p. 5
Beans
T Lazy S Margaritas, p. 23
Mexican Flan, p. 236

FRONT PORCH SUMMERTIME SUPPER
Canadian Bacon Sandwiches, p. 51
Jazzy Bean Avocado Salad, p. 102
Texas Tea, p. 20
Jan's Strawberry Ice Cream, p. 240

SCHOOL NIGHT SUPPER
Scalloped Potatoes with Pork Chops, p. 134
Broccoli Salad, p. 101
Sunflower Seed Whole Wheat Bread, p. 88
Mandarin Orange Cake, p. 198

MENUS

DINNERS & SUPPERS, Continued

QUICK SUPPER
Desperation Dinner, p. 129
Tossed Green Salad
Quick Onion Cheese Biscuits, p. 81
Easy Livin' Pie, p. 218

COLD NIGHT SUPPER
Mexican Cheese Soup, p. 43
Tossed Green Salad
Flour Tortillas
Quick Peach Cobbler, p. 229

BARBECUES & PICNICS

BACKYARD BAR-B-QUE
Chili Powder Cheese Roll, p. 15
Fruit Platter with Honey Lemon Dressing, p. 99
Hot Barbecued Ribs, p. 118
Long's Peak Beans, p. 168
Marinated Vegetables, p. 109
Herb-Buttered Bread, p. 81
Caramel Brownies, p. 209

BY THE LAKE PICNIC
Fresh Vegetables and Dip, p. 3
Teriyaki Chicken Sandwiches, p. 52
Fresh Strawberries & Park Springs Pound Cake, p. 201
Chilled Wine

LABOR DAY PICNIC
Texas Picnic Chicken, p. 144
Potato Salad, p. 113
Orange Sherbet Salad, p. 95
Marinated Black-Eyed Peas, p. 102
Favorite Chocolate Chip Cookies, p. 204
Famous Chocolate Ice Cream, p. 239

MENUS

HOLIDAYS

THANKSGIVING DINNER
Turkey, Dressing & Gravy
Sweet Potatoes & Marshmallows, p. 179
Spinach Souffle, p. 179
Orange Glazed Beets, p. 169
Pumpkin Muffins, p. 68 or Bran Muffins, p. 67
Cranberry Relish Mold, p. 94
Pumpkin Pie, p. 219

CHRISTMAS EVE DINNER
Shrimp & Crab Dip, p. 2
Speedy Spinach Mushroom Caps, p. 12
Standing Rib Roast
Broccoli with Walnuts, p. 169
Crab-Stuffed Potatoes, p. 177
Wined Fruit Medley, p. 100
Butter Buns, p. 83
Christmas Fruit Cake, p. 196

NEW YEAR'S DAY DINNER
Cream of Asparagus Soup, p. 40
Blue Creek Dove, p. 156
Home-Seasoned Wild Rice, p. 184
Fresh Spinach Salad with Sour Cream Dressing, p. 107
Black Eye Peas
Pan de Lote, p. 76
Raspberries Victor, p. 230

EASTER DINNER
Baked Ham
Poppy Seed Noodles, p. 186
Pineapple Casserole, p. 174
Asparagus Vinaigrette, p. 166
Corn Fritters, p. 172
Mandarin Orange Salad, p. 99
Strawberry Delite, p. 221

MENUS

HOLIDAYS, Continued

FOURTH OF JULY PICNIC
Fried Chicken, p. 145
Country Potatoes, p. 175
Picnic Beans, p. 168
Colorful Cabbage Salad, p. 103
Mississippi Mud, p. 197
Peppermint Ice Cream, p. 240

PARTIES

PINK AND BLUE BABY SHOWER
Strawberry Angel Food Cake, p. 202
Four Fruit Pie (use Blueberries, Strawberries & Bananas), p. 227
Petite Cheesecakes (Cherry & Blueberry), p. 227
Pinochle Club Strawberry Dessert, p. 231
Strawberry Punch, p. 19

ANNIVERSARY PARTY
Best of the West Spread, p. 9
Assorted Fresh Fruit Pieces with Fresh Fruit Dip, p. 7
Bacon Cheese Spread, p. 9
Party Tomatoes, p. 13
Zucchini Puffs, p. 184
Canadian Bacon Sandwiches (on Party Ryes), p. 51
Hot Mushroom Dip, p. 8
Anniversary Cake
Mints & Nuts
Pineapple Sherbet Punch, p. 18
Champagne • Coffee • Tea

SLUMBER PARTY
Individual Pizzas, p. 250
Tossed Green Salad with Italian Dressing
Caramel Corn, p. 254
Oatmeal-Raisin Cookies, p. 206
Hot Chocolate, p. 21

PARTIES, Continued

NEW YEAR'S EVE
Muchos Nachos, p. 14
Easy Guacamole, p. 5
Jalapeno Spread, p. 9
Fresh Vegetable Platter with Mozzarella Dip, p. 4
Tortilla Soup, p. 50
Chalupas, p. 129
Cream Cheese Brownies, p. 210

KIDS' BIRTHDAY
Party Time Banana Split, p. 234
Fruit Party Punch, p. 16

SCHOOL PARTY TREAT IDEAS:
Peanut Butter Popcorn Balls, p. 238
Peanut Butter Cupcakes, p. 198
Black Bottom Cupcakes, p. 192
Monster Cookies, p. 206
Cookies 'n Cream Cupcakes, p. 196
Krispie Bar, p. 212
Popcorn Balls of Favorite Color, p. 255

SUNDAY AFTERNOON FOOTBALL GAME PARTY
Harvest Dip, p. 7
Lone Star Cheddar Bites, p. 14
Sombrero Spread, p. 6
Creamy Seafood Dill Dip, p. 4
Beer Cheese Soup, p. 42
Southwestern Submarine Sandwiches, p. 53
Caramel Apple Pie, p. 216
Beer

AFTER TRICK-OR-TREATING PARTY
Hot Fried Cheese Sticks, p. 12
Candied Popcorn, p. 237
Plum Creek Applesauce Cake, p. 237
Hot Cranberry-Apple Cider, p. 20
Hot Chocolate, p. 21

MENUS

PARTIES, Continued

CHRISTMAS COFFEE
*(Your neighbors will love sampling an assortment of
these holiday goodies!)*

Petite Cheesecakes, p. 230
Christmas Fruitcake, p. 196
Rum Cake, p. 201
Miniature Pecan Pies, p. 219

Sandtarts, p. 208
Mississippi Mud, p. 197
Creme Wafers, p. 204
Toffee Bars, p. 213

Almond Roca, p. 233
Microwave Fudge, p. 236

Almond Cranberry Punch, p. 15
Coffee Rum Punch, p. 22
Daddy's Eggnog, p. 22

INDEX

A

ACCOMPANIMENTS
Apple Butter 91
Bar-B-Que Sauce 140
Bath Tub Pickles 59
Celebration Mustard-Ginger Glaze ... 141
Crab Apple Jelly 90
Dill Sauce 159
Hollandaise Sauce 28
Ray's Herb Butter for Chops 138
Salmon Sauce 159
Acorn Squash 181
Adele's Chicken 151
Aebleskivers 37
Almond Cranberry Punch 15
Almond Roca 233
Amazing Barbecued Chicken 144
Andy's Favorite Breakfast Drink 245
Angel Food Cake, Strawberry 202
Ape Shake 244

APPETIZERS
Bar-B-Que Beef Bites 14
Bacon-Filled Cherry Tomatoes 13
Calf Fries 11
Chili Powder Cheese Roll 15
Cocktail Franks 12
Crabbies 13
Dips
Bountiful Layers 2
Chipped Beef Dip 8
Creamy Seafood Dill Dip 4
Dilly Dip 3
Dip for a Crowd 5
Easy Guacamole 5
Fresh Fruit Dip 7
Fresh Vegetable Dip 3
Heather's Harvest Dip 7
Hot Crab Dip 7
Hot Mushroom Dip 8
Hot Nacho Dip 6
Mozzarella Vegetable Dip 4
Rio Grande Bean Dip 5
Roquefort Dip 4
Sombrero Spread 6
Southwestern Bean Dip 5
Susan's Shrimp & Crab Dip 2
Vegetable Dippers 3
Hot Fried Cheese Sticks 12
Lone Star Cheddar Bites 14
Marinated Mushrooms 10
Muchos Nachos 14
Oysters Florentine 11
Party Tomatoes 13
Quick and Easy Cheese Ball 15
Rocky Mountain Oysters 11
Speedy Spinach Mushroom Caps 12

Spreads
Baboon Butter 247
Best of the West Spread 9
Delicious Fruit 'n Cheese Spread 10
Easy Crab Spread 8
Jalapeno Spread 9
Lemon Pepper Cheese Spread 10
Pimiento Cheese Spread 57
Raisin Peanut Butter Spread 248
Vera's Bacon-Cheese Spread 9
Willie's Monkey Business 248
Apple Butter 91
Apple Cider, Hot Cranberry 20
Apple Coffee Cake 70
Apple Dumplings 221
Apple Jelly (Crabapple) 90
Apple Muffins, Baked 66
Apple Pie, Caramel 216
Apple Pie, Sour Cream 215
Apple Raisin Bars, Easy 208
Apple, Rome Cake 197
Apple Salad, Front Range 96
Applesauce Bread 62
Applesauce Cake, Plum Creek 190
Apple Strudel, Sarah's 223
Apples, Stuffed Cinnamon 97
Apricot-Glazed Carrots 171
Apricot-Lemon Sherbet 239
Apricot Nectar Cake 200
Apricot Salad, Dreamy 94
Arizona Soup 46
Asparagus Amandine 166
Asparagus Soup, Cream of 40
Asparagus-Tomato, Tangy 166
Asparagus Vinaigrette 166
Aunt Peggy's Beef Burgundy 122
Avery's Banana Boats 253
Avocado Soup, Chilled 40

B

Baboon Butter 247
Babysitter's Chicken Casserole 251
Bacon-Cheese Spread, Vera's 9
Bacon Filled Cherry Tomatoes 13
Baked Apple Muffins 66
Baked Beans 168
Baked Haddock 159
Banana Boats, Avery's 253
Banana Cake, Betsy's 191
Banana Split Popsicle 255
Banana Split, Party Time 234
Banana Split Stack 34
Bananas, State Fair Frozen Chocolate. . 246
Barbara's Vanilla Ice Cream 238
Barbecued Chicken, Amazing 144
Barbecued Pork Roast 135

Barbecued Ribs, Hot 118
Bar-B-Que Beef Bites 14
Bar-B-Que Beef Sandwiches 50
Bar-B-Que Sauce 140
Barn Raising Salad 106
Bath Tub Pickles 59

BEANS
Brandin' Beans 127
Hearty White Bean Chili 46
Green Beans Oriental 167
Green Beans Provencal 167
Jazzy Bean-Avocado Salad 102
Long's Peak Baked Beans 168
Nine Bean Soup 48
Picnic Beans 168
Red Beans and Rice 43
Rio Grande Bean Dip 5
Southwestern Bean Dip 5

BEEF
Aunt Peggy's Beef Burgundy 122
Bar-B-Que Beef Bites 14
Bar-B-Que Beef Sandwiches 50
Beef and Kraut Sandwich 57
Brandin' Beans 127
Calf Fries 11
Cavatelli 132
Chili in a Cup 252
Chipped Beef Dip 8
Chuckwagon Soup 44
Fajitas 130
German Cabbage Burgers 125
Great Beef Hot Pot 126
Grilled Cheeseburgers on Rye 51
Hero Sandwich 58
Hot Barbecued Ribs 118
Hot Roast Beef Sandwich 54
Lindy's Brisket 118
Liver & Onions 123
Marinade for Beef 121
Meatball Parmigiana, Veal or 133
Mom's Italian Delight 131
Monday Night Hash 126
Mushroom-Stuffed Steak 120
Pancho's Casserole 131
Pizza Burgers 56
Platte River Steak 119
Rocky Mountain Oysters 11
Running W Pepper Steak 121
Saucy Meatballs 119
Smothered Steak 'n Mushrooms 118
Snow Peas & Beef 123
Stock Show Steak 120
Stuffed Pasta Shells 132
Stuffed Peppers 124
Summit Meat Loaf 125
Working Woman's Roast 124
Zesty Beef & Zucchini 122
Beets, Orange-Glazed 169
Berry Good Cooler 244
Best Bran Muffins, The 67
Betsy's Banana Cake 191

BEVERAGES
A Berry Good Cooler 244
Almond Cranberry Punch 15
Ape Shake 244
Andy's Favorite Breakfast Drink 245
Champagne Punch 22
Christmas Coffee Punch 19
Cinnamon Cocoa Mocha Mix 21
Cranberry Orange Punch 16
Creamy Fruit Float 16
D & J Juice 245
Fruit Party Punch 16
Golden Summer Punch 16
Grape Punch 17
Hot Cranberry-Apple Cider 20
Hot Spiced Nectar 20
Irish Coffee Eggnog Punch 22
Joan's Coffee Rum Punch 23
Lime Cooler Punch 17
Lime Punch 17
Matt's Peanutty Shake 244
Orange Julius 19
Party Punch 18
Pineapple Sherbet Punch 18
Pineapple Upside Down Shake 245
Rum Slush 23
Sherbet Cooler 245
Strawberry-Pineapple Punch 18
Strawberry Punch 19
Bijou Springs Coffee Cake 70
Biscuits, Grandmother's Buttermilk 80
Biscuits n' Gravy 27
Biscuits, Heavenly 77
Blueberry Cream Pie 215
Blueberry Lemon Bread 62
Blueberry Lemon Pancakes 35
Blueberry Rolls, Lazy Morning 75
Blue Creek Dove 156
Bob's Bread Pudding 254
Boston Brown Bread 77
Bountiful Layers 2
Bowknots, Mrs. Van Husen's Orange 75
Brandin' Beans 127
Bran Rolls, Grandma White's All 83

BREADS
Quick Breads
Applesauce Bread 62
Blueberry Lemon Bread 62
Cache La Poudre Fruit Bread 63
Caribbean Nut Bread 63
Lemon Bread 64
Orange Nut Bread 64
Poppy Seed Bread 65
Pumpkin Date Bread 66
Quickscuits, Erin's 249
Strawberry Bread 65
Muffins
Apple Muffins, Baked 66
Bran Muffins, The Best 67
Cranberry Almond Muffins 67
Jalapeno Muffins 80

272

Peach Muffins 68
Pumpkin Muffins, Susan's 68
Rhubarb Muffins 69
Yeast Breads
Butter Buns 83
Crusty French Bread 86
Crusty French Rolls 86
Grandma White's All Bran Rolls 83
Harvest Batter Bread 84
Honey-Wheat Bread 85
Mrs. Van Husen's Orange Bowknots . . 75
No-Knead Breakfast Twists 74
Potato Rolls 84
Quick Caramel Sticky Buns 76
Raisin Bread 87
Sunflower Whole Wheat Bread 88
Whole Wheat Sesame Bread 89
Other
Apple Coffee Cake 70
Bijou Springs Coffee Cake 70
Boston Brown Bread 77
Cheese & Herb Bread 82
Cowboy Corn Cakes 78
Crunchy Granola Coffee Cake 71
Dutch Babies 69
Germaine's Quick Onion Rolls 79
Grandma Eaton's Coffee Cake 71
Grandmother's Buttermilk Biscuits . . . 80
Heavenly Biscuits 77
Herb Buttered Bread 81
Hamburger Buns 79
Judi's Pan de Lote 76
Lazy Morning Blueberry Rolls 75
Navajo Fry Bread 82
Orange Marmalade Bread 72
Parmesan Bread Sticks 78
Quick Caramel Sticky Buns 76
2 Quick Breakfast Coffee Cakes 73
Victorian Coffee Cake 72
Bread Pudding 222
Bread Pudding, Bob's 254
Breakfast Drink, Andy's Favorite 245
Breakfast Pizza 28
Broccoli Cheese Soup 41
Broccoli Delight 170
Broccoli Mushroom Souffle 170
Broccoli Salad 101
Broccoli Swiss Bake 169
Broiled Italian Tomatoes 182
Brownies, Caramel 209
Brownies, Cream Cheese 210
Brisket, Lindy's 118
BRUNCH
Aebleskivers 37
Banana Split Stack 34
Biscuits 'n Gravy 27
Blueberry Lemon Pancakes 35
Breakfast Pizza 28
Buttermilk Waffles 32
Cheese and Sausage Grits 32
Crustless Quiche 30

Eggs Fried Just Right 26
German Apple Pancake 36
Holiday Brunch Dish 34
Huevos Rancheros 28
Joanie's Birthday Brunch Sandwiches . 33
Longhorn Brunch Casserole 29
Old South Shortcake 31
Quick and Easy Quiche 30
Scrambled Eggs 26
Silver Dollar Pancakes 32
Spring Omelet 27
Strawberry French Toast 33
Swiss Bacon & Tomato Stacks 29
Butter Buns 83
Buttermilk Biscuits, Grandmother's 80
Buttermilk Waffles 32
Buttery Pie Crust 214

C

Cabbage Burgers, German 125
Cabbage Salad, Colorful 103
Cabbage with Apples, Red 171
Cache la Poudre Fruit Bread 63
Cajun Shrimp 161
CAKES
Apricot Nectar Cake 200
Betsy's Banana Cake 191
Carrot Cake 192
Charlotte's Nut Cake 197
Chocolate Cherry Coffee Cake 193
Chocolate Macaroon Cake 194
Christmas Fruitcake 196
Cookies 'n Cream Cake 196
Georgia's Rum Cake 201
Mandarin Orange Cake 198
Meredith's Crazy Cake 257
Park Springs Pound Cake 201
Pineapple Pudding Cake 200
Plum Creek Applesauce Cake 190
Rome Apple Cake 197
Strawberry Angel Food Cake 202
Suzie's Chocolate Sour Cream Cake . 195
Traditional Spice Cake 202
Western Slope Pear Cake 199
Calf Fries 11
Calico Salad 103
Canadian Bacon Sandwiches 51
CANDY
Almond Roca 233
Candied Popcorn 237
Charlie's Christmas Date Candy 235
Microwave Fudge 236
Quick Nut Candies 237
Peanut Butter Popcorn Balls 238
Pecan Clusters 235
Popcorn Balls 255
Sherrie's Monster Munch 256
Caramel Apple Pie 216
Caramel Brownies 209
Caramel Corn, Linda's 254

273

Caramel Ice Box Pie 234
Caramel Icing 203
Caramel Sticky Buns, Quick 76
Caribbean Nut Bread 63
Carrot Cake 192
Carrots, Apricot Glazed 171
Carrots, Susie's Tarragon 171
Cashew Chicken Salad 110
Castle Rock Chicken Casserole 148
Catfish, Fried 157
Cauliflower Salad 104
Cauliflower Soup, Cream of 41
Cauliflower Supreme 172
Cavatelli 132
Celebration Mustard-Ginger Glaze 141
Chalupas, Ritas 129
Champagne Punch 22
Charlie's Christmas Date Candy 235
Charlotte's Nut Cake 197
Cheese Ball, Quick & Easy 15
Cheese, Homemade Spread 6
Cheese Roll, Chili Powder 15
Cheeseburgers on Rye, Grilled 51
Cheesecake, Chocolate 224
Cheesecakes, Petite 230
Cheesecake, New York 225
Cheese & Herb Bread 82
Cheese & Sausage Grits 32
Cheese Sticks, Hot Fried 12
Cherry Cobbler; Ellen's 226
Cherry Salad, Ruth's 97
Chewy Oatmeal-Raisin Cookies 207
CHICKEN
Adele's Chicken 151
Amazing Barbecued Chicken 144
Babysitter's Chicken Casserole 251
Cashew Chick Salad wi Dijon Drsg . . . 110
Castle Rock Chicken Casserole 148
Chicken Breasts with Sour Cream . . . 152
Chicken Chimichangas 147
Chicken Club Sandwiches 53
Chicken Cordon Bleu 153
Chicken a la King 146
Chicken Breasts Mandalay 151
Chicken Pot Pie 145
Chicken Salad w/ Green Chilies 111
Chicken Stir-Fry 147
Chicken Stuffed Melon 111
Chicken Swisswiches 52
Chicken Tetrazzini 150
French Onion Chicken 149
Gourmet Chicken Breasts 154
King Ranch Chicken 148
Mandarin Game Hens 155
Marco Polos 57
Orange Chutney Chicken 153
Oven Lemon Chicken 152
Parmesan Chicken 154
Teriyaki Chicken 146
Teriyaki Chicken Sandwiches 52
Texas Picnic Chicken 144

CHILDREN'S FOOD (See KIDS' FOOD)
Chili Cheese Franks 251
Chili, Hearty White Bean 46
Chili Powder Cheese Roll 15
Chili in a Cup 252
Chilled Avocado Soup 40
Chimichangas, Chicken 145
Chipped Beef Dip 8
Chocolate Bananas, State Fair Frozen . 246
Chocolate Butter-Cream Bars 211
Chocolate Cheesecake 224
Chocolate Cherry Coffee Cake 193
Chocolate Frosting, Never Fail 195
Chocolate Ice Cream, Famous 239
Chocolate Macaroon Cake 194
Chocolate Peanut Butter Treats 237
Chocolate Pie, French 217
Chocolate Popcorn Squares 256
Chocolate Sour Cream Cake, Suzie's . . 195
Chocolate, Wolfensburger Pass Hot 21
Chowder; Cold Day 44
Chowder, Seafood 49
Christmas Coffee Punch 19
Christmas Date Candy, Charlie's 235
Christmas Fruitcake 196
Chuckwagon Soup 44
Cinnamon Cocoa Mocha Mix 21
Coastal Shrimp Salad 112
Cobbler; Ellen's Cherry 226
Cobbler, Quick Peach 229
Cocktail Franks 12
Coffee Cake, Apple 70
Coffee Cake, Bijou Springs 70
Coffee Cake, Crunchy Granola 71
Coffee Cake, Orange Marmalade 72
Coffee Cake, Stroh Ranch 71
Coffee Cake, Victorian 72
Coffee, Irish Eggnog Punch 22
Coffee Punch, Christmas 19
Coffee Rum Punch, Joan's 23
Cold Day Chowder 44
Colorful Cabbage Salad 103
Company Salad 101
Cookbook Kid's Snack 248
Cook His Goose 155
Cookies n' Cream Cake 196
COOKIES AND BARS
Caramel Brownies 209
Chewy Oatmeal-Raisin Cookies 207
Chocolate Butter-Cream Bars 211
Cream Cheese Brownies 210
Creme Wafers 204
Easy Apple Raisin Bars 208
Harvest Squares 209
Krispie Bars 212
Lemon-Butter Cookies 205
Molasses Cookies 205
Monster Cookies 206
Oatmeal Date Cookies 206
Oscar Mouse Cookies 257
Peggy's Lemon Bars 212

Peppernuts 207
Sandtarts 208
Toffee Pecan Bars 213
Corn Bread, Homestyle 78
Corn, Linda's Caramel 254
Corn Fritters 172
Cowboy Corn Cakes 78
Country Quiche 180
Courtney's Favorite Squash Casserole . 253
Crab Apple Jelly 90
Crabbies 13
Crab-Stuffed Flounder 158
Crab-Stuffed Potatoes 177
Cranberry-Almond Muffins 67
Cranberry Freeze 97
Cranberry Mousse 95
Cranberry Orange Punch 16
Cranberry Relish Mold 94
Crazy Cake, Meredith's 257
Cream Cheese Brownies 210
Cream Cheese Frosting .... 191 & 192
Creamy Fruit Float 16
Cream of Asparagus Soup 40
Cream of Cauliflower Soup 41
Cream Puff Dessert 226
Creamy Seafood Dill Dip 4
Creme Wafers 204
Crustless Quiche 30
Crusty French Bread 86
Crusty French Rolls 86
Crusty New Potatoes 175
Cucumber, Molded Salad 104

D

D & J Juice 245
Date Candy, Charlie's Christmas 235
Delicious Fruit 'n Cheese Spread 10
Desperation Dinner 129
DESSERTS
Bread Pudding 222
Cakes 190–203
Candies 233–237
Cookies & Bars 204–213
Frozen Desserts 238–240
Pies 213–221
Apple Dumplings 221
Avery's Banana Boats 253
Banana Split Popsicle 255
Bob's Bread Pudding 254
Caramel Ice Box Pie 234
Chocolate Cheesecake 224
Cream Puff Dessert 226
Ellen's Cherry Cobbler 226
Four Fruit Pie 227
Gingerbread 222
Lemon Fluff 228
Mexican Chocolate Ice Cream 241
Mexican Flan 236
New York Cheesecake 225
Peach Blueberry Shortcake 229

Peanut Butter Popcorn Balls 238
Peanut Parfait 255
Petite Cheesecakes 230
Pine Cliff Strawberries 231
Pinochle Club Strawberry Dessert ... 231
Quick Peach Cobbler 229
Raspberries Victor 230
Sarah's Apple Strudel 223
Summertime Lemon Dessert 228
Swedish Cream 232
Sweet Temptation 232
Dill Sauce, Grilled Salmon with 159
Dilly Dip 3
DIPS
Chipped Beef Dip 8
Creamy Seafood Dill Dip 4
Dilly Dip 3
Dip for a Crowd 5
Fresh Fruit Dip 7
Fresh Vegetable Dip 3
Heather's Harvest Dip 7
Hot Crab Dip 7
Hot Mushroom Dip 8
Hot Nacho Dip 6
Mozzarella Vegetable Dip 4
Rio Grande Bean Dip 5
Roquefort Dip 4
Southwestern Bean Dip 5
Susan's Shrimp & Crab Dip 2
Vegetable Dippers 3
Donnie's Original Wild Game Stew 139
Dove, Blue Creek 156
Dreamy Apricot Salad 94
DRESSINGS, SALAD
Fruit Salad Coating 98
Grand Marnier Dressing 111
Honey-Lemon Dressing 99
Lime Honey Dressing 111
Mayonnaise, Homemade 114
Mustard Vinaigrette 115
Ranch Style Dressing 115
Sesame Seed Salad Dressing 115
Dutch Babies 69
Dynamite Macaroni Salad 114

E

Easter Eggs, Sugar 258
Easy Apple Raisin Bars 208
Easy Crab Spread 8
Easy Livin' Pie 218
Eggplant Regina 173
Eggplant, Stuffed 173
Eggnog, Irish Coffee Punch 22
EGGS
Eggs Fried Just Right 26
Dutch Babies 69
Holiday Brunch Dish 34
Huevos Rancheros 28
Longhorn Brunch Casserole 29
Quick & Easy Quiche 30

275

Scrambled Eggs 26
Seafood Quiche 31
Spring Omelet 2
Eileen's Famous Chocolate Ice Cream . 239
Ellen's Cherry Cobbler 226
Equivalent Measures 283
Erin's Quickscuits 249

F

Fajitas 130
Family Fruit Salad 98
Family Time Stew 42
Famous Chocolate Ice Cream, Eileen's . 239
Fire & Ice Tomatoes 108
FISH
  Baked Haddock 159
  Clams
    Seafood Chowder 49
  Crab
    Crabbies 13
    Creamy Seafood Dill Dip 4
    Crab-Stuffed Avocado Salad 112
    Crab-Stuffed Flounder 158
    Crab-Stuffed Potatoes 117
    Easy Crab Spread 8
    Hot Crab Dip 7
    Joanie's B'day Brunch Sandwiches . . 33
    Lois Jean's Crabmeat Au Gratin 157
    Seafood Quiche 31
    Susan's Shrimp & Crab Dip 2
  Fried Catfish 157
  Microwave Fish Fillets 158
  Oysters
    Oysters Florentine 11
  Salmon
    Salmon Sauce 159
    Grilled Salmon with Dill Sauce 159
  Scallops
    Sandy Hook Scallops 160
  Shrimp
    Bountiful Layers 2
    Cajun Shrimp 161
    Coastal Shrimp Salad 112
    Seafood Chowder 49
    Seafood Quiche 31
    Shrimp Casserole 161
    Shrimp Etouffee 161
    Shrimp Tempura 160
    Susan's Shrimp & Crab Dip 2
  Trout
    Grilled Fillets with Tomato Butter . . . 162
  Tuna
    Good Ol' Tuna Casserole 162
    Molded Tuna Salad 113
    Tuna Burgers 251
Five Cup Salad 98
Flaky Pie Crust 213
Flan, Mexican 236
Florentine Chops 136
Flounder; Crab-Stuffed 158

Four Fruit Pie 227
Frances's Famous Lamb Chops 138
Franks, Chili Cheesy 251
French Bread, Crusty 86
French Chocolate Pie 217
French Onion Chicken 149
French Rolls, Crusty 86
French Toast, Strawberry 33
Fresh Fruit Dip 7
Fresh Spinach Salad w/ Sour Cr. Drsg . . 107
Fresh Vegetable Dip 3
Fried Catfish 157
Fried Okra & Tomatoes 174
Fritters, Corn 172
Front Range Apple Salad 96
FROSTINGS
  Caramel Icing 203
  Cream Cheese Frosting 191,192
  Never-Fail Chocolate Frosting 195
  Snow-Capped Icing 203
FROZEN DESSERTS
  Apricot-Lemon Sherbet 239
  Barbara's Vanilla Ice Cream 238
  Famous Chocolate Ice Cream 239
  Grand Marnier 238
  Ice Cream Sandwiches 256
  Jan's Strawberry Ice Cream 240
  Lemon Velvet Ice Cream 241
  Party Time Banana Split 234
  Peppermint Ice Cream 240
  State Fair Frozen Chocolate Bananas 246
  Watermelon Surprise 253
Fruit Bars 212
Fruit Bread, Cache la Poudre 63
Fruit Dip, Fresh 7
Fruit 'n Cheese Spread 10
Fruit Medley, Wined 100
Fruit Party Punch 16
Fruit Pie, Four 227
Fruit Platter 99
Fruit Salad Coating 98
Fruit Salad, Family 98
Fruitcake, Christmas 196
Fry Bread, Navajo 82
Fudge, Microwave 236

G

GAME
  Blue Creek Dove 156
  Cook His Goose 155
  Donnie's Original Wild Game Stew . . . 139
Gazpacho 45
Georgia's Rum Cake 201
Germaine's Quick Onion Rolls 79
German Apple Pancakes 36
German Cabbage Burgers 125
Gingerbread House 259
Glazed Beets, Orange 169
Golden Summer Punch 16
Good Ol' Tuna Casserole 162

Goose, Cook His 155
Gourmet Chicken Breasts 154
Graham Cracker Crust 220
Grand Marnier 238
Grand Marnier Fruit Dressing 111
Grande Potatoes 176
Grandma Cook's Peaches 'n Cream Pie 218
Grandma Eaton's Coffee Cake 71
Grandma White's All Bran Rolls 83
Grandmother's Buttermilk Biscuits 80
Granola Coffee Cake, Crunchy 71
Grape Punch 17
Great Beef Hot Pot 126
Green Beans Oriental 167
Green Beans Provencal 167
Grilled Cheeseburgers on Rye 51
Grilled Roast Beef Sandwiches 54
Grilled Salmon with Dill Sauce 159
Grilled Trout Fillets wi Tomato Butter ... 162
Grits, Cheese and Sausage 32
Guacamole, Easy 5

H

HAM
  Ham 'n Avocado Crescents 55
  Ham Loaf with Horseradish Sauce. ... 137
  Hoppin' John 136
  Potato Ham Soup 47
Hamburger Buns, Homemade 79
Harvest Batter Bread 84
Harvest Dip, Heather's 7
Harvest Squares 209
Hash, Monday Night 126
Hearty White Bean Chili 46
Heather's Harvest Dip 7
Heavenly Biscuits 77
Herb Butter for Chops, Ray's 138
Hero Sandwich 58
High Country Hot Dogs 55
Holiday Brunch Dish 34
Homemade Cheese Spread 6
Homemade Hamburger Buns 79
Homemade Mayonnaise 114
Home-Seasoned Wild Rice 184
Homestyle Corn Bread 78
Honey-Wheat Bread 85
Hoppin' John 136
Hors d'Oeuvres (See **APPETIZERS**)
Hot Barbecued Ribs 118
Hot Crab Dip 7
Hot Dogs, High Country 55
Hot Cranberry-Apple Cider 20
Hot Fried Cheese Sticks 12
Hot Ham Sandwiches 58
Hot Mushroom Dip 8
Hot Nacho Dip 6
Hot Potato & Wurst 128
Hot Roast Beef Sandwich 54
Hot Spiced Nectar 20
Hot Turkey Royale 58

Huevos Rancheros 28

I
Ice Cream, Eileen's Famous Chocolate . 239
Ice Cream, Lemon Velvet 241
Ice Cream, Peppermint 240
Ice Cream Sandwiches 256
Ice Cream, Jan's Strawberry 240
Ice Cream, Barbara's Vanilla 238
Icings (See **FROSTINGS**)
Italian Delight, Mom's 131
Italian Sausage Roll 56

J
Jalapeno Muffins 80
Jalapeno Spread 9
Jazzy Bean-Avocado Salad 102
Jan's Strawberry Ice Cream 240
Jelly, Crab Apple 90
Jenna's Magic Squares 246
Joanie's Birthday Brunch Sandwiches ... 33
Joan's Coffee Rum Punch 23
Judi's Pan de Lote 76
Judy's Tuna Islands 163

K
Kathleen's Lamb Stew 137
KIDS' FOOD
  Andy's Favorite Breakfast Drink 245
  Ape Shake 244
  Avery's Banana Boats 253
  Baboon Butter 247
  Babysitter's Chicken Casserole 251
  Banana Split Popsicle 255
  Berry Good Cooler 244
  Bob's Bread Pudding 254
  Chili Cheesy Franks 251
  Chili in a Cup 252
  Chocolate Popcorn Squares 256
  Cookbook Kid's Snack, The 248
  Courtney's Favorite Squash Casserole 253
  D & J Juice 245
  Erin's Quickscuits 249
  Gingerbread House 259
  Ice Cream Sandwiches 256
  Jenna's Magic Squares 246
  Linda's Caramel Corn 254
  Matt's Peanutty Shake 244
  Melon Boat 246
  Meredith's Crazy Cake 257
  Mother's Day Surprise Muffins 249
  Peanut Butter Toast 247
  Pineapple Upside Down Shake 245
  Pine Cone Bird Feeders 258
  Pomander Ball 257
  Oscar Mouse Cookies 257
  Raisin Peanut Butter Spread 248
  Ritzy Cracker 248
  Roasted Pumpkin Seeds 24

277

Sherbet Coolers 245
Sherri's Monster Munch 256
State Fair Frozen Choc. Bananas 246
Sugar Easter Eggs 258
Sunrise Juice 244
Sunshine Salad 250
Tanya's Pizzas 250
Tuna Burgers 251
Vegetable Surprise 252
Watermelon Surprise 253
Wesley Rabbit Salad 250
Willie's Monkey Business 248
Kika's Sunshine Vegetables 172
King Ranch Chicken 148
Krispie Bars 212

L

Lazy Morning Blueberry Rolls 75
LAMB
Frances's Famous Lamb Chops 138
Kathleen's Lamb Stew 137
Leg o' Lamb 138
Mustard-Ginger Glaze, Celebration . . . 141
Ray's Herb Butter for Chops 138
Lemon-Apricot Sherbet 239
Lemon Bread 64
Lemon-Butter Cookies 205
Lemon Chicken, Oven 152
Lemon Dessert, Summertime 228
Lemon Fluff 228
Lemon Pepper Cheese Spread 16
Lemon Pie, Sour Cream 217
Lemon Velvet Ice Cream 241
Leona's Pumpkin Pie 219
Lime Punch 17
Lime Cooler Punch 17
Linda's Caramel Corn 254
Lindy's Brisket 118
Liver & Onions 123
Lois Jean's Crabmeat au Gratin 157
Lone Star Cheddar Bites 14
Longhorn Brunch Casserole 29
Long's Peak Baked Beans 168

M

Macaroni & Green Pea Salad 115
Macaroni Salad, Dynamite 114
Magic Squares, Jennas 246
Main Dish Pasta Salad 113
Mandarin Game Hens 155
Mandarin Orange Cake 198
Mandarin Orange Salad 99
Margaritas, T Lazy S 23
Marinade for Beef 121
Marinated Black Eyed Peas 102
Marinated Mushrooms 10
Marinated Zucchini Salad 110
Matt's Peanutty Shake 244

Mayonnaise, Homemade 114
Measures, Equivalent 283
**MEATS (See BEEF, HAM, LAMB,
CHICKEN & FISH)**
Meatball or Veal Parmigiana 133
Melon Boat 246
Meredith's Crazy Cake 257
Mexican Cheese Soup 43
Mexican Flan 236
MEXICAN FOOD
Chicken Chimichangas 145
Dip for a Crowd 5
Fajitas 130
Gazpacho 45
Hot Nacho Dip 6
Huevos Rancheros 28
Jalapeno Spread 9
King Ranch Chicken 148
Margaritas, T Lazy S 23
Mexican Cheese Soup 43
Mexican Chocolate Ice Cream 241
Mexican Flan 236
Muchos Nachos 14
Pancho's Casserole 131
Picante Sauce 141
Rita's Chalupas 129
Tortilla Soup 50
Microwave Fish Fillets 158
Microwave Fudge 236
Millionaire Pie, Pineapple 219
Minestrone 67
Molasses Cookies 205
Molded Cucumber Salad 104
Molded Peach Melba 95
Mom's Italian Delight 131
Monday Night Hash 126
Monkey Business, Willie's 248
Monster Cookies 206
Monster Munch, Sherri's 256
Mother's Day Surprise Muffins 249
Mozzarella Vegetable Dip 4
Mrs. Kinsey's Ham Loaf 137
Mrs. Van Husen's Orange Bowknots 75
Mrs. Z's Strawberry Delight 221
MUFFINS
Baked Apple Muffins 66
Cranberry-Almond Muffins 67
Jalapeno Muffins 80
Mother's Day Surprise Muffins 249
Rhubarb Muffins 69
Susan's Pumpkin Muffins 68
The Best Bran Muffins 67
Muchos Nachos 14
Mushroom Caps, Speedy Spinach 12
Mushroom Dip, Hot 8
Mushrooms, Marinated 10
Mushroom Stuffed Steak 120
Mushroom Stuffed Tomatoes 182
Mustard-Ginger Glaze, Celebration 141
Mustard Vinaigrette 115

N

Nacho Dip, Hot 6
Nachos, Muchos 14
Navajo Fry Bread 82
Never-Fail Chocolate Frosting 195
New York Cheesecake 225
Nine Bean Soup 48
No-Knead Breakfast Twists 74
Nut Candies, Quick 237

O

Oatmeal Date Cookies 206
Oatmeal-Raisin Cookies, Chewy 207
Okra & Tomatoes, Fried 174
Old South Shortcake 31
Omelet, Spring 27
Onion Cheese Biscuits, Quick 81
Onion Rolls, Germai ne's Quick 79
Onion Soup, French 46
Orange Bowknots, Mrs. Van Husen's 75
Orange Cake, Mandarin 198
Orange Chutney Chicken 153
Orange Glazed Beets 169
Orange Julius 19
Orange Marmalade Bread 72
Orange Nut Bread 64
Orange Salad, Mandarin 99
Orange Sherbet Salad 95
Oscar Mouse Cookies 257
Oven Lemon Chicken 152
Oysters Florentine 11

P

Paint Mines Pork Roast 135
Pancakes, German Apple 36
Pancakes, Blueberry Lemon 35
Pancakes, Silver Dollar 32
Pan de Lote, Judi's 76
Park Springs Pound Cake 201
Parmesan Bread Sticks 78
Parmesan Chicken 154
Parmigiana, Veal or Meatball 133
Parsley Potatoes 178
Party Punch 18
Party Time Banana Split 234
Party Tomatoes 13
Pasta Primavera 187
Pea 'n Cheese Salad 105
Peach Blueberry Shortcake 229
Peach Cobbler; Quick 229
Peaches 'n Cream Pie, Grandma C's ... 218
Peach Melba, Molded 95
Peach Muffins 68
Peanut Butter Cupcakes 198
Peanut Parfait 255
Peanut Butter Popcorn Balls 238
Peanut Butter Toast 247
Peanutty Shake, Matt's 244

Pear Cake, Western Slope 199
Pear Crisp Pie 218
Pecan Clusters 235
Peggy's Lemon Bars 212
Pennsylvania Dutch Pork Chops 134
Peppermint Ice Cream 240
Peppernuts 207
Perfect Potatoes 178
Petite Cheesecakes 230
Pickles, Bath Tub 59
Picnic Beans 60

PIES

Blueberry Cream Pie 215
Buttery Pie Crust 214
Caramel Apple Pie 214
Easy Livin' Pie 218
Flaky Pie Crust 213
French Chocolate Pie 217
Graham Cracker Crust 220
Grandma C's Peaches 'n Cream Pie. . 218
Leona's Pumpkin Pie 219
Mrs. Z's Strawberry Delite 221
Pear Crisp Pie 218
Pineapple Millionaire Pie 219
Raspberry Chiffon Pie 220
Rhubarb Custard Pie 214
Strawberry Rhubarb Pie 220
Sour Cream Apple Pie 215
Sour Cream Lemon Pie 217
Pikes Peak Pork Tenderloin 135
Pimiento Cheese Spread 57
Pineapple Casserole 174
Pineapple Millionaire Pie 219
Pineapple Pudding Cake 200
Pineapple Sherbet Punch 18
Pineapple Strawberry Punch 19
Pineapple Upside Down Cake 200
Pineapple Upside Down Shake 245
Pine Cliff Strawberries 231
Pine Cone Bird Feeders 258
Pinochle Club Strawberry Dessert 231
Breakfast Pizza 28
Pizza Burgers 56
Pizzas, Tanya's 250
Platte River Steak 119
Plum Creek Applesauce Cake 190
Pomander Ball 257
Poppy Seed Bread 65
Poppy Seed Noodle Casserole 186
Popcorn Balls, Peanut Butter 238
Popcorn, Candied 237
Popcorn Squares, Chocolate 256

PORK

Barbecued Pork Roast 135
Florentine Chops 136
Paint Mines Pork Roast 135
Pennsylvania Dutch Pork Chops 134
Pike's Peak Pork Tenderloin 135
Pork Tenderloin in Normandy Sauce .. 127
Rita's Chalupas 129

279

Scalloped Potatoes with Pork Chops . 134
Pot Roast, Best Ever 124
POTATOES
Crab Stuffed Potatoes 177
Crusty New Potatoes 175
Grande Potatoes 176
Hot Potato & Wurst 128
Parsley Potatoes 178
Perfect Potatoes 178
Potato Cakes 175
Potato Ham Soup 47
Potato Rolls 84
Prairie Schooners 177
"Pretty" Stuffed Potatoes 176
Sweet Potatoes and Marshmallows . . 179
POULTRY (See CHICKEN)
Prairie Schooners 177
"Pretty" Stuffed Potatoes 176
Pumpkin Date Bread 66
Pumpkin Muffins, Susan's 68
Pumpkin Pie, Leona's 219
Pumpkin Seeds, Roasted 247
PUNCH
Almond-Cranberry Punch 15
Champagne Punch 22
Christmas Coffee Punch 19
Cranberry Orange Punch 16
Creamy Fruit Float 16
Fruit Party Punch 16
Golden Summer Punch 16
Grape Punch 17
Joan's Coffee Rum Punch 22
Lime Punch 17
Lime Cooler Punch 17
Party Punch 18
Pineapple Sherbet Punch 18
Strawberry Pineapple Punch 18

Q

Quiche, Crustless 30
Quiche, Quick & Easy 30
Quick Caramel Sticky Buns 76
Quick & Easy Cheese Ball 15
Quick & Easy Quiche 30
Quick Nut Candies 237
Quick Onion Cheese Biscuits 81
Quick Peach Cobbler 229

R

Rabbit Salad, Wesley 250
Raisin Bread 87
Raisin Peanut Butter Spread 248
Ranch Style Dressing 115
Rasberry Pretzel Salad 96
Rasbperries Victor 230
Ray's Herb Butter for Chops 138
Red Beans and Rice 43
Rhubard Custard Pie 214
Rhubarb Muffins 69

Rhubarb-Strawberry Pie 220
Rice, Home-Seasoned Wild 184
Rice, Spanish 185
Rio Grande Bean Dip 5
Rita's Chalupas 129
Ritzy Cracker 248
Roast Beef Sandwich, Hot 54
Roast Beef Sandwich, Grilled 54
Rocky Mountain Oysters 11
ROLLS
Butter Buns 83
Crusty French Rolls 86
Germaine's Quick Onion Rolls 79
Grandma White's All Bran Rolls 83
Lazy Morning Blueberry Rolls 75
Potato Rolls 84
Quick Caramel Sticky Buns 76
Rome Apple Cake 197
Roquefort Dip 4
Rum Cake, Georgia's 201
Rum Slush 23
Running W Pepper Steak 121
Ruth's Cherry Salad 97

S

SALADS
Molded
Cranberry Mousse 95
Cranberry Relish Mold 94
Dreamy Apricot Salad 94
Molded Cucumber Salad 104
Molded Peach Melba 95
Orange Sherbet Salad 95
Raspberry Pretzel Salad 96
Seafood Salad
Coastal Shrimp Salad 112
Crab-Stuffed Avocado Salad 112
Vegetable
Applewood Spinach Salad 107
Barn-Raising Salad . . . . ·106
Broccoli Salad 100
Calico Salad 103
Cauliflower Salad 104
Colorful Cabbage Salad 103
Company Salad 101
Fire and Ice Tomatoes 108
Fresh Spinach w/ Sour Cream Drsg . 107
Jazzy Bean-Avocado Salad 102
Marinated Black Eyed Peas 102
Marinated Vegetables 109
Marinated Zucchini Salad 110
Pea 'n Cheese Salad 105
Saucy Salad 105
Sesame Seed Salad 114
Susie's Tomato & Onion Salad 108
Fruit
Cranberry Freeze 97
Five Cup Salad 98
Front Range Apple Salad 96
Fruit Platter w/ Honey-Lemon Drsg . . 99

Mandarin Orange Salad 99
Orange Beet Salad 106
Orange Salad 100
Ruth's Cherry Salad 97
Stuffed Apples 247
Stuffed Cinnamon Apples 97
Sunshine Salad 250
Wesley Rabbit Salad 250
Wined Fruit Medley 100
Macaroni
Macaroni & Green Pea Salad 115
Dynamite Macaroni Salad 114
Main Dish Pasta Salad 113
Meat Salads
Cashew Chicken w/ Dijon Drsg 110
Chicken Salad with Green Chili 111
Chicken Stuffed Melon 111
SALAD DRESSINGS (See DRESSINGS)
Salmon, Grilled with Dill Sauce 159
Salmon Sauce 159
Sandtarts 208
SANDWICHES
Bar-B-Que Beef Sandwiches 50
Beef and Kraut Sandwich 57
Canadian Bacon Sandwiches 51
Chicken Club Sandwiches 53
Chicken Swisswiches 52
Chili Cheesy Franks 251
German Cabbage Burgers 125
Grilled Cheeseburgers on Rye 51
Grilled Roast Beef Sandwich 54
Ham 'n Avocado Crescents 55
Hero Sandwich 58
High Country Hot Dogs 55
Hot Roast Beef Sandwiches 54
Hot Turkey Royale 58
Italian Sausage Roll 56
Pimiento Cheese Spread 57
Pizza Burgers 56
Sausage & Cheese Sandwiches 59
Tuna Burgers 251
Southwestern Submarine Sandwich ... 53
Teriyaki Chicken Sandwich 52
Sandy Hook Scallops 160
Sarah's Apple Strudel 223
SAUCES
Bar-B-Que Sauce 140
Celebration Mustard-Ginger Glaze ... 141
Cheese Sauce 57
Chocolate Sauce 234
Dill Sauce 159
Hollandaise Sauce 28
Horseradish Sauce 137
Picante Sauce 141
Salmon Sauce 159
Saucy Meatballs 119
Saucy Salad 105
SAUSAGE
Cheese & Sausage Grits 32
Desperation Dinner 129
Italian Sausage Roll 56

Sausage & Cheese Sandwiches 59
Tanya's Pizzas 250
Wild Rice & Sausage 128
Sauteed Snowpeas & Mushrooms 179
Scalloped Potatoes w/ Pork Chops 134
Scrambled Eggs 26
SEAFOOD (See FISH)
Seafood Chowder 49
Sesame Seed Salad 114
Sesame Seed Salad Dressing 115
Sherbet, Apricot-Lemon 239
Sherbet Coolers 245
Sherri's Monster Munch 256
Shortcake, Peach-Blueberry 229
Shrimp Casserole 161
Shrimp & Crab Dip, Susans 2
Shrimp Tempura 160
Silver Dollar Pancakes 32
Smothered Steak 'n Mushrooms 118
Snow-Capped Icing 203
Snow Peas & Beef 123
Snow Peas & Mushrooms, Sauteed ... 179
SOUPS
Arizona Soup 46
Broccoli Cheese Soup 11
Chilled Avocado Soup 40
Chuckwagon Soup 44
Cold Day Chowder 44
Cream of Asparagus Soup 40
Cream of Cauliflower Soup 41
Cream of Spinach Soup 49
Family Time Stew 42
Hearty White Bean Soup 46
Gazpacho 45
Mexican Cheese Soup 43
Minestrone 47
Nine Bean Soup 48
Potato Ham Soup 47
Red Beans and Rice 43
Seafood Chowder 49
Tortilla Soup 50
Sour Cream Apple Pie 215
Sour Cream Lemon Pie 217
Sour Cream Noodles 186
Southwestern Bean Dip 5
Southwestern Submarine Sandwich 53
Spanish Rice 185
Spice Cake, Traditional 202
Spinach Salad, Applewood 107
Spinach Salad w/ Sour Cream Drsg. ... 107
Spinach Souffle 179
Spinach Soup, Cream of 49
SPREADS
Baboon Butter 247
Bountiful Layers 2
Delicious Fruit & Cheese Spread 10
Easy Crab Spread 8
Homemade Cheese Spread 6
Jalapeno Spread 9
Lemon Pepper Cheese Spread 10
Pimiento Cheese Spread 57

Raisin Peanut Butter Spread 248
Vera's Bacon-Cheese Spread 9
Willie's Monkey Business 248
Squash, Acorn 181
Squash Casserole, Courtney's 253
Squash Fluff 181
Squash, Sauteed wi Mushrms & Onions 180
Spring Omelet 27
State Fair Froz. Chocolate Banana 246
Steak, Chicken Fried & Cream Gravy .. 119
Steak 'n Mushrooms 118
Steak, Mushroom-Stuffed 120
Steak, Platte River 119
Steak, Stock Show 120
Stock Show Steak 120
Strawberry Angel Food Cake 202
Strawberry Bread 65
Strawberry Delite, Mrs. Z's 221
Strawberry French Toast 33
Strawberry Ice Cream, Jan's 240
Strawberry-Pineapple Punch 18
Strawberries, Pine Cliff 231
Strawberry Dessert, Pinochle Club 231
Strawberry Punch 19
Strawberry Rhubarb Pie 220
Stroh Ranch Coffee Cake 71
Strudel, Sarah's Apple 223
Stuffed Apples 247
Stuffed Cinnamon Apples 97
Stuffed Eggplant 173
Stuffed Pasta Shells 132
Stuffed Peppers 124
Submarine Sandwich, Southwestern 53
Sugar Easter Eggs 258
Summertime Lemon Dessert 228
Summit Meat Loaf 125
Sunflower Whole Wheat Bread 86
Sunrise Juice 244
Sunshine Salad 250
Sunshine Vegetables, Kika's 172
Surprise Muffins, Mother's Day 249
Susan's Pumpkin Muffins 68
Susan's Shrimp & Crab Dip 2
Susie's Tarragon Carrots 171
Susie's Tomato & Onion Salad 108
Suzie's Chocolate Sour Cream Cake ... 195
Swedish Cream 232
Sweet Potatoes & Marshmallows 179
Sweet Temptation 232
Swiss Bacon & Tomato Stacks 29

T

T Lazy S Margaritas 23
Tanya's Pizzas 250
Tarragon Carrots, Susie's 171
Tea, Texas 20
Teriyaki Chicken 146
Teriyaki Chicken Sandwich 52
Tetrazzini, Chicken 150
Texas Picnic Chicken 144

Texas Red Chili 43
Texas Tea 20
The Best Bran Muffins 67
Toffee, English 235
Toffee Pecan Bars 213
Tomato & Onion Salad, Susie's 108
Tomatoes, Broiled Italian 182
Tomatoes, Cherry, Bacon Filled 13
Tomatoes, Fire & Ice 108
Tomatoes, Mushroom-Stuffed 182
Tomatoes, Party 13
Tomatoes Rockefeller 183
Tortilla Soup 50
Traditional Spice Cake 202
Trout Fillets with Tomato Butter; Grilled .. 62
Tuna Burgers 251
Tuna Casserole, Good Ol' 162
Tuna Islands, Judy's 163
Turkey Royale, Hot 58
Two Quick Breakfast Coffee Cakes 73

V

Vanilla Ice Cream, Barbara's 238
Veal or Meatball Parmigiana 133
VEGETABLES
Acorn Squash 181
Apricot-Glazed Carrots 171
Asparagus Amandine 166
Asparagus Vinaigrette 166
Broccoli Delight 170
Broccoli Swiss Bake 169
Broccoli-Mushroom Souffle 170
Broiled Italian Tomatoes 182
Buttery Italian Green Beans 167
Cattlemen's Club Baked Potatoes 177
Cauliflower Supreme 172
Corn Fritters 172
Country Quiche 180
Country Style Green Beans 167
Courtney's Favorite Squash Casserole 253
Crab-Stuffed Potatoes 177
Crusty New Potatoes 175
Eggplant Regina 173
Fried Okra and Tomatoes 174
Grande Potatoes 176
Green Beans Oriental 167
Green Beans Provencal 167
Kika's Sunshine Vegetables 172
Long's Peak Baked Beans 168
Mushroom-Stuffed Tomatoes 182
Orange Glazed Beets 169
Parsley Potatoes 178
Perfect Potaotes 178
Picnic Beans 168
Pineapple Casserole 174
Poppy Seed Noodle Casserole 186
Potato Cakes 175
"Pretty" Stuffed Potatoes 176
Red Cabbage with Apples 171
Sauteed Snowpeas and Mushrooms . 179

282

Sour Cream Noodles 186
Spinach Souffle 179
Squash Fluff 181
Stuffed Eggplant 173
Sweet Potatoes & Marshmallows 179
Susie's Tarragon Carrots 171
Tangy Asparagus-Tomato 166
Tomatoes Rockefeller 183
Vegetable Surprise 252
Wheat Pilaf 185
Zucchini Casserole 183
Zucchini Puff 184
Vegetable Dip, Fresh 3
Vegetable Dippers 3
Vegetable Surprise 180
Vera's Bacon-Cheese Spread 9

W

Waffles, Buttermilk 32
Watermelon Surprise 253

Wesley Rabbit Salad 250
Western Slope Pear Cake 199
Wheat Pilaf 185
Whole Wheat Sesame Bread 89
Wild Rice & Sausage 128
Wild Game Stew, Donnie's Original 139
Willie's Monkey Business 248
Wined Fruit Medley 100
Wolfensburger Pass Hot Chocolate 21
Working Woman's Roast 124

Z

Zesty Beef 'n Zucchini 122
Zucchini Casserole 183
Zucchini Salad, Marinated 110
Zucchini Puff 184

EQUIVALENT MEASURES

3 teaspoons = 1 tablespoon
16 tablespoons = 1 cup
2 cups = 1 pint
2 pints = 1 quart
4 quarts (liquid) = 1 gallon
4 tablespoons = ¼ cup
5 tablespoons + 1 teaspoon = ⅓ cup
1 cup = 8 fluid ounces
Pinch or dash is less than ⅛ teaspoon
2 tablespoons = 1 fluid ounce
1 pound = 16 ounces

SUBSTITUTIONS

1 tablespoon cornstarch (for thickening) = 2 tablespoons flour (approximately)

1 cup sifted all-purpose flour = 1 cup + 2 tablespoons sifted cake flour.

1 square chocolate (oz.) = 3–4 tablespoons cocoa + ½ tablespoon shortening.

1 teaspoon baking powder = ¼ teaspoon baking soda + ½ teaspoon cream of tartar.

1 cup bottled milk = ½ cup evaporated milk + ½ cup water.

1 cup sour milk = 1 cup sweet milk into which 1 tablespoon vinegar or lemon juice has been stirred; or 1 cup buttermilk.

1 cup sweet milk = 1 cup sour milk or buttermilk + ½ teaspoon baking soda.

1 cup molasses = 1 cup honey.

1 cup sour cream = 1 cup evaporated milk + 1 tablespoon vinegar or lemon juice.

1 whole egg = 2 egg yolks + 1 tablespoon water (in cookies) or 2 egg yolks (in custards and similar mixtures).

1 tablespoon fresh herbs = 1 teaspoon dry herbs.

⅛ teaspoon garlic powder = 1 small fresh garlic clove, pressed.

1 cup fine crumbs = 24 saltine crackers, 4 slices bread, or 14 squares graham crackers.

To order *Kitchen Keepsakes* and *More Kitchen Keepsakes*:

Please send _____ copies @ $19.95 (U.S.) each $_____

   Plus postage/handling @ $3.50 each $_____

   Texas residents add sales tax @ $1.44 each $_____

Check or Credit Card (Canada-credit card only)   TOTAL $_____

Charge to my _____ Master Card or _____ Visa Card
Account # _____
Expiration Date_____   **MAIL OR CALL:**
Signature_____

                                           Cookbook Resources
NAME_____   541 Doubletree Drive
                                           Highland Village, Texas
ADDRESS _____   75077

CITY_____ST_____ZIP_____   **972 317 0245**

Please send _____ copies @ $19.95 (U.S.) each $_____

   Plus postage/handling @ $3.50 each $_____

   Texas residents add sales tax @ $1.44 each $_____

Check or Credit Card (Canada-credit card only) $_____

Charge to my _____ Master Card or _____ Visa Card
Account # _____
Expiration Date _____   **MAIL OR CALL:**
Signature _____

                                           Cookbook Resources
NAME _____   541 Doubletree Drive
                                           Highland Village, Texas
ADDRESS _____   75077

CITY _____ST _____ZIP_____   **972 317 0245**